Some Nautical Tales

by

Captain Wilbur H. Vantine

Copyright 2005

All Rights Reserved

Photographs are by the Author, unless otherwise noted

authorHOUSE®

AuthorHouse™
1663 Liberty Drive
Bloomington, IN 47403
www.authorhouse.com
Phone: 1-800-839-8640

First published by AuthorHouse   12/14/2011

ISBN: 978-1-4670-4112-6 (sc)
ISBN: 978-1-4670-4110-2 (ebk)

Library of Congress Control Number: 2011917613

Printed in the United States of America

This book is printed on acid-free paper.

Dedication

I dedicate this book to my Chief Mate. That is, my Lifetime Chief Mate, **Dorothy Marie Vantine.**

I could not have made a better choice, and I am very lucky that she said yes to my proposal back in 1956.

Although we married rather late in life, our long lives gave us the opportunity to live together 53 years and to grow old together. Dorothy died in 2009. I miss her very much but draw inspiration from my memories.

During all of this time, we loved each other. But more importantly, we genuinely liked, admired, and respected one another.

This is my favorite picture of Dorothy. It was taken in 1962, when we were living in Coco Solo, Canal Zone. She was about to attend the annual Atlantic Side Fashion Show where the ladies wore clothes and hats that they had made themselves.

Dorothy Marie Vantine (1962)

About the Author

Captain Wilbur H. Vantine was born in Quanah, TX, on March 16, 1925. He grew up mostly in Missouri.

In June 1943, when he was 18 years old, he joined the United States Merchant Marine and commenced training at the United States Maritime Service training facility at Sheepshead Bay, Brooklyn, New York. Two months later he was accepted into the U. S. Merchant Marine Cadet Corps and transferred to their Basic School at Pass Christian, MS. While in training as a Deck Cadet, he made two voyages, spanning eight months, on freighters carrying war cargoes to the South Pacific. He returned to the Academy to complete his training in July 1944. In April 1945, he graduated from the Merchant Marine Academy at Kings Point, NY, ranked first scholastically in his Section, and obtained his Coast Guard license as Third Mate in the U. S. Merchant Marine and a Commission as Ensign in the U. S. Navy Reserve.

Five years later he obtained a license, which was issued by the United States Coast Guard, as *Master of Steam and Motor Vessels of any Gross Tons upon Oceans.* The following year, at age 26, he was given the first of seven commands of tramp freighters engaged in worldwide trade.

In 1957 he became a Panama Canal Pilot. He took early retirement from that position in 1983, after having completed more than 4,800 piloting assignments in the Panama Canal. He continued living in Panama until 1997, working as a self-employed Marine Consultant/Surveyor and (until 1995) as a part-time Docking Master for Petroterminal de Panama, the Company that operated a pipeline across Panama for Alaskan crude. He handled more than 300 piloting assignments of tankers on the Alaska Oil Lift, ranging up to 300,000 tons displacement (with a length of 1,100 feet, a beam of 185 feet, a draft of 70 feet and with a cargo capacity of 1,860,000 barrels). All of his piloting jobs were handled without any reportable damage to the ships or any injuries to personnel.

Professional Associations—

Society of Naval Architects and Marine Engineers (Panel H-10, Ship Controllability); The Marine Society of the City of New York (Life Member); The Council of American Master Mariners; Navy League of the United States (served five terms as President of the Panama Council); Kings Point Alumni Association (Life Member, Past President of the Panama Chapter and 1945 Class Agent); International Organization of Masters, Mates and Pilots; and the Panama Canal Pilots Association (Past President).

About This Book—

Some Nautical Tales covers the adventures and experiences of Captain Wilbur H. Vantine, as he worked his way up from Ordinary Seaman and sailed as Ship Master on tramp freighters in the United States Merchant Marine.

Along the way he was able to "see the world" at a very interesting time in world affairs.

During WWII, he served on two ships in the war zones of the southwest Pacific and on another in the North Atlantic to the United Kingdom. He obtained his first command in 1951 at age twenty-six. While sailing as Ship Master, he did difficult navigation among icebergs in the far north; had his ship breaking up and losing three of its four lifeboats in a "super" storm; was confined with his crew on a Liberty ship, in ballast, during a winter-time crossing of the North Atlantic, when there was a killer virus on board; sailed to Korea before, during and after the Korean War; took action to minimize damage from an unavoidable collision and directed actions to separate the two ships which were connected by their anchor chains;

The author, Captain Wilbur H. Vantine, age 80, working on this book.

made an ocean crossing with growing cracks in the main deck threatening to cause his ship to break-up; steamed trans-Pacific with a cargo of coal undergoing spontaneous combustion; had his ship boarded and crew attacked by a large and angry mob in Yugoslavia; had a shifting cargo of army tanks threatening to knock out the sides of his ship during a storm; and had unique interaction with both ship and shore personalities.

This book was authored during Captain Vantine's 79th and 80th years, referring to notes and records that were made at the time of the events. It is all based on actual experiences. The numerous photographs were taken by the author, except where noted otherwise.

Some Nautical Tales

Table of Contents

Chapter I: WWII Adventures   **1**

Sheepshead Bay   4

The Merchant Marine Cadet Corps   6

Pass Christian Basic School   7

SS Davy Crockett   10
New Orleans, Panama Canal, Milne Bay, Port Moresby, Oro Bay, Milne Bay, San Francisco

SS Cape Chalmers   19
San Francisco, Noumea, Guadalcanal, Russell Islands, Pago Pago, San Francisco

Kings Point   23

SS Christopher Gadsden   31
New York, Liverpool, New York

Chapter II: SS Walt Whitman (My First Post WWII Voyage)   **34**

My Year Away from the Sea   34

SS Walt Whitman   36
Beaumont, Panama Canal, Long Beach, Kobe, Manila, Panama Canal, Galveston

Chapter III: SS Grays Harbor (Why I Didn't Sail Tankers)   **41**

Voyage with Heavy Drinking Shipmates
Lake Charles, Bristol, Houston

Chapter IV: SS George Clement Perkins (First Tour of Duty)   **50**

First Voyage   51
Galveston, Rotterdam, Galveston

Second Voyage   54
Galveston, Malmo, Norfolk

Third Voyage   55
Norfolk, Charleston, Santos, Tampa

Fourth Voyage   56
Tampa, Panama Canal, San Pedro, Kobe, San Pedro, Panama Canal, New Orleans

Fifth Voyage   57
New Orleans, Savona, Cueta, Rosario, Buenos Aires, Montevideo, Tenerife, Antwerp, Southampton, Norfolk, Baltimore

Chapter V: SS George Clement Perkins (Second Tour of Duty)   **61**

Sixth Voyage   61
New Orleans, Kingston, San Juan, New Orleans

Seventh Voyage   62
New Orleans, Panama Canal, Honolulu, Kobe, Yokohama, Tacoma, Seattle

Eighth Voyage   63
    Seattle, Yokohama, Longview
Ninth Voyage   64
    Longview, Otaru, Yokohama, Honolulu, Panama Canal, Galveston
Tenth Voyage   65
    Galveston, Gibraltar, Trieste, Gibraltar, New York
Eleventh Voyage   67
    New York, Hamburg, New Orleans
Chapter VI: SS Sea Leader (First Tour of Duty)   **69**

First Voyage   69
    Mobile, Galveston, Savannah, Charleston, Norfolk, LeHavre, Norfolk
        Penicillin   70
Second Voyage   70
    Newport News, Bordeaux, Norfolk
Third Voyage   71
    Newport News, Oran, Algiers, Charleston
Fourth Voyage   72
    Charleston, Panama Canal, Honolulu, Pusan, Sasebo, Honolulu, Panama Canal,
    Baltimore
        Old Spice   73
Fifth Voyage   74
    Baltimore, Jobos Bay, San Juan, Emden, Narvik, Baltimore, Norfolk
Chapter VII: SS Sea Leader (Second Tour of Duty)   **76**

Licensed as Master Mariner, Steam & Motor Vessels, Any Tonnage, Oceans
Sixth Voyage, The Isbrandtsen Charter   80
    Houston, Philadelphia, Newport News, Norfolk, Baltimore, Philadelphia, New York
    Cherbourg, LeHavre, Antwerp, Rotterdam, Bremerhaven, Emden, Hamburg, Bremen,
    Antwerp, Rotterdam, New York, Philadelphia, Baltimore, Newport News, Baltimore
        Our Ship's Paint Supply   84
Seventh and Eight Voyages   85
    Baltimore, Avonmouth, Baltimore, London, Norfolk
Chapter VIII: SS Thomas Sumter (My First Command)   **87**

First Voyage   91
    New York, Philadelphia, LeHavre, Rouen, Norfolk
Second Voyage   97
    Norfolk, Rotterdam, Charleston
Third Voyage   99
    Charleston, Bremen, Newport News
Fourth Voyage   100
    Newport News, Kiel Canal, Copenhagen, Kiel Canal, Falmouth, Baltimore
    (Meningitis aboard)

Fifth Voyage   114
Baltimore, New York, Malmo, New York (Super Storm)
Sixth Voyage   120
New York, Philadelphia, Bordeaux, Mobile (Ship Breaking Up)
Lay-up   124
Mobile, New Orleans, Mobile

Chapter IX: SS Waltham Victory (The Greenland Voyages)   **126**
First Voyage   132
Norfolk, Argentia, Thule, Norfolk
Second Voyage   146
Norfolk, New York, Narssarssuaq, Sondre Stromfjord, New York
Addendum   161
SS Waltham Victory, Captain's Standing Orders

Chapter X: SS T. J. Stevenson (First Tour of Duty)   **163**
First Voyage   169
Norfolk, New York, Praia (Azores), Gibraltar Genoa, Trieste, Sibenik, Philadelphia, New York
Second Voyage   183
New York, Norfolk, New York, Rijeka, Pula, Genoa, Savona, New York
Third Voyage   187
New York, Norfolk, Praia, Vila do Porto (Azores), Rijeka, Istanbul, Derince (Turkey), New York
Fourth Voyage   195
New York, Genoa, Naples, Tripoli, Casablanca, Dingwall (Nova Scotia), Baltimore
Fifth Voyage   202
Norfolk, New York, Casablanca, Leghorn, Sibenik, Gibraltar, Philadelphia

Chapter XI: SS T. J. Stevenson (Second Tour of Duty)   **213**
Sixth Voyage   213
Norfolk, Philadelphia, New York, Norfolk, Praia (Collision), Vila do Porto (Lost Anchor), Genoa, Naples,Tripoli, Piraeus, Tampa
Seventh Voyage (The States Marine Time Charter)   220
Tampa, New Orleans, Panama Canal, Long Beach, San Francisco, Seattle, Aberdeen, Yokohama, Yokkaichi, Kobe, Pusan, Sasebo, Keelung, Osaka, Yokohama
(The Matson Line Sub-Charter)   231
Yokohama, Honolulu, Mahukona, Honolulu, Panama Canal, New Orleans

Chapter XII: SS Kenneth H. Stevenson   **235**
First Voyage   235
New York, Praia, Casablanca, Genoa, Naples, Pula, Trieste, New York

Second Voyage   238
New York, Norfolk, (Nearly Losing the Ship), Casablanca, Cartagena, Tripoli, Rijeka, Norfolk
Third Voyage   244
Savannah, Naples, Norfolk

Chapter XIII: SS Sea Leader (as Master)   **247**

First Voyage   247
Houston, (Breakdown at Sea), Jacksonville, Gibraltar, Haifa, Gibraltar, Mobile
Second Voyage   254
Mobile, Panama Canal, San Pedro (Trans-Pacific with a Burning Cargo of Coal), Muroran, Moji, Inchon (North Korean Mine), Moji, Seattle
Third Voyage   262
Seattle, Olympia, Aberdeen, Panama Canal, New York, Philadelphia, Wilmington
Vacation/Honeymoon   267

Chapter XIV: SS Harold D. Whitehead (The First Cargo)   **270**

The Military Charter   270
San Francisco, San Pedro, Panama Canal, Aruba, Zeebrugge, Bremerhaven, St. Nazaire, Bordeaux

Chapter XV: SS Harold D. Whitehead (Second & Third Cargoes)   **279**

The Military Charter, Extended
Milford Haven, Livorno, Piraeus, Iskenderun, Livorno, Iskenderun, Piraeus, Casablanca

Chapter XVI: SS Harold D. Whitehead (Fourth Cargo)   **288**

The Military Charter, Extended Again
Bremerhaven, Suez Canal, Karachi, Suez Canal, Casablanca, New York

Chapter XVII: SS Federal Jurist (My Last Command)   **296**

First Voyage   298
Norfolk, Antwerp, Philadelphia
Second Voyage   304
Philadelphia, Dunkerque, Philadelphia

Chapter XVIII: Federal Bulkcarriers, Inc.   **307**

The End   313

List of Illustrations

Mrs. Dorothy Marie Vantine (1962) — Intro 2

The author, Captain Wilbur H. Vantine (2005) — Intro 4

Two Bedroom house in the country (1942) — 1

Letter from High School Principal (1943) — 3

Ordinary Seaman Wilbur H. Vantine (1943) — 5

Lifeboat Training (1943) — 9

Basic School Section (1943) — 10

Kings Point Room Mates (1945) — 25

Cadet Midshipman Wilbur Vantine (1945) — 26

Kings Point Graduating Section C-331 (April 1945) — 29

Letter from Captain John J. Kelly (1945) — 33

Letter from Motel Owner (1946) — 35

Letter from Captain P. J. Gennusa (1946) — 41

Letter from the Master of the *SS Grays Harbor* (1946) — 49

Picture with Brazilian Girl Friend (1947) — 55

Shipmates having dinner in Trieste (1949) — 66

Captain Elmer F. Goodlett and Chief Mate Wilbur Vantine (1950) — 78

Captain Demetrius Belesiotis and 2nd Mate Louis Murphy (1950) — 79

Deck Officers of the *SS Sea Leader* (1950) — 80

The *SS Sea Leader* berthed in Rotterdam 1950 — 81

Kings Point Alumni Letter that saved the author from the draft in 1951 — 83

Chief Engineer Richard Thompson (1951) — 88

Captain Wilbur H. Vantine (1951) — 91

Rouen Cathedral (1951) — 94

Place in Rouen where Joan of Arc was burned at the stake (1951) — 94

SS Thomas Sumter docked in Bremen, Germany (1951) — 99

The *SS Thomas Sumter* aground at Brunsbuttlekooog (1951) — 102

The *SS Thomas Sumter* transiting the Kiel Canal (1951) — 104

Port Area of Copenhagen (1951) — 105

Empty Liberty Ship in North Atlantic Gale (1951) — 110

Captain's Quarters, North Atlantic (1951) — 111

Horace and Ora Lee Netherton, the uncle and aunt who raised the author (1952) — 126

SS Watham Victory (1952) — 128

Illustration from the Internet showing what a whole Iceberg would look like (from internet) — 136

Typical Greenland West Coast Iceberg.(from the internet) — 137

Satellite Image of Greenland and Baffin Island (NASA) — 139

Example of the Aurora Borealis (from the internet) — 140

Thule Air Base in the Summer and Winter (from the internet) — 143

Icebergs that we encountered at the north end of Baffin Bay.(1952) — 145

Chart of south Greenland showing the channel to Narssarssuaq — 148

The port area of Narssarssuaq in Skovfjord (1952) 151
Chief Engineer Ira Sager fishing at Narssarssuaq 151
Membership Certificate in the Arctic Circle Masonic Club 152
East coast icebergs that we encountered off Cape Farewell (1952) 153
West coast of Greenland at the Arctic Circle. 154
View of Sondre Stromfjord looking astern at our wake (1952) 155
View of the bank of Sondre Stromfjord alongside the ship (1952) 156
Shoreline of Sondre Stromfjord (1952) 157
Stevenson Lines Smoke Stack Symbol 163
Captain's Bedroom and "Party" Room (1952) 166
Chief Mate Bunting & Third Mate Koerner (1952) 166
Radio Operator (Sparks) Raymond Brazner & Second Mate Joe Koller (1952) 167
Chief Engineer George Thomas & Donald Taylor, Third Assistant (1952) 168
Portuguese Bosun & Chinese/American Deck Maintenance Man (1952) 168
Genoa Harbor, Old Section. Passenger Ship *SS Andrea Dora*, far left (1952) 172
SS Andrea Dora, (1952) later sunk in collision the Swedish *MV Stockholm* (1952) 173
Italian Island of Stromboli (1952) 173
Superb British Troops in Trieste (1952) 175
Entrance to Sibenik Bay with City in distance (1953) (from the internet) 177
Climbing Sibenik Hill. (1953) 178
The Author scaling the old Castle Wall above Sibenik (1953) 178
View from the old castle above Sibenik (1953) 179
Krka Waterfalls six kilometers upriver from Sibenik (1953) 180
New Yugoslav Military Installation in Sibenik Bay (1953) 181
The author's Yugoslav friend, Ivan, sailing in Sibenik Bay (1953) 181
Yugoslav Women Work Gang with a (non-working) Male Foreman (1953) 182
Roman Coliseum in Pula, Yugoslavia (1953) 185
Bearing WNW from our anchored ship at Via do Porto (1953) 189
Aya Sofya, Church in Istanbul that was completed in 532 AD (1953) 191
The author posing in front of the "Blue Mosque" in Istanbul (1953) 192
Istanbul Harbor as seen from the Golden Horn. *SS T. J. Stevenson* in background 193
King's Palace, Tripoli (1953) 197
2,000 Year Old Ruins in Tripoli (1953) 198
Looking aft from the bridgewing when our ship was docked in Casablanca (1953) 199
Casablanca "Taxi" Stand (1953) 199
Rabat Street Scene (1953) 200
Rabat Laundromat (1953) 200
Rabat School Room (1953) 200
50 foot seas during Hurricane 1953 204
The Author testing the wind during a Hurricane 1953 204
Letter from Chief of Police in Sibenik restricting a seaman to the ship (1953) 207
Translation of Letter from Chief of Police (1953) 208
Writing on ship's side by a mob in Sibenik (1953) 210

Seas breaking on Genoa Breakwater just after we cleared the port (1954)   217

SS T. J. Stevenson in the port of Tripoli, Libya (1954)   218

Steps Leading up to the Acropolis (1954)   219

Author at Parthenon on 29th Birthday (1954)   219

Overhauling Jumbo Gear (1954)   221

Loading Heavy Lifts in New Orleans (1954)   222

SS T. J. Stevenson in Seattle (1954)   223

Picture that the author took of Mt. Fuji from Yokohama (1954)   224

English Sign in the Progressive City of Yokkaichi, Japan (1954)   225

Bow section of *SS Cornhusker Mariner* at Pusan Harbor Entrance (1954)   226

Stern section of *SS Cornhusker Mariner* being salvaged in Pusan (1954)   226

Tokyo/Yokohama Subway (1954)   228

Japanese Emperor's Grounds (1954)   229

Japanese Prime Minister's Official Residence (1954)   229

Japanese Diet Building (1954)   230

Interior of Japanese Upper House of Parliament   230

Loading sugar at Mahukona, Hawaii Island (1954)   232

Porpoises that we encountered in mid-Pacific   232

The Battleship, USS Wisconsin, in Gatun Locks (1954)   233

Taking the Local Apparent Noon Latitude Sights (1954)   235

Capo Spartivento at "toe" of Italian "Boot" (1954)   237

Capo Santa Maria de Lucia at the "heel" of the Italian "Boot"(1954))   237

After Deck Cargo following a Severe Gail (1954)   241

SS Kenneth H. Stevenson in Cartagena (1954)   242

Cartagena School Children (1954)   243

Rijeka Night Club on Christmas Evening (1954)   244

"New" Castle in Naples (1954)   245

The Author in Pompeii, Mr. Vesuvius in background (1955)   245

SS Independence, calling at Gibraltar (1955)   249

View of Mount Carmel from our ship at the dock in Haifa (1955)   250

View of Haifa from the top of Mount Carmel. (1955)   251

Bahia Temple, Haifa (1955)   251

Nazareth Street Scenes (1955)   252

Nazareth Butcher Shop with pigs for sale (1955)   253

US Army Launch using bow wave to wash mine away from anchored ship (1955)   259

Inchon, Korean Stevedores discharging cargo of hot coal (1955)   260

Shore Line in Shimonoseki Straits   261

The Author, Pastor Thomas Cruxton, Bride Dorothy (Wedding Day 2/1/56)   267

Stepson Dewey B. Whittaker, the Author, Bride Dorothy (2/1/56)   268

Our Parents— Horace L. Netherton, Ora Lee Netherton, Emma Schneck (2/1/56)   268

Port of Zeebrugge. The Breakwater was being further reinforced.(1956)   272

Municipal Buildings in Zeebrugge (1956)   272

Brugge is known as the "Venice of North Europe" (1956)   273

Swans in Brugge (1956)   273
Brugge Crystal Store where Author purchased Val St. Lambert Crystal set. (1956)   274
German Sub Pens in St. Nazaire (1956)   275
St. Nazaire Public Transportation (1956)   275
Street Scene in Nantes, France (1956)   275
SS Harold D. Whitehead docked in Bordeaux (1956)   276
Chief Engineer Pottinger on his Peugeot Motor Bicycle and Bordeaux Bell Tower   276
Beautiful Bridge near Bordeaux (1956)   277
Winery at Cadillac (1956)   277
Sunday Bicycle Race passing through Cadillac (1956)   277
One Legged Sheep Herder near Cadillac (1956)   278
The author castle exploring in Wales (1956)   279
Carew Castles near Milford Haven (1956)   279
The Acropolis, (1956)   281
The Parthenon (1956)   281
Porch of the Maidens (1956)   282
Bill Harris and his Land Rover in Iskenderun (1956)   282
Iskenderun Bus Station (1956)   282
Caves seen from road between Iskenderun and Antioch (1956)   283
Ruins of Church of St. Peter in Antioch, the very first Christian Church (1956)   283
Crusader's Fort near Antioch, Syria (1956)   284
Antioch Street Scene (1956)   284
Antioch Blacksmith Shop (1956)   284
Turkish Couple at Farmer's Market in Iskenderun (1956)   285
Statue of Ferdinand de Lesseps (1956)   289
The *SS Harold D. Whitehead* berthed in Port Said (1956)   289
The *SS Harold D. Whitehead* transiting the Suez Canal (1956)   290
Port of Karachi (1956)   292
Street Scene in Karachi (1956)   292
German Sailing Training Vessel in the English Channel (1956)   299
Author's wife, Dorothy, visiting *SS Federal Jurist* in Philadelphia   301
Letter from Mr. John F. Shea, Executive VP of T. J. Stevenson & Co., Inc. (1957)   302
Letter from Captain William J. Campbell, Operation Manager (1957)   303

Chapter I: My WWII Adventures

Pearl Harbor Reaction

When Pearl Harbor was attacked on December 7, 1941, my uncle and aunt, who had raised me, Horace Lafayette Netherton and Ora Lee (Kerley) Netherton, and I heard of it on our living room radio. We were living in the country in a two-bedroom one-bath house near Cole Camp Junction, MO. Horace Netherton was an Electrician (a very good one) for the Texas-Empire Pipe Line Company, that operated a pipeline for crude oil being pumped from Texas to the Chicago area. The pumping station at Cole Camp Junction had been shut down a couple of years earlier. The Company offered the Station Engineer's house, rent-free, to Horace. This would enable them to keep it insured and maintained for later use.

Like all Americans, we were shocked at the news, mad as hell at the Japs, and worried about our country. The news seemed to be all bad. We were losing everywhere.

We were caught up in the huge patriotic surge that suddenly engulfed the citizens of America. Although there was no one around to see it except us, my dad put up a flagpole and I gladly accepted the task of putting up our flag every morning, before breakfast, and taking it down every evening, after supper. In handling the flag, I was careful to never allow it to touch the ground, and folded it properly in the military manner.

Two Bedroom house in the country where author and his family were living when Pearl Harbor was attacked.

We accepted, with only minimal complaints, the shortages that developed and the rationing, first of gasoline, and later coffee, sugar, meat and other products. Many people planted "Victory Gardens" to grow their own vegetables. We already had a good sized garden but we more than doubled its size. We worked in it quite a bit.

I was working, after school and on weekends, at two gas stations at the junction of US 65 and Missouri State 52 (Cole Camp Junction), which was only about 300 yards from our home. Texaco Fire Chief cost 9.75 cents per gallon and Sky Chief was 12.75 cents. Those prices never changed during the three years that I worked there. We sold so little of the "expensive" Sky Chief that it didn't rate an electric pump. It had a ten-gallon visible glass tank, with markings every one-eighth of a gallon, that was pumped up manually. I kept a can close by the gas pumps into which I emptied gas remaining in the hose nozzles (after the customers left). When some foolish rich guy had his oil changed after only one or two thousand miles, I salvaged that also. It ended up costing me very little to run my 1933 Chevrolet coup (with a rumble seat). A further economy was obtained, after my dad changed my eighteen-inch wheels to sixteen-inch, so that I could use the old tires from his company car. In those days, the windshield always got wiped, after buying gas, and the customer was always asked if he wanted the oil checked. My wages were ten cents per hour, but after a year or so, I negotiated a fifty percent pay increase. Tips for doing your job were never given or expected.

I had turned sixteen the previous March, and so was too young to get into the fight at that time. But I sure did want to do something. Because of having to repeat the third grade (schooled in three states that year), I was a year behind in school for my age and was only a sophomore in the Cole Camp, MO, (population 875) High School, that was located four miles from where we lived.

During the summer of 1942, the pipeline pumping station was to be reactivated, so we moved eighteen miles to Sedalia, MO, (population 20,000), where I attended Smith-Cotton High School for my junior year. My ownership of a car (1933 Chevrolet coup with a rumble seat) enabled me to have many "friends".

I would turn 18 in March 1943 and so, as soon as school was out in May that year, I would be off to the war, with only three years of high school completed.

I wanted to get into an officer-training program, but my lack of a high school diploma was a big handicap. I had made real good grades in school and had taken five "solids" each year instead of the required four. Also, I had been president of my freshman and sophomore classes. The Principal of Smith-Cotton High School, Mr. Forest L. Drake, tried to help me and recommended me for the Navy V-12 pilot training program. I scored high on a qualifying test and went to Kansas City (70 miles away) for further processing. The Officer-in-Charge noticed that my high school transcript only had two years on it, since even my junior year was not yet completed. So, I was not going to be a Naval Aviator. Most likely my eyes would have caused me to fail the physical exam anyway.

SMITH-COTTON JUNIOR-SENIOR HIGH SCHOOL
SEDALIA, MISSOURI

OFFICE OF THE
PRINCIPAL

April 22, 1943

To Whom It May Concern:

Wilbur Vantine entered this school in September
from the high school in Cole Camp, Missouri. His
record from that school is very good and he has kept
his grades up to a high level this year. He tells
me that he has passed the V-12 test and is to report
April 27.

This boy is honest, very dependable and cooperative.
I am very glad to give him my unqualified recommendation
because he has done good work in high school and I am
sure he will continue to do his best wherever he is
placed. A transcript of his school record is enclosed.

Sincerely yours,

Forrest L. Drake.

Forrest L. Drake
Principal

FLD:nw
Enc.

**Letter from High School Principal recommending the author for the Navy V-12 Officer
Training Program**

A friend of our family, John Metcalf, had joined the Merchant Marine Cadet Corps and, in the spring of 1943, came home for a five-day leave, after completing the sea-going part of his training. That phase consisted of a minimum of six months on merchant ships. This was a program that ended with a graduate getting a Third Mate License for the Merchant Marine, and an Ensign Commission in the Navy Reserve. He looked real spiffy in his uniform and talked me into applying.

There was a three-month window of opportunity for me. During that brief time, my high school credits were sufficient to qualify, since I had taken extra science and math courses. Later, they raised the entry standards to require four years of English and that would have ruled me out.

So I applied and waited. And waited. But no news came, good or bad.

I did not want to wait to be drafted and had decided that I wanted to join the Merchant Marine. So I went to Kansas City, where they had a recruitment office, and joined. In June 1943, I rode a train to New York to go to the Merchant Marine training facility at Sheepshead Bay, Brooklyn.

Sheepshead Bay

General Information

There were about 10,000 recruits in training at that time. They had four programs of instruction, deck department, engine department, stewards department and a Purser-Pharmacist Mate course. The engine rooms were very hot and you couldn't see the scenery when on duty, so for me, that was not a good choice. I didn't like waiting on people, as the stewards department would be doing, so that also was not desirable. Paper work and medical chores, which were taught in the Purser/Pharmacist Mate course, also did not appeal to me. So, I chose the deck training. An added attraction was that the deck department could lead to being a Captain one day.

Our monthly pay was $50 and that was really all "spending money", since everything was provided. Overall, something like 90% of the pay that the trainees received was used to pay bar bills. Bars do well in wartime.

Frank Sinatra was becoming famous and his appearances in Manhattan were causing young girls to scream and faint.

I was only eighteen years old, which is a tender age to leave home. But millions of young men my age were doing just that all over the country, so no one thought much about it.

I did have some problems associated with being inexperienced.

Youthful Difficulties

They had us ship all of our civilian clothes home and gave us new sailor type white uniforms, new shoes, socks and underwear. I had always worn jockey type underwear and they issued boxer type to us. I found, to my great distress, that the boxer type shorts climbed and rubbed my crotch raw when we marched, in the summer heat, to learn proper military drilling. I was afraid to complain, or interrupt the marching, to tug my underwear away from my crotch. I was in miserable condition.

In the anterooms of each of the shower rooms, they had two Bendix washing machines. I had never seen one of these and, of course, didn't know how to properly use one. I put a whole (small) box of soap in a laundry load and soap suds ended up knee deep in anteroom, filled the large shower room and spilled into the hallway. As punishment, I was made "Captain of the Head". Along with that impressive title went the chore of cleaning the head (toilet).

Another distressful experience occurred when they gave us yellow fever shots. I had a severe allergic reaction and passed out. I was taken to sickbay and given a shot to counteract the vaccination. The next day I was fine.

One course of instruction that was very highly regarded was the small boat training, which was designed to enable us to properly use lifeboats. They had a large number of these boats and launching davits, similar to those on ships, lined up along a long pier. We practiced launching and rowing the boats and got very good at it. This training undoubtedly proved useful and saved lives when ships, these men later manned, were torpedoed.

For the first month, we were not allowed to leave the base. On one of the weekends, Mayor La-Guardia visited us and gave a speech. We were all standing in formation. My position was so far away from the speaker's stand and the loud speakers, that I could not hear what he said. I could just barely see the Mayor. He was short and fat, but was very well regarded.

Ordinary Seaman Wilbur H. Vantine
New York, July, 1943

Prior to leaving the base on liberty, we all had to pass "short arm inspection". It was an effective measure to prevent the spread of VD. We all lined up, single file, to have our penises inspected for chancres, and (self) "milked" to check for possible gonorrhea infections. Prophylactic kits were freely available and we were all shown a movie that instructed in the use of them and to warn about VD. The use of condoms was not pushed, I suppose because they had not yet been refined to the point that they were effective. Maybe they were not available.

These days you hear a lot about homosexuals and "gay rights", but back in 1943, at age 18, I had never even heard of them. Also, I had never heard the term "oral sex" mentioned, and if I had heard it, I would have assumed that it meant talking about sex. In all of my experience at the training facilities during the war, these subjects never came up. Also, the "f" word was seldom used and never in mixed company. Our values and activities have changed greatly and not all for the good.

My First NY Liberty

My first liberty in New York was a memorable affair. The day started with a boat trip out to the Statue of Liberty. In those days you could climb up inside the monument, which of course, we did. Then, in the evening, things took a step downward. One of my compartment mates (about sixty men to a sleeping compartment) was formerly the bandleader at the Park Central Hotel in Manhattan. He gave a buddy of mine and me, passes to the hotel ballroom. We were refused entry, supposedly because of our age, but I believe the real reason was that we were intoxicated. We were binge drinking and didn't hold our booze very well. I remember that I was drinking slow gin fizzes, and had had way too many of them. After being refused entry to the ballroom on the hotel roof, we retreated to the hotel lobby. There I threw-up on a coffee table, that was conveniently near the couch I was seated on. I remember some nice lady sympathizing about that "poor boy". Somehow, we managed to get the subway back to Sheepshead Bay and sleep off our misbehavior.

The Merchant Marine Cadet Corps

Joining

On the day that I left home to travel to Sheepshead Bay, a notice was mailed to my Sedalia, MO, address, stating that I had been accepted into the Merchant Marine Cadet Corps. As soon as it had been forwarded to me in Brooklyn, I commenced trying to get transferred.

Since Cadet-Midshipmen were in the Navy Reserve, and since the program culminated in receiving a commission as Ensign in the Navy Reserve, I had to first pass a Navy physical exam. They were conducted at 90 Church Street in downtown New York City. I got permission to leave the Training Station and go take my physical exam.

I had some special problems to overcome. I had been wearing glasses since I was in the second grade and, at that time, Naval Officers had to have 20/20 vision, and not wear glasses. So I put them away. My left eye was my best and was nearly 20/20. I failed the eye test, but made a point of memorizing some of the lines on the eye chart.

I wrote a letter to the Navy, stating that I had gotten a cinder in my eye in the subway, and asked to take the exam again. To my surprise, they allowed it.

This time, with the examiner standing behind me, I read the chart with my left eye twice, switching hands with the card but keeping the opening in front of my left eye. Of course, having memorized some of the eye chart lines helped. The examiner didn't notice my chicanery and passed me.

I had a couple of other problems to overcome. One was that the hearing in my right ear was poor. The examiner had you hold your hand over one ear at a time while he spoke some words softly. I easily passed with the left ear and then, instead of holding my hand over my left ear, I actually cupped it to aid hearing. It worked and I passed the hearing test.

Lastly, I had very flat feet, and that was also not allowed. They had us walking around naked all day, and I found that I could make an arch artificially, and did so. It was very tiring, and I was sure glad when they told our group to get dressed.

So, having passed the Navy physical examination, I was accepted into the Merchant Marine Cadet Corps.

They had three Basic Training Schools where new inductees were given three months of intense training, before being assigned to ships for a minimum of six months. One was at San Mateo, CA, one was at Pass Christian, MS, and one was at the Academy at Kings Point, Long Island, NY. Instead of sending me to the nearby one at Kings Point, I was ordered to proceed home to Sedalia, MO, and then to go to Pass Christian, MS. How did we win that war?

So, I was discharged from the Maritime Training Facility at Sheepshead Bay and issued seamen's papers. They qualified me to sail on U. S. flag merchant ships in the following capacities: Ordinary Seaman (deck department); Wiper or Coal Passer (engine department); and Messman (steward's department). I was issued a train ticket for travel from New York to Sedalia, MO, and a second one from there to New Orleans. I was allowed five days at home before proceeding on my way.

Pass Christian

Getting There

Instead of taking the train from my hometown (Sedalia), I decided to take it from Kansas City, after first visiting my sister, Frances Lee (Netherton) Asel, and her family who lived there. My brother-in-law, Arthur Asel, took me to the train station to catch a train at 2100. A fast premium train, the "Southern Belle" was to leave an hour later, but there were no seats available. That turned out to be most unfortunate.

The train that I took stopped at every little town along the track and never went very fast between towns. Not only did the "Southern Belle" that left an hour later pass us, but the "Southern Belle" from the next night also passed us. When we reached Texarkana, we had to transfer to a different train that was even worse than the first. It was a coal burner and the engine belched heavy black smoke. The weather was hot, so we had to keep the windows open, and soot badly soiled my white sailor's uniform. The second train had hard wooden benches. We finally arrived in New Orleans about 0400, after more than 31 hours of miserable travel.

I had made friends with a Navy sailor, who was sharing my misery on the train. We decided to economize by sharing a hotel room. We found a taxi driver, at the train station, and asked if he could take us to a hotel. He said that the regular hotels were all full, but he believed that he could find us a room in a small one, that wasn't top rate, but that was clean. So he took us to a small, run-down establishment, that had the toilet and shower down the hall. Our room had a very poor and sagging bed.

I was supposed to report to the Merchant Marine Cadet Corp's New Orleans office on Canal Street at 0800, so I had a short night. At 0700, I noted the name of the "hotel", and took a taxi the dozen or so blocks to the New Orleans office.

After checking in at the office and being issued a train ticket for travel that afternoon from New Orleans to Pass Christian, MS, I caught a taxi. I asked the driver to take me back to the hotel, so that I could retrieve my gear. The driver told me that there was no hotel by that name. I was in a real jam and quite worried. There was a street in the French Quarter with the same name, and the driver suggested that he drive up and down that street, to see if I could recognize the building. The idea was a good one and saved my day. I did recognize the "hotel" and was able to recover my seabag of clothes and personal belongings.

That night I arrived at the Pass Christian railroad station. A bus met the several of us who were new Cadets, and took us to the Basic School. It had been established in what was formerly a middle class motel/resort.

General Information

Over the next few days, we were issued uniforms and organized into Deck and Engine Sections of about thirty men each. On average, about half of each Section would be eliminated during the three month course, for either failing grades or for getting too many demerits. There were about four to five hundred Cadets in attendance. I remember that the Commanding Officer was Commander A. E. Champeau, USMS (U. S. Maritime Service).

The base was still under construction and on several of the weekends, work parties were formed to aid construction. My group unloaded a railroad car full of gravel on one of the occasions.

I was lucky in that I always had found school work (study and tests) to be easy and soon earned the nickname of "4.0 Vantine". It was not meant to be a friendly name because about half of my Section Mates, at the bottom end of the curve, were being expelled for low grades. I did not know how to handle this hostility. Did they expect me to purposely miss questions on exams? To make me even more unpopular, I got through the whole three-month course without getting a single demerit.

The heavy studying, while having to do without my glasses, caused me to have headaches for the first month or so. Doing without the "crutch" of glasses caused my eyes to improve dramatically. The headaches soon went away.

One of the methods, used to break us in for the hard world out there, was to deprive us of sufficient sleep. We were assigned to night "fire watch" duty about once per week. These were for four hour stretches in the middle of the night. On one my watches, I was stationed near the barracks of the Chinese Stewards Department. There was a strong sweet odor waffling from their quarters that I later was told was marijuana. I had never heard of the stuff. On another fire watch, I was stationed at the base perimeter near a swampy area. The mosquitoes we so vicious that they were biting me through my thick leggings, where I could not scratch. I get an allergic reaction to mosquito bites and that was a terrible night for me.

The Grudge Fight

One of my Section Mates picked a fight with me during a lunch break. It was observed and broken up by one of the School Officer/Instructors. He arranged for us to put boxing gloves on and have a "grudge" match. It took place in a raised boxing ring and was witnessed by many of the Cadets (light entertainment?). The match was to consist of three two-minute rounds and the gloves were heavily padded. My opponent thoroughly disliked me and was highly motivated. Some of his buddies were cheering him on, but nobody was cheering for me. He charged me, flaying away wildly. I braced and met his charge with a straight left, that landed well, and greatly slowed and impressed him. I had some boxing experience with my high school buddies and had received some coaching from my brother-in-law, Arthur Asel. I wasn't truly expert, but I was a lot better than this joker, and beat him decisively. This affair earned some respect for me and greatly eased the pressure.

Finishing Basic School Training

The Basic School training course was intense. It did about all possible to prepare us for shipboard duty, in the three months that were available.

Although the numerous ship sinkings were not being fully reported, word of mouth news about them was getting around. We all knew that we would soon be facing great danger, during our six months (minimum) sea training on merchant ships. A few Cadets (not

Lifeboat Training, Pass Christian (1943) Cadet Wilbur Vantine, left front, Cadet Dean Bruch, behind him at Tiller. Other Cadets unidentified. (USMMCC Photos)

9.

The Author's Basic School Section, Pass Christian, MS (1943)
Cadet William K. Morgan, Back Row, far left, Cadet Dean K. Bruch, Front Row, 5th from
left, Cadet Wilbur H. Vantine, Back Row, 6th from right. These three became Ship
Captains and later worked together as Panama Canal Pilots

in my section), due to an unusual circumstance, were able to get away with postponing shipping out. Cadets, who were not already circumcised, were required to have the surgery prior to leaving. Some were so apprehensive about going to sea that, after their surgery, they purposely worked up erections to (painfully) break the stitches, and thereby delay be declared fit for sea duty.

Very much against the odds, two of my Section Mates from that 1943 Basic School Section, remain good friends to this day, 62 years later. We all three ended up as Ship Masters and later worked together as Panama Canal Pilots. They were Captain Dean K. Bruch and Captain William K. Morgan. Dean and I are shown in the accompanying picture, which was taken during lifeboat training.

The SS Davy Crockett

New Orleans, Panama Canal, Milne Bay, Port Moresby, Oro Bay, Milne Bay, San Francisco.

Joining the Ship in New Orleans

The Basic School Graduates were sent to various ports to be assigned to merchant ships. I was sent to nearby New Orleans.

I had two or three nights on the town, which was a very wild place during the war. In one of the nightclubs, on Bourbon Street in the French Quarter, I encountered one of the former Cadets from my section at Pass Christian. He had flunked out because of low grades. He had joined the Army Transport Service and was wearing one of their uniforms, with the rank of Lieutenant Senior Grade. I believe that they used Navy style rankings but, if they used Army style rankings, it would have been the rank of Captain. He told me that he had been appointed Captain of a small landing craft and was to make a delivery trip with it to the South Pacific, traveling in convoy with several others, one of which would have a "Navigator" aboard. He was brave to undertake such a responsibility with very little training to prepare him.

We Cadets were all apprehensive about going aboard the ships, not only because of the danger, but also because we really knew very little about ships and didn't know what kind of reception we would get from the crews. One good thing, our pay of $65 per month would be increased to $82.50, while the ships on which we were serving, were operating in the various "war zones".

The *SS Davy Crockett*, to which I was assigned, had been built by the Todd Houston Shipbuilding Corporation. The keel was laid on July 18, 1941, and she was launched on April 19, 1942. There were about 2,700 Liberty Ships constructed in the United States for the war effort. Except for this one, they all looked the same from a distance. The *SS Davy Crockett*, apparently by mistake, had a second crow's nest installed on the Main Mast. These ships were supposed to only have one and it should be located on the Fore Mast. This difference made it easy for us to locate our ship in an anchorage crowded with Liberty Ships, even though all were painted the same shade of gray and did not have the names painted on their hulls. There were name boards installed on each side of the flying bridges on Merchant Marine ships, that were hinged in the middle, so that they could be closed to hide the name. She was being operated by the Lykes Brothers Steamship Company for the War Shipping Administration, which owned the ship.

Except for having two crow's nests, he was a standard vessel of the type, being 441 feet in length, 57 feet in beam, displacing about 14,000 long tons, when fully loaded. She was able to make about 11 knots in smooth water. The ship was not equipped with a gyrocompass, so it had to be navigated using only the magnetic compasses. Navigating without a gyro compass added great difficulty. We were pretty well doing it like Columbus did, except that we could get time-ticks, by radio, to keep our chronometers accurate.

The Merchant Marine crew consisted of 37 men plus, when assigned, two Cadets.

There were 16 men in the Navy Gun Crew, including a Lieutenant (jg) and a Gunners Mate. These Navy Crews were referred to as "shark bait" in the fleet, because so many of them were ending up that way.

These ships were armed with eight 20mm machine guns, a three-inch gun on the bow and a five-inch gun on the stern. Merchant Marine crewmembers were assigned to help load the guns during combat situations. My general quarters station turned out to be loader for the 20mm machine gun, located on the port side forward on the Flying Bridge.

The ship was loading general cargo into the 'tween decks, when I joined her at a New Orleans pier, on Monday, November 15, 1943. The lower holds had already been filled with drums of aviation gasoline. Two days later we finished loading cargo and sailed.

When available, both a Deck Cadet and an Engine Cadet were assigned to a ship. In this case, Engine Cadet Curtis Brooks and I joined the ship together. We were to share a room on the bridge deck, next to the Radio Operator (Sparks). Curtis was a good shipmate and roommate. We got along well for the eight months that we were destined to sail together on two ships. He is now a retired Stationary Engineer and we have recently corresponded.

After 62 years, I still remember the names of some key personnel— Captain Kelsen, Chief Mate Atwell, Chief Engineer Prichard, and Spark's surname was Celeste.

Captain Kelsen was a handsome man, in his early forties. He had a neatly trimmed mustache and dressed in nice clothes daily. He conducted himself with dignity and seemed to handle his job competently. He had almost nothing to do with me and barely acknowledged my existence. I would later encounter him, in the summer of 1946, in Manila, Philippines, when he was Port Captain there for Lykes Brothers Steamship Company, and I was acting Second Mate on a Liberty Ship, that called in Manila to discharge cargo.

Chief Mate Atwell was a lean, muscular man in his mid-forties. He was a true seaman and knew his job well. He kept me busy doing manual labor on deck and provided no officer training. He had a fixation on the song "Paper Doll", and hummed it constantly.

The Second Mate was an overweight New Orleans native in his late forties. He had a heavy local accent and was severe in his demeanor. He offered no instructional help to me and I suspected that he was not very competent at his job.

I was required to do some navigational calculations for my Sea Project, and my only source of instruction was the Third Mate. He was a nice man, in his late twenties, who had just obtained his Third Mate License, at the Fort Trumbell School in New York. He was willing to help, but unfortunately, he was not very skilled in these matters. His "help" caused me to have several errors in my Sea Project.

"Sparks", Mr. Celeste, our next-door neighbor on the ship, was about fifty and was very friendly to Curtis and me. He had lost his left hand, in an accident, and got along very well with just one. Like many others who had physical handicaps that kept them from qualifying for military service, he chose to serve his country, in this war, by sailing in the Merchant Marine.

Curtis and I had reported aboard in uniform and were told to immediately change into work clothes. We were provided with what are now called "jeans" for work, but in those days they were called dungarees.

We Cadets were required to do a "Sea Project" during this part of our training. To properly do it required about twenty-one hours weekly of intense study/work.

Captain Kelsen and Chief Mate Atwell were not "school ship" men and had, as the saying went, "come up through the hawse pipe". They did not approve of the Cadet training program and, rather than helping me with my studies, kept me busy 12 hours daily doing manual labor. They allowed me no ship's time to work on my Sea Project.

My daily routine started by unblacking-out the ship at dawn, which consisted of opening the portholes, with their dead light steel plates, in the public areas to increase ventilation (weather permitting). I next sounded the cargo bilges, port and starboard for each of the five cargo holds. Sounding number four lower hole required me to climb down into the engine room and into the shaft alley, where those sounding pipes were located. I then had breakfast at 0730 and at 0800 went to work under the Bosun, mostly chipping rust and painting. At dusk, I blacked out the ship, which required me to check all portholes, in the crew and officer quarters, to make sure that the proper blackout vents were in use, instead of the open ones that were used during daytime. After all of this, I was usually too tired to effectively work on my Sea Project. I was falling further behind schedule on it every day.

Passage #1— New Orleans, Panama Canal

We traveled from New Orleans to the Panama Canal alone, without any escort. This was a very dangerous passage, because many ships were being torpedoed in the Gulf of Mexico and the Caribbean Sea. A zigzag course was followed, to confuse submarines that might sight us. We swung the lifeboats out, and secured them against "puddings", to be ready for quick lowering. If we got torpedoed, we had to hope that it hit in the engine room, rather than in one of the cargo holds where we had drums of aviation gasoline. Of course, the "Black Gang" no doubt had reservations about this and probably hoped that any torpedo would hit anywhere but the engine room, so that it would not doom them.

We arrived at the Cristobal Breakwater just before sunset and were instructed, by flashing light, to proceed twenty miles back to sea and to return at daybreak. They dragged a submarine net across the entrance at night. A few nights later, a German submarine Captain discovered this "happy hunting ground" and sank ships outside the Cristobal Breakwater, one each on five consecutive nights. The Sub Captain wrote a book after the war and said that he had to depart because he had run out of torpedoes. We had no navy vessels available to counter this danger.

The SS *Davy Crockett* docked in Cristobal to take fuel and water. So, Cristobal, Canal Zone, and the adjacent Panamanian City of Colon, were my first foreign ports. Like most wartime seaports, it was a wild place, with crowded bars and nightclubs, which had downright raunchy floorshows.

The experience was educational for me in that I learned about "B" girls. I was buying drinks for a pretty young thing, She was giving enough encouragement so that I had hopes of getting to know her better, before the evening was over. Each time that they delivered a drink to her, they gave her a plastic token, about the size of a silver dollar, which she dropped into her purse. My funds ran out at about 2300, and she abruptly left my table to find another sucker. I returned to the ship, poorer but wiser.

We transited the Canal the next day. A Marine Corps detachment of about a dozen men was placed aboard. Two Navy CPO's rigged an independent telephone communication between the bridge the engine room. These steps were to guard against efforts to sabotage the canal, which was vital to our war effort.

A Panama Canal Pilot boarded to direct our maneuvers and a gang of Canal Seamen boarded to handle the lines at the locks. They all stayed aboard for the entire transit that took about ten hours.

I again got confirmation that the Deck Department was a better choice than the Engine Department. I got to see the interesting scenery of the Canal, while poor Engine Cadet Curtis Brooks was sweating profusely down in the engine room.

Passage #2— Panama Canal, New Guinea

After clearing the Pacific end of the Canal, we set a southwesterly zigzag course toward the southwestern Pacific war zone.

A few days later we crossed the equator and had the usual ceremony to initialize the "pollywogs". We were blindfolded and brought before King Neptune, who properly terrorized us. Sparks typed up Certificates for us and I kept mine for many years, but have now lost it.

This was a very long passage of over a month. We had both Thanksgiving and Christmas at sea. The Stewards Department did its best to present special meals for those two occasions. This was my first Christmas away from home and I felt rather homesick, but tried not to reveal it.

I remember that Venus and Jupiter were situated so that they were very close together and were spectacular in the early evening sky. Most of the time the weather was excellent, but we had one very strong gale with high seas, during which time, there were huge Albatrosses circling the ship. They were cleverly "playing" the air currents and never had to beat their wings. They were gigantic birds, with a wingspan of about twelve feet. They were at sea many hundreds of miles from the nearest land. Studies have shown that they only go to land every two years, where they nest and lay and hatch huge eggs. Their nesting areas have an "A" team and a "B" team, that come on alternate years. After a couple of years at sea, they land and take off running with their wings spread. It resembles airplanes landing on the decks of aircraft carriers.

The Navy Lieutenant (jg) was a schoolteacher from Kansas. He was what was commonly called a "90 day wonder". He was lazy and not steeped in Naval traditions. He ran his command poorly. At Captain Kelsen's urging, we did have one session of gunnery practice on this long passage. We dropped an empty oil drum overboard and tried to hit it with cannon fire. There were no other drills and he never once inspected the guns, to see if they were being properly maintained. He slept about twelve hours a day. When we finally got back to San Francisco, he would be in big trouble, due to the poor condition of the guns.

As we neared our destination, which turned out to be Milne Bay, New Guinea, I was checking the provisions in one of the lifeboats, when we were suddenly "buzzed" by a plane. Thankfully, it was one of ours, a P-38, which was a unique design that had twin fuselages. It came upon us very quickly and there was no way that we could have prepared a defense, if it had been a Jap plane.

New Guinea

Milne Bay provided a large secure anchorage at the extreme southeastern tip of New Guinea. When we arrived, it presented an amazing sight, with about 150 ships, many of them Liberties, at anchor. We were to spend about a month here.

During our afternoon "coffee time" break, many of us went swimming. We had to look out for schools of stinging jellyfish, that drifted by from time to time, and also for huge swimming coral snakes, that were about eight feet long and large in diameter. The Navy Lieutenant ordered his men not to go swimming. He took a long nap every afternoon and many of the Navy boys swam while he slept.

One afternoon, one of the Navy Armed Guard crew shot a large coral snake with his rifle. We had one of our lifeboats tied up at the foot of our gangway, so Chief Mate Atwell and I decided to retrieve the dead snake. I used a boat hook to drape it over the bow and was surprised at how heavy it was. I was also surprised to find out that it was not dead. I hurriedly pushed it back into the water and it swam away.

One of our Messmen had a serious problem, in that he had trouble urinating. Chief Mate Atwell and I took him ashore to see an Army Doctor. It turned out that his problem was related to an old case of gonorrhea. The Doctor passed a sound through his penis and pulled a lever to open three sharp blades. He then pulled it out to cut the passage open to allow proper flow. When he withdrew the instrument, there was nothing touching the operating table but the back of the Messman's head and the heels of his feet.

While we were at anchor, I got to witness a bit of history. There was a Norwegian tanker anchored near us. Three US light cruisers, *the USS Boise, the USS Phoenix* and a sister ship whose name I don't recall, came in to refuel. Two went alongside the tanker and the third one anchored nearby to await a berth. They each had several ship silhouettes newly painted on their bridgewings. They were just back from one of the first uses of radar in a naval engagement. Jap ships had been anchored in a "U" formation in a bay. The cruisers had, at night, made a "U" inside their "U" and sank several of them. The Japs did not know about radar and were taken completely by surprise.

The *USS Phoenix* was given to the Argentine navy after WWII. They designated it as a battleship. It was sunk, with heavy loss of life, by a British atomic submarine during the Falklands War.

While we were anchored in Milne Bay, there were some attempted Japanese air raids. We were told that our pilots defeated them, with heavy loss to the Japs. We had several air raid warnings, but they turned out to be false. The combined anti-aircraft firepower of 150 ships, most of which had eight 20mm machine guns, would have been impressive.

We had two "casualties" on board our ship during a night call to general quarters. One of the Navy Gunners ran into the Bosun, who weighed about 260 pounds, when the two were going in opposite directions on an outside ladder (stair). It seemed funny, but wasn't, because both suffered painful injuries.

After about three weeks, we shifted to a dock and discharged the general cargo from our 'tween decks. Australian Army personnel ran the cargo winches and directed the work. After taking Attabrin for a long time, in lieu of the unavailable Quinine, to avoid malaria, they had turned yellow in areas that they perspired heavily, such as in their armpits.

"Good Enough" Island is located a short distance off the coast in this area. Natives from that island were trained by the Australians to work as stevedores. They were small in stature, had dark black skin, and had no excess body fat. They had great posture and a graceful stride. Their heads were covered with extremely heavy hair, that earned them the nickname of "fuzzy wuzzies". They were barefooted and wore only loincloths. Many had ringworm infections. The New Orleans stevedores had left an old Life Magazine in with the cargo. One of the fuzzy wuzzies was looking at a picture of the New York skyline. To my surprise, he asked me, in English with a cultured English accent, if it were true. He told me that he was a "child of England" and that he had been taught English in a missionary school.

After discharging our 'tween decks, we again shifted to anchor. The only cargo still on board was the drums of aviation gasoline in the lower holds.

Our Purser was an 18-year-old recent graduate of the Purser/Pharmacist Mate course at Sheepshead Bay. As I recall, his last name was Williams and he planned to be a doctor one day. He went ashore, to where a lot of Japanese soldiers had been buried, and retrieved the skull of one of them. He cleaned it up, so that only the boney part was left, and had it proudly on display in his room. Don't tell anyone on the Geneva Convention about this.

One morning while making my rounds sounding the cargo holds, I saw one of the Navy Crewmen hammering on something on the main deck cap rail. I looked over his shoulder and to my horror, saw that he was trying to open a Japanese hand grenade with a hammer and screwdriver. I hurried to Gunnery Officer's room and told him. He stopped the idiot before he could kill himself and possibly some others.

While we were anchored, a small Panamanian flag freighter, the *SS Ponce,* which was about 300 feet long, came alongside us. They had been over here for a long time and were out of just about everything. It was determined that we could spare them some food and other stores.

They had a monkey and a tomcat as pets. Our Bosun had a pet pussycat and, without his knowledge, it was decided to breed some kittens. It was quite a show that we all watched.

An Ordinary Seaman on that ship was Bill Nehring, who years later would be a Panama Canal Pilot with me.

The Bosun's cat, Agnes, died before she could present us with kittens. She was in the habit of jumping from the Main Deck to the top of Number 4 hatch, which was about a four-foot leap. She did it one day when the hatch covers were off and fell to the bottom of the hole, about thirty feet. Our tough old Bosun was in tears. Some of the other, very tough, seamen were also very sad.

Agnes had a remarkable sense of balance. When the ship would be rolling heavily and we humans would be clumsily lurching from side to side and hanging on to the rails, she would be walking along and maintaining a graceful vertical stance, seemingly without any effort.

I needed a pair of work shoes and bought a pair from the ship's "slop chest". They fell apart the first time that I got them wet. I read the label and found that they had been made by the "American Paper Company".

After a few days, we were ordered to proceed to Port Moresby on the south coast of New Guinea. There we anchored in the harbor. They had vicious mosquitoes that were small enough to get through the screens in our porthole vents. We had no insect spray and no repellant, so were pretty miserable. We were all taking Attabrin pills, that apparently worked in keeping us from catching malaria. After staying at anchor for two or three days, we were ordered to return to Milne Bay.

Our cargo of aviation gasoline was needed at Oro Bay, a small indent on the north coast of New Guinea, which was near a recently constructed airstrip. The problem was that there were no stevedores available there. It was proposed that the ship's crew discharge the cargo, after which we would be free to proceed back to the U. S. We enthusiastically agreed to this proposition. Some oil drum cargo hooks were placed aboard for our use, and we moved up the north coast, and anchored at Oro Bay.

We were to drop the drums of gasoline into the water and army launches would push them to the nearby sandy beach, where they would be manhandled onto shore by Army personnel.

We were organized into shifts to work one hatch at a time 24 hours per day. It was decided to ignore blackout rules so that we could work at night. The need for the gasoline was urgent. The deck crew worked six hours on and six hours off. All other crewmembers also worked about four hours daily on the cargo, in addition to performing their regular duties. To make the work crews come out even, one person, who turned out to be me, had to work twelve hours on and twelve off.

I still have a knot on my head that was a result of that operation. I was working down in the hold and was walking into the hatch opening, with a load of dunnage on my right shoulder, while the Second Mate, who was tending hatch, was directing the lowering of the cargo hook into the hold. There was a heavy snatch block shackled to it, for added weight. The hook and snatch block hit me on the left side of my head, which could not move much from the blow because of the dunnage on my right shoulder. I actually saw stars like they draw in the cartoons. Strangely, although I was knocked down, I was not completely unconscious. I was able to return to work after a short time. Of course, during this time, I had no opportunity to work on my Sea Project, and was hopelessly behind schedule on it.

It took us more than three weeks, but we finally finished discharging all of the drums of gas. They were being trucked away from the beach to the nearby airstrip, but there was still a big concentration of them on the beach. We heaved anchor and again returned to Milne Bay, to take fuel from an anchored tanker.

We were ready to steam back to the USA. If we had had excess stores, they would have been off-loaded, but we just had enough food, etc. to make it back. We had previously transferred some of our stores to the starving personnel on the *SS Ponce*. After spending almost three months in New Guinea, we were about to head for San Francisco, and we all felt good about that.

I had a big worry in that my Sea Project was nowhere near up to date. The Kings Point Representative in San Francisco was likely to have me expelled. On the voyage back, I burned the midnight oil every night, after spending 12 hours daily doing my shipboard duties and work. It was impossible for me to catch up, but I did make progress.

San Francisco

We zigzagged our way back across the Pacific Ocean without incident. When we picked up the San Francisco Pilot, Captain Kelsen dressed up in his Navy Blue uniform for our arrival. The Pilot preferred working from the Flying Bridge, where the visibility was better. As we entered the channel, sea gulls were following the ship, riding the air currents, so that they almost never had to beat their wings. One of them dropped a white greeting on the arm of Captain Kelsen's dark blue uniform.

The date was Tuesday, 4/4/44.

As some of the Navy Crew had been predicting, our guns did not pass inspection and the Navy Lieutenant (jg) was in bad trouble. A fish starts smelling from its head and he had done a poor job of commanding this gun crew. I don't know what action they took against him, but he was removed from the ship. The Gunners Mate, who was the senior Enlisted Man, was also in trouble and was removed.

My oldest sister, Mrs. Blanche Parks, who was eighteen years older than me, lived in nearby Valejo, CA. She worked at the Mare Island Navy Base, repairing and maintaining Sperry Gyro Compasses. It was a strange occupation for a lady, but the gals did a lot of strange and hard duty to aid our war effort. Security at the Base was not very tight and she was able to get me in to see her work place, the Gyro Laboratory. In fact, while I was the area, the local newspaper ran an article telling how one of the workers, as a joke, put the picture of a monkey on his ID badge and had no trouble gaining entry.

Engine Cadet Curtis Brooks and I had completed five months duty on the *SS Davy Crockett*. Our tour of sea duty was required to last a minimum of six months, so we would be shipping out again. This was a break for me, because it would give me a chance to bring my Sea Project up to date. The Kings Point Inspector gave a pass, on being behind, when I explained that the Captain and Chief Mate had allowed me no ship's time to work on it, and that I had to do it all after working twelve hours daily for the ship. Chief Engineer Pritchard had been more generous with Curtis and had allowed him some ship's time to do his Sea Project. He was pretty well up to date.

The Inspector tried to find us a berth on a ship that would have a relatively short voyage. We were first assigned to the *SS Cape Alexander*, but were pulled off when it was found that the ship would undergo extensive repairs before sailing.

(Note: According to "The Liberty Ships" by Captain Walter W. Jaffee, the SS Davy Crockett entered the Suisun Bay Reserve Fleet on May 15, 1946 and was withdrawn on May 13, 1969. She was converted at Richmond, CA to a pipe laying ship and subsequently became a general barge/dockside facility at Crockett, CA. She retained the same name.)

The SS Cape Chalmers

San Francisco, Noumea, Guadalcanal, Russell Islands, Pago Pago, San Francisco

Joining the Ship in San Francisco

Next, we were sent aboard the *SS Cape Chalmers*, a C-1 type freighter that was a bit smaller and faster than a Liberty Ship. 173 of them were built, some with diesel engines. They were "upscale" from Liberties and had much nicer quarters and facilities.

After we boarded, she shifted from San Francisco to Benecia, CA, to take aboard a full load of 500-pound bombs. The detonators were loaded separately into a specially built compartment in Number 4 'tween deck.

While we were loading, a huge explosion occurred at Port Chicago, which was another ammunition handling port across the Bay from Benecia. Three ship loads and a munitions train blew up and many people were killed. It broke windows for miles around and many people thought that there had been an earthquake.

When the explosion occurred, I was riding a bus to Vallejo, CA, to visit my sister, Blanch Parks. We did not feel or hear the explosion on the bus, but in the towns we passed through, people were in the streets, awaiting after shocks from what they assumed was an earthquake. Many store display windows were broken. In my sister's house, which was about twenty miles from Port Chicago, the hatch to the attic and been knocked out of place. This accident very much brought to mind what could happen if our cargo of 500-pound bombs exploded.

The *SS Cape Chalmers* had a friendly Captain and was a happy ship. I don't remember the Captain's name. He was in his late fifties and was a bit overweight. He had a full head of wavy gray hair and wore a rumpled khaki uniform, without any insignia. He, at first, gave the impression of being an old "fuddy duddy", but he was actually rather sharp. He was interesting in training Cadets, which was a break for me. I was given three hours daily of ship's time to work on my Sea Project.

The Chief Mate, Mr. Christiansen, was a 35-year-old Norwegian-American with a heavy Scandinavian accent. "Chris" was a handsome man, blonde with blue eyes, over six feet tall and with good posture. He later became a Pilot in Los Angeles Harbor. He had me stand the 12-4 daytime watch with the Second Mate and had me help work up the noon position daily. I was given other helpful duties around the chartroom and bridge. I kept all of the brass on the bridge highly polished. In addition to the three hours of ship's time, I spent at least two hours of my own time on my Sea Project. In a month or so, I was all caught up and soon had it finished.

Although we were to conduct weekly Fire and Boat Drills, they seemed to be a waste of time. We all knew that, if we got torpedoed or struck a mine, there would be one tremendous explosion and that would be that. One happy thought was that it might take out the submarine that torpedoed us. We had more than 8,000 long tons of 500-pound bombs aboard.

Passage #1— San Francisco, Noumea, Guadalcanal

We left San Francisco on Thursday, April 27, 1944, and set a zigzag course for Noumea, New Calidonia. This was a French Colony and we saw quite a few French men and women there. It had been headquarters for Admiral Halsey for a while, but he had moved on.

The Third Mate and I took a small rowboat, that we had on board, and explored the harbor. The water was crystal clear and there were some interesting sunken ships to explore. There were vicious barracuda fish about, so we had to be careful. One sunken steamship had the engine exposed and it looked just like a smaller version of the triple expansion steam reciprocating engine of a Liberty Ship. The windlass was clearly labeled "SF Ironworks 1904", which we deemed to mean San Francisco Iron Works.

We next proceeded to anchorage at Guadalcanal where we had an interesting visitor. The Captain's 18-year-old son was in the Marine Corps and was stationed here. Arrangements were made for him to visit his father. He was my age and had already been in heavy combat against the Japanese soldiers. He was only allowed a short visit and a meal before he had to return to his unit.

The Russell Islands

We then steamed to the Russell Islands where our cargo was needed. The Seabees had recently cleared the jungle, and laid down steel mats to serve as a landing field/base, for B-24 bombers. They had also built a proper dock, to which we tied up, and commenced discharging our cargo of 500-pound bombs.

Every day we had a different group of Army Air Corps Pilots aboard, so that they could enjoy a hot shower and better, or at least different, food than they were used to.

The Third Mate and I took a walk ashore and passed three Seabees sitting at the entrance to their Quonset hut, which was painted up real fancy. They also had whitewashed rocks lining the walkway to the hut. They asked us if we would like a cold beer!!! Can you imagine, a cold Budweiser in the middle of this tropical jungle setting? These guys worked hard and when they were done, they played just as hard. They had worked a miracle in construction here and now miraculously produced cold beer.

That evening I attended an outdoor movie at a military camp. The audience sat on log benches. About half way through, the movie was stopped, and it was announced that the D-Day Invasion of Europe had commenced. The date was June 6, 1944. The Chaplain led us all in a heartfelt prayer for its success. No one was interested in seeing the rest of the movie.

Return Voyage— Russell Islands, Pago Pago, San Francisco

It took two weeks to discharge our cargo and we then set course for Pago Pago, Samoa, in ballast (empty). We were to load empty oil drums there to take back to the United States.

Back in the days when U. S. Navy ships burned coal, Pago Pago had been an important coaling station. There were many blue-eyed natives to prove it. The local Chiefs were designated CPO's (Chief Petty Officers), in the U. S. Navy, and had their own unique uniforms. One of the Chiefs was stationed aboard to act as boss of the stevedore gangs. I befriended the Chief assigned to our ship and invited him into the Cadet's room for a coke. He was about five feet eight inches tall and was very much overweight. He ended up drinking a whole case of warm Coca Cola, that I had no way to replace. He told me that all Chiefs had to get tattoos, to show their rank, and that they had to go to British Samoa to get a proper one. He dropped his drawers and showed me his tattoo. It consisted of black stripes radiating from the crack of his fanny. The black tattoos did not contrast much with his brown skin, and were not very impressive to me. He invited me to come back after the war and he would fix me up with a nice wife. He said that I could have a good life here.

We took aboard two passengers, the retiring station chief for Matson Navigation Company, and his native wife. He was in his mid-sixties and I imagine that his wife was younger than him. However, the native women here, although beautiful when they are young, do not age well. His wife looked like an 80-year-old woman.

They had a lot of empty oil drums here and we loaded them all, but there were not enough to completely fill our ship. Of course, they did not weigh much, so we were high in the water when we set sail for San Francisco. We had mostly good weather as we zigzagged our way back home. We did have enough rolling and pitching to make both of our passengers seasick.

The Navy Gun Crew on this ship had a proper Officer in command. They conducted many drills and we had several sessions of target practice during the voyage. This ship had armament similar to that on the *SS Davy Crockett,* namely eight 20mm machine guns, a three-inch gun on the bow and a five-inch gun on the stern. As before, I was loader for one of the 20mm machine guns on the Flying Bridge. The gunner let me fire a few rounds and that was a great experience.

We arrived back in San Francisco on Tuesday, July 18, 1944. The Kings Point Inspector boarded the ship and inspected our Sea Projects, which were now completed. The next day Engine Cadet Curtis Brooks and I were detached and sent on our way home for a five-day leave, after which we would travel to the Academy.

We had just over eight months of shipboard duty, two more than was required.

Leave

I rode a train from San Francisco to Kansas City and changed there to the Missouri-Pacific railroad, that ran through Sedalia, MO, my hometown. There were no seats available on the first train and I spent the entire passage sitting on my suitcase in the aisle. Many military personnel were doing the same.

The Academy had released my picture and a brief story to the local paper, *The Sedalia Democrat,* which ran it in an edition while I was home.

I had missed my senior year of high school, but my old classmates had graduated the previous May, They were now all off to the various military branches. So, none of my old friends were here to buddy around with. It was great to visit my family, but I was kind of lonesome for contemporaries.

There was strict gasoline rationing, so I couldn't use the family car much. Army, Navy, Marine Corps and Coast Guard personnel, on leave, could get extra gasoline ration tickets, but I was informed that Merchant Marine personnel did not qualify.

A widowed friend of the family, who was my God Mother, Mrs. Patricia Illgenfritz, had a fine old Packard automobile that she didn't drive much, and so had gas ration coupons to spare. She loaned me her fine automobile, and I was able to make the rounds of the local clubs. I found almost nobody that I knew.

The five days passed quickly and I boarded the Missouri-Pacific railroad for travel to St. Louis, where I changed to the Pennsylvania railroad to go to New York's Penn Station. There I took the Long Island Railroad to Great Neck, Long Island, and then a bus to the Academy at Kings Point.

Kings Point

General Information

The Academy is located on Long Island Sound at the beautiful estate of the late Walter P. Chrysler, plus adjacent land that had been purchased. The old Chrysler home served as the Administration Building and the resident of the Supervisor, Captain (later Commodore) Giles P. Stedman. He had been Commodore of the United States Lines and had been Captain of the *SS America*. Six three-story barracks buildings and a messhall had been constructed with connecting hallways. Also and large gymnasium and an additional (separate) barracks building as well as a stadium, gatehouse and buildings for classes had been provided. An extremely tall flagpole had been erected. It was said to be the tallest one in New England. A harbor for small craft, with an extensive pier, was in place to berth the *SS Emery Rice* and numerous other training vessels and boats.

There were about 1,200 Cadet-Midshipmen in residence at the U. S. Merchant Marine Academy at the time. They were divided into Three Battalions of Six Companies each. The Cadets were assigned four men to the rooms and organized into Sections of about thirty men, that would attend classes as a unit. There were two programs of instruction, Deck, which would lead to a License as Third Mate, and Engine, which would lead to a license as Third Assistant Engineer. After we finished the Academy courses and passed our final exams, the U. S. Coast Guard conducted the Merchant Marine License Examinations and issued the Merchant Marine Licenses. Graduates of both courses obtained a Commission as Ensign in the U. S. Navy Reserve.

On average, about half would be expelled during the nine month course at the Academy for getting a grade of 2.3 or lower, on any course, or for getting more than 50 demerits. This was after a similar failure rate at Basic School and many failing in their Sea Projects. Also, 144 were killed while sailing as Cadets aboard Merchant Ships. So, only about twenty-five percent of those who qualified to join the Merchant Marine Cadet Corps, ended up graduating.

Only one of my Basic School Section Mates, Craig Sharp, ended up in my Section at the Academy. Bill Morgan had lucked out with exactly six months of sea time and was two months ahead of me now. Dean Bruch ended up with ten months of sea time and was two months behind me. Most of the others were not around and I suspected that some might have failed to finish their Sea Projects. I heard that one had been lost at sea.

My First Demerits

On my first day back at the Academy from my Cadet Sea Duty in August 1944, I was assigned to Furuseth Barracks, along with others in the same category. Each sleeping room had about thirty or so two-high bunks with metal lockers along the walls.

In those days there were many more Cadets than could be accommodated in one seating at the mess hall, and I ended up being assigned to the second mess. When they sounded reveille at 0600 the next morning, I arose, made my bunk and started policing up the place. I noticed that some of the other second-mess Cadets stayed in their bunks another 15 or 20 minutes before getting up.

The next morning, I was just as tired as they were, so I did the same. Unfortunately, I looked up and saw the Barracks Officer, Ensign Sinesa, at the door. I shouted "attention" and jumped out of my bunk, as did several others. My bunk was near the door and I was the only one that he could be certain was in their bunk after reveille. That cost me 25 demerits. I never met or spoke to Ensign Sinesa after that one incident, but I remember his name to this day, 61 years later, although I'm not sure of the spelling. This incident would later have serious consequences.

The Routine

The routine at Kings Point was very demanding. The courses required hard concentration and much study. At the same time, we did hard physical training. I was again successful with the schoolwork part of our training and had the highest grade point average in my Section C-331. I was awarded a scholastic star to wear on the sleeve of my uniform.

Our weekend liberties were brief, from after the Saturday Review, which ended about noon, to having to be back aboard at 2200. If we went into Manhattan, we had to catch the 2100 Long Island train from Penn station. We were also allowed to leave the Academy grounds on Sunday afternoon for a few hours. On our 27th weekend, we were allowed an overnight liberty, and we all looked forward to that as a major event.

Every Saturday morning we had inspections in which those making the inspections made strenuous efforts to find something wrong. Their white gloves did their best to find dust over the door jams, behind the radiators, etc. Room inspections also occurred unannounced during the week, when we were in class. I fared pretty well on these inspections except that, during my turn every four weeks as room captain, I picked up three demerits for minor infractions. These were for such things as dirt in a washbasin or a smudge on a mirror— things for which the blame couldn't be easily assigned to an individual in the room.

The rooms in the barracks were designed for two occupants. There were two washbasins with mirrors, and room to accommodate two persons comfortably. During the war, four Cadets were assigned to each room. They were equipped with two double-decker bunks and a desk was placed in the middle of the room along, with four chairs, to use for study.

During the nine months that I was at Kings Point, our section got moved around a couple of times. My roommates after the final move were John Olson, Paul Neely and Walter Malone. I lost track of John over the years, but regretfully was informed that he passed away in 2003, while residing in Lincoln Park, NJ. Paul was very successful and was Chairman of his own firm, Arnheim & Neely, Inc., which was in the legal and real estate business in Pittsburgh PA. Walter and I have corresponded occasionally and we both attend the five-year Homecomings at

Kings Point. He had a successful career in the Navy and retired, as a Captain, to Virginia Beach, VA. After he left the Navy, he worked several years as a consultant to a defense contractor.

The Short Sheet Episode

While at the Academy, Walter, who had the bunk above me, developed a skill that the other three of us envied greatly and which irritated us no end. He was thin and was able to slip into and out of his bunk, without disturbing the sheets and blanket to the extent that the bed had to be remade.

Finally, when we had all that we could take, we struck back. We short-sheeted his bed when he was out

My three Kings Point Roommates, Left to Right, Walter J. Malone, Paul Neely and John Olson

of the room. To do this, you double back the bottom sheet and fold the edge of it back over the top sheet and blanket so that the bed looks like it is made-up normally. When lights out occurred and taps were sounded that night, the laughter and howls in our room were spectacular. It was a wonder that we didn't get in trouble.

The Hurricane of 1944

In September of 1944 a severe hurricane struck the Long Island area where the Academy was located. The town of Kings Point and the city of Great Neck were relatively wealthy areas, with many large homes that had spacious yards with big, beautiful trees. The storm caused extensive damage.

In the Academy harbor area, the devastation was awesome. The strong wind had fortunately blown on shore, so our many small craft had not been blown away, but most were now on our shore and badly beat-up. The *SS Emory Rice,* an historic old combination steam and sail vessel with a wrought iron hull, had been torn loose from her moorings and was now "high and dry". This interesting old ship had been the flag ship for Admiral Mathew C. Perry when, in 1853-54, he led an expedition that forced Japan to have diplomatic and commercial relations with the West, after more than two centuries of isolation. The Academy's seamanship department cleverly rigged huge block and tackle arrangements, so that several hundred Cadets pulling together, including yours truly, were able to pull the old ship back into the water.

After helping rescue the *SS Emory Rice,* I was assigned as a member of a work party, that went through the nearby town of Kings Point, to clear the streets of fallen big old trees. This was in the days before powered chain saws, so we were cutting up the trees the "old fashioned way", with handsaws and axes. My work group was invited into a very fine old home for a cup of tea and a drink of water. Our hosts were a nice old couple who appeared to be very wealthy.

A Chilling Experience

I had one very "chilling" experience while in training at Kings Point. The winter of 1944-45 was very cold in the U. S. Northeast. There were patches of sea ice in Long Island Sound.

On one extremely cold February morning, we were training in how to properly rig and use a Lyle Gun and Breeches Buoy. A Lyle Gun is a small cannon that is used to fire a projectile, to which a line is attached, from one location to another. Their main purpose is to rescue stranded people on a sinking ship, when seas are too rough to allow transfer by boat. We fired a Lyle Gun from one finger pier to a second finger pier and then swung up and braced booms, which were about twelve feet high, on both finger piers to anchor the endless pulley arrangement, to which the Breeches Buoy would be attached. Then, one person at a time could be transferred, over the water, from one finger pier to the other. I was unusually foolish that morning and volunteered to be the first passenger. When I was about half way between the finger piers, the tieback line on one of the booms let go and I ended up floating in Long Island Sound, along with the chucks of sea ice. It seemed to take forever for them to figure out how to retrieve me from the water. When I finally got on solid ground, it required a walk of several hundred wind-swept yards to reach the nearest shelter, which was a barracks building for the First Battalion. My Section was quartered in Jones and Barry Hall, which was at the far end so, in my freezing condition, I had to walk through the two barracks of the First Battalion, the Mess Hall, the two barracks of the Second Battalion and to the second and last barracks of the Third Battalion, before I could strip off my cloths and take a hot shower. I was about as cold as one could get without freezing to death.

Cadet/Midshipman Wilbur Vantine (1944)

My First Serious Romance

My best friend and liberty buddy, in those days, was section-mate Bob Bayless, whose father owned an automobile agency in southern California. We spent many Saturday liberties together, hitting the bars and looking for girls in Manhattan. Bob was more handsome than me and he had an easy way with the ladies. He always made the initial contact. Our favorite hangout was the bar in the Taft Hotel.

Except for the overnight liberty on our 27th weekend, we had to catch the 2100 Long Island train, from Penn Station, in order to be back at the Academy by 2200. This put a severe crimp in our "cruising" activities.

On one of our evenings at the Taft Hotel bar, we met two pretty girls, who were about our age, from Wilkesboro, PA. As usual, Bob made the advance and, of course, ended up with the one that he considered to be best looking, Ellen. I got the other, Helena, who fortunately was my first choice anyway. Both girls were very nice and had office jobs back home. They were in New York for the first time and were seeking adventure, as were we. We all hit it off very well and agreed to get together again, whenever the girls could get back to New York. Having to catch the 2100 train put a big hitch in our would-be plans for the evening.

A couple of weeks later, Ellen and Helena did return and we all got together again for a visit, which included some (innocent) time in their hotel room. Helena and I made plans to a serious get together during my 27th weekend overnight liberty.

For the big occasion, I made a reservation at the Riverside Hotel, that was in a beautiful location on the Hudson River, in northwest Manhattan. I was able to meet Helena's train at Penn Station and we took a taxi to the hotel. I was nervous about checking in (and also about some other things), but the hotel clerk did not question our Mr. and Mrs. status. Our room was on the fifth floor and had a beautiful view of the river.

We had a nice dinner in the hotel dining room and then adjourned to our room. I wanted to do things first-class and had obtained a bottle of champagne. There was some difficulty in removing the cork, but over all things went well. We were young and in love and things took their natural course. Helena was a virgin, but we tenderly overcame that difficulty.

During a trip to the bathroom about 0200, Helena left the hot water facet running in the lavatory with the stopper closed. About 0600 I was awakened by a heavy pounding on our room door. As I swung around and put my feet down, to my great surprise and distress, I found that our carpet was thoroughly wet and that steam was coming from our bathroom door. The water was running into the rooms on the floors below and they were working their way up to determine the source. They had found it.

Of course the costs of cleanup and damage from this occurrence was going to be great and I had very little money. My income was only $65 per month. We did not know what to do. The hotel management must have realized that there was nothing to be gained by pressing for recompense and did not suggest it. We got dressed and quickly and quietly checked out and made tracks away from the Riverside Hotel.

Helena was able to get to New York on a couple of more weekends prior to my graduation and also met me there for another tryst when I graduated and no longer had to catch that damn 2100 train from Penn Station. We continued to correspond for some time. She had wedding bells in mind, but I was not yet ready to settle down.

After not exchanging mail for a couple of years, I again wrote to her at her old address in Wilkesboro and got a reply. She was amazed that my letter had somehow been forwarded to her in Hawaii. She was happily married and had a baby boy.

My good buddy, Bob Bayless, did not graduate from the Academy. He was not dumb by any measure, but got expelled for getting a 2.3 grade in one of our subjects. For some time he had been teetering on the scholastic edge. I recall one incident in our Gyro class when the Instructor asked Bob a question to which he did not know the answer. I whispered it to him and the Instructor heard me. He announced that we would both get a 2.3 grade for that day. After class, I spoke with the Instructor and asked that he please not do that to Bob, since he had done no wrong and could not afford the 2.3 grade. Thankfully, he relented.

My Near Expulsion

A few weeks before our scheduled graduation, my section was, in our Naval Science Class, studying "Naval Courts and Boards". It is hard to imagine a more boring subject. The class occurred just after lunch. The room was overheated and my seat was in the back of the class. Unfortunately, I dozed off. The Instructor noticed and ordered me to put myself on report for "sleeping in class".

I checked up on this and found that it was a 25-demerit offense. It was going to put me over the 50-demerit limit for expulsion.

What should I do? Failing to obey an order was also an offense that would result in expulsion. Looking at the situation with today's perspective and values, it seems that I should have explained the situation to the Navy Officer, who ordered me to put my self on report, and request leniency. The atmosphere was such that this course of action never occurred to me or to any of my friends. Instructors were our enemies, intent on trying to give us a 2.3 grade, leading to expulsion. They did this to about half of my section mates. The administrators were likewise against us, seeking primarily to give out demerits, with their dismal consequences. It seemed to me, that the best and most "manly" way to handle the situation, was to do as ordered, and go out with as much honor and dignity as I could muster.

I kept watching the "Mast List", which was posted daily. My name didn't come up and it seemed like an eternity, while I waited and watched. Then, one evening, during study time, a Cadet whose name I wish I knew, knocked on our room door and asked for me by name. It seemed that he had been put on report and had fished his report slip out of the report box at the Battalion Office. Mine had come out with his. He assumed that I wanted it thrown away and that is what he had done with it. The Instructor in my Naval Science Class never checked to see if I had put myself on report. So, I lucked out.

Graduation

I now have fond memories of my time at Kings Point. We all tend to remember the good and forget the bad. Few women would bear a second child if this were not the case. But, when I seriously recollect my time at the Academy, I remember that the discipline made it a miserable place. This, coupled with the extremely hard physical and mental pressures, made it unpleasant. I felt a camaraderie with my roommates, section mates, and fellow cadets, but I hated the place and looked forward eagerly to graduation.

Our original section C-331 of 30 Cadets had been reduced to 17 by graduation day, which occurred on Friday, April 20, 1945. My buddy, Bob Bayless, was the last to drop out.

Graduation Picture of Section C-331, April 1945
17 Survivors of the 33 who had started nine months earlier
Cadet Wilbur Vantine, front row, far right
Cadet Walter Malone, 2nd row, far right

Two Deck Sections and two Engine Sections graduated every two weeks. Since they occurred so often, no big deal was made of the graduation ceremonies. Commodore Giles Stedman presented us with our diplomas.

The only recognition that I received, for being first scholastically in my section, was that Cornell Maritime Press gave me a certificate to purchase fifty dollars worth of books in their Manhattan store. That is a fine company, that is still very much into the business of publishing for the Maritime Industry.

My God Mother, Mrs. Patricia Illgenfritz, bought a class ring for me that cost the princely sum of fifty dollars.

After we had finished the (wartime shortened) course of nine months back at the Academy and had passed the final exams, we sat for the Coast Guard Examinations for Third Mate (for Deck Cadets) or Third Assistant Engineer (for Engine Cadets). These examinations took a week to complete.

The Coast Guard Commander who conducted the license exams was very severe in his demeanor. If you so much as looked up from your paper you were likely to get kicked out and absolute silence was required. We Deck Cadets faced a special difficulty in connection with the Coast Guard exam.

The biggest problem was the possibility of getting a certain "Day's Work" problem that started with a compass bearing and distance off Barnegat Lighthouse. This was similar to other "Day's Work" problems, in that you then sailed several compass courses for varying times at various speeds. You had to first find the position of the Light House (in the Light List), correct the compass bearing for variation and deviation and remember to reverse it, and to correct the various courses steered for variation, deviation (different on each heading), leeway and current. It wasn't such a difficult dead reckoning problem, but was tedious and there were many places where an error would cause you to be wrong in finding your final position. The difficulty with the Barnegat Day's Work problem was that the Coast Guard Commander had the wrong answer. The Academy knew this, but couldn't tell him without revealing that they illegally had the problem. If we were handed that one, we had to decide whether to work it out correctly, and get failed, or to give the Commander the answer that he had. If you took the latter course, you had to hope that he had not meanwhile discovered his mistake, and wonder how you came up with a wrong answer that exactly matched his previous wrong answer.

I had determined that, if I drew this one on the exam, I would solve it correctly and argue it out with the SOB. My Section Mates and I sweated this one out, but none of us got this problem.

Again, I lucked out and was home free. I happily left the Academy and went out to finish off Hitler and Tojo.

(Some years later, those of us who had obtained an unlimited Master or Chief Engineer license from the Coast Guard, were awarded a Bachelor of Science Degree in Nautical Science.)

Leave

I took a train home for two weeks leave before shipping out. While there, I called on Mr. Forest L. Drake, the Principal of Smith-Cotton High School in Sedalia, MO. I showed him the transcript of my credits and grades from Kings Point. He arranged for me to get a high school diploma based upon that.

The diploma was dated 1945, which causes some confusion when it is time for the high school class reunions. I had been a classmate with the group that graduated in 1944, not with the 1945 bunch. I attend the 1944 reunions, although I am only a half-ass member of that class. (As of this writing, I am planning to attend our 60th Class Reunion commencing October 30, 2004.) (Later update— I did attend the Class Reunion and enjoyed it very much)

VE Day, May 8, 1945, occurred while I was home on leave. We were all very proud of our boys in Europe that had defeated the formable German war machine. We all dreaded the expected carnage that was expected when we invaded Japan, but were confident that we would prevail.

The SS Christopher Gadsden

Joining the Ship in New York

I returned to New York and on Saturday, May 26, 1945, and was assigned to the *SS Christopher Gadsden,* a Liberty Ship freighter, as Third Mate. She was loading general cargo at a pier in Manhattan. Most of it was prominently stamped "Lend Lease".

She was a standard Liberty ship, similar to the 2,700 others that were built for service during the war. The ship was constructed by the North Carolina Shipbuilding Co. The keel was laid on November 15, 1942 and she was launched one month and three days later on December 18, 1942. She was operated by AGWI Lines (Atlantic, Gulf and West Indies Line) for the War Shipping Administration, that owned the ship.

A representative from the Masters, Mates and Pilots union boarded and signed me up for membership and, of course, collected my dues.

Captain John J. Kelly was in command. He was about forty years old and was just under six feet tall. His weight was about right for his height. He had a good head of brown wavy hair and brown eyes. He had a medium mustache. He had been torpedoed twice and these experiences made him very apprehensive. While we were at sea, he never took his clothes off, and he slept on the settee in the Chart Room. It was as though he expected to be torpedoed again, at any moment. This conduct continued, even though Germany had surrendered, and the submarines had been ordered to cease combat operations.

New York, Liverpool, New York

This voyage took us from New York to Garsten, England, which is a suburb of Liverpool. The weather was good and we, for the first time since the war started, did not have to worry about submarines. There were plenty of mines about, but they were mostly in the North Sea and along the European coast, areas that we would not visit on this voyage.

I was enjoying performing my duties as Third Mate and was good at it. I was earning the excellent wage of $218 per month. I stood the 8 to 12 bridge watches.

The Liverpool area had been heavily bombed by the Luftwaffe and severe damage was visible everywhere. Each block in the residential areas had a bomb shelter erected in the street. They were not very bombproof in that they were just brick structures about seven feet high with benches inside. This contrasted sharply with the bomb shelters, that I would later see in Germany, that had reinforced concrete walls many feet thick, that would give real protection during an air raid.

The people were largely of Irish extraction and everyone was very friendly to Americans. The British people very much appreciated the service that our Merchant Marine, and their own Merchant Service, was performing. Our Merchant Marine casualty rate was very high, but the British Merchant Service suffered an even higher one.

Miss Violet McGann, who was a very pretty young lady, invited me to visit in her home. These folks had very little to eat or in the way of luxuries, but were anxious to share what they had. I begged off in taking any of their food, since they had to get by on such small rations.

The whole area had a dingy and depressing aura. They heated their homes and cooked using coal, and everything had a dismal coating of coal dust and soot. A heavy rain was needed to wash the place clean.

I purchased, for about $120, a British Husun (brand) sextant. Most ships had a sextant, belonging to the ship, but they were usually not very good.

It took about two weeks to discharge our general cargo. We then loaded several tons of Scotch Whiskey, which was prominently labeled "Reverse Lend-Lease". The stevedores purposely dropped hard a few pallet loads of whiskey onto the main deck, for the purpose of breaking some of the bottles. They then raised the pallets a few feet above the deck and caught the drippings, or at least a large part of them, in tin cups. They immediately drank their loot. This was pilferage that did not show, since no cases were missing, and they were still sealed shut. I tried to stop them from doing this, but they ignored me and the authorities were not interested in the matter.

We arrived back in New York on Friday, August 3, 1945 and docked to unload our cargo of Scotch Whiskey. Here, the stevedores apparently didn't care about the niceties of not having any missing cases, as they openly pilfered the cargo. I tried to stop it but they informed me that I had better mind my own business. There was no support form higher authority so I desisted.

It was obvious that the war was winding down, and I wanted to get into college as soon as possible. My ambition was to be a chemical engineer. On Monday, August 6, 1945, I signed off the Articles of the *SS Christopher Gadsden*. Captain Kelley gave me a nice letter of recommendation. At Captain Kelly's request, I stayed on for a few more days until a replacement Third Mate could be obtained.

V-J Day occurred on Tuesday, August 14, 1945. I celebrated in Times Square with about a million other happy Americans. This horrific war had finally ended.

(Note: According to "The Liberty Ships" by Captain Walter W. Jaffee, the SS Christopher Gadsden entered the Beaumont Reserve Fleet on April 30, 1948 and was withdrawn on March 24, 1970. She was scrapped at New Orleans, LA, in November of that year.)

AGWILINES, Inc.

SS Christopher Gadsden
6 August 1945
New York N.Y.

To Whom it may Concern,

Dear Sir:

This is to state that Mr. W.H. Vantine was rated as 3rd Officer aboard the SS Christopher Gadsden from May 26, 1945 to August 6, 1945.

His duties consisted of Senior Watch Officer, Junior Navigator and assistant in the managment of the vessel, all of which he performed to the satisfaction of all concerned.

I regret to note that Mr. Vantine has chosen to leave my unit and our organization, however, I feel that with his ability and qualifications he will do well wherever he goes.

Sincerely:

John J Kelly

Master, SS Christopher Gadsden.

Letter of Recommendation from Captain John J. Kelly
(Note: This letter helped the author obtain a job as "Acting" Second Mate, when he returned to sea the next year.)

33.

Chapter II: SS Walt Whitman
(My First Post WWII Voyage)

My Year Away from the Sea

Since this section has little to do with "Nautical Tales", I will keep it brief.

After V-J Day, I caught a train from New York to my home in Sedalia, MO, and starting shopping for a college. I didn't have much money saved, but I was strong and healthy and could work while attending school. Also, it was widely presumed that a Bill of Rights, for the Merchant Marine, would be passed similar to the GI Bill of Rights that helped Armed Forces personnel with college expenses.

I did not know it, but I was legally supposed to be "frozen" in my profession in the Merchant Marine. I most likely left the sea illegally.

Commencing in September 1945, I attended the Missouri School of Mines in Rolla, MO, for two semesters, taking twenty-one hours and twenty-three credit hours of subjects. I again did well in schoolwork and made the Dean's List. I was on my way to become a Chemical Engineer.

I joined the Sigma Nu fraternity. I was the first of the war veterans to get into this college and the fraternity did not know how to deal with me. The other pledges were eighteen year olds fresh out of high school. I even heard talk, from the older members, that maybe vets were not suitable to become frat brothers. I put up with and endured the stupid hazing, including getting paddled. They gave me assignments (all at night) to gather a bushel of cow droppings, to put a chalk mark on every third telephone pole along the railroad track between Rolla and the next town six miles away, and to bring in a used man hole cover. For the later assignment, I got a girl that I knew to give me a Kotex with a little mercurochrome painted on it. Another pledge with this assignment rolled in a real one from the street.

I worked for three hours daily after classes at a Motel (Shuman's Tourist City) and also for twelve hours on Sundays and every-other Saturday. This was a good job for a student because I could study when not busy.

The anticipated "Bill of Rights" for WWII Merchant Marine Seamen did not come through. This was in spite of the fact that our all-volunteer service had a fatality rate of about one in twenty-six, higher than that of any of the armed services.

To better finance my education, I decided to temporarily go back to sea during the summer months of 1946.

SCHUMAN'S

TOURIST CITY

U. S. HIGHWAYS 63 AND 66

**ALL MODERN
MOTOR COURT CONVENIENCES**

ROLLA, MISSOURI

R. E. SCHUMAN, OWNER AND MANAGER

RADIOS

TELEPHONES

COMBINATION TUB AND
SHOWER BATHS

PRIVATE GARAGES

AIR COOLING SYSTEM
FOR SUMMER COMFORT

CENTRAL STEAM HEATING
SYSTEM FOR WINTER COMFORT

WATCHMAN ON GROUNDS
ALL NIGHT

MAIL SENT OUT ON
NIGHT TRAINS

May 25, 1946

TO WHOM IT MAY CONCERN:

The bearer of this letter, Mr. W. H. Vantine,
has been working here on a part time basis while attending
the Missouri School of Mines.

We have found him to be honest, dependable,
and a very likeable young man. We are glad to recommend him
to you as such, and will gladly answer any inquiries you
make care to make regarding him.

Very truly yours,

Owner

Letter from Motel Owner for whom the author worked during college

The SS Walt Whitman

Beaumont, Panama Canal, Long Beach, Kobe, Manila, Panama Canal, Galveston

Joining the Ship in Beaumont

When the second semester of college was finished, I took a train to New Orleans and went to the office of Lykes Brothers Steamship Company to apply for a job. This was a large and successful company and was the one for whom I had worked for five months as Cadet on the *SS Davy Crocket*.

Shipping was good and, although I only had one voyage under my belt as Third Mate, my Kings Point background, plus the letter of recommendation from Captain Kelly (of the *SS Christopher Gadsden)*, enabled me to land an Acting Second Mate job. It was on the *SS Walt Whitman*, a Liberty Ship freighter that was loading general cargo in the port of Beaumont, TX. She was a standard Liberty Ship similar to the other 2,700 built during WWII.

I took a bus to Beaumont and boarded the ship on Thursday, June 13, 1946.

The Master was Captain P. J. Gennusa, a nice man who was not competent to handle this job. He had never sailed deep sea before. His sailing career had been entirely on the Great Lakes. He knew almost nothing about celestial navigation, which was the only way we had in those days to find our position when out of the sight of land. He did not even own a sextant. He was completely dependent upon getting a Ship's Mate who could navigate. He was lucky to get me.

The Chief Mate was a Norwegian-American about sixty years old. He spoke with a heavy Scandinavian accent. He was a fine old seafarer and ran the Deck Department well. However, he was not a skilled navigator.

The Third Mate was also a nice guy. He was about forty years old and was about twenty pounds overweight. He was a "professional Third Mate" with no ambition to move higher. He was lazy and did the least possible to get by.

Passage— Beaumont, Panama Canal, Long Beach, Kobe

We finished loading our cargo and set sail for the Panama Canal. We had nice summer weather.

We went to anchor in Limon Bay, for an hour or so, and then transited the Canal, with no shore leave for the crew. A Panama Canal Pilot boarded to direct our maneuvers, along with the Canal Deck Hands to handle the lines at the locks. The Marine Guards were no longer put aboard for the transits of ships from "friendly" countries. The nine-hour transit proceeded without any problems.

After clearing the Canal, we set course for Long Beach, CA, where we were to take bunkers. My sister Juanita lived in the Los Angeles area, so I sent her a radiogram to advise her of our schedule.

The passage went well, except that we had a strong gale as we passed through the Gulf of Tehuantepec, Mexico, an area that is famous for having bad weather.

When we arrived at Long Beach, we went immediately to the berth and started taking fuel. My sister, Juanita, who was thirteen years older than me, was very resourceful. She had found our ship's berth and boarded us soon after docking. We had a good visit. I got kind of mad at the Third Mate, who tried to romance her. Juanita knew how to handle the situation and smoothed things out, with no hard feelings.

As soon as the bunkering was finished, we left the berth at about 2200, bound for Kobe, Japan. When I came on watch at midnight, the Captain had gone to bed. I discovered that he had made a mistake in transferring our position and course from a large-scale to a small-scale chart. He had set course for the middle of the blacked-out coast of Catalina Island. I corrected it and woke him up to inform him. I got a sleepy "thank you" and he went back to bed.

During the voyage, I was doing all of the celestial navigation, taking star sights every day at dusk and occasionally at dawn, when a morning navigational fix was important, such as when approaching a landfall. I also took sun lines in the morning and the latitude by sun observation at local apparent noon. The Third Mate also took morning sun observations and the latitude if local apparent noon occurred before he went off watch at 1200. The Chief Mate didn't take any star sights although dawn and dusk both occurred during his 4 to 8 watches. The Second Mate (me) stood the 12 to 4 watch.

One disgusting thing on this voyage was the problem of weevils in our bread. Each slice of our ship-baked bread had on average four black weevils that we picked out. When the flour was sifted, it was found that there were, on average six white weevils for each black one. The white ones were not visible in the bread, so if you ate a slice you were consuming about twenty-four weevils. The Second Cook & Baker refused to sift the flour unless he was paid overtime for the work. Captain Gennusa refused to authorize the overtime. So we got by without eating bread.

We enjoyed good summer weather for our passage.

Kobe

Upon arrival in Kobe, we proceeded to and made our bow fast to a large mooring buoy. We would discharge the cargo for this port into barges and "junks" which ranged from modern designs to ancient ones that looked like they came from the middle ages. Many of the old ones had families living aboard.

We were to discharge about half of our cargo here and the remainder in Manila, Philippines.

Kobe had been heavily bombed during the war and large areas of the city were still completely devastated, with the only standing structures being round industrial smoke stacks. The people were very subservient in their actions and attitudes. They treated Americans as "conquerors". We received many respectful bows as we walked down the streets.

The dollar was very strong against the yen, so I did a good deal of shopping. I bought a beautiful tea set for my parents, figurines and dolls for various relatives, and a Seiko Pocket Watch for myself. This was before Seiko had good quality control and the watch only lasted a few days before it stopped, never to run again. My main purchase was a beautiful Samurai sword that had jewels in the handle and a nice scabbard.

A Typhoon passed over Kobe while we were there. When the water taxi service was suspended in the afternoon, it caught the Captain, the Chief Mate and about half of the crew ashore. That left me in charge. Shore crews came out and assisted us in putting out more mooring lines to the buoy. The Bosun was aboard and I had him take all available deck hands and securely batten down the hatches and secure, as well as possible, all things that might blow away. I spent the night in the open on the bow, crouched down behind the bulwark, where I could observe the tension on the mooring lines. During the height of the storm we had very heavy rain. I kept telephone communication with the bridge to direct the helmsman and with the engine room to adjust the engine speed. For several hours, I had the engine on either slow ahead or dead slow ahead. On a couple of occasions, I increased to half ahead for a while. It blew very hard and the eye passed over Kobe. When that occurred, we briefly had a clear sky, with the stars showing, and a dead calm.

The mooring buoy and our lines held. A few things, such as some dunnage that had been left on deck, blew away, but we sustained no major damage.

An Army Lieutenant was stationed aboard to supposedly be a "cargo officer". He was actually with the Army CID (Criminal Investigation Division).

Unbeknown to me, before I joined the ship in Beaumont, the Captain, Chief Mate and the Chief Engineer, had gone together and purchased several cases of cigarettes, for the purpose of selling them overseas at an enormous profit. The person who sold them the cigarettes collected a reward for informing the U. S. Customs about the sale, who in turn notified the U. S. military authorities in Japan.

The Army CID took no action at first, because they wanted to also catch the Buyers of a transaction. I spent a lot of time visiting with the very friendly Army Officer and, I guess, that he was able to determine that I was not in on the deal. The smugglers were not able to find a contact that could handle the amount of "goods" that they had for sale. I suspect that the black market people ashore knew that they were being watched and avoided our ship.

On the afternoon before we were due to sail, while I was ashore, the Army CID took action. All of the crew, including the officers, was ordered to assemble at Number 4 Hatch while the quarters were thoroughly searched. They confiscated the several cases of cigarettes and arrested and took ashore, in handcuffs, the Captain, Chief Mate and Chief Engineer.

There were no replacements available for them, and after a few hours, the three were returned aboard, very shaken by the experience.

Soon after their return aboard, we let go the mooring buoy and left Kobe, bound for Manila.

We continued to enjoy good weather enroute to Manila.

Manila

We arrived off Manila Bay about 0200. Instead of waiting for daylight, Captain Gennusa entered the port in the dark and anchored. We had no radar and, of course, almost no commercial ships did at that time. At daylight, we found that we had been very lucky not to have struck a wrecked ship. There were the masts of more than fifty sunken ships sticking out of the water all around us. Most of them were not plotted on the chart that we had for Manila Bay.

We stayed at anchor for a few days and during that time, July 4, 1946, occurred. This was Independence Day for the Philippines. From aboard ship, we could not observe any celebrations for the occasion. We finally shifted in to a cargo berth and commenced discharging our cargo.

The Port Captain, for Lykes Brothers Steamship Company in Manila, boarded our ship. It turned out to be Captain Kelsen, who had been Master of the *SS Davy Crocket,* my first ship as Cadet, from November 1943 to April 1944. Our greetings for each other here were polite but reserved, because neither of us had thought much of the other during our previous time together.

The city of Manila was in ruins from the heavy fighting that had occurred here. The people had been psychologically brutalized and it was a dangerous place. Our berth was a good way from the center of the city, and the only available transportation was privatized jeeps, that came along from time to time, carrying passengers. They were usually full but always had room for one more. The fares were high, but could be negotiated downward.

A group of six or eight thugs surrounded the Third Mate, who had been drinking, and kept pushing him roughly from one to another, making great sport of it. They took his watch and money, and roughed him up some and then left him dazed and lying in a ditch. Some other Americans came along and helped him get back to the ship. His injuries were not serious.

We were warned not to go ashore alone, but always to be in groups of at least three persons, and to keep alert for possible foul play. The bars were full and many of the patrons, especially the Filipinos, were armed. There were many female "companions" available for the numerous single men.

We finished discharging our cargo and took aboard sufficient fuel for our voyage back to the U. S. We left the dock and the Pilot directed our zigzag course through the Bay, around the many wrecks, until we were clear.

We had not enjoyed our stay in Manila and were glad to leave.

It was a very long passage back to the Panama Canal. The weather was mostly good, but the morale on the ship was poor. The Steward department was not very good, and we still had the problem of weevils in the bread. The Captain, Chief Mate and Chief Engineer were very worried about what charges they might face in connection with the attempted cigarette smuggling incident in Kobe.

We transited the Panama Canal without any problems and proceeded to Galveston, TX, arriving Wednesday, September 25, 1946.

Galveston

Because of the attempted smuggling incident in Kobe, it was a sure thing that the U. S. Customs were going to give us special treatment when we returned. The so-called "forty thieves" boarded us at anchor and did a thorough search of the ship for contraband. They found none, which seemed to make them surlier than ever.

I declared the purchases that I had made in Kobe, including the beautiful Samurai sword. The Customs Inspector seized it, claiming that it was a "dangerous weapon". I requested a receipt and he said that he would give one when he was finished checking the other declared items. I never got the receipt and I suspect that the sword now graces the wall over the fireplace of that Inspector's heirs.

It turned out that the Captain, Chief Mate and Chief Engineer had been worrying unnecessarily. Nothing was said about the Kobe cigarette incident.

It was now too late to get enrolled for the fall semester at Missouri School of Mines. I determined that I had best continue going to sea until time for the next semester to start.

This voyage had been difficult for Captain Gennusa. His previous experience and education had not prepared him for the responsibilities of being Master on an ocean-going ship. He was basically a good person and he appreciated the essential help that I had provided in navigating his ship. He gave me a nice letter of recommendation which is reproduced below.

(Note: According to "The Liberty Ships" by Captain Walter W. Jaffee, the SS Walt Whitman had been built by the Oregon Ship Building Corporation. The keel was laid on March 31, 1942 and she was launched on May 11, 1942. She entered the Beaumont Reserve Fleet on August 1, 1949 and was withdrawn on May 19, 1972, She was scrapped in Brownsville, TX a month later)

Lykes Bros. Steamship Co., Inc.

OWNERS, OPERATORS AND AGENTS

Lykes L *Lines*

CABLE "LYKES"

SERVICES TO
WEST INDIES
NORTH COAST OF
SOUTH AMERICA
UNITED KINGDOM
CONTINENTAL EUROPE
MEDITERRANEAN
FAR EAST, SOUTH
AND EAST AFRICA

BRANCH OFFICES

ANTWERP	KANSAS CITY
BALTIMORE	LAKE CHARLES
BARCELONA	LONDON
BEAUMONT	MANILA
BREMEN	MEMPHIS
CHICAGO	NEW YORK
CORPUS CHRISTI	PITTSBURGH
DALLAS	PORT ARTHUR
FORT WORTH	ROTTERDAM
HAMBURG	SAN JUAN
HAVANA	TAMPA

September 27, 1946
SS Walt. Whitman

TO WHOM IT MAY CONCERN:

     W. H. Vantine has served aboard this ship from
June 11, 1946 to September 27, 1946 as Acting Second Mate.

     During this time I have found him to be sober,
reliable and attentive to his duties.

     Mr. Vantine is an excellent navigator and could
well handle the navigation aboard any ship.

P. J. Gennusa,
Master

Letter of Recommendation from Captain P. J. Gennusa
Master of the *SS Walt Whitman* (1946)

Chapter III: SS Grays Harbor
(Why I Didn't Sail Tankers)

How I ended up on a Tanker

In an attempt to get back to sea before the impending strike, I signed off the Articles of the *SS Walt Whitman* and immediately obtained a job as Third Mate on the *SS Nancy Lykes,* a C-2 class freighter (length 459 feet, beam 63 feet). The ship then shifted from Galveston to Houston.

On October 1, 1946, the Masters, Mates and Pilots union went on strike against the Dry Freight Shipping Companies. My ship had not been able to sail before the deadline, so it was caught in the strike. I checked into a cheap hotel and registered with the union for picket duty. I would have preferred to go home to Sedalia, Missouri, but that would have resulted in my being "black listed" by the union and most likely unable, in the future, to get sea-going jobs. Everyone thought that the strike would only last a few days, so I was not too concerned.

However, the Steamship Companies "hung tough" and the strike lasted the entire month of October. My school fund nest egg was fast going for hotel and restaurant bills. Don't tell my grandkids, but some of the money also went for bar bills.

On the morning of Tuesday, October 17, 1946, I stopped in the Union Hall to get my picket card punched, after having stood the midnight to eight watch at one of the Houston docks. The Picket Captain was a fellow, who eleven years later, would become my good friend and fellow Panama Canal Pilot, Edgar Carlson. He asked me if I was a "Tanker Man" and, having become financially desperate, I lied and replied yes. The strike was only against dry cargo shippers and tankers were not affected. There was a Third Mate job available on a T-2 tanker, that was berthed at the Cities Service Oil Terminal in Lake Charles, Louisiana.

(Note: I have recently (summer of 2005) had a telephone conversation with Captain Edgar Carlson who is a retired San Francisco Bar Pilot. He will soon be 87 years old.)

Background

When I was going to sea in the United States Merchant Marine (1943 to 1957), there were "Tanker Men" and "Freighter Men".

Tankers went to terminals that were usually out in the boon docks, because the powers that be wisely didn't want an explosion or fire, that might happen, to be near a population center. A second drawback in sailing them was that they usually had a quick turn-around in port, frequently 24 hours or less. The tanker operators had tight control over the cargo operations and were very efficient. And thirdly, you were usually sitting on a potential bomb. There were also some advantages. The pay scale was about ten percent higher than on freighters and the voyages were usually shorter, many being coastwise in the U. S. Also, more generous funds were provided to the Steward's department to provide better meals. When required to make an ocean passage without cargo, it was possible to ballast tankers down to a proper draft. This was not possible on freighters.

Freighters usually had much longer stays in port. The berths were usually convenient to cities, with all the interesting things contained in them. This was before the advent of container operations and break/bulk cargo handing varied greatly in efficiency. In many places, such as in Latin America, in France and in southern Europe, cargo operations did not take place at night, on weekends nor on the many holidays that were celebrated in different parts of the world. Most of the time the cargoes were not dangerous. Tramp freighters frequently went to different ports on successive voyages, and one could get to "see the world".

Of course, during WWII, I had no choice, but luckily was assigned to freighters rather than to tankers. After the war, I chose to sail on tramp freighters.

Joining the SS Grays Harbor in Lake Charles

Lake Charles, Bristol, Houston

Due to my desperate financial situation, I accepted the tanker assignment, rushed back to my hotel, packed my gear, and that afternoon boarded a bus to Lake Charles. The bus driver was knowledgeable about the area and told me that I had best get off at Sulfur, LA, and take a taxi from there. It was long $30 taxi ride and I arrived at the Cities Service Terminal at about 2200. I was a very tired 21-year-old, having stood picket duty midnight to eight that morning, and I was also very worried about my ability to handle this job, never having previously been aboard a tanker. Both my weariness and apprehension were soon to increase dramatically.

T-2 tankers were 523 feet in length and 68 feet in beam. When fully loaded they had a draft of about 32 feet and displaced about 23,000 long tons. They were a good bit larger than the Liberty Ship freighters, that I had been sailing on, which were 441 feet in length and 57 feet in beam. Liberties carried a loaded draft of about 27 feet 9 inches and displaced about 14,000 tons. This was before the advent of super-tankers, which would make these ships seem very small by comparison. Years later, I would pilot tankers ranging up to 300,000 tons displacement, with a length of 1,100 feet, a beam of 185 feet and a draft of over 70 feet. But in 1946, T-2 tankers were considered to be large ships and to my eyes that night, it appeared to be gigantic.

These tankers had the engine room and stack aft with the crew quarters divided between a midship house and the after quarters. The Captain, Chief Mate, Second Mate, Third Mate, Radio Operator and Purser were quartered in the midship house, which also contained the wheelhouse, chart room, radio shack, gyro room, a pantry and the hospital room. The Engineering Officers and all of the unlicensed crew members were quartered in the after house, that also contained the galley, officer's saloon (pronounced like the drinking establishments of the old west), the crew mess, the steward's storerooms and refer boxes.

Tankers, when fully loaded, do not have much freeboard (distance from the water line to the main deck) and therefore frequently take seas on deck. A raised catwalk connected the midship and after houses and also ran from the midship house to the forecastle. Sometimes, during stormy weather, it was not possible to safely move between the two sets of quarters, which meant that the unlicensed crewmembers, on bridge duty, could not get relieved, and that all persons in the midship house, had to subsist on what was available in the pantry.

There were nine tanks fore and aft, which were three across except at number one tanks, where the beam narrowed toward the bow, they were only two across. That made 26 tanks, each equipped with valves to control the flow of cargo to and from them, with various crossover and master valves. My knowledge of this system was nil.

Each tank had a hinged steel oval shaped cover about four feet by three feet which was mounted on a steel oval cowling that raised it about three feet above the main deck. When loading most cargoes, these tank covers were kept closed and the height of the cargo in the tanks was monitored by taking soundings in the nearby sounding tubes. However, the *SS Grays Harbor* was in the process of loading stove oil, which is not so volatile, and all of the tank covers were left open so that the level of the cargo could be visually observed.

There are a number of things that have to be considered when loading a tanker. For instance, if only forward and after tanks were first loaded, the ship would "hog" and break. If only midship tanks were loaded first, the ship would "sag" and break. Obviously, initial loading must be spread out appropriately throughout the length of the ship. Also, port and starboard loading must be balanced so that the ship does not develop a list.

With most cargoes, all tanks cannot be filled or the ship would be dangerously overloaded and too deep in the water. The number of tanks that are slack (partially filed) needs to be kept to a minimum to avoid "free surface", which can cause dangerous rolling. Ideally, all tanks should either be full or empty but, as a practical matter, there would have to be at least one partially full, so as to adjust to the maximum allowed cargo.

The final loaded trim of the ship should either be even keel, if draft was critical in the channels, or with a one to two foot drag for best fuel economy and ship-handling. The ship's fuel and water supplies can usually be shifted between fore and aft tanks, to somewhat adjust the final trim. All of this is further complicated by the specific gravity and expansion/contraction of the cargo, which varies with its temperature. I knew all of this from my studies at the Merchant Marine Academy, but had no idea on how to accomplish the needed results.

So, I climbed the gangway of the *SS Grays Harbor* and went aboard with great trepidation. I went to the Captain's quarters, to report for duty, but was informed that he and the Second Mate were ashore. The Third Mate, who I was relieving, had already left. The Chief Mate, as was his normal function, was busy overseeing the loading of cargo. The problem was that he was very drunk and getting more so by the minute. He assumed that I was a true "Tanker Mate". He told me that the cargo plan was on his desk and that he was going to lie down for a few minutes. In truth, he passed out and I could not rouse him.

My Adventures Loading the Tanker

The terminal was pumping cargo into the ship at full force. What was I to do? I sought out the Chief Pumpman who, as a rule, does not get involved in loading a tanker, only in its discharge. He was also very drunk.

What saved the day was that a seaman, who normally sailed as Chief Pumpman, had signed on as a Wiper (the lowest rating in the Engine Department) because of a slump in shipping. He was about 40 years old, sober, competent and willing to help. There is a general conspiracy in many circles, including on ships, to cover up for drunks and I guess that we were all actively pursuing that goal.

So, for the next several hours, the Wiper, following the cargo-loading plan from the Chief Mate's desk, directed the loading. As one tank would become nearly full, he would show me which valve to open on another tank as he simultaneously closed the one on the nearly full tank. The valves were of the rising stem type and were controlled by round handles about two feet in diameter. It took about twenty turns to change from full open to closed and it took considerable effort to turn them. If it appeared that two or more tanks would be nearing full at about the same time, we had to partially close some valves to reduce the flow, because we couldn't handle more than one simultaneous closing and opening. Of course, we had to keep several open at all times, so that the terminal's cargo pumps would not encounter excessive backpressure, and so that the ship could be loaded expeditiously.

A spill was, of course, a no-no. The deck scuppers were all plugged so as to retain any small spills on deck, but if anything went over the side, the terminal and Coast Guard would have to be notified. In that event, a fine would result and our environment would be damaged.

All during this time, I was anxiously running up and down the length of the ship, peering into the tanks with my flashlight. Three times during the loading, I had to arouse a few drunken deck hands to take in the slack in the mooring lines, and heave up the gangway bridles, as the ship's draft increased from the cargo loading. At about 0300, the Captain and Second Mate returned aboard, both very drunk. As the loading neared completion, I also had to go down on the pier to read the draft fore and aft.

At about 0700, we were almost fully loaded and were ready for the "topping-off" phase, when the loading is slowed to a trickle and the nearly full tanks are filled the rest of the way. I asked the terminal to shut down cargo pumping while we got ready. At this time, I was able to awaken the Chief Mate. He had recovered remarkably and told me that he was sure glad to get a competent "Tanker Man" aboard. He proceeded to take over the topping-off operation.

We were ready to sail at 0900. Normally, docking and undocking maneuvers are done with the Third Mate on the bridge (to operate the engine room telegraph and to keep the bell book) with the Captain, Pilot and an Able Seaman (to steer). The Chief Mate is forward together with the Bosun, Carpenter and about half of the deck crew. The Second Mate is aft with the other half of the deck crew. For this sailing, the Second Mate was too hung over to get up, so the Captain ordered me to the aft station. I never thought it possible, but I actually went to sleep standing up and caught myself, just in time, to avoid falling.

On three mate ships such as this one, the Third Mate stands the 8 to 12 watch, so after leaving the dock, I reported to the bridge to stand the rest of my watch. When the Second Mate relieved me at noon, I skipped lunch and slept the most sound sleep you can imagine, until I was called at 1645 to perform the Third Mate's normal duty of relieving the Chief Mate, on the bridge, at 1700, for about half an hour, so that he can go to the officer's saloon for dinner. When he returned to the bridge, I skipped another meal and again died in my bunk until called at 1930 to get ready for my next 8 to 12 bridge watch. By breakfast time the next morning, I was pretty well recovered from my ordeal and was very grateful to a certain Wiper.

Our Captain

Our Captain was a very complex person. He was in his fifties, about five feet ten inches tall, about five pounds overweight, had light blue eyes, a full head of mostly grey wavy hair. He appeared to be in good health. He was extremely competent, self-assured and was a genuine war hero. The Captain had an easy commanding way about him that came from years of being in command. He had a good voice and good posture. Some of the following information was obtained indirectly, but I believe all of it to be factual.

Before WWII, he was sailing as Master on tankers for the Standard Oil Company. The Navy needed tanker men, so he was inducted. His first assignment in the Navy was to serve as "Routing Officer", in Panama, for ships bound for the South Pacific. He was next assigned to be Commanding Officer on a dry cargo supply ship, ferrying supplies to Navy vessels operating in the Pacific. Sometimes you wonder how we won the war the way some of our assets, such as this man's expertise in tanker command, were wasted.

While serving as commanding officer on a Navy freighter supply vessel, he developed a method of resupplying, from ship to ship while underway, using an endless whip arrangement. His method was used extensively for such operations as transferring bombs to aircraft carriers, to replenish their supply. For this he received a Naval decoration.

During the invasion of Okinawa, his ship (a C-2 type freighter) was hit by a Japanese kamikaze plane and was severely damaged, with loss of life. Under his direction, his crew welded hatch covers across the broken areas of the ship and restored sufficient structural strength so that they could steam back to the U. S. west coast, all without outside assistance. For these efforts, the Navy again decorated him.

The Captain, at the time that I knew him, appeared to be a wealthy man. The stories that I heard were that the Standard Oil stock, that he had from before the war, had greatly increased in value, and also that he had married a very rich lady. He enjoyed sailing as shipmaster and did so mostly for the fun of it.

He was a good man all around. However, as we shall see, he had a drinking problem.

Adventures in Bristol, England

From Lake Charles, we proceeded to Bristol, England. The weather was reasonably good and the passage was made without problems.

Soon after the ship's agent came aboard, with the British pounds that the Captain had requested, a generous draw (an advance against wages) was passed out to the crew. The Captain let it be known that he would be staying in the best hotel in town (named the Adelphi as I recall) and, if anyone needed more funds, they could find him there. He took with him a large bundle of pound notes.

A number of us did seek him out for additional funds. I obtained pound notes from him, equivalent to about $120, to purchase a German Plath (brand) sextant. The Nazi swastika had been ground off of it, but otherwise it was like new, and it had terrific optics. It was far superior to the British Husan (brand) sextant that I had purchased during the war in Liverpool. He did not make a notation of my additional draw and it would have passed unrecorded, had I not later re-minded him of it. Others also got additional funds from him and, I suspect, that some had a "freebie".

When the Captain awoke the next morning in his hotel room, his money was missing. He immediately suspected the young lady, next to him, had something to do with the disappear-ance. He demanded that the hotel management call the police, which they did. The sweet young thing strongly and tearfully protested her innocence. After the hell raising was well progressed, he thought to look under the mattress. The money was there, where he had placed it, and he was very embarrassed.

The cargo discharge went well, without problems. But one thing bothered me very much, and that was the careless way smokers came and went on deck without extinguishing their cigarettes. There were ashtrays, just inside all of the exits, to make it convenient to extinguish cigarettes, but they were too often not used. I had also observed this during loading at Lake Charles. When challenged about this, the smokers always put the cigarettes out, and half-heartedly apologized.

Prior to sailing, the Captain ordered a generous supply of Scotch Whiskey delivered to the ship. There was at least a case brought aboard.

After a two-day stay in Bristol, we sailed for Houston, Texas.

Incident at Sea

About five days out, during my evening 8 to 12 watch, and while enjoying remarkably good weather, a series of unusual events occurred.

There was a loud drinking party going on in the Captain's office. His drinking buddies were the Purser and (surprisingly) the Chief Pumpman, who the Captain had apparently known from previous times. The Captain's quarters consisted of a two-room suite on the deck below the bridge. The door of his office faced the foot of the ladder (stairway) to the chartroom and bridge.

About 2200, the Chief Pumpman came to the bridge and said that the Captain said to stop the ship, because the Purser was going to get off. He went back down below and I, of course, did not take any action on the relayed order.

I started listening at the voice tube to the Captain's quarters and heard a violent argument between the Captain and Purser. The Purser said that he was going to his room to pack his suitcase. The Captain came to the bridge roaring that "when he said to stop the ship he meant god damn well *stop the ship!!!*" He moved the telegraph handle to the stop position and left the wheelhouse.

The Third Assistant Engineer responded on the telegraph, ordered his Fireman to douse the fires in the boilers and started closing the throttle on the steam line that supplied power to the turbines that drove the generators. T-2s had turbo-electric propulsion and were very maneuverable. The Third Assistant, of course, called the Chief Engineer, who hurriedly proceeded to the engine room.

Normally, the engineers are advised long before maneuvering will occur and are given a telegraph order of *Standby,* prior to the first maneuver. When running at full sea speed, all burners are operating at full capacity, a full head of steam is maintained and extra nozzles are opened to the turbines. An emergency stop such as this causes all sorts of problems and, soon after the stopping process started, the safety valves on both boilers started to blow, making an uncanny screaming noise. It was very loud on the bridge and must have been deafening in the after quarters. After about five minutes, the excess steam pressure had dissipated and there was an eerie silence. The sea was unusually calm.

I again started listening at the voice tube to the Captain's quarters. He and the Purser were making up and professing great admiration and affection for one another. The Purser, although his suitcase was packed, had now decided not to get off. I put the telegraph back on full ahead and we went on our way.

The Chief Engineer called the bridge on the telephone and demanded an explanation. There really none that I could give him that made any sense, but I assured him that everything was now okay.

The Chief Engineer logged this affair and made an official complaint to the Company (Pacific Tankers, Inc.) when we arrived in Houston on Friday, November 22, 1946. He fully expected that the Captain would get fired. Instead, the Chief Engineer did.

I signed off the ship. I now had sufficient sea time to raise my grade and I sat for the Coast Guard examination to obtain a Second Mate license.

I also firmly resolved that I would never again sail on tankers. And I didn't.

Follow-Up

After retiring from the Panama Canal Commission in 1983 (as a Canal Pilot), I piloted ships part time, until 1995, for Petroterminal de Panama. That was the company that operated a pipeline across Panama to transfer Alaskan crude from the Pacific to the Atlantic. It was much cheaper to use the pipeline than the Panama Canal, because larger ships could be used. The tankers bringing the oil from Alaska to our Pacific terminal ranged up to 300,000 tons displacement when fully loaded. The largest ones had a length of 1100 feet, a beam of 185 feet and carried a draft of a bit more than 70 feet. Their cargo capacity was 1,860,000 barrels. Our U. S. East Coast ports could not handle ships of this size so smaller ones were used in the Atlantic, but most of them were still too big and/or had a draft too great to use the Panama Canal.

Because of provisions in the Jones Act, which specified that coastwise and intracoastal commerce be transported in U. S. flag ships, this Alaskan crude was all carried on American tankers. As a consequence, I had experience on many of them.

The heavy drinking and partying that so distressed me in 1946 was no longer present. The downsizing, and competitive pressures, in the U. S. Merchant Marine has caused the drunkards and incompetent people to be eliminated from our ships.

The officers and crews now sailing American tankers are top rate. We can be proud of them

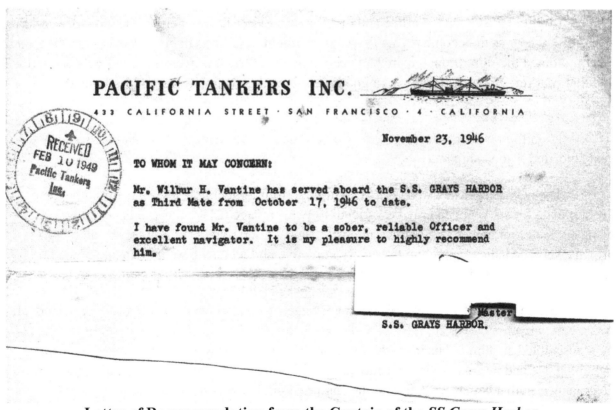

Letter of Recommendation from the Captain of the *SS Grays Harbor*

Chapter IV: SS George Clement Perkins
(First Tour of Duty)

Joining the Ship in Galveston

After leaving the *SS Grays Harbor,* I checked into a hotel in Houston and spent a week in intense study. I then sat for and passed, in three days, the Coast Guard Examination for *Second Mate, Steam and Motor Vessels of Any Gross Tonnage upon Oceans.*

I would have liked to go home for Christmas, but my funds were low and I needed a job as soon as possible.

I went to the MM & P (Masters, Mates & Pilots) Union Hall in Houston and got listed for a job as Second Mate. Shipping was good and there were only two Second Mates registered ahead of me. On Tuesday, December 10, 1946, I was assigned to the *SS George Clement Perkins,* a standard Liberty Ship freighter, that was loading cargo in Galveston, TX. The Permanente Metals Corporation, Yard Number 2, built the ship with the keel being laid on April 1, 1944. She was launched 19 days later on April 20, 1944. The ship was operated by T. J. Stevenson & Co., Inc., a New York Company that I had never heard of, but which would turn out to be my Employer for the next ten and a half years.

I took a bus the 70 miles or so to Galveston and then took a taxi from the bus station to the ship, boarding her that same day.

I went to the Captain's office and met Captain Elmer F. Goodlett, a fine old Norwegian-American, who was to become my good friend and mentor. He was in his late fifties and had also recently joined the ship. In fact, there had been almost a 100% turnover of the Officers and Crew, and that was very unusual. There was a good reason for this, which we would find out about in due time.

I don't remember the name of the Chief Mate. He was a competent man, about forty years old, and a good shipmate.

The new Third Mate was Louis L. Murphy, from Lynchburg, VA, who would become my shipmate for six years and my best friend. He was my age (21) and was a handsome man, being six feet, four inches tall, with good posture and a good voice. He was blonde and had brown eyes. The ladies found him to be very attractive and when we went "cruising" together, he always ended up with the best looking one.

The new Chief Engineer was Mr. Ira S. Sager, who also would become a good friend. He was a very large man, over six feet tall and obese at about 270 pounds. He was so fair that he almost resembled an albino. His hair was white and his skin color was very fair. His eyes were light blue. He had ramrod straight posture and a soft voice. He ran his department in an unorthodox manner, in that he never set foot in the engine room. He kept track of things by closely monitoring the Engine Room Log Book, and by speaking frequently and extensively with the

Assistant Engineers. Strangely, his method of operation worked fine, and the Engine Department ran very well.

I don't recall the first name of the Purser, but his surname was Bell. He would sail with us until all Pursers were removed from the ships, as an economy measure. The axe would fall in less than a year.

First Voyage

Galveston, Rotterdam, Galveston

We loaded a full cargo of wheat in Galveston, down to our WNA (Winter North Atlantic) Plimsoll (Load) marks. As soon as we could get secured for sea, we left port bound for Rotterdam, Holland. This was to be a wintertime crossing of the North Atlantic and there was no way to escape the bad weather. We did pretty well for the first several days and then we commenced having one storm after the other, some of them severe.

Our Chief Mate, who stood the 4 to 8 watch, took star observations at dawn and dusk when possible, which was not very often on this passage. I took morning sun lines and the latitude sights at Local Apparent Noon (when the sun momentarily bears due north or south), again only when the sun and horizon were both available for sextant observations. Third Mate Murphy, who stood the 8 to 12 watches, was a good navigator, and I found that his morning sun line observations were good, so I soon ceased taking them. After a while, I only took the latitude observations, and I kept the clocks set so that Local Apparent Noon would occur on my 12 to 4 watch. Captain Goodlett was allowing me to work up the noon position daily. At least half the time on this voyage, we had to rely on Dead Reckoning, because no celestial observations were possible.

There were many mines left over from WWII, and hardly a week went by that you didn't hear about a ship striking one of them. There were recommended routes to follow in the English Channel, and, in the North Sea, there were designated channels that had been cleared of mines. These channels were marked by buoys, but the stormy winter weather had moved many of them a considerable distance out of position. The lights of some of them were not working, so they were of no use at night. Radar would have been useful, but we did not have it.

After a slow passage, averaging only eight knots, we finally reached the Pilot Station for Rotterdam and proceeded up the channel to the port, where we tied up to large mooring buoys, fore and aft. A huge floating grain suction barge came alongside and almost immediately commenced discharging our grain cargo into barge/vessels, that had pointed bows and were self-propelled. They had the wheelhouse aft, where they also had living quarters, many with women and children living in them. They were all sized to just fit into the locks that connected the waterways throughout Europe. They were all neatly painted, with curtains in the windows, some even with white curtains. The families that we saw on them mostly wore pointed wooden shoes, that they left on deck when they went inside their quarters.

We now found out why there had been almost a complete change of crew in Galveston. This ship had come to Rotterdam on her previous voyage. The black market in cigarettes was big business. A carton of cigarettes that cost us less than a dollar tax-free on the ship could be sold ashore for about fifty dollars worth of Dutch Guilders. Some of the previous crewmembers had sold a whole case to the Rotterdam black market operators just before sailing. They had a few good cartons on top but most of the case was filled with cartons than contained cork that had been taken from lifejackets and cut to proper size. These were tough people, not to be cheated without consequences. The black market people did not discover what had occurred until the ship had left port and was proceeding down the channel to sea. They sent a high-speed launch to chase it and by megaphone warned that they would get revenge if this ship ever came back to Rotterdam. So, here we were, dumb and happy, not knowing anything about this.

A gang of seven or eight large and very tough-looking Dutchmen boarded us on the afternoon of our arrival. The weather was cold and they were all wearing long black overcoats, that made them look even larger and more sinister. They were seeking the individuals who had cheated them. They bulled their way into the quarters and started opening doors. The deal in dispute had been consummated in the Engine Room, so they also went down there. They were not able to find anyone that they recognized. We were able to convince them that there had been a complete change of crew, and that we had nothing to do with what had happened. We wondered if it would be safe for us to go ashore in Rotterdam, which was generally regarded to be a good liberty port for Merchant Seamen.

A middle-aged lady, known as "Rotterdam Mary", had come aboard to sell watches and other items of jewelry. She had Swiss watches, some with 21-jewel movements, for very reasonable prices. She sold several to our Officers and Crewmembers. We established good relations with her, which was important, because her brother was one of the "toughs" who had come aboard seeking revenge. She put in a good word for us and had the thugs called off.

The Purser, Mr. Bell, pried off the back of a watch that he bought from her and discovered that the movement did not have a single jewel in it. He had trouble getting the case closed and had to hammer it, which naturally stopped it from running. Using the pretense of shopping for another watch, he worked a switch on Rotterdam Mary to get an identical one that was at least running. Those of us who knew about this were terrified that she would find out about it and get her brother, and his friends, to rough us up ashore.

Mr. Bell and I went ashore in the same water taxi (called a Speedo) that Rotterdam Mary and her brother decided to take. On the way in, she noticed that one of her watches was not running and shook it and looked at it hard. Mr. Bell and I were on pins and needles. Fortunately she did not suspect what had happened.

In port, we almost always broke sea watches. The Deck Crew were all put on eight hours of day work and the Engine Crew watch standers changed to eight hour shifts. At least one of the Deck Officers had to be on duty at all times and the Chief Mate needed to take the day watch when the Deck Crew would be working. That left Third Mate Louis Murphy and me to cover the night hours and that meant that we could not go ashore together. We flipped a coin to see who would go ashore on the first night and I won. That was unfortunate for him, because we would be sailing before he had a chance for liberty.

After making some inquires as to where "the action was", Purser Bell and I took a taxi to the Ambassador Club. It was a large nightclub. There were about twenty gorgeous young ladies lounging around the bar. They were all available for shacking up but I, being an innocent country boy, did not realize this. The Purser and I teamed up with two of the beauties and moved to a table. The girls, like just about everyone in Rotterdam, spoke English. We both ended up going home with our "dates". Mine introduced me to her parents and I was shocked that they did not object to what their daughter was doing. They had been reduced to this behavior by the hard economic situation. She seemed to be a very nice person and was very much in love with a British soldier, who had returned to England.

Purser Bell and I had each taken a carton of cigarettes ashore with us that, when we sold them, fetched Guilders sufficient to pretty well pay for our evening on the town.

In about twenty-four hours, the huge grain suction barge had transferred all of our cargo of wheat, almost 10,000 long tons, to the fleet of barges. Soon thereafter, we let go from the mooring buoys and left port, bound back to Galveston.

It was another miserable, wintertime, stormy crossing of the North Atlantic. We arrived back in Galveston on Monday, February 3, 1947.

Galveston

Galveston was a wild town in those days. Post Office Street was world-famous. For about four blocks, every house on both sides of the street was a whorehouse. At the "high" end, the girls were all white and wore formal type dresses with some variations, such as extremely low fronts. As you moved down the street, the atmosphere became less and less formal. In the middle area the girls were mostly Hispanic and at the "low" end they were colored. All of the houses had bars, at which you could have a drink and look over the selection. Most also had dance floors and a jukebox. You were not required to participate fully.

In one of the local bars (not a whorehouse), I paid for a drink with a twenty-dollar bill that was equivalent to at least $100 dollar bill today. The change was not forthcoming and I protested to the Manager. He claimed that I had paid with a five-dollar bill and said that he had no twenties in the cash register. I went outside and found a policeman, who accompanied me back into the bar. The Manager opened his cash register and invited me to take any twenties that I could find. The policeman believed me, but said that there was nothing that he could do about it.

Second Voyage

Galveston, Malmo, Norfolk

We again loaded a full cargo of wheat that was, this time, destined for Helsinki, Finland. Most of the crew and all of the officers signed over for another trip. We set sail on Monday, February 10, 1947.

We again had a typical stormy wintertime crossing of the Atlantic, but things were quite different when we neared our destination. The winter of 1946-47 was extremely cold in north Europe. There was some sheet ice in the North Sea. The Kiel Canal was frozen closed, so we had to proceed around the north end of Denmark into the Kategat, that was about 80% covered with ice. When we reached the Sound, between Copenhagen, Denmark, and Malmo, Sweden, the ice was more than a meter thick with a couple of meters of snow on top of that. At first, a small Danish Icebreaker was escorting us, and then, a larger Swedish one relieved it. Even the larger one had less beam than our ship, so we kept getting stuck. It would turn back and circle us to break us free, and we could then go a mile or so before again getting stuck. Our propeller was badly damaged and we could only obtain about 50 RPM, instead of our normal 76 RPM. All of the Baltic Sea was frozen over and there was no way that we were going to be able to get to Helsinki. It was decided to divert us to Malmo for discharge and repairs to our propeller. We were to end up spending a month is this port.

Sweden at that time had their automobile traffic drive on the left side, as in Great Britain. It was the only country on the Continent that did this, and they would soon convert to driving on the right side.

They had prohibition, of a sort, in that you could only have two drinks at a restaurant and then, if you wanted more, you had to move to a different restaurant, and have another meal. This made it very difficult to get intoxicated and very expensive to try. Whenever this situation exists, it creates a market for bootleggers. I remember a huge man standing on the same street corner every night. The inside of his overcoat was lined with pockets containing bottles of aquavit, the local hard drink.

Our colored Galley Man had a talent that we did not know about. He became a star at a local nightclub. He could sing very well and the local fans adored him. He ended up going there almost every night. I halfway expected him to jump ship and start a professional singing career.

Chief Engineer Sager turned out to be an alcoholic. He obtained a case of whiskey and drank it all in a few days. He then had a terrific hangover. It was clear to all, especially to him, that he had to stay completely away from the stuff.

Soon after arrival, our ship proceeded to a dock, equipped with grain suckers, that discharged our cargo in a couple of days. We then waited for our turn in the drydock. When we finally got into the dock, we found that all of the ends of our propeller were bent over. We had a spare propeller aboard, but it was decided not to install it because, most likely, it would end up also being damaged. They cut off an equal portion of each blade, removing the bent portions, so that we could proceed back to the U. S.

While we were in Malmo, my 22nd birthday occurred on March 16th. I kept it a secret.

An icebreaker again escorted us back through the Sound and Kategat. The ice had melted some and this time we did not get stuck. After another stormy crossing of the North Atlantic, we arrived in Norfolk on Tuesday, April 29, 1947.

Third Voyage

Norfolk, Charleston, Santos, Tampa

We were going to have to drydock to change our propeller and, since the ship was due soon for a drydock inspection to keep in Class with the ABS (American Bureau of Shipping), the two procedures were combined.

When the shipyard work was completed, we sailed for Charleston, SC, and loaded several hundred tons of general cargo for Santos, Brazil. We left Charleston on Saturday, May 24, 1947 and went to Trinidad, where fuel was cheap. After taking bunkers, we proceeded on our way to Santos.

In Santos, we discharged the general cargo and started taking a partial cargo of coffee, in 50 kilo sacks. The cargo smelled good. It would take three weeks to load it.

I met a girl here, who it seems, fell very much in love with me. I switched watches with Third Mate Murphy so that I could go to Sao Paulo with her over a weekend. It was a beautiful city with outstanding architecture in the buildings and mosaics in the sidewalks. We stayed overnight with a married couple, who were her friends. We traveled both ways by bus, but the trips were quite different. We went up on the new modern road and came back on the old one, that was full of hairpin curves. Our bus driver coming back was a crazy man, and I didn't think that we were going to make it.

I was swapping watches with Third

**Picture with Brazilian Girl Friend (1947)
Note the ring which purposely, but incorrectly, made it appear that we were engaged.**

55.

Mate Murphy so that I could spend about every other night ashore with my girl friend. She kept after me to wear my uniform and have a picture taken with her. I finally agreed and we had the portrait made. The photographer had us pose with me seated and with her standing alongside with her left hand on my arm. I did not notice, but she was wearing a ring on her left ring finger, that gave the impression that we were engaged. It stood out like a sore thumb against the background of my dark blue uniform. That was the impression that my mother had when the picture arrived at my home by mail from Santos. It was signed on the back "from the Brazilian Girl Who Loves You". I had to do a lot of explaining. The picture that caused all of the trouble is reproduced here.

When all of our cargo of coffee was aboard, we left Santos and proceeded to Tampa, FL, arriving there on Tuesday, July 8, 1947.

Fourth Voyage

Tampa, Panama Canal, San Pedro, Kobe, San Pedro, Panama Canal, New Orleans

In Tampa we quickly discharged our partial load of coffee and took on a full load of wheat for Kobe, Japan. It didn't take long to dump the cargo in, from huge grain elevators, and we sailed on Saturday, July 12, for the Panama Canal. We transited soon after arrival and had no shore leave in the Canal Zone.

We then proceeded to San Pedro, CA, to take bunkers. As usual on this run, we had a good blow when passing through the Gulf of Tehuantepec, Mexico. Otherwise, the weather was good. We docked upon arrival at San Pedro and our fueling only took about seven hours, after which we set sail for Kobe, Japan. We had reasonably good weather for our crossing of the North Pacific Ocean.

I had been in Kobe a year earlier and was amazed at how quickly the city was being rebuilt. There were a huge variety of interesting goods available for sale in the stores. The idea occurred to me that I should start a company to import some of these products into the United States. If I had followed through on that idea, I would probably be a rich man today.

At that time, there were no grain suckers working in Kobe, so our cargo of grain had to be discharged using canvas slings, that were emptied into barges alongside the ship. They worked twenty-four hours per day at all five hatches and discharged us in five days. One strange thing about the Japanese stevedores, which I had also observed on my previous time here, was that instead of sitting as we do, they squat and sit on their heels. For instance, instead of sitting on the main deck cap rail, as we would, they get up there on their feet and squat. They were very diligent workers and never took a break from their labors.

Soon after discharge was finished, we set sail and retraced our path to San Pedro, for bunkers, and the Panama Canal. As before, our stay in San Pedro was brief and our transit of the

Panama Canal proceeded without delay and with no shore leave. We finished up in New Orleans on Tuesday, September 23, 1947.

Fifth Voyage

New Orleans, Savona, Cueta, Rosario, Buenos Aires, Montevideo, Tenerife, Antwerp, Southampton, Norfolk, Baltimore

This was to turn out to be an interesting and long voyage.

It started on a sad note. All Pursers were to be terminated, so we had to bid goodbye to our friend, Purser Bell. We hated to see him go, as he had done a good job as our ship's "doctor", in addition to doing a proper job with the paper work. This change threw more work on the Captain, much of it having to be done when approaching port, when he should be concentrating on the safe navigation the ship. I decided that I had better become a good typist, so that I could help properly, and practiced by typing the Nautical Rules of the Road over and over. This also helped me study for my next license exam.

We loaded wheat in New Orleans and sailed on Thursday, October 2, 1947, for Savona, Italy, which is located about twenty miles southwest of Genoa.

Our Ocean crossing went well, for the time of year, with only a few moderate gales.

Savona was a very good and friendly liberty port. Since they did not work cargo at night or on weekends, we had enough time to enjoy the pleasures. Most of the crew hung out at the nearby Scandinavian Bar. The local girls were very friendly and many romances occurred.

Some of the other Officers and I discovered a jewel of a small hotel on the coast not far from the city. The food and scenery were great and we all found pretty and enjoyable companions.

After our cargo was discharged, we commenced on what we expected to be a normal return to the USA. Instead, we were ordered by a radio message to stop in Ceuta, Spanish Morocco, and to take maximum bunkers for a voyage to Rosario, Argentina.

Ceuta was a typical Muslim city, with narrow winding streets and much obvious poverty. There were no tall buildings and all of them were painted white. The women were heavily veiled.

Our voyage from here to Argentina would be a very long passage with mostly good weather.

For some time, I had made a hobby of trying to take a navigational observation of every star in the Nautical Almanac. This voyage to the southern hemisphere gave me a chance to take many that had not been visible in the northern hemisphere. At night at sea, where there are no distracting lights, the stars are brilliant and beautiful. I never ceased to enjoy studying them.

When we arrived at the Rio Plat in Argentina, we first proceeded to Buenos Aries to clear customs. Captain Goodlett did not pass out enough cigarettes and bottles of whiskey to satisfy the boarding officials, so they decided to give us a hard time. They claimed that we had insulted the Argentine Navy by not dipping our flag when we passed a pier that had a small navy ship, which, we had not noticed, tied up at the far end, over 1,000 feet away. They fined our ship for that and required that we make a detailed store list, counting every nut, bolt, tool and can of paint in our deck and engine stores, as well as all of the Stewards stores. Then they came back aboard to closely check it. This was the corrupt regime of Dictator Juan Peron, when he was in power the first time. They would have called all of this harassment off for a sufficient bribe, but Captain Goodlett was furious with them and determined to give them nothing more.

After a delay of three days, we were finally cleared to proceed the 1,000 miles up the Rio Plat to Rosario. We had two Argentine Pilots aboard, who alternated duty, directing our maneuvers up the river. In the narrow upper reaches, we anchored at night. It took us five days to travel up river.

We docked port side to a pier at a grain elevator to load corn. They had an ancient conveyor system that dropped much of the grain into the river between the ship and the dock. Therefore, in this area, we had very fat corn-fed fish. We caught many of them, with hand lines, from the stern of our ship. The dominant fish was a catfish with the adults weighing about fifteen pounds. They barked like a small dog when being pulled from the water. The reason that they were dominant was that they were truly designed by Mother Nature for fighting. They had razor sharp fins and three sharp spikes on each side of their tails.

Another prominent type of fish in the area was sunfish. They were shaped in about the same proportion as a person's hand but were large at about fifteen pounds. Their shape gave them tremendous swimming power and they really put up a struggle when hooked. There were also normal looking catfish weighing in at about ten pounds. We had several avid fishermen aboard and they filled our Fish Reefer Box completely up. They then starting giving fish away to the area's residents.

The dollar was very strong against the Argentine peso and food in the restaurants was cheap. I frequently skipped the free dinner aboard ship and ate very good steak, eggs and fried potato meals ashore, for the equivalent of about thirty-five cents.

Our ship's Agent and the Ship Chandler here were both of British descent and were more British than the people are in England. They liked to visit with Captain Goodlett to practice their English. One evening they invited him and me to have dinner with them in their English Club. It was like an English pub, complete with dartboards and snooker tables. No Spanish was heard anywhere.

We had a good dinner with plenty of liquid refreshment. Captain Goodlett didn't hold his booze too well and wasn't being very sharp. The Ship's Agent proposed that he and the Ship

Chandler, play Captain Goodlett and me, a game of snooker for a fifty-dollar wager. I tried to nix the idea, but Captain Goodlett, who could hardly stand, thought it was a good idea.

While I was attending high school, I worked part time racking balls in a pool hall in my hometown of Sedalia, MO. It was called the "Smoke House", and had eight pool tables and a billiard table. They paid me twenty-five cents per hour and allowed me to play free whenever a table was vacant, which was most of the time. I had a lot of practice and got to be real good. I hadn't played pool in about four years, but it is a skill that you retain.

I had never played snooker and didn't know the rules. The table was larger than a pool table. The balls and holes were smaller, but basically the cue work was similar to pool. I was mad at these two for taking advantage of Captain Goodlett, and was therefore motivated to concentrate hard on the game. I shot better that I ever did before (or since), and ran the table, defeating these two shysters. They were not gracious in their loss and, at first, refused to pay, claiming that I was a "pro" who had suckered them in. I reminded them that they had proposed the match and that I had tried to stop it. I had support from some of the bystanders, and they were shamed into paying.

We spent three weeks loading a partial cargo. We could not take a full load because the depth of the river was not sufficient. When the proper amount of cargo was aboard, we left Rosario and proceeded down river to Buenos Aires. It had taken five days to come up the river but we went down in four. We docked in Buenos Aires to top off with more corn.

We spent a month here while the stevedores went through a ridiculous "make work" routine. Truckloads of corn would arrive alongside the ship, on an irregular schedule, and the workers would then sack it and sew the sacks closed. They would then load the sacks onto pallets and transfer them into the ship's 'tween decks, where other workers would open the bags and dump them out. We spent a month doing this and moved an amount of cargo that would be handled in a modern port in a couple of hours.

The city was beautiful with very wide streets and nice modern buildings. Mounted police, in groups of three or four, were present on many street corners. It was clearly a repressive dictatorship.

After a couple of months in Argentina, we shifted across the Plat Estuary to the city of Montevideo, Uruguay, to take fuel. This was also a beautiful city and the attitude of the people was friendlier than in Buenos Aires. We got the impression that no one in Latin America was in a hurry. We ended up spending a couple of days here taking fuel, a job that would only have taken a few hours in an efficient port.

When we sailed, we were able to observe the wreck of the German Pocket Battleship, *Graf Spee*, which had been scuttled here during WWII, to avoid facing the British Navy, that was gathering a force outside to battle them.

Our cargo of corn was destined for Antwerp, Belgium. We would have to refuel enroute at Tenerife in the Canary Islands.

Tenerife Island, as seen from sea as you approach it, is spectacular. It is the largest of the Canary Islands but is not very big. It has a mountain near its center that is over 12,000 feet high. Rising that high just a short distance from the coast is amazing. Gran Canara Island, not far away, is also impressive, being over 8,000 feet high. These islands are owned and administered by Spain. The population on Tenerife appeared to be very poor and many people, dressed in rags, came to our ship's side to beg for food.

We were only docked for a few hours and the authorities did not allow any shore leave. We finished taking fuel and left port, bound for Antwerp.

We had been having nice summer weather in the southern hemisphere but now suddenly we were encountering winter storms in the northern hemisphere. This winter was not as severe as the previous one, but the weather in Antwerp was cold, cloudy and dreary.

In Antwerp, we had returned to the efficient commercial world. The cargo of corn, that had taken a couple of months to load in Argentina, was pumped out of the ship by grain suckers in a little over a day.

The city appeared to be well run and the people prosperous. The population here was mostly Flemish and they spoke a language similar to the Dutch. In Brussels and the part of Belgium adjoining France, French is the dominant language.

The price of Bunker "C" in Antwerp was very high, so it was decided to have us stop at Southampton, England for fuel. That was another efficient operation and we were in and out in a few hours, with no shore leave allowed.

We faced another wintertime crossing of the North Atlantic and finally arrived in Norfolk on Sunday, February 15, 1948. This voyage had taken three and a half months. It was going to be a good payday.

The ship moved up the Chesapeake Bay to Baltimore to load a cargo for the next voyage. I departed the ship there and checked into the Lord Baltimore Hotel. The Manager there was a good friend of the Chief Steward on the ship, and he took good care of me.

Only twelve months were required and I now had over fourteen months sea time as second mate. I could sit for a Chief Mate license examination, and I did so in Baltimore.

I had the Rules of the Road memorized and was pretty well studied up on all of the other subjects. I passed the exam in three days without any problems. I then caught a train to go home to Sedalia, MO, to await the return of the *SS George Clement Perkins*. I was scheduled to resume my job as second mate.

Chapter V: SS George Clement Perkins
(Second Tour of Duty)
Sixth Voyage
New Orleans, Kingston, San Juan, New Orleans

The *SS George Clement Perkins* returned from its voyage without me to New Orleans. I rejoined it there as Second Mate on Friday, April 30, 1948.

We loaded a few hundred tons of general cargo for Kingston, Jamaica, and sailed on Sunday, May 2, 1948. It was too early for hurricane season and we enjoyed beautiful summer weather.

The population of Jamaica is mostly descendants from African slaves. It was formerly a British colony and English is the dominant language.

There was a strike in progress, against the public bus system, and pickets warned us that they would put our eyes out if we rode the bus. So we walked to town.

In those days men wore hats. A young man ran up from behind and snatched the Stetson off my head and made off with it.

Over all, our time in Kingston was not very pleasant.

After a two-day stay there, we proceeded to San Juan, Puerto Rico. We were still experiencing nice summer weather.

Here we loaded about five thousand tons of sugar in cloth bags weighing 100 Kilos each. The cargo operations took about a week. San Juan is an interesting city, with several forts and other large structures, dating back to the days when it was a Spanish colony.

Several of us were drawn to the Normandy Hotel and its bar, because the building is shaped somewhat like a ship. One evening I was delayed aboard ship and agreed to meet some of my friends later in the Normandy bar. Prior to my arrival, they had arranged with the bartender to fix my rum and coke so as to be almost entirely 190 proof rum. I gagged when I tasted it and they all chimed in saying that the drinks had at first been too weak and that they finally got the bartender to make them properly. They urged me not to complain. I suspected their plot, but decided to go along with it and managed to get the drink down. I watched the bartender closely when he made the next one, to make sure that didn't happen again. If my buddies expected exaggerated reaction from their chicanery, they were disappointed because, in those days, I could hold my booze well.

We loaded sugar for five days and then left San Juan bound back to New Orleans, arriving there on Thursday, June 3, 1948, and immediately commenced discharging our cargo of about 5,000 long tons of sugar.

Seventh Voyage

New Orleans, Panama Canal, Honolulu, Kobe, Yokohama, Tacoma, Seattle

After the sugar was discharged, we shifted to a grain elevator and took on a full cargo of wheat for Kobe, Japan. We left New Orleans on Sunday, June 6 and proceeded to the Panama Canal. We transited without incident and again there was no shore leave.

We stopped in Honolulu for bunkers and this was my first time in the Islands. An old friend of mine, Judson Banks and his wife, Leloy, and child lived here. I was glad for the chance to visit him. Judson and I had been buddies in high school and had been members, together, in the Boys Choir at the Calvary Episcopal Church, in our hometown of Sedalia, MO. As sixteen year olds, we had traveled together by train during the summer of 1941 to Washington, DC, and stayed there with his married sister and her husband. We spent three weeks sightseeing. Our Washington, DC, visit occurred only six months before Pearl Harbor. During our ship's stay at the Honolulu fuel berth, Judson had time to drive me around the Island and showed me some of the major sites of interest. He and his wife, who had been his high school sweetheart, loved living on Oahu. Judson had a good job as a draftsman and Leloy was a happy housewife.

After bunkering, we left Honolulu and proceeded to Kobe, Japan. This was sort of getting to be my homeport. This was my third visit to Kobe and they had all been about a year apart in the summers of 1946, 1947 and now in 1948. The rapid rebuilding of the city and the huge variety of interesting goods in the stores again impressed me.

There was still no grain sucking mechanism in this port, so we again discharged our cargo of wheat into barges, using canvas slings. We were tied up to a large mooring buoy.

An interesting incident happened with some of our crewmembers. Five of them went ashore together. One of the group was a huge ordinary seaman, whose surname was Simpson. He must have weighed at least 270 pounds. They ended up shacked up, all five of them and their girl friends, in the same room. They were using straw mats on the floor. Simpson asked that the lights, which were bare bulbs in the ceiling, be turned off. When his repeated request was ignored, he took action by reaching up and yanking the wiring loose from the ceiling. This not only turned off the lights, but also started a rapidly spreading fire. They had to immediately evacuate and did not have time to get dressed. In the dark, and due to the urgency of the situation, some of them could not find their clothes. A number of them received minor burns on their bare backs and buttocks.

The door to the room was hinged to open in, but Simpson hit it running and converted it to opening the other way.

The fire department and police arrived on the scene quickly, as did a large crowd. The firemen were able to keep the fire from spreading, but the flimsy building, which they had been in, burned down. They spent the rest of the night in detention and were a sorry looking, half naked group, when a police launch returned them to the ship the next morning.

In most ports and countries, a claim would be made and the culprits would be required to pay for the damage that they had caused. Japan was still under US occupation and, I guess, that they thought that they had to put up with this sort of thing. No claim was made and no criminal charges were filed.

Our cargo was discharged in five days and we then sailed to Yokohama to take bunkers. There was no shore leave here and, after taking fuel, we left Japan bound for Tacoma, WA.

Since it was summer time, we took a great circle route that we modified a bit so as not to go up into the Aleutian Islands.

After a mostly fair weather passage, we arrived at the Straits of Juan de Fuca on a clear day and we were treated to the most beautiful scenery imaginable. There were snow-capped mountains all around, magnificent green forests along the coast and pretty blue water.

We picked up a Pilot at Port Angeles and proceeded to Tacoma. The plans for us to load cargo there did not work out, so after a day we shifted to Seattle where our voyage payoff occurred on Tuesday, August 24, 1948.

Eighth Voyage

Seattle, Yokohama, Longview

We again took on a full cargo of wheat and set sail for Japan on Friday, August 27, 1948, for a port to be named via radio. After a week or so, we were advised that our discharge port would be Yokohama. We again went via great circle but our nice summer weather was coming to an end. We had several gales that caused heavy rolling and pitching and slowed us considerably.

As we neared Japan, we had to contend with a very unusual Typhoon. We were closely monitoring the weather reports from both the American authorities, who were based at Guam, and the Japanese. They kept reporting the eye to be in different locations, some thirty to forty miles different. It turned out that this Typhoon had two well developed centers, that were sort of playing a "dance" with each other. The normal thing that you try to do when at sea in a typhoon or hurricane is try to maneuver so to place your ship in the left or "navigable" semi-circle. In the northern hemisphere, this is usually in the west or southern side of the storm. On the right side, the forward progress is added to the counter-clockwise rotational velocity and on the left side it is subtracted. This difference is usually about twenty or thirty knots of wind speed and, in some cases, it is much more. Since we were well to the east of the storm, our strategy had to be to slow our forward progress and wait for the typhoon to pass. We had winds of about 100 knots for several hours. It blew from the same direction for an extended period of time so the seas developed a pattern of huge waves, sort of like moving ridges of water about fifty feet high. It was not as bad as you might think because the pattern was consistent and the waves were spaced far enough apart so that we had time to recover from one before the next one hit. We steamed at reduced speed, trying to keep the seas about ten degrees on our port bow.

We reached Tokyo Bay, picked up a Pilot near Fort No. One and proceeded to a dock in Yokohama. This port, like Kobe, did not have any grain suckers and we again discharged our wheat using canvas slings. The cargo was hauled away from shipside by trucks that were efficiently and constantly available. This area had been heavily bombed during the war but there was hardly any wartime damage now visible. The country was being rapidly rebuilt.

The port area was remote from any points of interest or good shopping centers. I did not go ashore much in Yokohama but did take a train to Tokyo and did some sight-seeing there.

Our cargo was discharged in five days and we again left Japan and headed back to the US West Coast. About half way across the Pacific, we received orders to proceed to Longview, WA. After a stormy passage, we arrived on Monday, October 11, 1948. The crew was paid off the following day.

While in Longview, I, along with some shipmates, attended a local high school football game. The visiting team was from Olympia, WA. Every time that their team did something spectacular, their cheerleaders would lead a cheer, "It's the water, it's the water". Someone had to explain the significance of this yell to us. That is the selling slogan for Olympia beer.

Ninth Voyage
Longview, Otaru, Yokohama, Honolulu, Panama Canal, Galveston

We again loaded wheat for Japan but the destination was to be a place quite different than the ports that we had been to on Honshu Island.

After loading a full cargo, we left Longview bound for Otaru, Japan, a port that is located on the southwest coast of Hokkaido Island. It is the most northerly one of the major Japanese islands and the one most sparsely populated.

We did not go on a great circle route this time, but still had one storm after the other. From the weather reports that Sparks picked up, it was even worse farther north. We finally arrived at Otaru, picked up a Pilot, and proceeded to a dock. The port was protected by a massive breakwater.

The weather was cold and snow was on the ground.

The local culture here was quite different than it had been in Kobe and Yokohama. In those other ports, the men all wore western type clothes, as did some of the women. In Otaru, the men wore traditional Japanese robes and all of the women wore kimonos. I saw several instances in which the man of the family was strolling along with his wife following a respectful distance behind him, with her arms crossed in front of her and with her hands in the opposite sleeve. The ladies had their faces turned down toward the ground in front of them and never looked up or to either side. They walked with rapid short steps that looked strange. Here the husbands ruled the roost decisively.

We had a Finish-American AB (Able Seaman) in our crew whose surname was Pulei. I don't remember his first name and I probably am spelling his last name incorrectly. It was pronounce like "pulley". He was an interesting guy, in his mid-forties, and a bit of a "rounder" when in port. He was on the 12 to 4 watch with me and had told me some interesting things about his background. During WWII, he was working aboard a Norwegian flag merchant ship. His ship was in port in Norway when the Germans invaded. The Captain and Crew of his ship decided to make a break for it and they left port in the dark of night and made it to England and spent the rest of the war helping the Allied cause. He had obtained his American citizenship and was a very good seaman.

One evening he went ashore in Otaru and ended up shacked up for the night. As in all Japanese establishments, he was required to leave his shoes at the door. The next morning he found that his shoes had been stolen during the night. This was a serious matter because it was very cold and the ground was covered with snow. His girl friend could offer no help in the matter. So, he went out barefooted and the first Japanese man that he encountered, he forcefully removed his footwear, which turned out to be a pair of rubber boots. They were a bit tight but he managed to hobble back to the ship.

While we were in this port, a severe winter storm occurred. There wasn't much snow with it but the wind blew very hard. Fortunately it was from a direction that forced our ship against the pier instead of away from it. In spite of the huge breakwater that protected the port, heavy seas were striking our ship and the surge was causing some of our mooring lines to part. I was standing the midnight to eight watch and most of this trouble occurred during that time. The seas were striking the breakwater and transferring the energy through it, creating similar waves on the inner side. I had the entire Deck Department crew up for several hours replacing lines. It was a big job because we also had to put men on the dock to handle the shore end of the operation. Overall, we parted six of our eight-inch (circumference) manila mooring lines. I wrote to the US Hydrographic Office about this occurrence and they published it in one of their Notice to Mariners.

It took a week to discharge our cargo and we then left Otaru, enroute to Yokohama to take fuel. Fuel was expensive here so we only took enough to enable us to reach Honolulu, where we again took fuel. I was able to again have a short visit with my boyhood friend, Judson Banks, who lived there. We had Christmas at sea as we proceeded to the Panama Canal, where we transited without incident and without any shore leave. We ended the voyage in Galveston, TX, arriving there on Saturday, January 8, 1949.

Tenth Voyage

Galveston, Gibraltar, Trieste, Gibraltar, New York

We again took aboard a full load of wheat that this time was destined for Trieste. That port city was, at the time, a city without a country. Both Yugoslavia and Italy claimed it but the dispute had not yet been settled. The population was overwhelmingly Italian, but Italy had been on the wrong side during WWII, while Tito, and his Yugoslav forces, had fought bravely and effectively against the Germans. We had a typical wintertime crossing of the Atlantic to Gibraltar, where we took fuel, before proceeding on to Trieste.

The people were very friendly and this was a good liberty port. I became acquainted with an Italian gentleman who invited me to his home for a visit and some good wine. I was shocked to see that he had a large portrait of Mussolini on his living room wall. As soon as I could politely do so, I excused myself and left.

Italian Lira was the currency in use in Trieste. The black market exchange rate for the dollar was about four times the official rate so, I am ashamed to say, most of us exchanged some money illegally. Some of us suffered due to our greed. Three of us, namely Third Mate Murphy, Third Engineer Neugebauer and I were suckered in by a scam and we felt pretty stupid. Two black marketers offered us a super good exchange rate and we followed them up an alley. They showed us a big roll of Lira notes and inquired how many dollars we wanted to exchange. We each wanted fifty dollars worth and handed over our money. They said that they didn't have enough Lira with them and one of them left and took our money with him to get it changed. After he was safely away, the other one ran for it and, although we gave chase, we soon lost him in the dark alleys. Our $150 was gone.

While we were in Trieste, a storm occurred that is called a "Bora". The north Adriatic Sea is well known for these winter storms, during which the wind reaches hurricane strength. The port authorities came aboard to warn us of the approaching storm and had men on the dock to assist us in putting out every mooring line possible. Fortunately, our berth was well sheltered and we had no trouble staying alongside the dock. Another ship in port did break loose and suffered serious damage.

Trieste had no working grain suckers, but they did have electrically driven cranes which were used to discharge our cargo of grain. It was loaded into railroad cars using canvas slings. The cranes were not very tall and when our ship got high in the water, we had to put a list on her so that the cranes could reach over the side. This list made ship-

Shipmates having dinner at the Garibaldi Restaurant in Trieste Gentlemen, left to right, Charlie Hippman, 2nd Egr., Louis Murphy, 3rd Mate, Walter Neugebauer, 3rd Engr., Wilbur Vantine, 2nd Mate

board life miserable for a few days. It took almost two weeks to unload the cargo.

We left Trieste and again stopped at Gibraltar for fuel. After a stormy crossing of the North Atlantic, the voyage ended in New York on Wednesday, 3/9/49.

Eleventh Voyage

New York, Hamburg, New Orleans

We took aboard another cargo of wheat, this time for Hamburg, Germany. We left New York on Saturday, March 12 and had a reasonably good crossing of the Atlantic. My twenty-fourth birthday occurred on March 16, but I did not tell anyone.

In Hamburg, we immediately went alongside a berth which was next to a grain elevator that was equipped with efficient grain suckers. They had our ship empty in a little over twenty-four hours.

The city of Hamburg had been almost entirely destroyed by bombing during WWII. On one occasion, there had been 1,000 planes over the city, day and night for twenty-four hours, and over 200,000 people died in the resulting firestorm. Much rebuilding had been done, but a lot of damage was still apparent.

The city was famous for its red light district so I took a look at it. There was a walking street area three or four blocks long that had a walk-around barricade at each end. Throughout the length of the street, on each side, were storefront type display windows, in which professional ladies were posing in a provocative manner on chairs, couches and beds. They came in all shapes and sizes and were in various stages of dress and undress. They catered to a number of different fetishes. The area was a principal tourist attraction and many people that I saw along the walkway, were just sightseeing (as I was).

Soon after our cargo was discharged, we left Hamburg and proceeded back across the Atlantic to New Orleans, arriving there on Wednesday, 4/27/49.

One of the duties of the Second Mate is to keep the charts and nautical publications such as Light Lists and Sailing Directions up to date. At the time this was complicated. You had to make arrangements to receive the various publications from both the US Hydrographic Office and the British Admiralty and to systematically process the information. The British disseminated the information regarding the mines in European waters and there were frequent updates. To make these tasks easier for others, I prepared an outline to instruct how to best perform this duty. I sent it to the Hydrographic Office and, to my surprise, they published it without change. It completely filled the back of one of the Pilot Charts that they issued.

We did not know about a traumatic development that was about to occur until we arrived in port and it was a big shock. The operation of the *SS George Clement Perkins* was to be transferred to another company. All of the ship's crew was to be terminated from the payroll immediately after the voyage payoff.

Captain Goodlett, who had not had a vacation in over two years, went to visit his friends and relatives in Wisconsin. Third Mate Louis Murphy, who had also been two years without a vacation, went home to Lynchburg, VA. He was going to use the time off to get his Second Mate license. I went home to Sedalia, MO. We three, particularly, vowed to keep in touch as we hoped to sail together again. We were told that T. J. Stevenson & Co., Inc. would find another ship for us soon. All of the other officers and crew scattered to their homes or registered with the various unions, seeking another job.

(Note: According to "The Liberty Ships" by Captain Walter W. Jaffee, the SS George Clement Perkins entered the Olympia Reserved Fleet on July 18, 1949 and was withdrawn on January 26, 1951. She remained under the American flag but had several name changes; the SS Seamonitor, the SS Grain Trader, the SS Maria H, the SS Mount Rainier, and the SS Duval. On 6/26/57, she was aground in Inchon, Korea and suffered severe bottom damage. In August 1969 she was scrapped in Kaohsiung, Taiwan.)

Chapter VI: The SS Sea Leader
(First Tour of Duty)

Joining the Ship in Mobile

I had had a Chief Mate License for over a year but, at age 24, was considered too young for the job.

About the middle of June, I received a call from Mr. John A. Moore, the Personnel Manager at T. J. Stevenson & Co. in New York. He offered me the Chief Mate job on a Liberty Ship, the *SS Sea Leader,* which was being taken out of the lay-up fleet in Mobile, AL. To make things even more interesting, Captain Goodlett was going to be Master and Louis Murphy was going to be Second Mate. Captain Goodlett had arranged this and I could not have been more pleased.

The original name of the *SS Sea Leader* was the *SS Joseph I. Kemp.* She was built by the New England Shipbuilding Corporation. The keel was laid on April 5, 1944 and she was launched on May 16, 1944. The ship had been bought from the U. S. Government by the Whitehall Steamship Corporation that only owned this one ship. She was to be operated by T. J. Stevenson & Co., Inc.

I traveled by train to Mobile and checked into the Battleship Hotel on Monday, June 20, 1949, where I met Captain Goodlett. The next morning we took a taxi to the ship that was being made seaworthy at a lay pier in a local shipyard. There was no power on the ship. It was closed up and very hot. A new Chief Engineer, First Assistant Engineer and Chief Steward were also assigned, and we met them all aboard ship.

My first task was to inventory the Deck Department stores and equipment. The storerooms were extremely hot. I got a thermometer and checked the temperature in the forepeak storeroom and it was 120 degrees. The deck above and the surrounding hull were painted black, which really soaked up heat from the sun. There was no ventilation. After a day of this work it was great to get back to the air-conditioned hotel and take a shower.

In time we completed the inventory and prepared requisitions for the items that we would need to operate the ship.

First Voyage

Mobile, Galveston, Savannah, Charleston, Norfolk, Le Havre, Norfolk

We crewed up the ship, including my old friend Louis Murphy as Second Mate, fired up the boilers, took stores and sailed on Coastwise Articles on June 29, 1949. We proceeded to Galveston, Savannah, Charleston and Norfolk, loading general cargo. In Norfolk we signed foreign articles and on Wednesday, July 26, 1949 sailed for Le Havre, France.

We were having nice summer weather and, since the ship had been laid up for a long time, a lot of catch-up maintenance work was needed and done.

We had another fair weather crossing and arrived back in Norfolk on Saturday, August 27, 1949.

Penicillin

We all were very grateful for the miracle drug Penicillin that became widely available after WWII. It was issued to Merchant Marine ships in syringes in quantity, mainly to use in the treatment of Gonorrhea and to a lesser extent to start treatment of Syphilis.

It is now widely known how Penicillin lost its effectiveness over time, i.e., by being over-prescribed by Physicians; by some patients being prescribed too small a dosage to be effective; and by other patients stopping the medication, by mistake, before an effective amount had been taken. By these actions, super germs were created that could resist Penicillin.

In the time frame that I am covering here, gonorrhea was by far the most prevalent VD. It was usual to have two or three cases show up aboard ship, after sailing from ports where "romances" had blossomed.

In 1949, an interesting development occurred. Penicillin became available to us on ships in tablet form. By taking a prophylactic dose, we suddenly had a freedom for sexual activity without risk of catching VD in any form that Penicillin curried. An additional "blessing" was that this could be achieved without having to first catch it and then get that long "barbed" needle stuck in our behinds. It was a sudden freedom, somewhat like the "pill" offered the girls many years later.

I am not very proud of the contribution that I made in diminishing the effect of penicillin, but this is a "tell all" tale.

Before going ashore in Le Havre, I took a "sturdy" prophylactic dose of penicillin tablets. I met a beautiful girl ashore and, having no fear of catching VD, had a romantic interlude with her. Soon after sailing, I developed a suspicious sore in a "private area". In alarm, I got my good buddy, Second Mate Louis Murphy, to give me a shot of Penicillin. The suspicious sore got worse and more developed. I then had Murphy really fill me up with Penicillin. In spite of this, my condition continued to worsen.

Upon arrival in Norfolk, I beelined it to the Marine Hospital to get checked. The Doctor was amused at my alarm and informed me that I did not have VD, but only an allergic reaction to the Penicillin.

Second Voyage

Newport News, Bordeaux, Norfolk

We shifted to Newport News and took on a full load of coal and on Thursday, August 30, 1949, sailed for Bordeaux, France.

As we were approaching port, we were advised by radiogram that, because the river current was unusually strong, it would be necessary for us to disconnect one of our anchors, so as to be able to connect an anchor chain to a mooring buoy in the Gironde River, at the port of Pauliac. This was a difficult task and could not be done with even a small bit of rolling or pitching. So we anchored at the approach to the Gironde River to perform the task. I had the booms for Number One Hatch raised and rigged with a running block so as to evenly distribute the weight of lifting the anchor between the two five-ton booms. I was afraid that the anchor and chain combined might be too heavy for one boom. We then backed the starboard anchor out a bit, put a man over the side in a bosun's chair, and attached a sling from our running block to the anchor. We then paid out the anchor chain while lifting the anchor up and landing it on deck. Then came the difficult task of unshackling the chain from the anchor. We had to get help from the Engine Department to heat, with a torch, the large shackle pins to loosen them so that we could drive them out. I knew of no other port that put us to this much trouble. It took us half a day to get ready.

A French Pilot then directed our transit up the Gironde River to Pauliac, where we made the anchor chain fast to the buoy. The tie-up people had no power winches to assist in the operation and we had to pass a messenger line from the end of the chain to the buoy and back to the ship so that we could heave it to the buoy. This operation took a couple of hours. The current was strong, but I am confident that our regular mooring lines would have held. For sure our wire Insurance Cable would have sufficed and would have been a lot easier than the anchor chain to rig. The Insurance Cable was rated strong enough to tow the ship if that became necessary.

Using the ship's cargo gear, we discharged into barges. Discharge took two and a half weeks. I did not bother to go ashore. When the coal was all out of the ship, we disconnected from the Buoy and steamed back down the Gironde River and anchored for half a day while we reconnected the starboard anchor to the anchor chain. We then set course for Norfolk and arrived there on Wednesday, October 5, 1949.

Third Voyage

Newport News, Oran, Algiers, Charleston

We shifted to a Newport News lay berth and started laying off the crew because there was no profitable cargo available. Freight rates had dropped to below the break-even rate.

I had purchased a case of Piper Heidseck champagne, in France, that I did not want to abandon on the ship. I had our ship's carpenter make a wooden case to put it in and disguise it. I then labeled it "Electronic Equipment- Do Not Jar", and took it to the Railway Express office in Newport News, for shipment home to Sedalia, MO. As things turned out, I would not get home for another seven months. At that time, I proposed that we have the champagne with the family reunion dinner that we were having. It turned out that there were only two bottles left. The story that I got from my sister, Frances, and mother, was that the family dog, Cookie, must have gotten into it and drank those other ten bottles.

When I returned to the ship from the Railway Express office, everything had changed. A cargo had been found. We crewed up and shifted to a coal loading dock and took on a full load for Algeria, North Africa.

We left for sea on Thursday, November 24, 1949, and proceeded toward the Straits of Gibraltar. This was a wintertime crossing and we had the usual winter gales. After entering the Mediterranean Sea and, as we proceeded along the north coast of Africa, we observed that there was a continuous and heavy oil slick left by tankers, that cleaned their tanks while enroute back to the Suez Canal from Europe. This was massive large-scale pollution that no one was doing anything about.

We first stopped in Oran, where we discharged about half of our cargo of coal. It was a dangerous place for shore liberty. There was strong agitation to gain independence from France and a war was brewing. There were many thieves about and you had to constantly fend off pick-pockets. In the old section of the city the streets were narrow and winding, some were on steep hills, and the streets were a series of stair steps. I saw several burros hauling goods in these areas. The buildings were all white and did not have many windows. The women were all fully veiled and only their eyes were visible.

After a week in Oran, we continued up the coast to Algiers, the capital of Algeria. It was a repeat of Oran, except that there was a good-sized part of the city that had modern streets and buildings. I had conversations with the Head Stevedore, who made no secret of the fact that he hated Frenchmen. He hinted that he had killed some and would kill more in the near future.

After a week in Algiers, our cargo was all discharged and we departed for Charleston, SC. We spent Christmas at sea while we were having a strong northerly gale that caused so much rolling that serving and eating Christmas dinner was difficult. We arrived in Charleston on Wednesday, January 4, 1950.

Fourth Voyage

Charleston, Panama Canal, Honolulu, Pusan, Sasebo, Honolulu, Panama Canal, Baltimore

In Charleston we loaded a full cargo of phosphate and were told that it was to be discharged in Fusan, Korea.

We obtained charts of Korea and could find no port by that name. I got out a magnifying glass and did find a Fusan on the north east coast, but it did not appear to be a large enough port to handle ocean-going freighters. This was before the Korean War and we knew nothing about it being divided into a Communist North and a Democratic South. I suggested to Captain Goodlett that he ask the Charterers to provide the Latitude and Longitude of the discharge port. When we got that information, we found that the chart showed the name of the port in that location to be Pusan. The explanation was that the Japanese, who had occupied Korea for about fifty years, had called the port Fusan and the Koreans had changed it back to the original name of Pusan. It would have been interesting if we had gone to Fusan, North Korea. That incident would have no doubt made us famous.

We departed Charleston on Saturday, January 7, 1950 and proceeded to the Panama Canal. We transited without incident and with no shore leave. We stopped in Honolulu for bunkers and then went on our way to Pusan. Our time in Honolulu was short and mostly at night so I did not get to visit with my local friend. This was a wintertime crossing of the North Pacific and we had our share of gales.

Our Saloon Messman this voyage was Puerto Rican man, about thirty years old, whose first name was Juan. He was about six feet tall and was about thirty pounds over weight. He was an extremely good waiter, who had worked several years at fine restaurants in New York. He could take and remember several orders at once. He could and did load up large trays in the Galley and expertly carry it over his head, balanced on one hand, to the Officer's Saloon. I will never forget an incident that occurred during some heavy rolling during a gale. As he entered the door on the port side of the Officer's Saloon, carrying a large tray of food, the ship took a heavy roll to starboard. He ended up racing down hill across the room with the tray held high over his head and crashed into the bulkhead on the starboard side. The resulting crash and mess were impressive.

Korea at that time was a very poor country. The weather was very cold and the restaurants and hotels were not effectively heated. As in Japan, the people sat on the floor and took off their shoes when entering a building.

Some of our crew went to see some public executions, which were done by beheadings. They were conducted at the edge of town. I am not sure that it was accurate information, but we were told that executions occurred weekly. It was too grizzly a spectacle for me and I did not go.

Bunker "C" fuel was not available here, so we went to Sasebo, Japan, to take bunkers. From there we proceeded to Honolulu and Ahukina, Hawaii to load sugar. While in Honolulu, I got to again visit my friend, Judson Banks, and his wife Leloy. We loaded about 6,000 long tons and set sail for the Panama Canal. We had another good transit of the Canal, without shore leave, and went to Baltimore to discharge our cargo of sugar, arriving there on Thursday, April 20, 1950.

Old Spice

On this voyage we had a Radio Officer (Sparks) whom it was easy to dislike. His most notable fault was that he never bathed, and to try to mask his BO, he splashed on copious quantities of Old Spice after-shave lotion. The odor of an unwashed body, mingled with the smell of Old Spice shaving lotion, was overwhelming and most unpleasant. Prior to knowing him, I liked Old Spice after shave but now, even these many years later, cannot stand it.

He was a good looking man in his middle twenties, about five feet, ten inches tall and weighed about 175 pounds. He had a round face with good features, black hair and brown eyes.

It was impossible to insult him. We tried everything that we could think of to get him to take a bath. We called him "Spice" instead of "Sparks".

When we were bound for the Panama Canal and were about a day and a half away, an interesting situation developed. The planet Venus is frequently visible during daylight, but is not generally seen because we don't know where to look. On this occasion, it was located in a position that was easy find in relation to the moon, that was also visible that day. I called "Spice" to the bridge and showed it to him and suggested that it might be a flying saucer. He swallowed the bait "hook line and sinker" and was busy watching it with binoculars and estimating its height, course and speed in relation to clouds that passed by from time to time. He excitedly called Captain Goodlett to see it and wanted him to authorize a message to the authorities at the Panama Canal. I gave Captain Goodlett a wink and he played along with the game. "Spice" was very frustrated that Captain Goodlett would not send a message regarding the "flying saucer".

On another occasion, "Spice" needed some maintenance work done on the ship's radio antenna. The antenna, when at sea, was stretched between a communication mast, which was about twenty feet tall, on the Flying Bridge and the top of the Main Topmast. When it was last hoisted into place, a twist and kink had developed at the end near the communication mast. Someone needed to climb the mast to undo the kink. The mast had steps built-in and could easily be climbed, but "Spice" was chicken and was afraid to do it. He tried to get me to order the Bosun to do it, but I counter-offered to have him heaved up in a Bosun's Chair to do the job. He reluctantly agreed to be hoisted up. He easily cleared the kink and requested to be let down. I told him that we would not let him down until he promised to take a bath. He could have easily climbed down but was afraid. After an hour, and after having braved a rainsquall, he agreed and we lowered him down.

We all complemented him at dinner that evening on how nice he smelled. But, as I said, it was impossible to insult him.

Fifth Voyage

Baltimore, Jobos Bay, San Juan, Emden, Narvik, Baltimore, Norfolk

After discharging our cargo of sugar, we departed Baltimore in ballast (empty) on Wednesday, April 26, 1950, bound for Jobos Bay and San Juan, Puerto Rico, where we took a full cargo of sugar for Emden, Germany.

We had pretty good weather for this ocean crossing.

Emden had been very heavily bombed during the war and had not yet been completely rebuilt. A huge bomb shelter was the most prominent building in the center of the city, and it was truly impressive. It was then being used as a cheap hotel. The shelter was several stories high and the walls were of reinforced concrete many feet thick. It was about the only structure in the city that was not demolished by the bombing. It occupied prime real estate, and needed to be removed, but that would be an extremely difficult task.

After discharging in Emden, we proceeded, in ballast, to Narvik, Norway, to load Swedish Iron ore, that is shipped by rail from the mines in Sweden.

Narvik is located farther north than the Arctic Circle. We were there on June 21st, Midsummer's Day, a holiday to celebrate when the sun is at its summer solstice. If there were not mountains north of the city, we would have been able to see the sun at midnight. Much of the population, on that night, climbed a small mountain known as the "Sleeping Queen", to see the midnight sun. The mountain was so named because, if you used your imagination, you could make out the outline of a reclining female figure.

The iron ore is very dense and heavy. It was dumped from railroad cars on high tracks into the ship and did considerable damage as it landed in the ship. You could easily load a ship down to her marks and only have a relatively small pile of ore in the lower holds. This would make the ship dangerously stiff and cause very rapid and sharp rolling. Therefore, some of it had to be loaded into the 'tween decks. The 'tween deck ore has to be trimmed to prevent shifting. This is expensive and pressure is put on the Captain to minimize the amount to be loaded in the upper part of the ship. Captain Goodlett stuck by his guns and insisted that a proper amount of ore be loaded into the 'tween decks.

We took this cargo of iron ore to the Sparrows Point terminal of the Bethlehem Steel Company in Baltimore, arriving there on Tuesday, July 11, 1950. After discharging the cargo, the *SS Sea Leader* moved down the Chesapeake Bay to Norfolk where she was to load cargo for the next voyage.

I now had enough sea time, as Chief Mate, to sit for my Master's License, and I left the ship in Norfolk.

Chapter VII: The SS Sea Leader
(Second Tour of Duty)

The Master's License

On Wednesday, July 12, 1950, I signed off the Ship's Articles as Chief Officer of the *SS Sea Leader,* after serving in that capacity for an unbroken period of one year and thirteen days. I now had the required sea time to qualify for taking the examination for Master Mariner. Although there was no likelihood of being assigned a ship command at the tender age of 25, I never-the-less studied for, took and passed the Coast Guard examination for *"Master of Steam and Motor Vessels of Any Gross Tons upon Oceans",* as soon as I qualified. After a four-and-a-half day exam, the license was obtained in Norfolk, VA, on Friday, August 4, 1950. I was kind of proud of passing the exam in only five days, because most applicants go well into a second week to complete it.

Possessing a Master's license had the advantage of making it easier to obtain a position as Chief Officer, since I would be qualified to take over for the assigned Captain, should he become ill or disabled. This could result in a steamship company saving the major expense, and delay involved, in transporting a new Captain to wherever in the world the ship may be, when the need arose.

Norfolk

I was staying at the Monticello Hotel and was all alone in Norfolk. There was no one with whom to celebrate the accomplishment. Norfolk was not known as a friendly city or a good liberty town for seamen. It was famous for signs demanding that "sailors and dogs keep off the lawn". In fact, I've heard it said that "if the Good Lord decided to give the world an enema, he would stick the hose in at Norfolk". That was probably too harsh a view of the city, which I am sure, had some good qualities.

There was a large U. S. Naval presence in the area. Also, many merchant ships called to load coal, which was a major export. There was, additionally, a large and active Army Base, from which supplies were shipped to our military forces throughout the world.

It was a seven or eight block walk back to my hotel from the Customs House where, on the second floor, the Coast Guard conducted the examinations for Merchant Marine licenses. There were a number of bars along the way. They were limited to selling beer and wine and were frequented mostly by U. S. Navy sailors and Merchant Marine seamen. It was about 4:00 in the afternoon, and I decided to stop in one and hoist a couple to mark the occasion. As I entered, the only other occupants were the barmaid and a lady who appeared to be her friend. Both were in their mid-twenties and neither appeared to be of the "nice girl next door" type.

I parked on a convenient bar stool that was about three or four away from the other customer. As I drank my draft beer, I could, without really eavesdropping, hear the conversation between the barmaid and her friend. The friend, who was obviously hung over, had been partying the night before. Her boy friend had gotten her drunk and taken her to a tattoo parlor. She had a tattoo on her arm and she had no idea what it said or depicted. I looked over and observed a 4 x 4 bandage taped on the inner side of her left forearm. She was having a very bad day and it somehow made me feel guilty for having such a good one.

I no longer felt like celebrating. I suddenly realized that I was very tired, from the heavy studying, and hard concentration required for the Master Mariner's exam.

I returned to my hotel, called home to tell my mom and dad in Sedalia, MO, the good news, had a good dinner and then went early to bed.

The next day I boarded a train to go home and await the return of my ship, the *SS Sea Leader*. I was scheduled to resume my job aboard as Chief Officer.

My Vacation

The only way to get a vacation in the Merchant Marine during my seagoing days (1943 to 1957) was to take a trip off. The length of the vacation therefore depended on the greatly varying lengths of time that a tramp freighter may take for a given voyage. In my experience with T. J. Stevenson & Co., Inc., the company for which I worked the last ten and a half years that I spent going to sea, voyages usually took from a month and a half to two months, but they could be longer. Vacation pay, on the other hand, was exactly defined. After a year of service, you received one week's vacation pay, except that the Captain got two week's pay.

I had left the ship in Norfolk, VA, on July 12, 1950. About October 20th, my Company's Chief of Personnel, Mr. John A. Moore, called to tell me that the *SS Sea Leader* would be arriving in Houston in about four days, and that I should be prepared to resume my old position as Chief Officer. This had been too long, for a mostly unpaid vacation, and I was glad to hear that I still had a job. So, I took a train to Houston and signed back on as Chief Mate on Wednesday, October 25, 1950.

Rejoining the *SS Sea Leader* in Houston

One thing that distressed me upon my return was that my old friend, shipmate and role model, Captain Elmer F. Goodlett, was being relieved by Captain Demetrius Belesiotis, a Greek-American who was part owner of the ship. I had sailed with Captain Goodlett since December 10, 1946, when I signed on the *SS George Clement Perkins* as Second Mate. I had sailed with him two years in that capacity and then a little over a year as Chief Officer on the *SS Sea Leader*. During all of that time, Captain Goodlett had not taken a voluntary vacation. He apparently had no strong home ties or close family.

During WWII, Captain Goodlett had sailed as Master throughout the war without getting a scratch. His only war "injury" occurred after attending a pre-sailing Convoy Conference in Halifax, N.S. After the conference, he hoisted a few too many in a local bar. When he returned to the ship, he slipped into his bunk and fell into a sound sleep. The blanket was pulled tightly over his bent-back toes and when he awoke, he was temporarily but very painfully crippled.

Captain Elmer F. Goodlett and Chief Mate Wilbur Vantine (1950)

He was, in 1950, about 65 years old and was being put out to pasture. There were no pensions, other than Social Security, for us in those days and I was worried about whether or not he had enough money to survive. He was a fine Norwegian-American whose father was said to have been the first white man to born in Wisconsin. I loved that old man and felt that he was being treated unfairly.

Captain Belesiotis was also a good man. He was, perhaps, even more competent that Captain Goodlett and he also became a good friend. He was in his mid-fifties and had many years experience sailing as Master on Greek flag ships. He had obtained an American Master Mariner's license, issue #1-1, based upon his time in the Greek Merchant Marine, which was highly regarded. He had obtained his American citizenship and, of course, had passed the Coast Guard examination for Master. This was to be his first experience on an American ship.

Captain Belesiotis had some difficult adjustments to make, changing from the Greek to the American Merchant Marine. He was a personal friend of the Greek citizen, Mr. Teriosis, who

Captain Demetrius Belesiotis and 2nd Mate Louis Murphy (1950)

was the owner of the *SS Sea Leader,* and had been deeded a 7% ownership in the ship, as an incentive to perform well as Master. My Company, T. J. Stevenson & Co., Inc., operated the ship under contract and also did the same for a number of other Owners who had one or two ships.

One of Captain Belesiotis's first difficulties occurred when he requested that his Deck Officers wear Eisenhower type jackets, with epaulets to indicate their ranks, three stripes for the Chief Mate, two for the Second Mate and one for the Third Mate. He wore such a jacket himself with four stripes. He even offered to buy the jackets with his own funds. Actually, it was a good idea, as it would enable stevedores and others conducting business, to be able to identify who were the ship's officers. It was common practice in foreign merchant marines. We should have agreed, but we resisted fiercely. He reluctantly and gracefully conceded the point.

He also had to adjust to the fact that being Master on an American ship carried with it much less prestige than being Master of a Greek ship. Crews on Greek ships treated their Captain with great, verging on excessive, respect. Also, American crews, in the 1950's, were not as conscientious or hard working as the Greek crews. Greek ships frequently had crews that were all from the same island, many of whom were related. Often, even low ranking crewmembers, were part owners of the ship.

Deck Officers of the *SS Sea Leader* (1950)
Left to Right, Third Mate Charles Stukenberg, Second Mate Louis
Murphy, Chief Mate Wilbur Vantine (the Author)

Sixth Voyage

The Isbrandtsen Charter—Houston, Philadelphia, Newport News, Norfolk, Baltimore, Philadelphia, New York, Cherbourg, LeHavre, Antwerp, Rotterdam, Bremerhaven, Emden, Hamburg, Bremen, Antwerp, Rotterdam, New York, Philadelphia, Baltimore, Newport News, Baltimore

At the time that I rejoined the *SS Sea Leader,* she was newly time-chartered to the Isbrandtsen Company. There was an extensive "On Hire" Survey that required my climbing up and down, and thoroughly inspecting, all of the cargo compartments.

Throughout the Charter, they worked the ship and us very hard. We proceeded from Houston to Philadelphia, Newport News, Norfolk, Baltimore, Philadelphia and New York, loading general cargo in each of these ports for various ports in Europe, The Cargo Plan became very complicated. We we sure could have used a computer, but they would not come along for many more years. It was difficult and tiring to arrange and run all of these sailings and arrivals.

The Charterer had an "Expeditor" working for them by the name of Mr. Mossack. He frequently boarded us, at all hours, to make sure that we were performing properly. He had a belligerent manner that we all found offensive. We were diligently doing our jobs, but nothing seemed to please him. More about him later.

We sailed from New York on Monday, November 27, 1950, and for the next two and a half months, we all worked very hard. We proceeded to Cherbourg and LeHavre, France; Antwerp, Belgium; Rotterdam, Netherlands; Bremerhaven, Emden, Hamburg and Bremen, Germany; then back to Antwerp and Rotterdam. We discharged cargo in these ports and also loaded in some of them for several U. S. ports. The tricky part was to load cargo, that may be for the second, third, or fourth port, so that it will not block access to cargo for a port that is worked before it. As I said, we sure could have used a computer for the Cargo Plan.

I could not understand how this operation could be profitable for the Charterer. In some ports we only discharged or loaded a few slings of cargo. How could this possibly justify the port and other expenses involved? I guess that their operations were not profitable, because Isbrandtsen Company later went bankrupt.

The *SS Sea Leader* berthed in Rotterdam 1950
(The Author served 2 years as Chief Mate on this vessel and later as Captain)

We were in the port of Bremen on Christmas. The German people have a strong tradition of celebrating Christmas, quite similar to the way that we do in America. I met a beautiful and lonely German girl on Christmas Eve, who invited me to go home with her. She lived alone and had a large Christmas tree in her modest apartment. Before we went to bed, she lighted all of the ten or so candles on the tree, and turned off the room lights. It was beautiful and romantic, but I was terrified that the tree would catch fire. Before going to sleep, and over her objections, I put out all of the candles.

The winter of 1950-51 was very cold in north Europe. There was even some sheet ice in the North Sea. Ice kept us from getting hard alongside several of the docks. The frequent dockings and undockings, at all hours and in very cold weather, took a toll on all in the Deck Department.

An example of our problems occurred when we were about to pick up the German Pilot for the Elbe River. The weather was very cold and the wind was blowing hard. Captain Belesiotis had maneuvered the ship to make a proper lee for the pilot boat. The seamen putting the pilot ladder over the side had cold and stiff fingers, and they accidentally dropped it into the water. That was our only one that was long enough for the freeboard that we then had, so we had to bend two shorter ones together, hurriedly, on that cold windy open deck. Did I mention that this had to be done in the dark?

During this time I was having an additional personal problem. While at sea enroute between two of our European ports, I received a radiogram from my parents, advising me that the Draft Board in Sedalia, MO, had reclassified me as 1-A.

At the time, in spite of the fact that the Merchant Marine WWII casualty rate exceeded that of all the armed forces, my WWII service in the Merchant Marine, starting in 1943, did not count for anything. We were considered to be draft dodgers. According to data gathered by the American Merchant Marine Veterans (organization), during WWII about 250,000 men served in the United States Merchant Marine, over 9,750 gave their lives, 11,000 received disabling injuries and 710 were taken prisoner with only 62 returning home. Some 43 years after the war, on January 19, 1988, those who served on ocean-going vessels during WWII were finally granted veteran status by Congress. By that time in our lives, we no longer had need for assistance in getting college educations or cheap mortgage rates, which were the principal advantages of veteran status.

Between the next two ports, I received a radiogram stating that my induction notice was in the mail. I was going to be removed from my position as Chief Officer on an ocean-going freighter and drafted to be a private in the Army.

I sent a radiogram to the Alumni Association of the Merchant Marine Academy at Kings Pont, NY, and asked if they could help with this situation. They were able to explain the extensive training that I had received and convinced my Draft Board that I would be more valuable to our war effort in Korea by serving as a ship's officer rather than as an army private.

When we arrived in New York, I did not know that the Draft Board had relented. As soon as the ship was docked and before the mail could be delivered, probably with my induction notice, I went ashore with the intention of going to 90 Church Street to request immediate active duty in the Navy, utilizing my commission in the Navy Reserve as Lt.(jg). The Deck Department was temporarily left in the capable hands of Second Mate Louis Murphy.

COPY   COPY

ALUMNI ASSOCIATION OF THE UNITED STATES MERCHANT MARINE CADET CORPS

25 SOUTH STREET, NEW YORK 4, N.Y.

January 22, 1951

Local Draft Board #84
Sedalia, Mo.

Dear Sir:

Mr. W.H. Vantine a graduate of the United States Merchant Marine Cadet Corps, and as
Lt. (jg) in the United States Naval Reserve, has forwarded the enclosed radiogram to
me from the S.S. Sea Leader a vessel that he is now sailing with as Chief Officer.
Apparently he is concerned that induction proceedings possibly will be instituted
since he has notified us of his 1-A classification. According to my information
from Selective Service Headquarters memo #20 as supplemented by memo #22 of September
8, 1950, he will receive an indefinite postponement of induction proceedings, and
his entire file will be forwarded to Washington where it is held subject to review
by the Navy. I would appreciate a confirmation of this proceedure in order for me
to inform Mr. Vantine.

As a member of the Naval Reserve (M.M.R.) he is not in a position to join an organized
or volunteer component of the reserve, but is considered as a merchant marine reservist
to be continually trained although a member of the inactive component.

Sincerely yours,

Wheatley N. Hemmick, Jr.
Executive Vice-president

WNH:m
enc.

Kings Point Alumni Letter that saved the author from the draft in 1951

Luckily, I first called home from a phone on the dock and got the good news. So I returned aboard for the continued hard duty under the Isbrandtsen Charter.

When I returned to the ship, I was surprised to see Mr. Mossack, Isbrandtsen's Expeditor, acting very subdued and standing at the foot of the gangway. It seems that he had boarded earlier and found that I had gone ashore. He had charged up to Captain Belesiotis' office and demanded that he fire me. The good Captain read him the riot act, told him how hard we had been working under this charter and ordered him off the ship. Captain Belesiotis was a powerful man and was prepared to physically eject him if necessary. Mr. Mossack's bluff had been called and he had backed down completely. He was politely asking if I would please relay his apology to the Captain and could he please be allowed to come aboard. I was able to smooth things out. We all shook hand and he was asked aboard for a cup of coffee.

We discharged our cargo in New York, Philadelphia, and Baltimore, finishing up in Newport News, where we had an exhaustive "Off Hire" Survey. We were glad to be finished with the Isbrandtsen Charter.

Our Ship's Paint Supply

We had taken voyage stores in Baltimore, while calling there to load cargo for the Isbrandtsen Charter, and were delivered paint manufactured by some company, of which we had never heard. I had specified International Brand paint on the requisition, which I knew to be a good brand.

Although our schedule and the winter weather had not given us much opportunity to do maintenance work on deck, we did have a fair spell on our homebound passage from Rotterdam. I had the deck crew chip, scrape, wire-brush and red lead the rusty areas on the after house. When we then painted it, half way through we ran out of International Brand white paint and had to finish up with the new stuff. The contrast was great. The old paint gave a high quality finish and the new stuff was awful.

We still had an unopened five-gallon can of International Brand red lead and found that it weighed about twice as much as the off-brand red lead.

I told Captain Belesiotis about these things and we agreed that we should refuse to accept any more of this junk. The labor of our Deck Department was being wasted.

Another incident strengthened our resolve in this matter. Prior to arrival back in the U. S., I used to have the decks of the inside passageways painted, on the night before arrival, with a fast drying red paint called "Padalac". We would paint the entire length of the passageways on one side and, by the time we finished it, that side would be dry on the end where we had started, and we could then paint the other side. We ran out of International brand and had to do most of the second half with the new stuff. Again, the International brand was excellent and the other was terrible.

We again took voyage stores in Baltimore. As before, the same off-brand paint was substituted for the International Brand that I had specified. This time I refused to take delivery.

Well, we got our comeuppance and found that we were not so powerful as we thought. Mr. John F. Bernard, the Marine Superintendent for T. J. Stevenson, & Co., Inc., came down from New York to straighten us out. He came aboard with the Chief Chemist and the three top executives of the off-brand paint company.

I went through my routine of showing them the poor paint on the after house and on the passageway decks. I also showed them difference in weight between the International Brand red lead and their product. The personnel, from the paint company, seemed surly and advanced the ridiculous argument that I had not properly prepared the surfaces.

After the tour, Mr. Bernard got me aside, in my room, and explained that none of this made any difference. Mr. T. J. Stevenson, the Owner of our Company, was a heavy investor in this paint company and we would use it, whether we liked it or not. That was that.

Seventh and Eighth Voyages

Baltimore, Avonmouth, Baltimore, London, Norfolk

We next made two simple and easy voyages carrying coal from Baltimore, first to Avonmouth and then to London, England.

I had long wanted to visit London. While we were in Avonmouth, we were going to have a weekend without cargo discharge. Of course, I didn't know that our next voyage would be to London, so I asked Captain Belesiotis for permission to travel by train to London. He agreed.

The train travel was through lush farm land. You could have mistaken the scenery for Indiana. My time in London was very limited, so I had to set priorities. I first caught one of the water taxis, in the Thames, and traveled up to Greenwich, where I reveled in Nautical History and Traditions. The Observatory and Museum there are great, and of course, Admiral Nelson's flag ship, the *HMS Victory,* is open for inspection. Back in London, I found that I had to go to two restaurants and have two meals, to feel as though I had consumed a proper dinner. During WWII, the British got used to small rations, and that habit was continuing. I spent Sunday morning at the British Museum, and then had to catch the train back to Avonmouth.

During this time, many ships were being taken from the Lay-up Fleet (better known as the Bone Yard) to serve in the sealift, transporting war supplies to Korea. It occurred to me that, in spite of now being only 26 years old, perhaps I could get a command of my own. I wrote a letter to T. J. Stevenson & Co., Inc., stating that I felt capable of handling the job.

Actually, I only felt capable of competently navigating a ship and in following the Nautical Rules of the Road, which I had memorized, and about which I had studied many court decisions. I felt somewhat confident about handling crew relations since I had managed to have a happy and productive Deck Department while serving as Chief Mate. I was worried about conducting ship's business (dealing with Customs and Immigration Officials, Charterers, Stevedores, etc. in many countries and also about preparing crew payrolls, cargo manifests, Notices of Readiness, etc). And I was particularly worried about ship handling. At the time there was no training available, that I knew of, and no really good books available to instruct in the subject.

Captain Belesiotis was kind enough to attach a letter highly recommending me.

While we were enroute to Norfolk from London, I was advised by radiogram that I should sign off upon arrival (Wednesday, May 23, 1951) and that I would indeed be assigned as Master of a Liberty Ship.

I was happy with the promotion, but also very worried about my ability to handle the job.

There was to be about three weeks before my new assignment, so I went home to Sedalia, MO. I spent the time studying what material was available about ship handling and ship's business.

On Friday, June 8, 1951, I received a call from Mr. John A. Moore, Personnel Manager at T. J. Stevenson & Co., Inc. (in New York). He informed me that I should arrange travel so as to report to the Company's office at 80 Broad Street, in down town Manhattan, at 0900 on the following Thursday, June 14th. I would be taking command of the *SS Thomas Sumter* on or about that date. The travel would, of course, be at my expense.

So, on June 12th, I caught the Missouri Pacific Railroad from my home at Sedalia, MO to St. Louis. There I changed to the Pennsylvania Rail Road, with a sleeper compartment, to Penn Station in Manhattan. I reserved a room at the Governor Clinton Hotel, just catty-corner across Seventh Avenue from Penn Station. I checked into the hotel about 1300 on June 13, 1951.

In addition to regular luggage with clothing an personal effects, I always traveled with my trusty sextant.

Chapter VIII: SS Thomas Sumter
(My First Command)

Joining the Ship in Brooklyn

At 0900 on June 14, 1951, I reported to the offices of T. J. Stevenson & Co., Inc. at 80 Broad Street, in downtown New York City. I had an extensive interview with Captain William J. Campbell, who was the Operations Manager. I liked the "cut of his jibe" and he seemed pleased with me. He then went into the office his boss, Mr. John F. Shea, Vice President for Operations. The door was left open and I could hear Mr. Shea, rather loudly say, that a 26-year old could not possibly have enough experience to serve as Ship Master. Captain Campbell's voice was much softer, but I did hear him say that Captain Belesiotis had highly recommended me, and that I had been with the company for over four years as Second and Chief Mate.

Mr. Shea reluctantly agreed to my appointment. I am sure that the fact that there was a desperate shortage of qualified shipmasters was a factor in his acquiescence.

So, on Thursday afternoon, June 14, 1951, I went aboard my first command, the Liberty Ship *SS Thomas Sumter.* She was being reactivated at a pier in Brooklyn. The company doing the work was a small one, known in the trade as a "bicycle shop".

The ship had been laid-up since soon after the end of WWII. She had served as a troop ship and had temporary wooden quarters installed in the 'tween decks. All the troop quarters were being torn out.

She was a "standard" Liberty Ship, similar to about 2,700 others that were built for service during WWII. She was constructed in 1942 in Wilmington, NC, by the North Carolina Shipbuilding Company. The length was 441 feet six inches, beam 57 feet, summer draft 27 feet 8 7/8ths inches, summer displacement 14,300 long tons and she had a deadweight capacity (cargo, fuel, water, stores) of 10,800 long tons. Long tons, 2,240 pounds, were used in the Maritime Industry instead of short tons of 2,000 pounds. The engine was a steam triple expansion reciprocating one of 2,500 horsepower. Cruising speed, at 76 RPM, was eleven knots (12.7 mph) in smooth water.

One thing aboard that was about to be removed, but which I was able to retain, was an old Raytheon wartime radar. The government authorities agreed to leave it, but would not put it in working order, maintain it, nor supply any parts. I was fortunate to have a really good Radio Officer, Lawrence Hacy, who volunteered to work on it. There was a whole room full of spare parts, many of which Larry used. He was able to get it working just fine.

This was my first experience with radar. The unit was installed on the port side of the wheelhouse facing inboard. It had a vertical four-inch scope, with switchable ranges of 2, 4, 8, 20, 40 and 80 miles. It was a useful navigational aid. For instance, I once picked up Pico Island in the Azores 78 miles off. The bearings were only approximate, but were helpful. It was extremely noisy and I did not use it for collision avoidance in fog, because I could not hear fog signals, which I considered to be more important. Even if I had known at the time how to plot and calculate courses and speeds of radar targets, the scope was too small for this, and there was no variable distance-measuring device or movable bearing line. It only had the distance rings, at fixed intervals, and relative bearing degree markings around the outer edge.

The only crewmembers at first, in addition to me as Captain, were the Chief Mate, the Chief Engineer, the First Assistant Engineer and the Chief Steward.

The identity of the Chief Mate was a big surprise to me. For some time, I had been dating a young lady in New York, who worked as a telephone operator. My best friend and former shipmate, Louis Murphy, was dating her sister, who was also a telephone operator. My girl friend told me about her father, who had sailed as Master during WWII, but had been out of work for a long time. His story was a sad one indeed. While he was off at sea during the war, and sending the maximum amount of salary home in an allotment, his wife, the mother of his two daughters, was spending his money on a boy friend.

When the father came home one time unexpectedly, he found that his wife had locked the girls in the attic, while she was out with her boy friend. He filed for divorce, but his wife's lawyer, while he was back out at sea, bribed his lawyer to let some legal deadlines go by without action. The result was that his wife got what was left of his money, the house and the car. He got custody of the girls, whom she didn't want. Clearly, he needed a job, and my girl friend asked me to put in a good word for him with the Personnel Manager at my Company. Although I had never met the man and only knew a little about him, the fact that he had sailed as Master during the war, gave him considerable prestige in my eyes. I gave his name and address to my Company's Personnel Manager. Imagine my surprise when I found that Mr. Carroll, the 65-year-old father of my girl friend, was to be my Chief Officer.

He made a good first impression, being about six feet tall, thin, with a full head of wavy gray hair, and possessing a pleasant voice. I would soon learn why he had been unemployed for so long.

The Chief Engineer, Richard Thompson, was small in stature, and was a nice quiet man about 65 years old. He had been working ashore for several years, and was coming back to sea to help answer the call to man ships for the Korean War effort. He had a tough job ahead, because the engine and boilers in this ship were not so good. Our fuel consumption, when loaded, would turn out to be almost a barrel per mile, and that was much too high. The general quality of crews for tramp freighters, including the Assistant Engineering Officers, at that time, was not so good. Perhaps, if we had gotten top-flight

Chief Engineer Richard Thompson (1951) Photo taken in Rouen

Assistant Engineers, the engine room efficiency could have been improved. As it turned out, the ship's fuel consumption would remain excessive for the entire year that she would run before being returned to lay-up status.

The Chief Steward, whose name I can't recall, was an old Dutchman about 70 years old. He was about six feet tall, about twenty pounds overweight and spoke with a heavy Dutch accent. He had a great sense of humor and was a delight to be around. He ran a good department, and I was fortunate to have him as my Chief Steward.

Our government was in the process of reactivating many ships and had standardized the process pretty well. They had a uniform set of stores that they supplied. We had to check the lists, against what was actually delivered, and also to see if there were any other items that would be essential to ship operations. Having been an active Chief Mate for the last two years, I was very competent in knowing what the Deck Department needed. I found that my new Chief Mate, Mr. Carroll, did not know what he was doing, and I ended up doing his job in addition to my own. For instance, he had not ordered any slushing oil for the wire cargo runners, and didn't seem to know that it was needed. He seemed to have a good attitude about things and there was a severe shortage of Chief Officers. Besides, I had recommended him and he was the father of my girl friend. I had to retain him and hope for the best.

We crewed up the ship and prepared for sea. The unlicensed crew belonged to the National Maritime Union (NMU); the Engineering Officers belonged to the Marine Engineers Beneficial Association (MEBA); the Radio Officer also belonged to a union, but I can't recall its name; and the Deck Officers (including me) belonged to the Masters, Mates & Pilots Union (MM & P). Licensed officers, both Deck and Engine, could be either assigned by the company (preferable), with union clearance, or directly by the unions in response to company requests for specific ratings. In this case, the Chief Mate and I were the only company assigned crewmembers. The unlicensed crew was always ordered from the Union Halls.

The manning scale for a Liberty Ship at that time was as follows:

- 1 Master
- 1 Chief Officer (4-8 watch)
- 1 Second Officer (12-4 watch)
- 1 Third Officer (8-12 watch)
- 1 Bosun (day work)
- 1 Deck Maintenance Man (day work)
- 6 Able Seamen (2 on each watch)
- 3 Ordinary Seamen (1 on each watch)
- 1 Radio Officer
- 1 Chief Engineer
- 1 First Assistant Engineer (4-8 watch)
- 1 Second Assistant Engineer (12-4 watch)
- 1 Third Assistant Engineer (8-12 watch)

- 1 Deck Engineer (day work)
- 3 Oilers (1 on each watch)
- 3 Firemen/Water-Tenders (1 on each watch)
- 2 Wipers (day work)
- 1 Chief Steward
- 1 Chief Cook
- 1 Second Cook and Baker
- 1 Galley Man
- 1 Saloon Messman
- 1 Crew Messman
- 1 Bed Room Steward

That made a total of 36.

Until about three years before, there was also a Purser in the crew. He took care of the ship's paper work and most of them were also qualified as Pharmacist Mates, and therefore acted as the ship's "doctor".

Today's crews (circa 21st Century) are much smaller. All ocean-going ships now use "Iron Mikes" to steer the vessel, and a helmsman is only needed when maneuvering in port. The engine rooms are automated, and maneuvering is controlled directly from the Bridge. Machinery is self-lubricating and pretty much maintenance-free. Mooring lines are rolled up on large powered drums, that greatly reduce the effort needed to deploy, retrieve and stow them. Most cargo operations are now done with shore cranes, and ships that do carry their own cargo gear usually have cranes that are easy to prepare for work or secure for sea. Metal cargo hatch covers are easily opened and closed and are watertight, making it no longer necessary to cover them with tarpaulins, which had to be battened down. Ship gangways are now easily deployed and secured. Pre-prepared dinners (TV type) and self-service, even for the Officers, are now the order of the day. Now that easy voice communications are available at great ranges, the Radio Officers are no longer needed.

Some of these changes resulted in downgrading of shipboard life, but they were balanced by a great improvement in the quality of shipboard quarters and conditions. Just about everyone now has a private room, and many also have private baths. Washing machines and clothes dryers are provided, and most ships have gyms and recreation rooms. Movies are available on VHS and DVD formats. Email is readily available to keep in touch with friends and family. Instead of the one (or two for Masters) week vacation time per year, that was available when I was going to sea, many crews now work on a half-year basis, with paid time off equaling time worked. And very important, the ship's quarters are now air-conditioned.

One thing that I noticed when I looked over the crew list, on that June day in 1951, was that I, at age 26, was the youngest man aboard. Even the ordinary seamen, the wipers and messmen were older than me. All three of my Deck Officers were in their sixties.

Our First Voyage

New York, Philadelphia, LeHavre, Rouen, Norfolk

First Passage— New York, Philadelphia

We sailed from New York in ballast (empty) on Monday, June 18, 1951, for Philadelphia, taking departure at 0000 on June 19th. We arrived at Overfalls Light Vessel at 1518 that afternoon, after having to reduce speed for a while, due to engine problems.

This was the first time that I had ever given any telegraph orders to maneuver a ship's engine. It was fairly simple. Full Ahead when we dropped the New York Sandy Hook Pilot, and then Half Ahead, Slow Ahead, Stop, Half Astern and Stop when picking up the Delaware Pilot to proceed to Philadelphia. As you can readily understand, in slowing a ship for arrival, considerable forethought is needed. Ships don't stop on a dime and when you back the engine, on a single screw ship, they usually (but not always) turn sharply to starboard. These characteristics vary greatly, depending mainly on how much cargo is aboard. Of course, if you slow down too soon you waste valuable time and will get the reputation of being a "slow poke". Anyway, my first baptism under fire went well, and I was able to make a proper lee for the Delaware Pilot.

One short-coming of my three sixty-year-old (plus) mates, was that none of them remembered the Morse Code well enough to answer the flashing light signals that, in those days, was a standard challenge when approaching a pilot station. In these days of easy voice radio communication, it is hard to realize that, not long ago, the only radio communication from and to ships was by dots and dashes via the ship's radio operated, by the ship's Radio Officer. All Deck Officers should have been proficient in operation of the bridge signal light, but these three were not. So, in addition to handling the safe navigation of the ship when approaching port, I also had

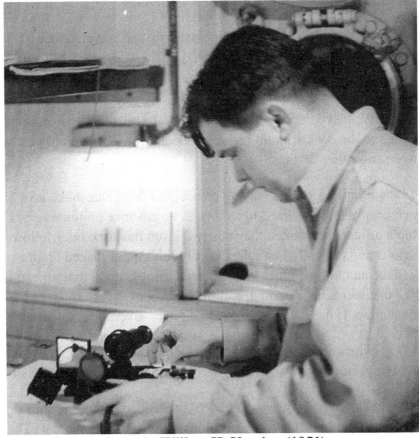

Captain Wilbur H. Vantine (1951)
reading observed sextant angle to calculate a line of position.

to climb up to the Flying Bridge and use the signal light to announce the identity of our ship, and get information regarding pilotage.

In Philadelphia we loaded a full cargo of coal for a port of ports to be named in North Europe. Since this was the first loading of this ship for me, I wanted to carefully gage the actual deadweight. The water in Philly is, of course, usually still, not choppy, so very accurate draft readings could be taken. I again found that my new Chief Mate was not so competent, in that he did not know how to measure the specific gravity of the water, and calculate our proper fresh water allowance. My notes show that it turned out to be entirely fresh, so our full fresh water allowance of 7 1/4 inches was appropriate. This is the allowance for the fact that ships ride deeper in fresh water than they do in salt water. We loaded 10,039 long tons of cargo and our deadweight, which included cargo, fuel, water and stores, worked out to be 10,809 long tons.

Second Passage— Philadelphia, Le Havre, Rouen

We sailed from Philadelphia on Tuesday, June 26, 1951. We headed in the general direction of the English Channel, following a Great Circle route, since this was summer time and good weather could be expected. A Great Circle track, which is the shortest route, takes you into high latitudes, that are best avoided in the winter when stormy weather is likely. A week or so later, I received notice to proceed to LeHavre, France, and that discharge would be partly there and partly in Rouen.

We had a nice summer time crossing and traversed the 3,336 miles in 13 days and three hours, averaging 10.59 knots.

Le Havre

We picked up the French Pilot to take us into LeHavre on Monday, July 9, 1950, and proceeded to the dock without undue incident. We were berthed port side to a very long pier, between two other ships.

Prior to arrival, I had the crew union delegates make up a "draw list", showing how much each crewmember wanted to receive as an advance on his wages. I personally asked each of the ship's officers how much they desired. From this time on, I followed a similar routine in the various ports of call. As a rule, the only limit that I placed on draws was that they could not exceed the amount of wages that had been earned, up to that time, minus any allotments (to wives, etc.) that had been specified, and slop chest purchases. Calculating the amounts was a bit time-consuming. If the stay in port extended over several days, I would grant additional draws.

When the Ship's Agent boarded, he had the funds, in French Francs, that I had requested, and I gave out the draws in an orderly manner in the Officer's Saloon.

Discharge of our cargo of coal proceeded, using the ship's gear. This was, after all, France, so the work was only done on one shift during the day. The stevedores took a very long lunch break, and they had their big jugs of wine, that they drank from as they worked. The winch drivers, at times, drunkenly and noisily raced the ship's steam winches, and that greatly worried me. However, they had a lot of practice drinking wine and handled it pretty well.

About three o'clock the first afternoon after docking, the Chief Steward came to me, and stated that the Deck Engineer had taken a large bag of sheets from the Steward's storeroom, and was proceeding down the dock with them. I ran to the port bridgewing and observed that this was true. I raced ashore and down the long dock and reached the police guards, at the head of the pier, just as the Deck Engineer did. I requested that they arrest him, which they did. He resisted arrest and it took three policemen to subdue him. Unfortunately, they kept the sheets as evidence.

The Deck Engineer was a large black man, about forty years old from Trinidad (in the West Indies). He was extremely angry with the Chief Steward, who had followed us to the head of the pier. He said that he was "going to kill that son-of-bitch". He further stated that he (the Steward) had sure better keep his door locked, because he was going to get him.

To be confined aboard ship, at sea, with a violent person who had threatened murder was a serious matter. I wanted to have him detained and not allowed to return to the ship. I consulted with the Union Delegates from the three departments (Deck, Engine and Steward). They all agreed with me, and the four of us proceeded to the American Consulate's Office in Le Havre to request this.

The Consulate was not a representative of which a red-blooded American would be proud. He was over-dressed, over-weight, had a silly little mustache, a high-pitched voice and was wimpish in his manner. He clearly did not want to retain the man in jail. I suspect that his reason was that it would cause trouble for him. He had visited the Deck Engineer in jail and had found him to be a nice peaceful fellow. The diplomat stated that he was sure that the Deck Engineer would not harm anyone on the ship. I asked, if the fact that he had been caught red-handed stealing government property, was of any significance and the reply was, "no, not in this case". I never the less submitted the petition, signed by the three Union Delegates and me, declaring our fear that this man would harm or possibly murder the Chief Steward, and we formally requested that he not be allowed to return to the ship. I further guaranteed, in the name of my Company, his return fare to the United States. The Consular Officer said that he would take the matter under consideration.

My other principal problem at the time was that Chief Mate Carroll was constantly drunk. Discipline in the Deck Department was consequently nil. Essential work was not being done. I searched his quarters and, over his strong objection, removed a couple of bottles of wine. Like most alcoholics, he was resourceful and managed to continue to stay drunk. I now understood why he had been unemployed for so long. It was also clear that I was going to have to fire him and that would most likely end my romance with his daughter.

Rouen

After unloading cargo in Le Havre for four days, our draft had been reduced to the point that we could proceed up the Seine River to Rouen, to complete discharge. We left the dock at 0531 on Friday, July 13, 1951.

Our passage up the river was one of those extraordinary experiences that you remember for a long time. The weather was perfect and the scenery was magnificent. When nighttime came, there was a full moon. It was Bastille Day and all of the villages along the way were celebrating, some with torchlight parades, complete with marching bands.

We docked in Rouen at 0100 on Saturday, July 14, 1951

Rouen is a beautiful city with a magnificent cathedral and many beautiful buildings, placed on wide tree-lined streets. The spot where Joan de Arc had been burned at the stake is well marked and, of course, we all had a look.

Rouen Cathedral (1951)

Place in Rouen where Joan of Arc was burned at the stake (1951)

Unless you spoke French, the people were, for the most part, down right unfriendly. The one exception was the French prostitutes, who were very friendly and were among the few locals who spoke English. But they took strong exception to my excluding them from being able to ply their trade aboard my ship. They were quite vocal about it, shouting up some rather unfriendly remarks to me from shipside. Some of my crew would have likewise preferred a more hospitable attitude on my part.

94.

Except for the fact that I had to contend with drinking stevedores and that the Chief Mate continued on his drunken spree, the stay in this unique French city was pleasant. It was perfect summer weather. We finished discharging our cargo of coal on Thursday, July 19th, and departed the dock at 1700 that afternoon.

Guess what happened as we were in the process of pulling up our gangway. The French police delivered our errant Deck Engineer aboard!!! I was furious and worried about the safety of my old Dutch Chief Steward. There was nothing I could do about the situation. It brought to mind the widespread sentiment of the time, namely, that "if you really needed help, you went to the British Consulate rather than to the American one".

Our Passage Home— Rouen, Norfolk

We sailed back down the beautiful Seine River and took departure from the LeHavre Outer Anchorage Buoy at 0112 on Friday, July 20, 1951. We were still enjoying nice summer weather.

My first order of business, after breakfast, was to have the Deck Engineer brought to my office for a lecture. I told him that there were several witnesses, including me, who had heard him threaten the Chief Steward and that, if any harm befell him, he (the Deck Engineer) would be in serious trouble. I further told him that if he displayed any threatening moves against the Chief Steward, I would have him place in irons (handcuffs) for the rest of the voyage. He was mostly silent but glared at me the whole time. I decided to take the ship's .38-caliber revolver out of the safe and keep in under my pillow when sleeping.

A few days later, when we were within easy radio range of the U. S. East Coast, I sent a message to the Coast Guard in Norfolk, requesting that they meet the ship upon arrival and deal with this matter.

Prior to sailing from Rouen, I dispatched a letter to Captain William J. Campbell, Operations Manager at T. J. Stevenson & Co., Inc., and told him about the drunken performance of Chief Mate Carroll. I requested a replacement, and mentioned that my first choice would be Louis L. Murphy, with whom I had sailed the last four years. He had been Third Mate when I was Second Mate and Second Mate when I was Chief Mate and had now obtained his Chief Mate License. He was a great guy, very competent and was my best friend during those years. Most steamship companies did not allow friends to sail together in key positions, but Captain Campbell recognized that we made a good team and arranged it.

Chief Mate Carroll had real withdrawal pains when he no longer had any wine to drink. He became very hostile to me and, I must admit, I was hostile to him. A few days before arrival in Norfolk, while I was asleep, he sneaked into my office, during his morning 4 to 8 watch, and got into my correspondence file. He located a copy of the letter that I had sent to Captain Campbell requesting that he be replaced. He let it be generally known around the ship about the letter and took great exception to it. Our relationship was tense to say the least.

We had good weather for our passage to Norfolk and covered the 3,322 miles in 11 days, 12 hours and 48 minutes, averaging 12.0 knots. We arrived at Cape Henry at 0800 on Tuesday, July 31, 1951.

Norfolk Events

A Coast Guard Official did in fact board the vessel soon after we docked. He questioned me and examined my log entries and correspondence regarding the Deck Engineer. He also questioned him. The Deck Engineer and I were both issued subpoenas to appear at a formal hearing two days later.

When I appeared for the Coast Guard hearing, the Deck Engineer was there, together with the Norfolk Port Agent and another official of the National Maritime Union, who were representing him. As the proceeding progressed, you would have thought that I was on trial instead of the Deck Engineer. It was brought out that he had been torpedoed during WWII. His toes had been frozen in a lifeboat, and that they had to be later amputated. I was an abusive Ship Master who was bullying this poor war hero. The fact that he had stolen property from the ship, and threatened to kill the Chief Steward, seemed to be glossed over as insignificant. The final decision of the Coast Guard Hearing Officer was that the Deck Engineer would have his seaman's papers suspended for 30 days.

Meanwhile, the Operations Vice President at T. J. Stevenson & Co., Inc., Mr. John F. Shea, was looking suspiciously into matters, as he did not believe that a 26-year-old should be sailing as Ship Master. He sent word for me to call him on the phone. He wanted to know why all three Mates were leaving the ship. That did not look good. I explained that the Chief Mate was fired for drinking, the Second and Third Mates, both of whom were in their sixties, had been ashore for some years, and had taken this voyage to get reacquainted with the ways of the sea. The Second Mate had a Chief Mate license, and signed off planning to get a Master's license. The Third Mate already had a Master's license and would be looking for a ship of his own. Mr. Shea reluctantly accepted my explanations and didn't fire me. Again, I believe that what saved me was the fact that there was a severe shortage of competent Masters. Also, Captain Campbell, the Operations Manger, supported me.

You may be wondering about my romance with the former Chief Mate's daughter up in New York. We never corresponded after the bad events of that voyage to France. Daughters love their fathers and I didn't want to diminish their loving relationship. Most likely, she would have supported him instead of me anyway. Also, it was to be a long time before I got back to New York and I was very busy handling my job.

Second Voyage

Norfolk, Rotterdam, Charleston

Passage #1— Norfolk, Rotterdam

We crewed up again and this time had a much better one.

My best friend, 26-year old Louis L. Murphy, was my new Chief Mate.

Another notable new crewmember, about whom you will read more later, was Bosun Wallace E. Ebanks, a resident alien from the Cayman Islands.

As an aside— Resident aliens in those days had a really good deal working in the American Merchant Marine. Number one benefit was, of course, our wage scales were higher than those in foreign merchant marines. In addition to that, they did not have to pay any U. S. Income Tax on the part of their wages that were earned outside of the U. S. The only tax, that I withheld from their pay, was the tax on the relatively small portion earned while in U. S. ports.

It was surely good to have a sober and competent Chief Mate to run the Deck Department. Although this was Louis Murphy's first job as Chief Mate, he knew his stuff. For instance, he knew how to measure the specific gravity of the water at our loading pier and calculate our fresh water allowance. On this occasion the brackish water allowed us to load 4 1/4 inches deeper than our summer Plimsoll mark. We loaded 10,073 tons of coal and our deadweight this time worked out to 10,930 tons, 120 more than on the last loading.

(Note: At the instigation of one of its members, Samuel Plimsoll, a merchant and shipping reformer, the British Parliament, in the Merchant Shipping Act of 1875, provided for the marking of a load line on the hull of every cargo ship, indicating the maximum depth to which the ship could be safely loaded. Application of the law to foreign ships leaving British ports led to general adoption of load-line rules by maritime countries. An International Load Line was adopted by 54 nations in 1930, and in 1968 a new line, permitting a smaller freeboard (hull above waterline) for the new, larger ships, went into effect. The load line marks are generally referred to as the Plimsoll line, in honor of Samuel Plimsoll. The reforms that he instigated saved countless seamen from the watery graves, where greedy shipowners would have sent them in dangerously overloaded ships)

We took departure from Cape Henry at 2042 on Tuesday, August 7, 1951.

Again our stated destination was a port or ports in North Europe. A few days out, I was ordered to proceed to Rotterdam for discharge.

We had good summer weather for the entire passage. We arrived at the Rotterdam Pilot Station on Tuesday, August 21, 1951, at 2106. We covered the 3,534 miles in 13 days, 18 hours and 24 minutes, giving us an average speed of 10.7 knots.

Our rate of fuel consumption was troubling and worked out to be 0.881 barrels per mile. That was much too high and Chief Engineer Thompson was at a loss to explain it.

Rotterdam

Our ship was moored fore and aft to mooring buoys in the harbor. The crew and others traveled to and from shore in motor launches called "Speedos".

On a return Speedo ride back to the ship, I overheard seamen from another ship discussing, in jovial terms, a terrible thing that they had done. Now days we are told to avoid salt, but in those days salt consumption was encouraged. Dispensers for salt tablets were placed next to the water fountains aboard ships. These low-life characters had convinced their girl friends in Rotterdam, that these salt tablets were actually new magic pills that would keep them from becoming pregnant.

The Dutch were much more efficient that the French. The cargo of coal was discharged around the clock by large floating cranes that transferred the cargo into barges. The barges were unique in that they were actually small ships, self-propelled with a wheelhouse and quarters aft. Many of them had a family living aboard. Even though they were hauling a dirty cargo, like coal, they were neat as pins, some even having white curtains in the windows. These barges could and did deliver cargo throughout Europe, via the various waterways and canals.

Rotterdam was a good friendly port for merchant marine seamen, but the quick turnaround time was not so good for liberty purposes. All of the public places, even including rest rooms, were clean as a whistle, again a great contrast with France.

My old Dutch Chief Steward was in his glory here. He got to visit friends and relatives that he had not seen in many years.

Passage #2— Rotterdam, Charleston

We took departure from the Rotterdam Pilot Station at 2230 on Thursday, August 23, 1951, bound for Charleston, SC.

During this passage, we encountered a couple of moderately strong gales and had to slow the engine to avoid pounding. We arrived at the Charleston Pilot Station on Saturday, September 8, 1951, at 1942, having covered 3,822 miles in 16 days, 3 hours and 12 minutes. This gave an average speed of 9.87 knots and our fuel consumption, even in ballast, was a high 0.851 barrels per mile.

Overall, this, my second voyage as Master, had gone well. The Operations Vice President, Mr. Shea, must have been satisfied because he did not question me about any problems. My relationship with the Operations Manger, Captain Campbell, continued to go well. After each trip, I wrote a "Voyage Letter" to Captain Campbell, which detailed events that seemed to be of interest. I surely do wish that I had kept a copy to peruse in my later years.

Third Voyage

Charleston, Bremen, Newport News

Passage #1— Charleston, Bremen

We loaded a full cargo of coal in Charleston. An unusual situation, for bulk cargo, came about in that our cargo spaces filled completely up, without getting the ship down to her summer load marks. We were only able to load 9,441 long tons of coal, which was about 600 tons short of what we would normally be able to lift. This had a bright side in that we didn't have to skimp on fresh water and could be generous in our fuel calculation, without cutting out cargo capacity.

We took departure from the Charleston Sea Buoy on Friday, September 21, 1951, at 2342, again bound for a port or ports in North Europe. In due time I received orders to proceed to Bremen, Germany.

After having better weather than can usually be expected this time of year, we arrived at the Weser River Pilot Station on Sunday, October 7, 1951, at 1318. We covered 4,059 miles in 15 days, 7 hours and 36 minutes, giving an average speed of 11.17 knots. This good speed was in spite of a stoppage at sea of 4 hours and 24 minutes for engine repairs. However, our fuel consumption was a dismal 0.925 barrels per mile.

Bremen

I had spent the previous Christmas in Bremen (as Chief Officer on the *SS Sea Leader)* and I was impressed by how quickly the city was being rebuilt, after the catastrophic bombing damage of WWII. In just the ten months since my last visit, remarkable progress had been made. It was a clean, bustling and modern city with almost no signs remaining of war damage.

I purchased a sporterized 7mm Mauser bolt-action rifle, that had a unique second "hair" trigger, in a local store. I prized this gun and kept it for many years until I, while working as a Panama Canal Pilot, had to sell it when Panama took over the Canal Zone. Panama, like, New York, had strict gun control laws. I sold it to a U. S. Army soldier, who was stationed in Panama and could legally own it.

The port operations were, like those in Rotter-

SS Thomas Sumter docked in Bremen, Germany (1951)

dam, very efficient. Large shore cranes discharged our cargo of coal in less than two days. The weather had turned bad, and our crew had to secure for sea in miserable cold and rainy conditions.

Return Passage— Bremen, Newport News

We took departure from the Weser River Pilot Station on Wednesday, October 10, 1951, at 0524 with orders to proceed to Hampton Roads for orders. We experienced good weather for most of the passage and arrived at Cape Henry Junction Buoy on Thursday, October 25, 1951, at 1142, covering 4,191 miles in 15 days, 12 hours and 18 minutes. Our average speed was 11.25 knots and fuel consumption averaged 0.724 barrels per mile.

Fourth Voyage

Newport News, Kiel Canal, Copenhagen, Kiel Canal, Falmouth, Baltimore

Passage #1— Newport News, Kiel Canal

We loaded a full cargo of coal at Newport News. Due to the season, we could only load to our WNA (Winter North Atlantic) Plimsoll mark and took on 9,602 long tons.

After all cargo was aboard, we shifted to anchor to await completion of the crew. All we needed was a Third Assistant Engineer and he was enroute by air from New York. I went ashore and waited in the Agent's office for his arrival.

The crew list was partially done and was in an electric typewriter awaiting completion. It was a Saturday afternoon and most of the office staff was not on duty. Since I knew how to type, I offered to work on it and the Agent gladly accepted. That was a bad mistake on his part. I had never before used an electric typewriter, and it seems as though I unknowingly and frequently, pressed a little on the "j" key. This did not matter on a manual typewriter, but it had serious consequences on an electric. Since there were several carbon copies being made along with the top one, each time I typed a "j" that didn't belong, a difficult erasing was necessary, on the copies as well as on the original. We soon reached agreement that I should cease "helping".

Finally, the Agent's driver arrived with the new Third Assistant Engineer, a Mr. O'Quien. He was about forty years old, dressed poorly, smelled bad, obviously needed a bath, and had no luggage. I offered to shake hands and he informed me that he didn't shake hands. He offered me his elbow, which I declined. He was about five feet eight, 160 pounds, and his nose was very much pushed to one side. I surmised that someone had probably knocked it that way. His Coast Guard License had a "D-5" after the issue number, indicating that he had lost his license and had it replaced four times.

Anyway, we got him signed on the Articles, finished the paper work, went aboard and got underway on Thursday, November 1, 1951.

A new twist this voyage, was that we already knew what our discharge port would be, and it was Copenhagen, Denmark, generally regarded to be the best liberty port in the world. All of the crew was in a happy mood.

Although the time of year was such that we could expect a stormy passage, we had good weather. We arrived at the Elbe River Pilot Station (enroute to the Kiel Canal) on Saturday, November 17, 1951, at 0618. We had covered 3,786 miles in 14 days, 23 hours and 24 minutes, giving an average speed of 10.53 knots. Our fuel consumption was a terrible 0.921 barrels per mile.

A bad day in the Kiel Canal

The Kiel Canal was completed in 1895. It is 61.3 miles long, originally had a width of 144 feet, and has a controlling depth of 36 feet. The channels have been enlarged to a width of 336 feet. A central portion has been further widened to 531 feet and mooring stations have been installed. Ships bound in one direction can tie up in the central portion, to allow ships bound in the opposite direction to proceed. The Canal runs approximately east-west through flat, lush farmland. When transiting, you see impressive looking cows grazing on both sides. It connects Brunsbuttelkoog, near the mouth of the Elbe River (which discharges into the North Sea), with Holtenau, near the city of Kiel, on the Baltic Sea. Kiel is famous for being the home of Germany's renowned submarine fleets.

Using the canal avoids having to go around the north end of Denmark and saves about 300 miles steaming for ships, bound from the English Channel or North European ports, to ports in the Baltic Sea. Lock Chambers on each end adjust the outside water level to that of the Canal and vice versa. Two Canal Pilots come aboard in the lock chambers. They have their own (two) Quartermasters to steer the ships. They take turns conning and steering, while their partners rest.

This was to be my first experience with the Kiel Canal and, except for enjoying pretty scenery, it was to be most unpleasant.

The Elbe River Pilot took us to an anchorage off the Canal Entrances, of which there were two. The Canal runs at roughly 90 degrees to the river. The down river approach channel, which we would use, had a left curving route from the river. It joined the other channel, from up river, which had a much more shallow turn to the right. It was used mostly by ships coming to the Canal from upstream.

At this stage of my career, I knew very little about shiphandling, which was unfortunate, because I should have intervened with the incompetent first Canal Pilot that handled my ship. As I (later) understood their system, the Kiel Canal Plots assign their most junior and inexperienced men, to take ships from the anchorage into the lock chambers. Then two more senior ones (plus two Quartermasters) come aboard in the locks to transit the Canal.

As we were proceeding in the left curving channel, we reached the junction with the other channel, where a further left turn of about 30 degrees was required. This junction was, as I recall, about half a mile from the locks. The arrangement was awkward, from the standpoint of maneuvering a single screw ship, because you likely would have to increase power to make the turn, and thereby add undesired speed when near the locks. A backing maneuver at the junction would be counter-productive, as it would probably cause the ship to turn to starboard.

Our Pilot was probably not used to handling steam ships, because almost all foreign ships had diesel engines. He had put too much headway on the ship and had (belatedly) put our engine on stop to drift some of it off. When we reached the junction, he ordered "hard port rudder" and "dead slow ahead" engine. Dead slow on a steam ship is usually only about 10 rpm giving power for only about two knots. On most diesel ships, dead slow is 40 rpm or more giving power for six or more knots and, when commencing from stop, provides a strong initial surge, giving very good rudder response, as the prop wash hits the rudder. When our ship did not respond to his commands, the Pilot panicked. Instead of ordering more power ahead to start the desired turn, he ordered "full astern" and ordered the port anchor dropped.

I should have intervened and ordered a brief "half ahead" to start the turn, but I did not do so. His maneuver guaranteed that we would run aground on the opposite side of the channel. So, we ended up crossways in the channel, with our bow aground in what fortunately turned out to be soft mud. A tugboat, which was stationed nearby, came over, put up a line to our stern, and pulled toward the river as we heaved the anchor, which pulled us away from bank.

The *SS Thomas Sumter* aground at Brunsbuttlekoooog (1951)

Our troubles were just beginning. After getting properly aligned with the channel, we let the tug go, and proceeded into the very large Canal Lock Chamber. We were to be the first ship in the lockage and were to tie-up starboard side to the lock wall, leaving room astern of us for a similar size ship. Smaller vessels would later tie up port side to the wall on the left side of the lock chamber.

Our Pilot now approached the Lock Chamber with too much speed, for a deeply loaded low-powered ship such as ours. Again, I should have intervened but didn't. He ended up having to go "Full Astern" at the last minute, to avoid running into the lock gate ahead. This caused a violet swing, bow to starboard, which in turn caused heavy contact with the lock wall, putting a good-sized dent on our starboard side forward. This heavy backing also caused us to wash well away from the lock wall.

We finally got secured alongside. The Lockmaster came aboard with a paper for me to sign, taking responsibility for knocking loose some of the large concrete blocks in the lock wall. Thus, instead of me having a claim against the Canal for damaging my ship, they were making a claim against the ship for damaging the locks. (This was in direct contrast with the Panama Canal, where the Canal pays for any damage to a ship caused by pilot error.)

I asked to confer with my ship's Agent regarding this matter.

While the discussion was going on, the Tugboat Captain appeared and asked me to sign his "bill". Fortunately, I read it before signing. It was a Lloyd's salvage agreement, giving his company salvage rights on my ship and cargo. I typed and signed a statement describing the services performed and gave that to the Tug Master. He was belligerent and not at all happy with me.

The Ship's Agent finally showed up and advised that I must sign the Lock Master's Claim, or my ship would not be allowed to proceed. I made a note that I was signing under protest and did so.

Meanwhile, the water level in the chamber had been adjusted to the level of the Canal. The smaller vessels tied up on the left side of the chamber proceeded. The Pilot, on the ship astern of us in the chamber, also elected to proceed around us into the Canal. This was a reckless maneuver and he should not have done it. As he passed us, the hydraulic force caused all of our mooring lines to part. They had been in warehouses for several years and, although they appeared to be in new condition, were actually pretty rotten. We were suddenly adrift, surrounded by concrete, and couldn't use our engine, because lines were in the water aft. Our deck crew was called out to quickly pull them aboard. We had to maneuver back alongside, so that the Agent and Lockmaster could debark, and also to reclaim the shore end of our parted mooring lines.

November 17, 1951, was a miserable day all around. The sky was heavily overcast, it rained intermittently all day plus it was windy and cold. Our troubles in the Kiel Canal had been notable, but were not over.

A new problem now surfaced. This was the first time that we had had steam on deck during cold weather. It was needed to run the windlass forward and the after mooring winch. The steam lines commenced developing breaks, with severe leaks, on both the fore and after decks. The Chief Engineer had his crew out patching the leaks as best they could. Of course, steam had to be shut off deck in order to fix the leaks. This meant that if we dropped the anchor, we could not pick it up. We were scheduled to tie up at the mid-point moorings to allow traffic to proceed in the opposite direction. Anchors were routinely used to maneuver to the tie-up pilings. Also, without steam on deck, we would have no power to the mooring winches to heave alongside the pilings.

Fortunately, when it came time to tie up, we did have steam power on the fore deck (but not aft). The Pilot did a good job of berthing, and was able to accomplish it without dropping the anchor. He maneuvered the ship alongside the pilings but our crew, working in cold rainy weather, had to pull the

The *SS Thomas Sumter* transiting the Kiel Canal (1951)

slack out of the wet and very heavy 8-inch (circumference) sisal mooring lines aft by hand. That took all hands from the Deck Department, and some clever rigging with a block and tackle. Again, my good friend, Louis Murphy, proved his worth as Chief Officer and Bosun Wallace Ebanks, did a great job of running the deck crew.

One smart and advanced (for the time) procedure in the Kiel Canal, was that one of the Quartermasters climbed up on the foremast and installed a kerosene powered red light, on the port side of the mast, to aid steering after dark. Many years later, principally due to my recommendations as Chairman of the Panama Canal Pilot's *Canal Improvements Committee,* the Panama Canal Commission commenced requiring steering lights on transiting vessels. We used blue steering lights, instead of red, so as not to be confused with the ship's running lights. A steering light forward aids greatly in determining, after dark, your heading relative to the channel and objects ahead. A change in the heading can be immediately detected, as the steering light moves (swings) against the background lights. Without this help, the person navigating a ship in the dark lacks sufficient information to safely guide it in narrow channels.

Another activity of the off-duty Quartermasters was not so praiseworthy. They toured all of the showers in the crew quarters and stole the soap from the soap dishes.

We finally cleared the Canal at 1136 on Sunday, November 18, 1951. That had been a terrible experience, but now we looked forward to Copenhagen

Copenhagen

It was 197 miles from Holtenau to Copenhagen, via the deep channels, and we arrived at the Pilot Station on Monday, November 19, 1951, at 0700. We were about to spend six days in what was called the "Paris of North Europe". Having been to Paris three times, I can state with authority, that from a seaman's point of view, Copenhagen was much better that Paris.

The people were very friendly and just about everyone spoke English. These were the same great people that did so much to save Jews from the Nazi thugs during WWII. When the Germans decreed that Jews had to wear a yellow Star of David on their garments, the King appeared in public, on his bicycle, wearing one himself. The word spread quickly and soon everyone started wearing one. It drove the Germans batty. Many Jewish people were smuggled from here to Sweden, which was not under German occupation. This was done mostly at night, in fishing boats, at great personal risk, and usually for little or no monetary payment.

The city was beautiful and well kept. The Tivoli Gardens are magnificent and, of course, we all saw the famous "Little Mermaid" statue in the port. In the part of the city near the docks, there seemed to be a nice bar on every corner.

An important element that made Copenhagen such a good liberty port was the many gorgeous and very friendly girls. I guess that you could criticize their morals, because many of them shacked up with casual acquaintances, such as seamen, but most of it was not done as prostitution. It was done because they were having fun and enjoyed the experience also. The Danish people genuinely appreciated what America had done during WWII.

Port Area of Copenhagen (1951)

105.

One favorite sport of the Danes was to take advantage of drunken Swedes, who arrived by ferry from Malmo, just across the Sound. Sweden had prohibition of a sort. You could have two drinks with a meal and then, if you wanted more, you had to move to a different restaurant for another meal. As I recall from a previous time in Sweden, some of these meals could be brief and not fully consumed. Never the less, it was difficult and very expensive to get intoxicated. As soon as the ferry left the dock in Malmo, the bar opened. By the time it reached Copenhagen, there would be a ferry load of very drunken Swedes to off-load.

I did have one unfortunate experience in Copenhagen. There was some urgent ship's business to conduct with the Agent, so I took a taxi to his office in late afternoon. Although in was only about 1630, the sun had set, but the streetlights had not yet come on. The area was very dark. I proceeded briskly toward what I took to be the door to the building, but it turned out to be a ceiling to floor window over a down stairway to the basement. I ended up taking a head first fall down the steps. There were no broken bones, but I was pretty well skinned up and bruised. My clothes were a bloody mess. I was able to climb back up and found the door. The Agent and his staff give me proper first aid. The weather was cold, so I was wearing an overcoat, and that kept my injuries from being more severe.

Third Assistant Engineer O'Quien was performing as I expected. He had not done one bit of work since our arrival. He was either ashore or, when aboard, passed out drunk. The Chief Engineer was keeping a record of his misdeeds and I would later log him two for one for the days that he missed work.

All of the crew, except for one member, was very much enjoying the pleasures of Copen-hagen. The one notable exception was Bosun Wallace E. Ebanks. This was his third voyage on the ship. He was a devoted family man who sent the maximum amount of an allotment back to his wife in the Cayman Islands. Wallace was about five feet ten inches tall and a little on the thin side. He was about 45 years old and his health appeared to be good. He worked all available vol-unteer overtime (mostly on ship's maintenance), so that he could earn more money. Almost all of his payoffs from the two previous voyages, amounting to several hundred dollars, had been en-trusted to me to keep in the ship's safe. During our stay in this fine port, Wallace did not even go ashore.

The First Leg of Our Return Voyage— Copenhagen, Falmouth

We departed Copenhagen on Sunday, November 25, 1951, at 1154. Since we were now in ballast, I could follow a more direct route back to the Kiel Canal and the distance traveled was 149 miles, compared to 197 miles going the other way. We arrived at the Kiel Light Vessel on November 26, 1951, at 0300.

Our transit of the Kiel Canal this time was without undue incident. We took departure from the Elbe Light Vessel, in the North Sea, on Monday, November 26, 1951, at 1700. The sky was heavily overcast and there was rain from time to time. There was a moderate gale blowing from the North, which cause some rolling,

106.

One annoying distraction was that the Third Assistance Engineer was not standing his watches. Together with the Chief Engineer and the Chief Mate, I searched his room for booze but could find none. The Chief Engineer had also searched places that he thought the Third Assistant might have hidden his supply. We found none, but he continued to stay drunk from some source for several more days.

As we were proceeding across the North Sea, enroute to the English Channel, our Radio Officer copied an SOS from a Danish vessel, not far from our position. We diverted a total of 91 miles searching for it, but without success. At length, after darkness came, we gave up on the search, and proceeded on our way. Other ships were also searching, including ships of the British Navy.

Chief Mate Louis Murphy reported to me that he was concerned about the Bosun, who had been sick in bed all day. Murphy had trained to be a Purser/Pharmacist Mate prior to going into the Deck Department. He was skilled in medical matters and had been taking the Bosun's temperature and pulse at regular intervals. The temperature was then 103 degrees and his pulse was shallow and rapid. There were no other symptoms, except that he felt headachy and listless.

From the North Sea, it was not possible for our radio to reach the U. S., to get advice from the U. S. Public Health Service. I therefore sent a message to the British Health Authorities. Their tentative diagnosis was rheumatic fever, and they suggested that I put into Falmouth, England, for emergency medical assistance. Falmouth is an English Channel port located on the southwest coast of England.

The Bosun continued to get worse and had to be restrained in his bunk as he thrashed about. His roommate (the Deck Maintenance Man), the Chief Mate and the Third Mate took turns retaining him in his bunk. His fever seemed to increase, but we couldn't measure it because he could not hold still. From time to time, there was a discharge from his mouth and nose that was wiped away.

We arrived at the Falmouth anchorage Friday, November 30, 1951, at 0312, having travel 723 miles since departing the Elbe River. It was, by now, a dark and stormy night, with intermittent rain. The wind was from the north, which thankfully gave us the lee of the land. I did not have a large-scale chart of Falmouth and was nervous about approaching this port in the dark and with no good radar. I did so while taking frequent cross bearing on the navigational aids, and constant soundings with our Fathometer. I was, of course, under pressure to get there quickly so as to get medical attention for the Bosun.

Soon after anchoring, a Doctor Dickinson came aboard. I met him at the head of the gangway and wanted him to immediately go to the Bosun, who appeared to have just died. He said that he wanted to see the Captain first. When I told him that I was the Captain, he still wanted to confer with me in my office. So, we climbed up two decks to my office and had a brief conversation, after which he accompanied me to the Bosun's room. The Doctor confirmed that he was dead. The inside of his mouth was blistered and his skin was still hot to the touch. Doctor Dickinson and I returned to my office.

To be hospitable, I put a bottle of Scotch whiskey on my desktop, along with a couple of glasses. That turned out to be a bit of a mistake. The Doctor was apparently an alcoholic, and started pouring himself enormous drinks.

I asked him what he thought had killed Bosun Ebanks, and he replied that the human body was like a piece of machinery. Once it stopped, you couldn't tell what the trouble was without going inside of it.

He then asked me what the daily operation costs were for the ship, and stated that he had the authority to keep the ship in port for up to three days. It was obvious that he wanted me to bribe him to release the ship to proceed. I told him that if he thought what killed the Bosun was contagious, I wanted him to hold the ship three days, or as long a necessary, to avoid more deaths.

About this time the Ship's Agent boarded and came to my office. The Doctor stated that he didn't think that the Bosun had had any contagious disease. It was decided that the body would be sent ashore for an autopsy. The Agent promised to radio me the results as soon as they were available.

We placed the body of Wallace E. Ebanks in our ship's basket stretcher and lowered it to the Agent's boat. The Doctor and Agent went ashore, taking the corpse of our late Bosun.

Final Passage of Voyage #4— Falmouth, Baltimore

We took departure at 0524 that same morning, and headed out into the now very stormy North Atlantic Ocean enroute to Baltimore.

I promoted the Deck Maintenance Man to Acting Bosun.

With the Deck Maintenance Man and the Union Deck Delegate as witnesses, I inventoried and packed the belongings of Wallace Ebanks. We counted the money from the safe, that he had left with me. As I recall, it was about $700. That was an amount that would be helpful to his family in the Cayman Islands.

Business is business, so I compiled a detailed file including the medical charts that Chief Mate Murphy had made of the periodic temperature and pulse readings. Also included were copies of the radio messages and a narrative of our medical emergency call in Falmouth, leaving out the part about the bribery solicitation by the good Doctor. I was doing all of this to protect my Company against a possible lawsuit, claiming negligence on our part. I calculated the pay and overtime due to him up to the time of his death. I had asked the Falmouth Agent to notify my Company by cable of the occurrences. I presume that they then cancelled the next scheduled allotment payment to his wife in the Cayman Islands.

During the first several post WWII years, American flag ships routinely carried full cargoes from our shores, but usually returned in ballast (empty). Most freighters do not have sufficient ballast tanks to enable them to the attain anything approaching an ideal draft, when they have no cargo. In stormy weather, they become virtually uncontrollable and can make little or no headway.

When light draft ships pitch in high seas, the propeller comes substantially out of the water, causing the engine to race, which in turn causes heavy vibration throughout the ship. The watch engineers stand a "Butterfly Valve Watch", during which time they try to anticipate when the engine will race, and partially cut off steam power, via a butterfly valve. It is difficult duty.

Pitching also produced another unpleasant and dangerous phenomena known as "pounding". The bow at times lifts completely out of the water, and the flat bottom of the ship slams down with a big crash, violently shaking the ship. It was very important to minimize pounding, and that could usually be accomplished by slowing the engine and/or changing course.

Rolling was also very unpleasant but not structurally dangerous. It was not unusual for my toilet lid to fall to the down position during a roll, but when it fell back up again, I knew that we had had a heavy roll.

Sleeping on a Liberty Ship in ballast during stormy weather was very difficult. The beds of the officers were aligned fore and aft. I used to place pillows under both sides of my mattress to make a sort of cup, or pocket, that would restrain side motion during rolling. The bunks of the unlicensed crew were aligned athwartships. This meant that they would scoot,, in their skin, back and forth as the ship rolled. There was little that they could do about this, and most went sleepless, until they became so fatigued that they could sleep, even under these trying conditions. Liberty ships had four large deep tanks in the bottom of #1 cargo hold. They were normally used to carry dry cargo. When we were to be making an ocean crossing, in ballast, during the winter, I routinely had them filled with seawater. Another useful measure was to put seawater in #5 lower hold, up to a level a little below the top of the shaft alley. Prior to doing this, we had to remove the cargo battens, that lined the inside of the ship's hull for the purpose of keeping cargo away from the ship's skin. I never did it, but some Liberty Ship Captains also put water in the bottom of #4 hold. The only additional measure possible was to put seawater into empty double bottom fuel tanks. When this was done, we pumped it out prior to arrival in port, polluting the ocean in the process.. This was routinely done by all, and was not even against the law.

Unless really necessary, I avoided ballasting the fuel tanks because it caused water pollution of the fuel, when we later put bunkers in these same tanks.

So, we sailed from Falmouth headed for a stormy wintertime crossing of the Atlantic.

The shortest route was, of course, to follow a great circle course that would take you into high northern latitudes. That would not be feasible because of the severe winter storms up north. The conventional wisdom, to which I subscribed, was that the best way to proceed was to commence on a southwesterly heading, until you reached about 35 degrees north latitude, and then go due west until you neared the U. S., at which time you would angle northwestward to the port of destination. Some Captains routinely went on down to 30 degrees north latitude. I usually tried 35 degrees, and kept the option open to go farther south if the weather patterns indicated it should be done.

But now we had a special problem. What had killed Bosun Ebanks? He was the only man on the ship that had not gone ashore in Copenhagen. He had gone from apparent good health to death

Empty Liberty Ship in North Atlantic Gail

in only three days. The British Doctor had not believed that it was anything contagious, but we should take what precautions that we could in case he was wrong.

We threw his mattress, bedding and work clothes overboard. We scrubbed down his room with Lysol solution. We also thoroughly scrubbed down the galley, the crew mess hall, the crew recreation room (the old gun crew mess), the officer's saloon and the deck department toilets and showers.

Then we waited for news from our Agent in Falmouth.

We waited four days, while we beat our way toward the area of the Azores, where we hoped to find better weather. On the fifth day, I had grown impatient of waiting and was coming to believe that the Falmouth Agent had forgotten us. I sent a radio message to him inquiring about the cause of Wallace Ebank's death.

The answer came back that he had died of Pleurisy and Meningitis. So, I got out the ship's medical books, and started reading up on these two diseases.

I read that Pleurisy is an inflammation of the pleura, which is a thin membrane surrounding the lungs and the inside of the chest wall. It is essentially a secondary ailment caused by other things, such as pneumonia. It did not appear to be contagious.

Meningitis was another story.

A five-year-old niece of mine, Judy Ann Asel, had died of Meningitis in 1945, on the same day that President Roosevelt died. She was the only known case in Kansas City, MO, and had gone from apparent perfect health to death in three days. No one knew how she could have become infected. Bosun Ebanks had also gone from apparent perfect health to death in three days. He had not left the ship since we departed Newport News on November 2nd, 28 days before his death.

I read that Meningitis, if untreated, can lead to death within hours, and that "Small epidemics may occur in such environments as military training camps, college dormitories and other small groups of people in close contact". A ship at sea battened down for winter storms certainly fit into the latter category.

One way that it is spread is from secretions from the mouth and nose. That meant that certainly the Deck Maintenance Man, Chief Mate Murphy, and the Third Mate had been exposed as they acted to retrain Ebanks in his bunk, and wiped away the discharge from his mouth and nose. The Third Mate was a nice young Mexican-American whose surname was Bustamente. He had volunteered during his watch below to help with the Bosun. I don't recall his first

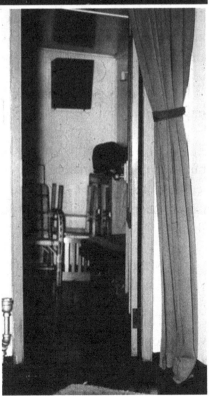

Captain's Quarters, Winter, North Atlantic

111.

name.

So here we were, bouncing around on a light Liberty Ship, in the middle of the stormy Atlantic Ocean. There was no way that we could get help from any quarter.

I sent an urgent radio message to the U. S. Public Health Service for advice. I told no one aboard about our situation, except Chief Mate Murphy. Of course Sparks (the Radio Officer) knew, but I swore him to secrecy.

The USPHS inquired how many sulfa pills were on board. I forget whether this was sulfa thiazode or sulfa dyazide, but it was one or the other. I had a full bottle of 500 and about 200 more in a partly used bottle. They instructed that I should give all hands two pills twice a day, at twelve-hour intervals, until the supply was exhausted. They stressed that this was a prophylactic measure, and that it was extremely important that no one miss their medication. If someone skipped a dosage, and then came down with the illness, they could infect all the rest, and our pills to fight it would be gone.

Sparks was allergic to sulfa drugs and they instructed that he should take a course of penicillin tablets instead, but that sulfa was preferable for those who could tolerate it.

The symptoms to watch for were sore throats, fever, stiff necks and headaches.

I set up a daily routine to dispense the pills from 0745 to 0815 and from 1945 to 2015, to all hands. I personally observed each man take his pills. The Officers were instructed to bring the drinking glasses from their rooms, and each Unlicensed Crewman was issued a glass for his personal (only) use.

The only person that resisted taking the pills was the Chief Engineer, and I had to become very forceful with him.

Only three of us knew what symptoms to watch for and we all three developed them. The mind can play remarkable tricks on us. My throat actually got sore and I developed a fever, stiff neck and headaches. Chief Mate Murphy and Sparks did likewise. It would have been funny if it had not been so serious. We all three thought that we would be facing the same death as Bosun Ebanks.

Meanwhile, our ship was rolling and pitching violently, as we were slowly making our way across the ocean. The Engineers were standing "Butterfly Valve Watches".

Third Engineer O'Quien had run out of booze finally, and was standing his watches. His two-for-one loggings were so heavy that I would have to reduce them at payoff, so that he would come out even. When we had bits of good weather, we ran the engine wide open to hurry our passage. No one was enjoying the ride.

Our supply of sulfa pills became exhausted on the fifth day. After that we could only hope and pray.

Some crewmembers were claiming to hear and see the ghost of Bosun Ebanks. They said that he was calling out for his money, that was in the ship's safe. This was, of course, ridiculous, but it was seriously believed by several of the crew. They swore that they had actually seen and heard him. Was it any more crazy that the psychosomatic symptoms that Chief Mate Murphy, Sparks, and I were experiencing? We were all feeling spooky and afraid. Most of all, we felt helpless against this microbe that had invaded our ship.

By the time that we ran out of sulfa pills, we were only about three days out from Baltimore. The weather had improved, and we cranked the engine to maximum speed to hurry to the relative safety of shore. As yet, no one else had come down with Meningitis, so it looked like we might all survive.

We arrived at the Chesapeake Light Vessel on Wednesday, December 12, 1951, at 0042. It had been a long 13 days, 1 hour and 18 minutes since we had departed Falmouth. We had traveled 3,236 miles at an average speed of 10.44 knots. Our fuel consumption was 0.905 barrels per mile, extremely high for running in ballast. Part of this high consumption was due to running wide open when the weather permitted.

We all breathed a sigh of relief to have reached port and to still be alive.

Since there had been a death on board during the voyage, I was required to make a detailed report to the Coast Guard Authorities. I turned over all documentation, along with his gear, the wages that he had earned on this voyage, and the $700 or so that I had been holding for him. The Coast Guard Officer, with whom I dealt, was very dour in his demeanor. He offered no comment regarding how I had handled the matter. I felt that I had done a good job and so did the Operations Manager, Captain Campbell, back at the Company's head office.

At payoff, Third Engineer O'Quien was falling down drunk. I had reduced his loggings and he paid off with about $30. He left, leaving his license in the license-posting frame on the ship. On his next job, he would have a "D-6" (duplicate 6) after his license issue number.

Baltimore

There was no cargo immediately available for our ship, so all of the crew was laid off, except for the Captain (me), the Chief Mate (Murphy), the Chief Engineer (Thompson), the First Assistant Engineer and the Chief Steward.

The *SS Thomas Sumter* was safely berthed at a pier within walking distance of restaurants, stores, movie theaters and bars. The five of us moved to a hotel in town and commuted to the ship daily for duty. A night watchman was hired to guard the gangway at night and on weekends. The five of us were on full wages plus subsistence, which was a good deal for all of us.

I became acquainted with a real attractive bar maid, whose name was Sandy. She told me that her husband was in prison, having been convicted of passing bad checks. On about my third visit to the nightclub where she worked, she invited me to go home with her after closing, which was at 0100. It was a Saturday night, and she was very attractive, so I readily agreed to the tryst.

Her apartment was on the second floor of a four story walk-up apartment building. It was a nice evening, and she proposed that we go up on the roof and enjoy the full moon and the night air. She walked me up to the roof, and then went back below to get blankets and pillows. A few minutes after she left, the occupants of the apartment on the fourth floor returned home. They were having a big loud party with several guests. The door to that apartment opened on to the hallway, immediately opposite the stairway to the roof, and they left the door open. I was more or less trapped on the roof, and Sandy never came back. There was a large skylight that opened into Apartment #4 and I could observe the party goings-on. It was quite an affair with several couples, all in their twenties, living-it-up.

What was I to do? I was hoping and expecting that Sandy would return, but she didn't. The people in apartment #4 might take strong exception to an outsider (me) being in the building and spying on their affairs. So, I spent two about two hours waiting for the party to die down, so I could slip past their door unnoticed, and leave the building. The wait was not completely un-pleasant because the city was beautiful in the moonlight, and there were impressive clocks, in steeples, that rang the hours loud and clear.

So what had happened to Sandy? A few nights later I returned to the club and she was on duty. She told me that when she went to her apartment, she was surprised to find her husband there. He had been released from prison. Naturally, she had to cancel our meeting, and was thankful that she had taken me to the roof, instead of to her apartment.

Fifth Voyage

Baltimore, New York, Malmo, New York
Loading for Voyage #5

Right after Christmas, a cargo was found for our ship. We crewed up, fired up the boilers, and shifted to a coal-loading berth in Baltimore on Friday, December 28, 1951.

We again took a full load of coal and, due to the time of year, were again limited to our WNA (Winter North Atlantic Plimsoll Mark). The terminal stated that we took aboard 8,847 long tons. Their tonnage figure was way short of what had actually been put into the ship.

Loading coal, in U. S. ports, usually was done by dumping the cargo from railroad cars, one at a time, into the ship. The cars were usually of about 70 long tons capacity. The most effi-cient operation was at the ports where the bottom of the cars opened up, and dumped into a chute that fed into the ship's holds. That way, the train could be moved ahead one car length at a time with all cars remaining coupled. The coal pier, that we loaded at in Baltimore, uncoupled each car and physically raised them up and turned them on their sides (plus few degrees more to insure complete emptying), to dump the coal onto a chute.

This coal was very dry, and great clouds of black coal dust rose with each dumping. To reduce the amount of dust, the terminal constantly poured water onto the coal as it entered the chute. The added, and unrecorded, weight of this water was to cause me a great deal of grief.

Fuel prices in Europe had become very high, and it was determined that we should bunker in the U. S. for the round trip. Also, quotes in New York were sufficiently below those in Baltimore, that money could be saved by making a stop there to take bunkers. So, when loading our cargo, we had to leave sufficient freeboard (the distance from the water line to the main deck) to allow for the later fueling operation.

The normal procedure when loading bulk cargo was, upon arrival, to notify the Cargo Terminal Supervisor how much tonnage we calculated that we could lift. This figure was based on our deadweight, which was a constant and known amount, and the amount of fuel, fresh water and stores that would be required for the voyage. I always included the Chief Engineer in the process when making these calculations, so that he would be satisfied and not tempted to keep some fuel or water "up his sleeve". When loading had progressed to within about two hundred tons of the amount that we had specified, the loading would cease while the Chief Mate checked the draft. A calculation would then be made as to how many more cars, if any, could be dumped. The tons per inch immersion for a Liberty Ship was 50 long tons.

It was a windy day in Baltimore, and the water was choppy. When Chief Mate Murphy went to check the draft, he had to observe the water level, fore and aft, for a while, to get an approximate reading, as the waves rose and fell. What he came up with was alarming. It seems that we were already several inches deeper in the water that we should be.

The Terminal Foreman was adamant in claiming that they had only put 8,847 long tons of coal into the ship, which was about 100 tons less than we had informed them we could load. We sounded all of the bilges in the cargo holds and the Chief Engineer sounded all of the fuel and water tanks. Everything checked out normal. The explanation had to be that they had added several hundred tons of water, with the constant wetting down of the coal as it was being dumped.

To have to discharge coal back out of the ship would be extremely expensive, and would be a first class screw-up, resulting for sure in Chief Mate Murphy and me being fired.

What to do? I am not very proud of what I did do, which was nothing. We would not be overdraft sailing from Baltimore, but would be several inches deeper that our winter marks after taking bunkers In New York. The Baltimore National Cargo Bureau Surveyor tried to measure our freeboard, and he questioned our deadweight calculation. He did not press the matter because the choppy water made accurate draft and freeboard readings impossible.

My only excuse for inaction was that I did not believe that the additional draft would put the ship and its crew in any danger. Many shipmasters purposely overloaded their ships to earn more revenue. We were to bunker by barge, at anchor off Staten Island in New York, and no authorities there would be checking our draft. We could get away with it and we did. I would later very much regret this chicanery.

Coastwise Baltimore to New York

We sailed from Baltimore on Sunday, December 30, 1951 at 0038, and took departure from the Chesapeake Light Vessel at 2312. I was ordered to proceed at reduced speed to time arrival in New York after the New Years Day holiday. We took arrival at Scotland Light Vessel on Wednesday, January 2, 1952 at 0724. We had traveled 235 miles at an average speed of 4.5 knots. We had anchored for 3 hours and 57 minutes due to fog during this passage.

We anchored off Staten Island. A fuel barge was brought alongside and we took aboard 4,797 barrels of Bunker C. This amount, when added to the 4,213 barrels already aboard, should be sufficient to fuel our voyage to Europe and back.

Passage #1— New York to Malmo (encountering the Super Storm)

We heaved up our anchor and sailed from New York, taking departure form Ambrose Light Vessel on January 2, 1952, at 2054.

Our discharge port this trip was to be Malmo, Sweden, across the Sound from beautiful Copenhagen. Normally, I would have set course for the English Channel, and plan to use the Kiel Canal enroute to Malmo. My Company, T. J. Stevenson & Co., Inc., had purchased a revolutionary service (for the time), that studied and predicted weather patterns, and suggested routing of ships to best take advantage of the patterns. Their recommendation was to take a Great Circle route, go north of Scotland, round the north end of Denmark and proceed through the Skagerak, Kategat and Sound to Malmo. This routing in the dead of winter would normally be unthinkable but I had to assume that they knew what they were doing. They almost did.

For the first ten days or so, the weather was much better than can normally be expected in January. I was becoming a believer in this new service. We were saving many miles of running distance by going this way, and the conditions were tolerable.

When we were about 60 miles from Scotland, the most unusual and severe weather pattern imaginable suddenly developed. It occurred without any warning from the British Ocean Weather Service, that was usually very reliable. I have been at sea in some hurricanes and typhoons, but they all paled in comparison with what was about to occur.

By now we probably had burned enough fuel to pretty well bring us up to our legal winter load line marks but, of course, if we had left New York with proper draft, we would now be lighter and therefore more safe in the coming storm.

The wind suddenly picked up to Beaufort Force 12 (hurricane strength) and commenced to frequently change direction. The sea became extremely high and, since the wind kept changing direction, had no pattern. In the hurricanes and typhoons that I have experienced, the wind blew, for a significant period of time, from one direction, and the sea developed a pattern, to which you could adjust your maneuvers. With a steady high wind, the ocean develops moving ridges of waves that, although high, are evenly spaced and are of uniform height. In this storm, the seas were of irregular height, with some being taller than our cargo masts, over 50 feet high. They were hitting us from all angles and the ship was uncontrollable. My main concern was to keep sea distance from the islands in the area, and what maneuvering I did accomplish was with this in mind. The ship bounced around like a ball in water. It made no difference whether the rudder was hard left or hard right. Since there was no control anyway, I reduced engine power to lessen the strain on the ship.

Darkness came and the storm's fury, unbelievably, continued to increase. The barometer was falling fast and got down to a final reading of 26.73 inches. I had never before seen it reach even 28 inches and had never heard of it dropping to 27 inches. Our ears were popping like they do at times in an airplane when it changes altitude.

Then it was reported to me that the ship was breaking apart. In the athwartship passageway on the Second Deck (the one below the Main Deck), in the area of the Steward's storerooms, you could hear, from the direction of #3 'tween deck, metal grinding on metal as the ship worked in the seaway.

It was essential to save the ship, because use of lifeboats in this weather would not be possible. I not only had the very heavy responsibility to somehow save the ship, but also carried the guilt that my sailing overdraft from New York might cause the death of all of us.

Then one tremendous sea struck our port side and caused a heavy roll to starboard. For a time the entire ship, except for the top of the smoke stack and the upper part of the masts, was under water. That sea carried away both lifeboats from the port side and the after one on the starboard side. It cracked the porthole in the Radio Shack, and smashed in the heavy wooden door on the Boat Deck that led to the passageway by the Chief Engineer's Office. It tore the name boards off both sides of the Flying Bridge. Sparks had the mushroom vent, from the overhead in his room to the Flying Bridge open, and he got a sudden deluge of cold seawater from it. Something, perhaps the water pouring into the passageway on the Boat Deck, shorted out some electrical circuits, and we were plunged into darkness.

It surely appeared that we were not going to survive this night and would not even be able to send an SOS, not that it could have been responded to by anyone.

After the longest night of my life, daylight finally came and the storm subsided a little. It was still blowing so hard that blown spray limited visibility to 100 feet or so. Our Engineers were able to get the lights working again, and we rigged a temporary closing for the broken door by the Chief Engineer's office. We got rid of the water that was sloshing around in the passage-ways.

I was later told that the weather instruments, in the nearby Hebrides Islands, registered wind velocity of 160 knots (184 mph), before being blown away.

The weather moderated a bit more and we could see, from the Bridge, that our Main Deck had cracked at the two after corners of #3 Hatch. The cracks were about four feet long. We could observe bubbles in the water as seas washed over the area and we could still hear the grinding noise of metal on metal. Now that I could again control the ship's heading, I steered so as to only roll the ship and to minimize pitching to the extent possible.

I was grateful to have survived this storm and felt great guilt and shame for having sailed from New York overdraft. It is not certain that the extra weight made our situation so critical, but it very well could have. I vowed never to do that again. And I didn't.

The weather continued to moderate and we were able to round the north end of Scotland, cross the North Sea to the Skagerak, round the north end of Denmark into and through the Kategat and into the Sound, arriving at the Malmo Pilot Station on Friday, January 18, 1952, at 0406. We had covered 3,731 miles in 15 days, 1 hour and 12 minutes, averaging 10.34 knots. Our fuel consumption was 0.890 barrels per mile.

Malmo

I had previously been in Malmo. It was during the extremely cold winter of 1946-7, when I was serving as Second Mate on the *SS George Clement Perkins*. At that time the Kategat was about 80% covered with ice and the Sound, between Copenhagen and Malmo, was frozen solid with ice at least one meter thick, with about two meters of snow topping that. We had to be es-corted by icebreakers and we badly damaged our propeller.

The winter of 1951-2 was much more mild and we did not encounter sea ice anywhere.

Like other ports in northern Europe, Malmo was efficient and shore cranes discharged our cargo in less than two days. The next six days were spent undergoing repairs to our heavy weather damage and obtaining replacements for our three lost lifeboats.

We discovered that cracks had formed in the Main Deck at the after corners of #2 Hatch, all four corners of #3 Hatch and the forward corners of #4 Hatch. The cracks at the after corners of #3 Hatch were very pronounced and extended about four feet outward into the deck plating. Below the Main Deck, in #3 'tween deck, the welding on a principal structural strength athwart-ship beam had broken loose from the main fore and aft beams. This was the source of the heavy grinding noise that we had heard during the storm.

The Swedish Surveyor for the American Bureau of Shipping was brought in to draw up specifications for repairs that would make the *SS Thomas Sumter* seaworthy.

The repairs essentially amounted to welding up the cracks in the Main Deck at the hatch corners and rewelding where the original 1942 welding had given way in #3 'tween deck.

Chief Mate Murphy and I were not pleased with the quality of the welding being done. When we put water hose tests on the welding that they had completed at the hatch corners, we found that they were not even watertight. This, of course, indicated that they were also not very strong and furthermore, that seawater on deck would find its way into the cargo holds.

We required them to lay more weld into the seams until they were at least waterproof. We had unhappy welders, who were not cooperating with us. The work was taking far too long.

The ABS Surveyor came aboard and acted as through he had been pressured to get the ship out more quickly. I got the impression that he was ready to certify seaworthiness with the imperfect work and expected me to be happy about it, and perhaps to reward him.

Murphy and I stuck by our guns and would not sign the bills until all of the hatch corners were at least watertight.

Our Return Passage— Malmo, New York

The half-ass repairs were finally completed and replacement lifeboats had been obtained and provisioned. We took departure from the Malmo Pilot Station on Saturday, January 26, 1952, at 2400, bound for the Kiel Canal.

We arrived at the Kiel Light Vessel on January 27, 1952, at 1148, having covered 148 miles in 11 hours, 48 minutes, giving an average speed of 12.54 knots. We proceeded to transit the canal and did so without incident. We took departure from the Elbe Light Vessel, in the North Sea on Monday, January 28, 1952, at 0236.

When we cleared the English Channel, I proceeded on a southwesterly course down to 35 degrees north latitude, and then sailed due west until it was time to head northwest to our destination, New York. We had one storm after the other and we did not arrive at Ambrose Light Vessel until Friday, February 15, 1952, at 0830. It had taken us 18 days, 11 hours and 54 minutes to travel 3,786 miles from the Elbe Light Vessel. Our average speed was only 8.53 knots and our fuel consumption was a whopping 1.039 barrels per mile, which was a terrible performance for a ship in ballast. Part of the heavy consumption rate was because at times we could make no headway against strong headwinds, although the engine was plugging away.

We proceeded to a lay pier in Brooklyn for repairs.

New York

I was again in serious trouble with the Operations Vice President, Mr. John F. Shea, and had to explain about the heavy weather damage that my ship had suffered. He had to be convinced that I had not improperly forced the ship in heavy seas and caused the damage. I was requested to bring the ship's logbooks to the Office for examination. When Operations Manager,

Captain William J. Campbell, read our log and saw the barometer reading of 26.73 inches, he knew that we had been in a catastrophic storm. Fortunately for me, he was able to convince Mr. Shea that I should not be fired.

There was no cargo immediately available, so the ship was put on idle status. All crewmembers were laid-off except for the Captain, Chief Mate, Chief Engineer, First Assistant Engineer and the Chief Steward. There was no steam on the ship to heat the quarters, so we all spent our evenings at the St. George Hotel in Brooklyn. It was said to be the largest hotel in the world. It had only a few clients and appeared to be a failing enterprise.

There was a huge indoor heated swimming pool in the basement that I used a couple of times, once as the only customer. Some time later the St. George Hotel was closed and torn down. We commuted daily between the hotel and the ship, by taxi, to oversee the repair work.

All of the welding done in Malmo was bad and was going to have to be replaced.

Apparently, someone high up in the Maritime Administration decided to use the *SS Thomas Sumter* as a guinea pig for a big experiment. They hit upon the theory that the reason that we developed cracks at the hatch corners, was because they were too stiff. When the ship was constructed, doubler plates were installed at all hatch corners, making the deck in those areas twice the thickness of the plating in the surrounding Main Deck. This was the standard ship construction procedure. Since they were going to be working on many of the hatch corners anyway, they decided to remove all of the doubler plates and insert new plating that was the same thickness as the Main Deck. The idea was, as I was told, that the plates would flex, and therefore not crack.

While we were on Idle Status, the work on our hatch corners proceeded. The Coast Guard inspected and approved our three new lifeboats from Sweden, but they had to be reprovisioned to U. S. specifications.

The company doing the repairs supplied us with electric power aboard and loaned us an electric heater for use in the Officer's Saloon. We congregated there when we were not overseeing work on deck or in the Engine Room. The weather was quite cold.

A cargo was finally located for us in Philadelphia. We crewed up again on March 6, 1952, fired the boilers and again brought the ship to life. The repairs were completed on March 7, 1952, at 2300.

Sixth Voyage

New York, Philadelphia, Bordeaux, Mobile
Coastwise— New York, Philadelphia

We left the dock at 2330, and proceeded toward Ambrose Channel. From 0113 to 0210 on March 8, 1952, we calibrated the Radio Direction Finder. I had found it to be so far off that it was useless. Satellite Navigation has now made these obsolete, along with sextants, but they were very useful in their day. Many lighthouses and light ships emitted distinctive radio signals (a series of dots and dashes), upon which ships could obtain bearings. If two or more were properly spaced from where you were at sea, cross bearings could give you a rough fix. We dropped the Sandy Hook Pilot and took departure from Ambrose Light Vessel on Saturday, March 8, 1952, at 0236.

We traveled 123 miles to the Overfalls Light Vessel, enroute to Philadelphia, and arrived at the Pilot Station at 1312. We anchored in Philadelphia Harbor on March 8, 1952, at 2106.

Passage #1— Philadelphia, Bordeaux

On March 12, 1952, we shifted to the coal loading berth and commenced loading at 1545. At 0825 the next morning we had completed loading 9,404 long tons. We were on our winter load marks plus an inch for inland navigation. We left the dock at 0900 and proceeded to sea, taking departure from Overfalls Light Vessel on Thursday, March 13, 1952, at 1942.

My 27th birthday occurred on March 16th but I did not tell anyone about it. My youthful appearance was a handicap in my job as Shipmaster and I tired to look older. Ship Captains were frequently referred to by the crewmembers as "the Old Man". I grew a mustache but it was not a good one. It was thin and wispy so I shaved it off. But, as I have a number of times told my grandchildren, youth is a temporary handicap. I eventually overcame it.

After leaving Philly, we immediately ran into an easterly gale that caused the ship to pitch moderately for the next couple of days. When the gale subsided and we could get on deck to inspect our new hatch corners, which Chief Mate Murphy and I both regarded as suspect, we found that almost all of them had developed cracks, extending varying distances out into the surrounding deck plating. This was a serious problem and I decided that I was going to have to minimize the amount of pitching. I would have to run the ship in the trough, which meant lots of rolling but little pitching. It also meant that we could not always go on a direct course toward our destination, which was to be Bordeaux, France.

The other action that we took was to drill holes at the end of the cracks to stop their progress. We then plugged the holes with boiler tube plugs. We drilled as many holes as we could until the next storm drove us inside. The experiment of removing the doubler plates from the hatch corners was a dismal failure.

Our pattern for this passage turned out to be two or three days of gales and then a day hove to when we could get on deck to drill more holes at the end of the cracks. Meanwhile, there was lots of unpleasant rolling, but only minimal pitching.

We eventually used up all of our drill bits and could do no more drilling. The many holes that we had drilled stopped many cracks and probably saved the ship from breaking up.

A good many cracks continued to develop and lengthen after we had exhausted our supply of drill bits. A number of them were four to five feet long. The ones that I worried most about were at the after end of Number 3 Hatch. They were lengthening daily and were over eight feet long. If they extended another seven feet, they would reach the junction between the deck and hull. If they then continued into the hull, there was a real chance that the ship would break up and sink.

The worst storm of this passage occurred in the Bay of Biscay, when we were only about 100 miles from our destination. It was an easterly gale, so I could not proceed toward Bordeaux without causing heavy pitching. So, we ended up hove-to, running dead slow ahead, on a northerly heading. The ship was rolling heavily in the trough. From the bridge, we could observe that the cracks at the after end of Number 3 Hatch were growing. The storm showed no signs of letting up. I was on the verge of sending an urgent radio message (just short of an SOS), requesting that some ship in the vicinity standby us, in case we had to abandon ship. The weather finally moderated and made this measure unnecessary.

Finally, on Thursday, April 3, 1952, at 1500, we arrived at the Gironde River Pilot Station. There was no Pilot available, so I went to anchor. It had taken us 20 days, 7 hours and 6 minutes to cover 3,329 miles, averaging only 6.83 knots. Our fuel consumption averaged 0.959 per mile.

Bordeaux

The Pilot boarded at 1947 and we got underway ten minutes later. We proceeded part way up the river and anchored at 2240 to await a favorable tide. The tidal currents in the Gironde River are extremely strong and great care has to be taken. The next morning, April 4, 1952, we got underway at 1036 and proceeded to a dock in the city of Bassens, a suburb of Bordeaux. We finished tying up at 1612 and immediately commenced discharging our cargo of coal, using the ship's cargo gear.

As was the case when we were docked in Rouen, the French prostitutes had access to the pier and wanted to do their work aboard the ship. When I prohibited this, they rather nosily protested from ship's side. They stated, among other things, that I had better not let them catch me ashore.

We again had the problem of what to do about the cracks at our hatch corners. As before, an American Bureau of Shipping (ABS) Surveyor was brought into the picture to make recommendations. It was decided that to make the ship seaworthy enough to proceed back to the US in ballast, it would only be necessary to weld up all of the new cracks, of which there were many. All twenty hatch corners had a least one crack and some had several. The welding could not commence until we had finished discharging the cargo, but everything was lined up for a quick start and hopefully a proper and thorough job.

On Wednesday, April 9, 1952, at 1700 cargo discharging was completed and the repairs of the heavy weather damage commenced. We had the same trouble with poor welding that we had had in Malmo. Each time that they said that the work on a hatch corner was completed, we would hose test it and find that it was not even watertight. This went on until 1325 on April 11,

1952. At that time, the ABS Surveyor declared us to be, in his judgment, seaworthy. I deemed that we were not totally seaworthy, but were in good enough condition to make a passage in ballast back to the United States.

While we were at the discharge berth, we had an interesting visitor. The U. S. Army Officer in charge of our military port operations (supplies for our troops in Germany largely came through this port) came aboard and introduced himself. It was Colonel Richard Dick USA. He had been cycling through the area and the name of our ship caught his eye. He had been repatriated home on this ship after the end of WWII. He and Chief Mate Murphy and I had a good visit. He ended up inviting us to have dinner with him and his wife and his second in command (a Major) and his wife, at a fine restaurant in Bordeaux.

The French do know how to run a proper restaurant and this was one of the best.

A funny event happened during the meal. The two ladies excused themselves to go to the Ladies' Room. Soon afterwards, Colonel Dick and the Major went to the Gentlemen's Room. A thin wooden partition type wall, a bit over seven feet high, separated the two restrooms. Hearing the wives talking next door, Colonel Dick though it would be amusing to pop his head over the top. He asked the Major to give him a boost up. As soon as his head reached the top, he saw a strange woman entering the Ladies' Room, and tried to duck back down. The Major, who was a very strong guy, thought that he was slipping, and boosted him higher. This action caused a good deal of bumping and scrapping on the partition, so the strange lady naturally looked up and saw a man, apparently peeping into the Ladies' Room. She screamed and reported it to the Manager. It was embarrassing and funny, and I don't think that they were able to properly explain their actions, especially since none of them spoke much French.

On April 11, 1952, we left the dock at 1333 and proceeded to Paulliac, a small port/city on the Gironde River, and anchored to take bunkers by barge. We finished bunkering on April 12, 1952, and got underway for sea at 0534.

Final Ocean Crossing for the *SS Thomas Sumter*— Bordeaux, Mobile

We took departure from the Gironde River Sea Buoy on Saturday, April 12, 1952, at 1000, and proceeded toward Mobile, AL.

On this, which was to be her last ocean crossing, the old *SS Thomas Sumter* performed at her best. The weather was pretty good. The ship made good speed and the fuel consumption was reasonable, for a change.

The need for additional ships, during the Korean War, was easing and some were to be returned to lay-up status. Although we had not been hauling cargo to Korea, we were replacing a ship that had been pulled from the Atlantic trade routes for service there. This ship had major structural problems and burned fuel excessively. She was an obvious candidate for the bone yard, and that was where she was going. We had not been informed of this, but I didn't expect that the people in authority would want to authorize the huge expense of redoing all of our hatch corners.

For one thing, it would bring unwanted attention to the stupid blunder that had been made of removing the doubler plates and installing single plating.

On Thursday, May 1, 1952, we took arrival at the Mobile Bay Pilot Station at 0554.

This had been our finest ocean crossing. It had taken us 18 days, 21 hours and 54 minutes to travel 4,691 miles. Our average speed was 11.33 knots and our fuel consumption was a respectable 0.694 barrels per mile.

Lay-up

Mobile, New Orleans, Mobile

In Mobile, we proceeded to the Adsco Dock. The crew was paid off and laid off, except for the Captain (me), the Chief Mate, the Chief Engineer, the First Assistant Engineer and the Chief Steward. The boilers were secured. The five of us moved to the Battleship Hotel and commuted by taxi daily to the ship for duty.

There was a large lay-up fleet in Mobile Bay, so it made sense to do the lay-up work there, but that is not what happened. A company in New Orleans bid substantially lower than the Mobile shipyards, where the managers apparently thought they could charge monopoly prices. So, we crewed up again, fired the boilers, and on May 13, 1952, steamed down Mobile Bay, the 90 miles over to South Pass, and then up the Mississippi River to a New Orleans lay pier, to prepare the ship for lay-up.

The crew was again paid off and laid off except that the same five key personnel were kept on the payroll. We moved to hotels and commuted to and from the ship by taxi.

Time was no longer critical, so the lay-up preparation work was only done during regular daytime working hours, and without hiring any additional personnel. It was not completed until June 11, 1952. All of this expense was wasteful, because this ship would never operate again and would end up as scrap.

This month in New Orleans was a good deal for the five of us still on the payroll. We were drawing full wages, plus subsistence, and were having a high old time in a party city. The shipyard was supplying electricity to the ship. We set up a hot plate in the Officer's Saloon. The Chief Steward had salvaged some goodies remaining from the stores of our final voyage. We had several pretty good steak lunches, thanks to his diligence.

The *SS Thomas Sumter* was to be towed back to the Reserve Fleet in Mobile Bay. Everyone except me was terminated from the payroll. A riding crew of three men was put aboard to accompany me in taking the ship, as a dead tow, back to Mobile Bay. Food, water, ice, bedding and a chemical toilet were put aboard for our use. We had kerosene navigation lights to rig after dark and we, of course had flashlights and lanterns.

A single seagoing tugboat took us in tow on Thursday, June 12, 1952, using a bridle forward that connected to a single towline. The current in the Mississippi River was running strongly and the tug, having paid out too much line, lost control at one of the bends in the river, causing us to go aground. We were pulled back off without any problem and, since it was soft mud, probably no damage was done.

The weather in the Gulf of Mexico was excellent and the 90-mile run from South Pass to the Mobile Bay entrance went smoothly.

It was an eerie sensation to be underway at sea on a dead ship, having complete silence, lacking any control and having no contact with the outside world. We did not even have communication with the tug. Remember, this was long before walkie-talkie radios had been developed.

When we arrived in Mobile Bay, two harbor tugs relieved the seagoing tug. A Mooring Pilot and crew boarded, to conduct the maneuver to a berth in the Reserve Fleet. At the proper time and place, both anchors were let go. We were pulled astern away from them, as the chain was paid out, until we reached a position alongside another Liberty Ship, that was moored in the opposite direction. We were then tied up alongside her. The berthing was done very expertly. There were hundreds of other ships there, all neatly moored in rows in the same fashion. The whole towing operation had taken a little over two days.

I felt a mixture of pride and sadness as I left the *SS Thomas Sumter*. I had been her final Captain and had served for one year and two days.

The date was Sunday, June 15, 1952.

(*Note: According to "The Liberty Ships" by Captain Walter W. Jaffee, the SS Thomas Sumter, which was constructed by the North Carolina Shipbuilding Company, had her keel laid on February 25, 1942 and was launched on May 31, 1942. She was withdrawn from the Mobile Reserve Fleet (where I had left her on June 15, 1952) on June 16, 1971, and was scrapped at Panama City, FL, in August that year.*).

Chapter IX: SS Waltham Victory
(The Greenland Voyages)

Vacation

After leaving my first command, the SS Thomas Sumter, securely berthed in the Lay-up Fleet in Mobile Bay, AL, on June 15, 1952, I went home to Sedalia, MO, for a deserved vacation. I had had an interesting and somewhat draining year, and needed some carefree time.

What I refer to as my "home" was really the home of my aunt and uncle who had raised me since I was a baby. My mother died when I was about a month old and her youngest sister, Ora Lee (Kerley) Netherton and her husband, Horace Lafayette Netherton, took me to raise. I called them mom and dad and they called me son. They had a daughter, Frances Lee, who was nine years older than me. We were to develop a brother/sister relationship. Ora Lee and Horace wanted a son and were pleased to take me in. My own father, James Theodore Vantine, already had four children, three girls and one boy, ranging in age from 11 to 18, to look after. What with now being a widower, he really had his hands full. So, it was a good arrangement all around. There was no formal adoption and I kept the name Vantine. I remained on good terms with my natural father and siblings and visited them in Quanah, TX, from time to time.

Horace L. and Ora Lee Netherton, the aunt and uncle who raised the author (1951)
Photos by Cecil's Photo Studio, Sedalia, MO

Although it was great to be on vacation, it wasn't long before I began to be strongly aware that there was no income, and I worried about when I would get another job. In those days, after a year of service, a ship captain only received two weeks pay. The rest of the crew just got one week's pay.

Ships that had been brought out of lay-up for the Korean War were being deactivated. It did not seem likely that I, as a very junior shipmaster, with only one year's experience under my belt, would be able to get another command any time soon. It appeared that I would be lucky to get a Chief Mate's job and I would have jumped at the first opportunity for one.

About July 1, 1952, I received a phone call from Mr. Eugene Mooers, Assistant to the Operations Manager at T. J. Stevenson & Co., Inc., in New York. He asked if I felt capable of serving as Master on a Victory Ship running to Greenland from the U. S. East Coast. Although I was uneasy about assuming such a task, I acted confident on the phone. This was going to entail difficult navigation, lots of bad weather, and for the first time in my life, icebergs. Also, it was to be a different type of ship than the Liberty Ships that I had been sailing on. Mr. Mooers told me that there was a possibility that there may be an opening coming up and that he would be in touch.

A few days later, I received a call from Mr. John A. Moore, Personnel Manager at T. J. Stevenson & Co., Inc. He told me to proceed to Norfolk, VA, and that I would be taking command of the SS Watham Victory on or about July 8, 1952. I should proceed first to the office of their Norfolk Agent, Hasler & Co., who would give me documentation and direct me to the ship's location.

The SS Watham Victory

Joining the Ship in Norfolk

The Norfolk Agent, Hasler & Co., that T. J. Stevenson & Co., Inc., used was unique. Their office was very modest and was run by Robert Hasler, Sr., a man in his late fifties, and his son, Robert Hasler, Jr., a man in his thirties. They were both amenable to long hours of intense work. The two of them did almost all of the "leg work", typing, phone answering, etc. that goes with running a steamship office. They were very good at their profession and certainly managed to keep overhead and employee expenses to a minimum.

As I had been instructed, I proceeded to their office. I had become acquainted with both of the Haslers while sailing as Master of the SS Thomas Sumter. We had had a good and cordial relationship and we were all glad to see each other again. They presented me with my orders, which had been mailed down from New York. The Captain that I was relieving was a gentleman in his sixties. He had declined the Greenland run, stating that it was too demanding for a man of his age. He had made an intelligent decision and had already departed the scene.

The Haslers did give me some great news. My best friend and long time (five years) shipmate, Louis Murphy was to be my Chief Mate. He had also been looking for a job since we had laid up the SS Thomas Sumter the previous month

The ship was berthed at the Norfolk Army Base and was loading general cargo for destinations that were classified. A U. S. Navy Officer and three Enlisted Men were to be added to the ship's complement. The Naval Officer would supply information regarding our destinations.

So, I proceeded to the Norfolk Army Base (by taxi) to join my ship. The taxi was not allowed to enter, so I had to carry my luggage and sextant from the gate to the ship. That was before the advent of roller luggage so it was no easy task. The distance, as I recall, was about half a mile. This was annoying but was typical of how the U. S. Military treated Merchant Marine personnel.

As her name suggests, the SS Watham Victory was a Victory class ship. She had been built in 1945 at Richmond, CA. She was a bit longer (455 vs. 441 feet), a bit wider (62 vs. 57 feet) and could carry a deeper draft (summer, 28 feet 6 1/4 inches vs. 27 feet 8 7/8 inches) than the Liberty ships. In spite of the greater dimensions, the deadweight (cargo, fuel, water and stores) capacity was similar, about 10,800 long tons. The reason for this was that the hull of a Victory ship was more streamlined (for greater speed) than that on a Liberty ship. These ships had two boilers supplying steam to high rpm turbine engines that drove the single propeller through reduction gears. Some Victories had engines that produced 8,500 horsepower and some than had 6,000 horsepower. This ship had the 6,000 hp engine that gave a speed of about 15 knots (17.3 mph) at 100 rpm. The more powerful models had larger propellers and could make about 17 knots.

For economy reasons, steam turbine ships are not fitted with as powerful an engine for going astern as they are for maneuvering ahead. Their backing power is only about two-thirds of

SS Watham Victory (1952)

128.

the ahead power. Changing from ahead to astern propulsion is much more cumbersome and time consuming than it is on a reciprocating steam engine, such as those on Liberty ships.

Until now, all of my seagoing experience had been with commercial enterprises. A ship's time is considered to be very valuable and the object in the commercial world was always to either have all of the cargo gear working to capacity, or to have the engine telegraph on Full Ahead. Only at those times would the ship be operating at maximum efficiency and earning her way. When arriving in port, we always had the cargo gear ready to commence work. When the cargo was all discharged or loaded, we got secured for sea as quickly as possible and sailed at the soonest possible moment.

Now we were on a government owned and operated ship. Things were going to be different and it would take some getting used to.

When operating under a military charter, I found that it was more important to be able to set a sailing schedule days in advance that could be easily adhered to, rather than to get out of port as soon as cargo operations were completed. No ship could sail until all of the cargo manifests were completed and put aboard, even when this caused many hours of delay, and when the papers could have been sent by air.

I met the Navy Lieutenant (jg) who was to travel with us. He had three Enlisted Men under his command that would operate a voice radio that they had brought aboard. It would be used to communicate with the shore authorities at our ports of discharge. This was state-of-the-art equipment at the time. The radio was battery powered, in a heavy container and had a khaki colored cloth cover. It stood about three feet high, was about two and half feet wide and had about a ten inch depth. It must have weighed about sixty pounds. To use it, a flexible wire antenna would be run up one of our flag halyards on the Flying Bridge. The microphone was connected via a coiled wire and there was a built-in speaker. The range of operation was only a few miles.

I liked the appearance of the Navy Lieutenant, who was about my age (27), and I expected to have a cordial relationship with him. This turned out not to be in the cards.

I inquired of him what would be our ports of call. He wouldn't tell me!!! I was the ship's Captain and had to navigate to these places and he would not tell me!!! I told him that I had to be sure that we had the necessary charts. He told me that he had all of the charts in a bundle that would be given to me after we had sailed. There were other considerations also, such as figuring the fuel, water and stores needed for the voyage. I was adamant and so was he.

I told our Norfolk Agent, Mr. Robert Hasler, Sr., about this ridiculous situation. He arranged for me to have a meeting with an Army Colonel at the Norfolk Army Base. The Colonel told me that our ports of discharge would be Argentia, on Newfoundland Island, and Thule, Greenland.

This part of the world was foreign to me and I had to look these places up in an atlas.

Argentia is a port on the south coast of Newfoundland Island. It was being used as a military base for both Naval and Air Forces. It was a well-developed area with normal navigational aids, channels, docks, etc.

Thule (pronounced "TWOlee") was an air base that was being developed and would become the principal eastern anchor of the DEW (Distant Early Warning) Line that was to be constructed across northern Greenland, Canada and Alaska. It was an extremely important forward air base, in that it was the nearest one to the Soviet Union. At that time, the Cold War was intense. Thule is located in North Star Bay on the northwest coast of Greenland at 76 degrees and 33 minutes north latitude. That is only 807 miles from the North Pole. Safely navigating a ship there and back was going to be quite a challenge.

I told the Navy Lieutenant that I had been informed about our ports of discharge and requested that I be allowed to check his bundle of charts to be sure that they were complete. He again refused. So, I sent the ship's Second Mate to the Chart Store with orders to purchase complete chart coverage for a voyage from Norfolk to Argentia and Thule (after first checking what was already in our Chart Room drawers). It is fortunate that I did this because it turned out that the Lieutenant had no charts at all for Newfoundland and there were skips in his coverage for the west coast of Greenland.

Another further annoyance, that I would not find out about until much later, was that a number of radio beacons had been established at points along Greenland's west coast. They would have been a great aid to navigating those waters. He kept them secret from me.

Louis Murphy had already joined the ship as Chief Mate. Loading of general cargo was well progressed. It was mostly miscellaneous supplies for our military bases. It appeared that there were no special problems with the cargo. There were no heavy lifts requiring us to rig our heavy lift gear and no dangerous cargo. There were some vehicles and boats that needed to be properly shored and lashed in place. Murphy was looking after all of this and I was fortunate to have him on duty.

The identity of the Chief Engineer surprised and pleased me. It was Mr. Ira S. Sager, with whom I had sailed in 1946-7, when he was Chief Engineer on the Liberty Ship, SS George Clement Perkins, and I was Second Mate. He was now about 60 years old. We had gotten to know each other very well and he had had a strong influence on me. Back in 1947, he had convinced me (rightly so) that I was avaricious in my financial dealings with others, always pressing for the best and sometimes unreasonable deal. Thanks to his influence, I became a much more financially generous person.

However, I did have some concerns about him being my Chief Engineer. He operated his department in a most unusual manner. He never set foot in the engine room!!! He monitored everything closely from the log entrees and by frequent conversations with the Assistant Engineers. I had strong reservations about his method, but could not criticize the results. His department ran flawlessly.

I also had another concern. When our ship was docked in Malmo, Sweden in 1947, Chief Sager had obtained a case of whiskey, and drank it all in less than a week. Then he had a gigantic hangover. He was obviously an alcoholic and had to stay completely away from the stuff. Except for that one slip-up in Malmo six years earlier, as far as I knew, he had never touched another drop of booze.

A key person, that would enable me to have a "happy ship", was Chief Steward Jeffrey J. Jenkins, a small black man about forty years old, who lived in Norfolk. He was a big family man and had six or seven children spaced about nine months and five minutes apart. He had pictures of his family displayed prominently in his quarters, and they were all good looking. Fortunately, the kids took after their mother, because J. J. was quite homely. He recruited good cooks from the NMU (National Maritime Union) hiring hall for our ship and he ran a top operation. The crew and I were very happy with the food and service.

Victory ships carried four Deck Officers (Mates) and four Engineering Officers (Assistant Engineers). Liberties only carried three of each. Having four mates and assistant engineers allowed the Chief Mate and First Assistant Engineer to be free of having to stand a watch at sea. They could more thoroughly supervise and monitor the ship's maintenance work and were available to assist in other ways. The fourth mate was called the Junior Third Mate and the fourth engineer was known as the Junior Third Assistant Engineer.

This would be my first experience with a good radar set. The ship was newly equipped with a Raytheon "Path Finder" radar, probably the best available at the time. It would prove to be a very useful navigational aid on the forthcoming voyages.

I had received no training in radar use nor had any of the other ship's officers. Because of this general lack of radar training, many collisions were occurring during bad visibility between ships equipped with the best radars. To properly use radars to assess risk of collision at sea, it is necessary to plot radar targets at regular intervals, for instance every six minutes, on a graph that also plots and projects your own ship's positions at those same times. After a few such plots, it is possible to determine the other vessel's course, speed and closest point of approach. No one on this ship knew how to do this and there were no radar plotting sheets aboard.

My company, T. J. Stevenson & Co., Inc., and many other steamship companies, refused to authorize the expense of equipping their ships with radars. Many of the marine accidents of the day were called "radar assisted collisions". The radars gave the Captains the misplaced confidence to speed in fog, but they did not know how to properly interpret the radar information. The SS Watham Victory was owned and operated by the U. S. Government and so the expense of radar installation had been approved, I believe wisely, so as to increase the safety while navigating among icebergs.

First Voyage

Norfolk, Argentia, Thule, Norfolk

Norfolk to Argentia Passage

We sailed from Norfolk on Saturday, July 12, 1952. Except for some fog, we had excellent weather, with only slight to moderate seas, for the entire passage.

Soon after sailing, the Navy Lieutenant presented me with his secret bundle of charts and secret orders. As expected, I was ordered to proceed to Argentia for initial discharge of cargo and then, we were to rendezvous at a specified position off the west coast of Greenland with a Coast Guard icebreaker. Together with it and a Mission Class tanker, we were then to proceed to Thule.

I checked his bundle of charts to see if he had anything additional or of later vintage than what we had purchased at the Chart Store in Norfolk. I found nothing new, or additional, except for instructions regarding special settings for the Sperry Gyro Compass when operating in latitudes higher than 60 degrees north. When I pointed out to him that he had no charts for Newfoundland and that there were gaps in his coverage of the Greenland coast, he should have been embarrassed. If he was, he was very good at concealing it.

While running in moderate fog at night in the Grand Banks area, we observed a radar target traveling from east to west at what seemed to be an impossible speed. Our calculations put it doing about forty knots. We later found out that it was the SS United States on the return leg of her maiden voyage to Europe. She had set a new trans-Atlantic record on the eastbound leg of 35.59 knots (40.96 mph) and had taken the "Riband" from the SS Queen Mary. That fine old ship had held it since 1935. The SS United States was then in the process of setting a new record for a westbound crossing. (About nine years later, I, as a Panama Canal Pilot, would board her for docking in Cristobal, Canal Zone. Although her 990-foot length could have fit (barely) in the 1000 foot long Canal Locks, she never transited the Canal.)

On the morning of Tuesday, July 15, 1952, we arrived at the Argentia Pilot Station. We had traveled 1,170 miles at an average speed of 14.53 knots. Our fuel consumption was a reasonable 0.774 barrels per mile.

Argentia

When the Pilot reached the bridge, I greeted him with a handshake and a cup of hot coffee. He informed me that he was a Chief Petty Officer in the U. S. Navy and not a pilot. He was just there to point out the dock to me.

With that sobering information in mind, I entered the buoyed channel. Fog had visibility limited to about half a mile, and this soon reduced to about a quarter mile. The CPO informed me that there was no outbound traffic and that the channel was clear. Our radar was working perfectly. It showed the channel buoys and confirmed that there was no other traffic ahead. We proceeded at slow speed, about four knots.

Suddenly, the CPO pointed out our berth. It was on the port side ahead three or four hundred yards. My knowledge of shiphandling was almost nil, but I got lucky. I put the ship on half astern and she behaved beautifully. She backed straight (unusual). After the headway was reduced to about one knot, I stopped the engine. The ship then answered the rudder as she drifted with bare headway (also unusual). I was able to steer alongside where another half astern bell, coupled with checking the forward spring line (which had been secured on the pier), stopped us in proper position. This had been my first docking maneuver and I thought that, "Boy, this shiphandling is easy!!!" I was standing at least seven feet tall.

We were to spend a week in Argentia discharging general cargo, using the ship's gear. This was much longer than the tonnage moved justified. If it had been a commercial operation, we would have been out in two or three days.

The weather was pleasant with daily high temperatures in the upper sixties and nighttime lows in the low fifties (Fahrenheit). The surrounding countryside was hilly and heavily wooded, with very large trees. The local citizens, whom I encountered, appeared friendly and to have been hardened by their severe climate. The economy was closely tied to and dependent on the fishing industry.

Preparing for the Difficult Navigation Ahead

I was very apprehensive about the upcoming passage from Argentia to Thule. We were now at 47 degrees north latitude and were going to travel up to 76 degrees and 33 minutes north. In addition to the icebergs, fog and storms, there were a number of other navigational problems to overcome.

Thule is almost as far north as the north magnetic pole, which is located in northern Canada. The Magnetic Pole is slowly but constantly moving. The magnetic compass needles, of course, point to the Magnetic North Pole instead of to the Geographic North Pole. The difference in these two bearings is known as "Variation". As I recall, in 1952 the Variation in Thule was about 80 degrees westerly.

The horizontal magnetic pull on a compass decreases in strength as the distance from the Magnetic Equator increases, and is zero at the Magnetic Poles. So, when a ship operates in very high latitudes, the other principal compass error, that caused by the resident magnetism in the ship (called "Deviation"), becomes relatively much stronger. The Deviation at Thule's latitude could easily exceed 20 degrees on some headings. If the Deviation and Variation were in the same direction (westerly in this case), the magnetic compass headings (and compass bearings) could be 100 degrees or more different from the true heading (or bearing).

Since gyro compasses, which indicate true courses and bearings, came into general use, commencing in the 1940s, the magnetic compasses were used mostly as a back-up, in case the gyro failed. Clearly, it was not going to be a very reliable back-up on this voyage.

But there was also a major problem with the gyro compass. The Sperry gyro compasses, that were used aboard most American (and many foreign) ships, were designed to operate only up to 60 degrees latitude. The gyro's operation depends on the earth's rotation. The rotational "fling" is maximum at the equator and zero at the earth's poles. There were settings on the gyro compasses to adjust for the different latitudes (up to 60), which were different for north and south. There were also settings to adjust for the different ship speeds. The "secret" papers, that were given to me by the Navy Lieutenant, gave settings to use at the high latitudes. They didn't make much sense. For instance, at 65 degrees north latitude and a speed of 15 knots, the setting might be 20 degrees south latitude with a speed of 25 knots. We would later find that the gyro did not closely follow large course changes and that it would take several minutes, sometimes many minutes, to settle down.

Those were the days before satellite navigation. We were dependent on celestial observations (with a sextant), dead reckoning (your estimated course and speed made good) and coast piloting (cross bearings of two or more shore objects or trigonometric calculations based upon changes in bearing of one object while running a known distance and course).

There were also special problems with these methods that were exaggerated because of the upcoming operation in very high latitudes.

Normally, when the weather permitted, star sights were taken at dawn and dusk, during the period of time when both the stars (and planets) and the horizon could be seen. When properly calculated, and with referral to navigational tables, each celestial observation would give a line of position at right angles to the bearing of the object. The lines were actually arcs of position, but for a short distance a straight line could be used, and was more convenient. These lines of position would then be adjusted to the same time by moving them along the course line, and if they crossed in about the same place, a navigational star fix had been obtained. During daylight, lines of position could usually only be obtained from observations of the sun. Morning sun lines would be advanced on the course line to the estimated 1200 position. At "local apparent noon" (which would normally be no more than about 30 minutes ahead or behind 1200 ship's time), when the sun would momentarily bear due north or south, an accurate latitude could be calculated from the sextant altitude. The local apparent noon latitude line of position would then be moved along the course line to adjust it to 1200. If the weather had been clear and the observations and calculations done properly, an accurate "noon position" could then be obtained. At times, the Moon and Venus can also be observed during daylight and, if their bearings are sufficiently different from that of the sun, a navigational fix can be obtained.

All sextant celestial observations have to be corrected for the height of eye of the observer above sea level and also for refraction, the bending of light rays by the earth's atmosphere. Sextant altitudes below 18 degrees are less reliable because of increased refraction. On the upcoming leg, there would be days without any sights and I would feel lucky to get one at 10 or 12 degrees altitude. When we got far enough north, daylight would last 24 hours a day so there would be no star sights. And the sun would never be very high in the sky.

Ships are equipped with Fathometers that measure the water's depth by sending electronic signals to the bottom, and measuring the time interval for them to bounce back. Now days, depths are mostly measured and charted in meters, but in my sailing days we used feet and fathoms. A fathom is six feet. We can blame the British for foisting such an awkward system onto us. In areas of the world where depth soundings have been extensively obtained and charted, this information can sometimes be a useful navigational aid. An example would be crossing the charted "100 fathom curve line" when approaching a landfall. Soundings along the Greenland coast were few and far between, so there would be no help from this quarter. We knew that the water was generally very deep because of the huge icebergs drifting about.

Radio beacon bearings are one additional aid that would have been very useful if the Navy Lieutenant had not kept secret from me the information regarding them. Aero beacons had been established, along the Greenland coast, to aid the aero navigation. Ships could also use their radio direction finders to take bearing of them, especially when they are located on points of land near the shoreline. These beacons had been constructed with and were maintained with material brought from sea, and so were located ideally for our use.

Finally, since we had an excellent radar, radar profiles of coastal features could sometimes help determine your location. That would not be possible, along the northern part of the Greenland coast, because pack ice along the coast would also send a radar echo and distort the image.

One thing that gave me some comfort was that we were to rendezvous with a Coast Guard icebreaker, which would then escort us to Thule. The Commanding Officer of that vessel would be experienced in these waters and would, no doubt, have the latest and best navigational equipment for use at high latitudes.

Icebergs

Up to this time in my nautical career, I had never seen an iceberg. I would soon see hundreds and I needed to learn what I could about them.

Greenland is mostly covered by a huge ice cap that in places is over 11,000 feet thick. There is so much frozen water there that, if it were to all melt, it is estimated that the height of the world's oceans would rise from six to seven meters (19.7 to 23 feet). The tremendous weight pressing down in the center of this ice cap causes glaciers to flow outward. At the end of the glaciers, as they flow to the coast, ice breaks off from time to time and falls into the ocean, giving birth to icebergs. This process is called "calving". The ice in these bergs is very compressed and they float about 7/8ths submerged. Approximately 40,000 medium to large size icebergs calve annually in Greenland. Only about one to two percent (400-800) of those make it as far south as 48 north latitude (St. Johns). The numbers vary greatly from year to year and seasonally. Most are seen off Newfoundland in the spring and early summer.

Glaciers feeding from the east coast of Greenland are not as productive as those on the West Coast. However, the numbers of east coast bergs are significant and they can be terrifying, as I would find out on my next voyage to Greenland. After calving, the east coast bergs and growlers (small bergs) drift southward and around Cape Farewell (at the southern tip of Greenland) and then northward up the west coast to join those produced there.

I recall reading that one glacier named, I believe "Unimak", located in Disko Bay, produced about 44 million tons of icebergs per day. I recently checked information on the internet and believe that same, very productive, glacier is now called "Jakobshavn Glacier". Other info from the Internet follows in the next paragraph.

"The west coast of Greenland has the fastest-flowing glaciers on earth. The one known as the Quarayaq Glacier flows at a velocity of between 66 and 72 feet per day. Jakobshavn Glacier at approximately 70 degrees north latitude (in Disko Bay) produces about 10 percent of all Greenland icebergs. It also flows at about 66 feet

Illustration from the Internet showing what an Iceberg might look like if you could see the whole thing. They are 7/8ths submerged.

per day. The icebergs accumulate in a fjord and are periodically pushed from this fjord in groups, accompanied by noise that can be heard for several miles. This greatest iceberg producing glacier measures only four miles along its front and is about 295 feet about sea level."

The icebergs drift northward along the west coast of Greenland to the north end of Baffin Bay, then move westward to near the coast of Baffin Island, and commence to drift southward.

By the time they can reach the shipping lanes and lay in wait for another SS Titanic, the west coast bergs are at least two years old and any east coast bergs, that made it that far, would be at least a year older. Only a small percentage of them survive to get that far south but a few have made it all the way to the area of the Azores Islands. After the Titanic disaster, an International Ice Patrol was established to keep watch on bergs that can pose a danger in the shipping lanes.

Typical West Coast Greenland Iceberg (Illustration from Internet)
This ice began as snowfall on the Greenland ice cap twelve to fifteen thousand years ago.

Of course, as they age, icebergs lose mass through melting caused by the sun's heat, and they also do some calving of their own. You can see streams of water running off them, but a lot of this is frozen back onto them, because the temperature of the surrounding seawater is below the freezing point for fresh water. They keep changing shape and some of them look pretty weird. When they get into a warm current, such as the Gulf Stream, they deteriorate very rapidly and disappear in a few days.

A typical Greenland iceberg weighs about 1,000,000 tons when it is calved and some are much larger. I would later measure the height of one to be 447 feet above water. Remember, it was 7/8ths submerged!!! I measured the length of another to be 1,280 feet. These were the biggest that we observed nearby, but there were larger ones out there. My measurements were calculated by trigonometric calculations, based upon measured sextant angles and distance off by radar.

One obvious lesson, from my research, was that a navigator must not approach any closer than about half a mile to a large iceberg. Since they are 7/8ths submerged, they might extend a very long distance, under water, in any direction.

Argentia to Thule Passage

We finished discharging the cargo for Argentia and sailed on Saturday, July 19, 1952.

Soon thereafter, I received a radio communication that did not make me very happy. The rendezvous with the icebreaker was cancelled. We were to proceed to Thule on our own.

The previous winter had been relatively mild and this summer had been relatively warm. The result was that there was not much sea ice, so the icebreaker escort was unnecessary.

The weather for this entire six-day passage was pretty good, except for frequent fog. We commenced seeing a few icebergs on the second day out from Argentia. These were mature bergs, two and three years old, very weathered and with odd shapes.

I figured that if I more or less proceeded up the middle, about half way between Greenland and Baffin Island, I would encounter the fewest icebergs. On the third day we commenced seeing many of them and, from time to time, had to change course to keep a safe distance from them. During darkness and in fog, I ran at half speed (about 8 knots), to give more reaction time for avoidance maneuvers. The biggest worry was the "growlers", small bergs that did not show up very well on the radar. Some of them had rounded tops that reflected radar pulses poorly. Any one of them could have wrecked our ship. I kept a bow lookout posted around the clock.

On the morning of the second day, we passed the very decomposed remains of a dead whale. That afternoon, we passed another dead whale. This one had died recently. Sea birds and sharks were having a feeding frenzy. It was a great mystery as to what could have killed these great mammals of the ocean.

To my great surprise, we encountered several Portuguese fishing vessels. They were only about 200 feet long and were a long way from home. These hardy people work very hard and face great danger to earn a living. We wondered if perhaps they had killed the whales.

What I remember most vividly about this passage was the remarkable refraction of the atmosphere. Many times we would see an iceberg and an image of that same berg upside down, immediately over it. A few times, we saw the same berg again, right side up, over the inverted image.

At times, the horizon would appear to undulate in very long and slow waves. Sometimes the upper part of a wave would seen to separate with jagged edges, which would properly mesh if you could somehow push them back together.

At night, before we got far enough north for 24-hour daylight, we had some spectacular displays of the aurora borealis. Since we were heading north and it occurs in the north, we didn't miss any of the shows. The following paragraph states some information obtained from the internet regarding this phenomenon.

"The sun gives off high-energy charged particles (also called ions) that travel out into space at speeds of 300 to 1200 kilometers per second. A cloud of such particles is called plasma. A steam of plasma coming from the sun is known as the solar wind. As the solar wind interacts with the edge of the earth's magnetic field, some of the particles are trapped by it and they follow lines of magnetic force down into the ionosphere, the section of the earth's atmosphere that extends from about 60 to 600 kilometers above the earth's surface. When the particles collide with

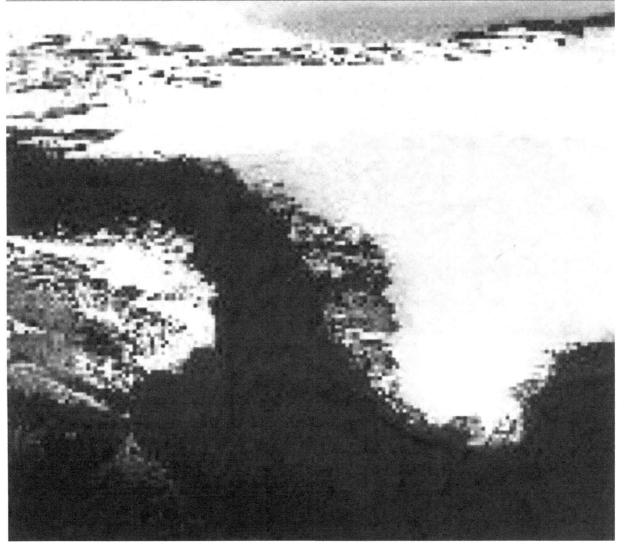

Satellite Image of Greenland and Baffin Island (NASA)
The massive ice cap is more than 11,000 feet thick in places

the gases in the ionosphere they start to glow, producing the spectacle that we know as the auroras, northern and southern. The array of colors consists of red, green, blue and violet."

One day we were observing a large mountain in Greenland and were trying to figure out what we were seeing. We finally found it by switching to a small-scale chart. It was a mountain 144 miles away!!! Refraction was bending its image over the horizon for an incredible distance, and the air was super clear.

All of this was pretty and interesting, but it made getting an accurate line of position by celestial navigation very difficult. I had to rely very heavily on dead reckoning, which was complicated by changing course many times going around icebergs, and by slowing down in fog and darkness. Also, our gyro compass was getting more and more sluggish at following course changes, as we got farther north.

Example of the Aurora Borealis copied from the Internet

I was doing heavy 24-hour duty on the bridge. I allowed Chief Mate Louis Murphy to relieve me and take the conn a number of times when conditions were good. I knew that I could trust him to keep an alert watch and to give the icebergs proper respect. I then got some much-needed rest. He was willing to do more and was very capable, but the heavy responsibility was mine, and I couldn't pass that on to anybody.

At the north end of Baffin Bay, where the current causes the icebergs to move from the Greenland coast westward to the Baffin Island coast, we had them pretty much "wall to wall". These were mostly huge young bergs. Many had straight sides, flat tops and square corners. It was difficult to find a path through them, that would not pass too close to one or more. We had to do some heavy zigzagging. The sluggish reaction of the gyro compass was very troubling. At least we had good weather, and 24 hours of daylight, to see what we were doing. Stormy weather at this time would have caused great danger.

Finally, on the sixth day, we were nearing our destination and necessarily had to close in on the coast of Greenland. Ahead on the starboard side appeared a very tall, two hundred feet or so, sharp pointed rock island, off the coast about two miles. Such a feature as this was bound to be plotted, but I could not find it on the chart. Was I lost? Had I passed Thule, and was on my way to the North Pole? We had not had a good navigational fix for three days and I was feeling a bit panicky.

Most of the charts for the northern part of this voyage were standard white navigational plotting sheets, with the shoreline sketched in, a few geographical features (such as mountains) drawn on them, and a few scattered soundings entered. I was nearing the upper (northern) edge of this chart, so I checked the next one and, to my great relief, there was a "Conical Rock" plotted on it. The charts overlapped enough so that it should have appeared on the other chart also, but it had been left off.

So, I had the first good navigational fix in days. We were nearing the point where we would be turning eastward into North Star Bay, where Thule was located. Our Navy Radiomen ran the antenna up a flag halyard, rigged the voice radio and established contact with Thule Base.

I remember the exact words that greeted us. "The old timers welcome you to North Star Bay. We like smartness, surety and safety". In an attempt at humor, I replied, "Gee, we must have come to the wrong place, because we like wine, women and song". I expected a chuckle or two, but there was absolute silence. At the time I believed they might be laughing with the microphone turned off, but I later concluded that they took everything very seriously and had no sense of humor. This dour regimen was most likely imposed by a very severe Commanding General, who had the crushing responsibility to build and defend this vital airbase, during a time of intense confrontation with the Soviet Union.

The next communication ordered us to proceed to the "DeLong" pier and to dock in the available berth. A "DeLong" pier was a very clever design of large, rectangular shaped, covered steel barges. They were equipped with long steel pilings at the four corners, that could be raised or lowered. They could be towed, with the steel corner pilings in the raised position, and when in location at the destination, they could be secured in place by lowering the pilings. A number of them could be joined, end to end, to make a suitably long dock. I did not know about them and asked the rather dumb question, "What is a DeLong pier and (not so dumb) where is it?"

At this point, my buddy, the Navy Lieutenant, said that he had a "secret" overlay for the chart, and went to his room to fetch it. So, at the last minute, as we were approaching the port and had ice all around, I had to go into the chart room and study his "secret" overlay. I could have cheerfully thrown him overboard. If I had known about the "secret" aero radio beacons that he had kept from me, I probably would have.

Our berth was to be starboard side to the dock, between two other ships. A very large U. S. Navy seagoing tug (as opposed to a handy-sized harbor tug) came up on our port side to make fast and assist in the docking maneuver. The Captain of the tug, probably a Chief Petty Officer, handled his vessel skillfully. It was really more like a ship coming alongside a ship. The tug was much too large for this assignment and kept dragging us to port. With a megaphone, I made arrangements with the Tug Captain that I would signal him with a mouth whistle, one whistle push, one whistle stop, two whistles back, and one whistle stop. He had no problem with these signals, and we proceeded to the dock. This was only my second berthing experience and I certainly was not very skillful at it. Anyway, we got safely docked and I breathed a big sigh of relief. It had been a difficult passage. I was very tired.

Our arrival date was July 26, 1952. We had covered a distance of 2,112 miles since departing Argentia 6 days, 13 hours and 12 minutes earlier. Our average speed was 13.44 knots and our fuel consumption averaged 0.842 barrels per mile.

Thule

Although I needed to get to bed, I had to first deal with the Boarding Authorities.

The General in command of Thule Air Base had ordered that there would be no shore leave for Merchant Marine personnel. A military guard was posted at our gangway to enforce the order. Our crew was not even allowed to stretch their legs on the dock.

This action was typical of the way the U. S. Military treated Merchant Marine personnel. Our little crew would not have overburdened the military clubs ashore and a little R and R would have improved morale.

Discharge of our cargo for Thule, using ship's gear, commenced in due time with no problems. I turned ship operations over completely to Chief Mate Murphy and hit the sack. He had "No Shore Leave" notices duly posted and put a "Do Not Disturb" sign on my door, that he enforced vigorously.

Considering our location, the weather was remarkably mild. At mid-day, you could get by in shirtsleeves. The temperature got up into the sixties (Fahrenheit) and the 24-hour sunshine kept things from cooling off much, even at midnight. During our stay, the air was mostly calm with little of no breeze. It was hard to visualize that in a few months there would be no sunshine here, there would be raging blizzards and the temperature would be 50 to 70 degrees below zero.

The countryside that we could see from the ship was truly desolate. There was no vegetation in sight and not a tree anywhere. I had heard that there was a very hardy fern-type growth, that survived in this harsh climate, but we could not see any from the ship.

The ship at the dock ahead of us was a C-4 class freighter (520 feet long) operated by MSTS, the Military Sea Transport Service. These ships had civilian crews that were Civil Service Employees. If I remember correctly, it was the SS General Han.

The Master of that ship, Captain Hansen, came over for a visit. He was an old hand in these waters and knew the local politics enough to be able to leave his ship and visit us. We had a good talk.

He introduced himself as being probably the only person that I would ever encounter that had had a geographical feature named for him. That turned out to be true, at least for the next 53 years and into my 80th year. A year or two earlier, he had been in command of a C-2 class freighter (459 feet long), and was making an entry into Sondre Stromfjord, which is located on the west coast of Greenland at the Arctic Circle. Until that time, only smaller Danish ships (Greenland was a colony of Denmark) with lighter drafts had gone into that body of water. But the U. S. was building an air base at the head of the fjord, so bigger ships would be entering. Straight out from the entry were shoals that had previously been unknown. Now they are named "Hansen's Shoal". He had discovered them the hard way, by running aground.

Ranges had later been set-up to guide ships into the fjord around "Hansen's Shoal". On my next voyage to Greenland, I would personally use that range.

I had one other visitor of note. The American Bureau of Shipping had stationed a Surveyor in Thule to check the ice damage done to ships calling there. He was a lonesome civilian at a military base, and he really needed someone to visit with and talk to about ships. When he entered my office, he announced that he was there to survey and note our ice damage. I told him that we had none, since we had been able to get to Thule without touching a single bit of ice along the way. He found this to be incredible, and said that we were the first ship that he had heard of that had managed to do that. That bit of information made me feel really good.

Our cargo discharge took a week. A commercial operation would have done it two or three days.

Thule Air Base, summer and winter
(from Internet)

On the morning of August 2nd, 1952, at 0800, we were secured for sea and ready to sail. Conditions were ideal. The fog had lifted and the tide had taken out the sea ice. Stupid military rules, that no one seemed to be able to countermand when indicated, would keep us at the dock until 1700. By then, the fog had set in again and the tide had brought the sea ice back into the port.

Six wooden-hulled launches, that were not suitable for use in this location, had been shipped up in our cargo. They had been reloaded back into our #4 Tween Deck. We could not sail until the Cargo Manifest for them had been made up, properly certified and delivered aboard. Planes were leaving the airbase several times daily, and surely these documents could have been sent on one of them. I was furious.

After a couple of hours of this needless delay, I started calling the Commanding Officer on our voice radio. His code name was "Marksman". I knew the charter rate for the ship, and with each call I informed him how much this unnecessary delay had cost the U. S. taxpayers up to that point. After my third call, they refused to answer me.

I had support for my impatience from the Commanding Officer of a Coast Guard ice-breaker, that was waiting to take our berth. My recollection was that it was the USS East Wind, but it may have been the USS West Wind. They were going to take fuel and supplies for an ex-ploratory voyage farther north. They had my admiration for embarking upon such an adventure, but I was sure glad that I was not going to be their navigator.

Thule to Norfolk Passage

The Cargo Manifest was finally delivered to us and we were ready to sail at 1700 on Sat-urday, August 2, 1952.

The big U. S. Navy seagoing tug came over and offered assistance. I thanked the Tug Captain and told him that we would not need any help leaving the dock. He wished us bon voy-agè. Actually, I would have been better off without his assistance in our docking maneuver. This was not the fault of the Tug Captain. It was just that his boat was too big and heavy.

To leave the dock, I had our forward spring line doubled-up and, after letting go all other lines, I worked the engine dead slow ahead with hard right rudder. When we had developed a sufficient angle away from the dock, I had the spring lines let go and we backed away from the dock without any problem. This was a simple maneuver, but I was very inexperienced in these matters and was pleased how well it had gone.

The Commanding Officer of the icebreaker was close at hand to take the empty berth. He was using the same voice radio frequency that we had, so I wished him well on his voyage far-ther north, and he wished us well on our voyage south.

We had to pick our way around patches of sea ice for two or three hours, until we were a ways out to sea. I could still say, at this point, that we had not touched a single piece of ice.

The psychology of the southbound passage was much different than that of the north-bound one. The hardest part of the leg was at the beginning, and conditions would progressively get better each day.

My biggest worry was getting by the mass of young icebergs at the north end of Baffin Bay, which lay just ahead. Again, I was lucky with the weather. The fog lifted and there was only a moderate breeze. With these ideal conditions, I was able to zig zag my way through these bergs without difficulty. I was relaxed enough to take measurements (trigonometric calculations based on sextant angle and distance off by radar) of some of the biggest ones as reported earlier in this narrative. They were immense. Even when you were half a mile or so away from them, you could feel their coolness. I had to keep reminding myself that there was seven times that visible bulk under the water.

The southbound navigation was much less critical than northbound. All I had to do was go in a southerly direction and keep between Greenland and Baffin Island. Eventually we would get far enough south so that the gyro compass would work properly and we would be able to take normal celestial observations. The main thing was not to hit any icebergs or growlers. We devoted intense effort to accomplish that. And we succeeded.

When we got far enough south to lose the 24-hour daylight, I ran at half speed during darkness when there were icebergs about. We had only brief foggy spells and were able to run at full speed (15 knots or 17.25 mph) most of the time.

I had decided to save a few miles and go through Belle Island Strait, on our return voyage, and go south along the west coast of Newfoundland Island instead of the east coast. There was a large iceberg grounded near the entrance to Belle Island Strait, and that would be the last one that we would see on this voyage. Upon reaching the south end of Newfoundland Island, we exited the Gulf of St. Lawrence and went back into the Atlantic Ocean through the Cabot Strait.

We had made a round trip to Thule without touching a single piece of ice.

We arrived at Hampton Roads on Monday, August 11, 1952. We had taken 8 days, 15 hours and 42 minutes to travel 3,090 miles. This gave an average speed of 14.88 knots. Our fuel consumption was 0.678 barrels per mile. The Labrador Current had given us a good boost as shown by the fact that we had negative slip of 1.2%. The ship had actually traveled farther than the propeller had pushed her. When there is no current or wind affecting performance, the resistance encountered, while pushing the hull through the water, causes a positive slip of about four

Iceberg Field at the North End of Baffin Bay (1952)
These were very large, young bergs. The one far left measured to be 1,280 feet long.

to eight percent, depending mainly on the ship's draft. To have negative slip for such a long passage was unusual.

We proceeded to a lay pier in Newport News, to await the availability of a berth at the Norfolk Army Base. We paid off the crew, signed on a new one and stored for the next voyage. All of the officers, except for one Assistant Engineer, and most of the unlicensed crew signed over for the next trip. While at the lay berth I took the picture of the ship, which was shown earlier in this chapter.

Second Voyage

Norfolk, New York, Narssarssuaq, Sondre Stromfjord, New York

Preparing For Our Second Voyage to Greenland

On Thursday, August 14th,, we shifted from the Newport News lay berth to the Norfolk Army Base, and commenced loading general cargo for a second voyage north. Our discharge ports were not secret this time, and were to be Narssarssuaq, on the south coast of Greenland, and Sondre Stromfjord, on the west coast at the Arctic Circle. The United States had built airbases at both locations. We were able to obtain large-scale charts of both areas.

Again there were no special problems with the cargo. There were no heavy lifts and no dangerous cargo.

Government run ship operations were unbelievably inefficient. We would spend 20 days loading general cargo for two ports in Greenland. Commercial operations would have had us loaded and out in less than a week.

Finally, on Wednesday, September 3, 1952, the cargo was all aboard, and we sailed coastwise to New York, where we were to take bunkers (fuel oil). We departed Norfolk in the wee hours September 4th, and arrived in New York later that same day.

Again, the government operations astounded me. We should have been back out to sea on September 5 but would not sail until September 7.

New York to Narssarssuaq Passage

We finished taking bunkers and sailed from New York on Sunday, September 7, 1952.

One day out we ran into an easterly gale that caused a bit of rolling and pitching. The cargo appeared to be well secured and there were no signs of any shifting about.

I again decided to save some miles, and get out of the rough seas of the Atlantic, by proceeding via the Gulf of St. Lawrence. We entered through Cabot Strait, went up the west coast of Newfoundland Island, and exited back in the Atlantic Ocean through Belle Island Strait. We had smooth water while inside, but it got rough again as soon as we cleared Belle Island Strait. The iceberg that had been grounded there when we passed this way southbound was gone.

The entry channels to Narssarssuaq (61° 09' N, 45° 26' W) were complicated. They consisted of a series of fjords or maybe they could be called multiple channels or reaches of one fjord. In the final area of the port, the fjord was quite wide but there were narrow channels and several turns, two of which were of about 90 degrees, before getting there.

There were no leading ranges, lighthouses or buoys. The entry from sea would have been just about impossible to find, except that some rocks had been piled up in the shape of a small pyramid to mark it. Similar small pyramids marked intersections in the fjords where sharp turns were necessary. The inland navigation channels were about sixty-five miles long. There were active glaciers that calved growlers and ice chucks into the area. This entry could obviously only be safely negotiated during clear, daylight hours.

I at first tried to make arrival on September 12, 1952, early enough to get through the channels before dark on that date. When it became clear that the gales we had encountered had slowed us too much to be able to meet that schedule, I reduced speed, intending to enter early daylight on September 13th.

Two bad things happened as we neared the south coast of Greenland. We commenced to encounter many icebergs that had been calved on the east coast. They were not as big as those west coast monsters, but they were plenty big enough to wreck our ship. On the night of September 12, a very severe westerly gale suddenly developed. We were in the midst of many icebergs. The big problem was that the gale whipped up the sea so much, that the clutter of "sea return" on the radar screen became excessive. It made it impossible to locate any bergs, even large ones, within three miles or so from the ship. This, of course, meant that growlers would go completely undetected.

It would take a lot of luck to get through the night without a disaster. I decided to reverse course at slow speed, allowing for estimated leeway, to try to retrace the route that we had followed northbound. After all, we hadn't hit anything coming up. It was a terrifying night and we were sure glad when daylight finally came the next morning. It revealed that we had indeed been fortunate, not to have struck or to have been struck by an iceberg. There were many of them in the area.

With daylight, I again reversed course and ran full speed (15 knots) toward the Narssarssuaq entrance, changing course a number of times to keep icebergs at a proper distance. The gale had moderated and was still blowing from the west, causing considerable rolling, but not slowing us down much. When we got close to the coast, I reduced speed and commenced looking for the little pyramid of rocks that marked the entrance. Our radar was helpful in that it clearly showed the coastal features. There was no pack ice along this coast to confuse the issue.

At about 1000, we found the entrance and proceeded in at half speed (8 knots). Our large-scale charts proved accurate, and the rock pyramids were all in place as charted at the turns in the channel. It was essential that we complete the passage before dark, so I ran at full speed (15 knots) in the straight stretches. There were good-sized chucks of ice in the fjords, but fortunately they were clear of the channels. After about six hours of inland steaming, we arrived at the very wide fjord (Skovfjord), where Narssarssuaq is located. We saw the dock and we were to berth starboard side to it. This would be my third docking experience, and I was about to embarrass myself terribly. It was, without doubt, the most humiliating experience of my maritime career.

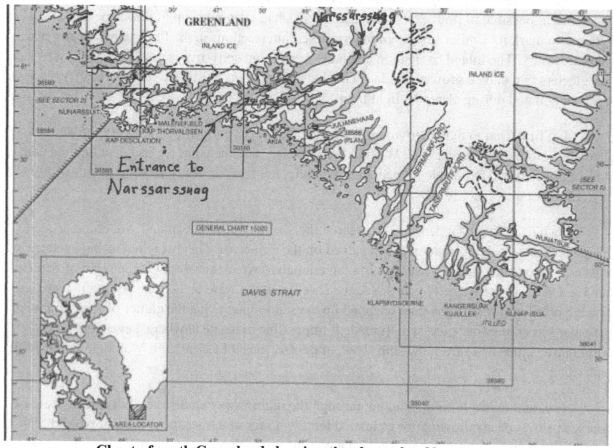

Chart of south Greenland showing the channel to Narssarssuaq

In my defense, I should point out that docking pilots in busy ports, where they constantly berth and unberth ships and gain great experience and expertise, they have at their disposal and use tugboats. For docking a single screw ship of our tonnage starboard side to the dock, they would normally use two tugs. Port side to the dock, under ideal conditions might only require one tug. Starboard side dockings are more difficult because the final astern movement, with the single screw, will cause an exaggerated swing of the stern away from the dock. The backing prop wash then travels mostly up the starboard side, thereby washing the entire ship away from the berth.

So, here I was, with very little experience and no training, being required to dock the ship in a port where I had no knowledge of the currents or tidal conditions, and without any tug assistance.

At this stage in my nautical career, I had no proper feel for the weight that I was handling. In my two previous dockings, the ship had not been heavily loaded, and that makes a big difference on how long she carries her headway and how difficult she is to stop.

We were now deeply laden and displacing about 14,000 long tons. As we approached the dock (with the engine stopped), we were not passing any objects that would have served as reference points to help judge our speed. I was not yet adept at "reading the water" to judge the amount of headway. Anyway, I approached the dock with too much speed. When I was a ship length away, I should have had the headway down to one or two knots. Instead, I was making four or five knots. By the time I realized I was in trouble, and backed full astern, it was too late. We sailed right by the dock and gave it a glancing blow with our starboard side forward,.

Needless to say, that experience shook my confidence. But the ship had to be docked and there was no one else to do it.

So, we made a circle to the left and again got lined up with the dock. Luckily, the fjord in this location was wide enough to allow us to make this circle to the left. This time, when were nearing the berth, I had Chief Mate Murphy drop the port anchor, with one shot of chain (15 fathoms or 90 feet), and then set the windlass brake. We dragged the anchor along the bottom as we approached the dock, and this worked well. It slowed our headway and allowed me to use "steering kicks" ahead with the engine, without putting on too much headway. I very much wished that I had done this on the first attempt.

My first approach had been excessively fast, and this time I was excessively slow. We finally get berthed and I was very embarrassed and ashamed of my performance.

The Dock Master was a civilian contractor. He was very gracious and did not make a big deal about the damage that I had inflicted upon the wooden fendering on his dock. He said that his people could fix it as good as new with no problems.

The damage to the ship's hull was negligible. Only the paint was scuffed a little.

Narssaraauaq

The whole atmosphere in this port was friendly and relaxed, a great contrast with Thule. Shore leave for the crew was allowed and escorted tours to the nearby ruins of Eric the Red's colony were arranged. The Commanding Officer of this base ran a "Happy Ship".

This part of Greenland is the most fertile on the island and vegetation, although sparse to our eyes, is relatively abundant. But there are no trees.

The fertility of this region was the reason that Eric the Red chose to live in south Greenland in about 985 AD, after he had been expelled from Iceland.

According to the sagas, it was Eric the Red who named this island Greenland. After he had lived for three years in this region, he returned to Iceland, and wanted to convince his fellow countrymen of the fine opportunities for starting a new life here in this "Green Land". The colonies that he established lasted for about 500 years, but eventually all of the inhabitants perished.

As the tide ebbed and flooded, the relatively small growlers calved from the active glaciers in the area entered and left the port area. I took the following photograph from our ship. Note the complete lack of trees.

The airbase here had been established in 1942, as an intermediary stop for planes being ferried to England during WWII. It would be deactivated in 1959, and become an international airport.

We were to spend eleven days discharging cargo in this port. The daily high temperatures were in the upper fifties and at night got down into the forties (Fahrenheit). We had some rain, but most of the time it was partly cloudy, with considerable sunshine.

After about five days, a Danish freighter of the famous Laurensen Line arrived, and was skillfully docked on the inner side of our berth. It was a small freighter about 350 feet long. The ship had been built for the Greenland trade and had a reinforced icebreaker bow. After my own disgraceful docking, it was with great interest that I watched the Danish Captain maneuver his ship into the dock. All of that company's ships had their hulls and smoke stacks painted bright red. The deckhouses were painted white

Being just across the dock from each other, the crews of the two ships naturally socialized. Being Danish, they all spoke English and were very friendly.

The Danish Captain, who was a very vigorous man in his late forties, invited my Chief Officer and me over for cocktails and hors d'oeuvrés, in the afternoon. We, in turn, invited him and his Chief Officer for dinner on our ship. Also invited, were two attractive lady passengers. The ladies, who were in their early twenties, were on the way to a Danish settlement up the coast named, as I recall, Fredrickshavn. They were to marry men there that they had never met, but they had corresponded with them, and had pictures. As I said, they were attractive and in the wilds of Greenland, they appeared to be gorgeous.

The Danish Chief Officer had to attend to important ship's business and declined our invitation.

After dinner, it turned into a bit of a wild evening. The Danish Captain got very drunk and was extremely loud. The young ladies gave Murphy and me encouragement, and so we were romancing them. Actually, only trying to romance them, since we never actually scored. The Danish Captain took his role as chaperone very seriously, and was loudly cursing (in Danish) and searching on our ship for the lady passengers. He roamed up and down our ship's passageways, shouting their names and slamming the palm of his hand on the closed doors, which made a loud noise.

The port area of Narssarssuaq in Skovfjord. (1952)
Active glaciers in the area calve small "growlers" that the tide carries in and out of port.
Note the complete lack of trees.

Murphy and I were distressed at the situation, but the ladies thought it was amusing to hide from him. Murphy and his "date" were hiding in the Chart Room, and my "date" and I were hiding in the ship's Hospital Room. A couple of times, things calmed down when the Danish Captain went back to his ship, probably for another drink or two, and passed out for a while. During one of the "quiet spells", my lady and I went up to the Flying Bridge and watched the aurora borealis, which was spectacular that night. At about 0100, it appeared that the Danish Captain

Chief Engr. Ira Sager, fishing in Narssarssuaq (1952)

had passed out for the final time, and the ladies quietly went back to their quarters on the Danish vessel.

The following afternoon, the Laurensen Line freighter sailed. I waved goodbye to the Captain but he did not return my wave. The young ladies stayed out of sight.

Mr. Glen E. Ball, the Port Official with whom I dealt, inquired if I was a Mason. When I replied in the affirmative, he invited me to become a member of the Arctic Circle Masonic Club. I did join and to this day, more than 53 years later, I still have and prize my membership certificate. A copy of it is reproduced here.

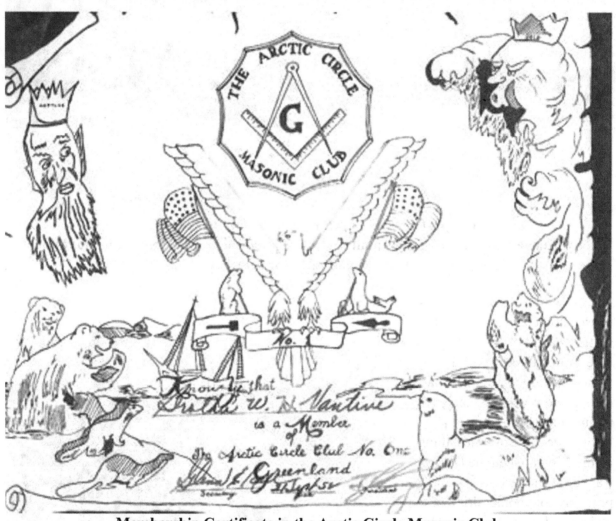

**Membership Certificate in the Arctic Circle Masonic Club
Presented to Brother Wilbur H. Vantine on September 21, 1952**

Narssarssuaq to Sondre Stromfjord Passage

We finished discharging cargo and sailed from the dock, early morning on Wednesday, September 24, 1952. We wound our way through the fjords and exited into the Atlantic Ocean without incident. The chucks of ice were still all outside the channels.

Three days before, September 21st, had been the Autumnal Equinox, when the sun's declination changes from north to south. On that day, everywhere on earth has 12 hours of sunlight and 12 hours of darkness. Now daylight on each successive day, until December 23rd, would become shorter in the northern hemisphere, dramatically so in high northern latitudes.

There were still many East Coast icebergs concentrated around Cape Farewell and I photographed some. They had been terrifying on the stormy night of September 12th, but presented no problem now in nice weather.

**East Coast Greenland Icebergs
that we encountered off Cape Farewell (1952)**

It would be almost a two-day run up the west coast of Greenland to the entry to Sondre Stromfjord. This stretch of the coast had fewer icebergs than most. The very active west coast glaciers are farther north, so only east coast icebergs that had drifted around the south end of Greenland, were present. A small portion of the warm Gulf Stream comes up this way, and prevents pack ice from forming along the coast.

There was a moderate easterly gale blowing, but since we had the lee of the land, the seas were only moderate. That meant that we had good radar signals to help watch for icebergs. I never the less ran at half speed (8 knots) after dark, to guard against the possibility of suddenly running up on a growler. I also adjusted our speed to time arrival at the fjord's entrance to be soon after dawn.

Sondre Stromfjord is located right on the Arctic Circle (66° 39' north latitude). This is the farthest south latitude, from which the sun can be seen over the North Pole at midnight on June 21st, when it is at its summer solstice (23° 21' north). It is also the farthest south latitude at which there will be no sun visible at noon on December 23rd, when the sun is at its winter solstice.

The only geographical feature that I have seen that is more spectacular than Sondre Stromfjord, is the Grand Canyon. This fjord is 110 miles long and runs inland in an almost straight line. Throughout most of its length, the fjord is about 500 feet wide. The inner half is ex-

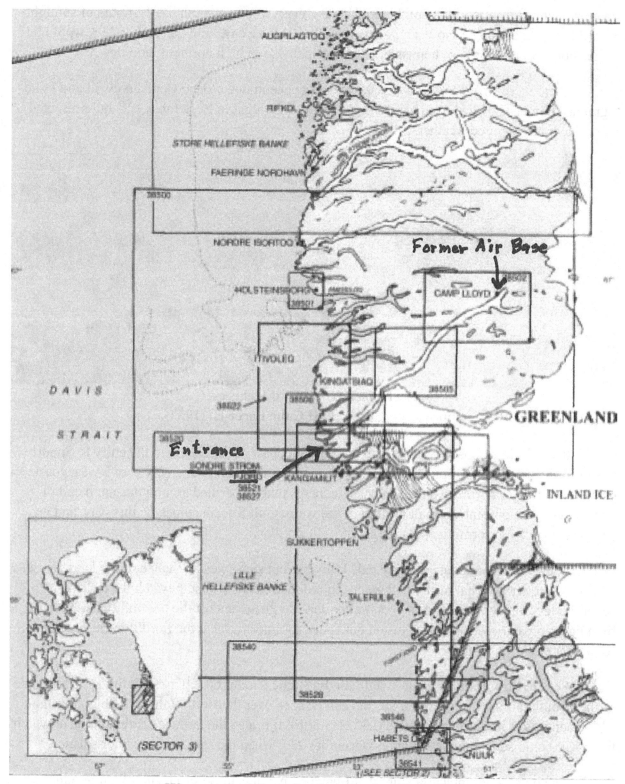

West coast of Greenland at the Arctic Circle.
Sondre Stromfjord extends inland 110 miles to the location of a former Airbase.

154.

tremely deep, so deep that a ship's anchor could not reach the bottom even with all of the chain paid out. Thus, the anchors would be of no help in case of engine or rudder failure.

The glacier that dug this fjord still exists at its head, but is now in retreat.

Because of the physical layout, there is a very strong tidal action in the fjord, with currents running as much as seven knots. The swift current, plus "Hansen's Shoal' being located straight our from the mouth of the fjord, makes entry and exit hazardous.

As Captain Hansen had mentioned to me in a conversation back in Thule the previous July, leading range markers had been set up to guide ships around the shoal named in his honor. To get lined up with it, I had to steam past the fjord entrance, turn right about 135 degrees, and proceed on a southeasterly heading. The range markers were not very large and I needed binoculars to see them until we got pretty close. We would follow this range until reaching the mouth of the fjord, at which time a turn to the left of about 90 degrees would be required.

I do not know if any "Sailing Directions" had been published for this part of Greenland but, in any case, I did not have any. Consequently, I had no warning about the extremely strong tidal current. It surprised, amazed and nearly shipwrecked me. I was approaching on the range at

View of Sondre Stromfjord looking astern at our wake.
We were past the halfway point (about sixty miles inland). The fjord was about 500 feet wide and the water was about 1,000 feet deep. (1952)

half speed, about eight knots. As we neared the entrance, we suddenly started "crabbing" sideways toward Hansen's Shoal. I immediately ordered full ahead and steered to the left to try to stay lined up with the range markers. Even steering 45 degrees to the left of our intended course and on full ahead, we were still being set down on the shoal. It was ebb tide and the current was pouring out of the fjord at great speed, seven or eight knots. It was by far the strongest current that I had ever seen. We gave the engineers a "jingle" on the telegraph, to request all possible power. We managed to reach the mouth of the fjord, and turned left another 45 degrees, and so were then directly stemming the current. We were then out of danger, but that had been a close call!!!

In preparation for this run up the fjord, I had the ship's carpenter build a special plywood chart table, for me to use at the forward bulkhead of the wheelhouse. On this run, there was not going to be time to go into the chart room to take a look at the chart.

There were only a couple of places in the fjord where I had to favor one side to avoid rocks. These were near the entrance, and for the remainder of the passage, I could just run up the middle.

View of the bank of Sondre Stromfjord alongside our ship.

156.

It took us about nine hours, running at full speed (15 knots through the water), to reach the head of Sondre Stromfjord, where the airbase was located. For most of this passage we had the tidal current flowing against us. I would have been more comfortable running at half speed, but deemed it essential to get to the anchorage, at the head of the fjord, before dark, and while we had reasonably good visibility.

During this time we had just about every conceivable kind of weather, except hot. It included clear sky, rain, fog, snow, sleet and hail. Also, the wind ranged from dead calm to strong gale. The depths in the inner half (fifty miles or so) were over 100 fathoms (600 feet). The scenery was fantastic, with snow-covered mountains in the distance, and very rugged high rocky banks on both sides of the channel.

When we reached the head of the fjord, we could see the glacier ahead, in the distance. It had retreated three or four miles from the water's edge.

There was no dock for this port, so we anchored. The depth had shallowed up to about fifty feet.

Our cargo for this port would have to be discharged into "ducks", amphibious trucks that could take it from alongside directly to where it was needed, or would be warehoused ashore.

**Shore line of the Sondre Stromfjord alongside our ship
as we made our way inland 110 miles. (1952)**

My understanding was that the main purpose of this airstrip was to provide an alternate landing place, in case of trouble on a plane bound to or from Thule. Duty here must have been about the loneliest anywhere.

There would be no shore leave here but nobody much wanted to go anyway. The cargo operations would take four days.

Sondre Stromfjord to New York Passage

We finished discharging our cargo and sailed on Wednesday, October 1, 1952, bound for New York.

I was now familiar with the 110-mile channel in the fjord and was not too worried about navigating it. What worried me was negotiating the exit at the mouth of the fjord. I would not have the leading range markers ahead to refer to. They would be astern and would be much harder to get, and keep, lined up. I did not know whether the current would be flowing into or out of the fjord and that would make a tremendous difference. It could be seven knots or more in either direction. As soon as we left the entrance, we needed to turn sharply to the right almost 90 degrees to a northwesterly heading. If we did not turn soon enough, we would ground on Hansen's Shoal. If we turned too soon, and the current was flowing in, we would ground on the rocks near the entry.

From watching the ripples on the banks of the fjord, I judged that the tide was ebbing and would be setting us down on Hansen's Shoal. This was further confirmed when I checked our speed and found that we were doing about 20 knots over the ground.

As we neared the exit, I stationed myself on the port bridgewing where I could observe the range marks and try to judge our turn so as to follow the proper channel out.

Unbeknown to me, the excellent Quartermaster that was on the wheel was relieved, just at this moment, by one who was not so good. I was outside and did not know about it. The Third Mate, who was on watch, should not have allowed the change at that critical time.

When I judged that the proper moment had come, I shouted in the order "Hard Right Rudder". As soon as I heard the acknowledgment from the slow-witted Quartermaster, I knew that I had a problem. I rushed into the wheelhouse and ordered the Third Mate to take the wheel, and to turn it quickly.

It took three and a half turns of the steering wheel to move the rudder from amidships to hard over (35 degrees), and to do so quickly took considerable effort. When the ship had swung about 70 degrees, I eased the rudder, and as we approached our desired heading, I ordered 10 degrees left rudder to steady-up.

I had judged the turn pretty well and the range markers were almost lined up astern. I adjusted the heading ten degrees, and we were soon perfectly lined up. Shortly, we cleared the shoal, and could turn left, and set a southerly course for Belle Island Strait, enroute to New York.

There was a moderate gale blowing from the north, which didn't bother us much except that it caused sea return clutter on the radar screen, possibly hiding growlers from us. For the first two days, I ran at half speed after dark because of icebergs and growers being in the area.

A few times during the years that I sailed as a ship captain, my intuition acted to prevent a probable disaster. This was the first of those times. On our second day out from Sondre Stromfjord, we were steaming along under ideal conditions, with not many icebergs about. After lunch, I decided to take a nap. I reminded the Third Mate, who was on watch, to give all bergs a wide berth and to call me if there were any problems. After just getting asleep, I suddenly awakened and felt that something was wrong. I quickly went to the bridge to find that we were about to pass close to a good-sized iceberg. I was just in time to alter course. I chewed out the Third Mate royally. Was he stupid, reckless, psychologically unable to give a rudder, order or was he a ship wrecker? It was clear that I could never again trust him and I resolved to fire him when we got into port.

We reached Belle Island Strait and proceeded through the Gulf of St. Lawrence, exiting back into the Atlantic through Cabot Strait. We had now made two round trips to Greenland without touching any ice.

Two days before arrival in New York, I received a radiogram informing me that I was to leave the ship in New York, and that I would be taking command of the SS T. J. Stevenson, the Company's flagship. This was incredible news. At age 27 I was to be Captain of the flagship of T. J. Stevenson & Co., Inc.

Chief Mate Louis Murphy

There was also some down side to this development. Chief Mate Louis Murphy would be staying on this ship. We had been shipmates for more than five years and had shared some remarkable experiences. We were best friends, but would never sail together again. After one more voyage, he would get off and obtain his Master Mariner's License.

Our Company had Murphy scheduled for a command of his own in the near future, but then a stupid thing happened. He got drafted into the Army. At age 18, he had joined the Merchant Marine in 1943, the same year that I did, and had sailed on merchant ships ever since. In spite of the fact that the all-volunteer Merchant Marine had a casualty rate during WWII higher even than that of the Marine Corps, we were considered to be draft dodgers.

Murphy and I had observed that the Army Officers assigned as "Cargo Officers", to oversee military cargo operations on our ships over the years, were not very knowledgeable about ships or stevedoring. With this in mind, Murphy requested to be assigned to that branch, where his expertise might do some good. Instead, since he knew how to type, he was made a Company

Clerk in an Army Division stationed in Germany. I suspect that they didn't want an Enlisted Man knowing more that the Cargo Officer.

About four years later, when my ship was berthed in Leghorn, Italy, Sergeant Louis Murphy drove down from Germany, in his Oldsmobile (that he had shipped over to Europe), for a visit. We had a real good one that included a drive to and overnight in Florence.

After he was discharged from the Army, T. J. Stevenson & Co., Inc., did give Louis Murphy a command, a T-2 class tanker (523 feet by 68 feet). The Grace Line passenger ship, the SS Santa Rosa, collided with his ship in dense fog off the East Coast of the U. S., with loss of life on the tanker. Newspapers around the world ran pictures of the SS Santa Rosa arriving in New York harbor with the smoke stack of Murphy's ship impaled on its bow. The subsequent inquiry determined that the passenger ship Captain was solely at fault for the collision.

When he later got married and wanted a shore job, Murphy found one as Head Surveyor for the National Cargo Bureau in Duluth, MN. He was scheduled to take over their very busy and important Norfolk office.

I wanted him to come to Panama to be a Canal Pilot with me, but his wife would not go. He died much too young, before his fortieth birthday, of an enlarged heart.

The other downside of my new assignment was that I would be off the payroll for about six weeks, awaiting the return of the SS T. J. Stevenson from her current voyage.

We arrived in New York on Thursday, October 9, 1952.

Leaving the Ship

The new Captain relieved me. The SS Waltham Victory was going to make another voyage back up north. I did not envy them. Murphy later wrote to me that they had run aground at Goose Bay, Labrador.

Being in the port of New York, I was able to visit the Company Headquarters at 80 Broad Street, in downtown New York City. I had a good chat with the Operations Manager, Captain William J. Campbell. I suspected that he was the one behind the scenes arranging for my assignment to the SS T. J. Stevenson. I also touched base with several other key executives including, of course, Operations Vice President, Mr. John F. Shea, who had thought me too young for the job back in June 1951.

On my occasional stops in New York, there were four things that I always tried to do.

- 1.   Take a trip to the top of the Empire State Building with a camera and a pair of binoculars.
- 2.   Have a steak dinner at the Black Angus.
- 3.   Have a lobster dinner at the Lobster Restaurant on 45th Street.
- 4.   See the current show at the Radio City Music Hall.

After a couple of days, and after having accomplished the above, I boarded a train at Penn Station to go home to Sedalia, Missouri, to await the return of the SS T. J. Stevenson to the United States.

Addendum

SS Waltham Victory, **Standing Orders**

1. Keep a good lookout and see that your lookouts do likewise. When it is necessary to go into the chartroom in connection with navigation, piloting, or to study the chart, etc., take a good look around with the binoculars before leaving the bridge. Never, under the best circumstances, stay in the chartroom more than four or five minutes without looking for traffic, etc., yourself. Do not rely on your lookouts too much. Often they are not responsible men or they may have bad eyesight.

2. Obey the Rules of the Road at all times. Give all ships a wide berth. When meeting or crossing with another vessel, take bearings of it and change course early enough to avoid any situation when a last minute misunderstanding could cause disaster. Read over the Rules of the Road at least every three months, or else you will forget them.

3. When at sea, have the man on the wheel check the gyro with the magnetic compass, every half-hour, and report same to you. Check it at least twice a watch yourself. When making a landfall or running along a coast, have your quartermaster steer by both the gyro and magnetic compasses, keeping a constant check for any unaccountable change. If the compasses change more than the changing variation would warrant, steer by the magnetic and call the Second Mate and me. When the helmsmen are changed, have them repeat both the gyro and magnetic courses to each other and to you. When you are relieved, give the gyro, magnetic and course to make good to your relief. When changing the watch at 0400 and 1600, check the Master Gyro with the Repeaters. The gyro compass, like any other piece of equipment, will go out of order occasionally. If we don't notice promptly when it breaks down, we could very well get involved in a serious accident.

4, When possible, take an azimuth each watch (both day and night) and enter it in the compass observation book together, with the deviation of the Standard and Steering compasses (in addition to the gyro error).

5. Never steer a course blindly. Study the chart before taking over a watch and check the proposed courses and distances. Note the description and characteristics of the navigational aids you will see and/or use,

6. When the wind changes sufficiently to affect the course being made good; when making a landfall or coasting, call me; when on the open sea, call me if I am up, if asleep, allow the leeway you deem necessary.

7. Never force the ship in heavy weather. When the vessel starts laboring, or (when light) pounding or taking substantial seas, call me. If you can't reach me immediately, reduce speed and/or change course as necessary to ease the vessel in the seaway.

8. When the visibility gets bad, start the radar, put the engine on standby, post a lookout on the bow and start giving whistle signals. There is no need to leave your duties to call me as I will hear the whistle and come to the bridge to reduce speed as necessary. If, for some reason, I am detained, and do not come promptly, you may reduce speed as you may deem necessary.

9. Look after the ventilation of the cargo holds. Different cargoes require different care along this line, so no set rules can be made. Keep alert for rain squalls and try to have the ventilators properly trimmed before the rain begins.

10. Use good seamanship, which is the same as good common sense. If the wind is increasing, make sure things likely to blow away are secured. If the sea is making up, be sure that things are properly battened down and that the watertight doors on the main deck are dogged tightly closed, etc.

11. Please feel free to call me at any time you are in doubt about anything. In case of emergency, give three rings on my telephone and I will rush to the bridge without delaying to answer the phone.

12. Study these Standing Orders, and after you understand and agree to them, please acknowledge by signing on one of the lines on the opposite page.

W H Vantine

Captain Wilbur H. Vantine

Chapter X: SS T. J. Stevenson
(First Tour of Duty)

Background

T. J. Stevenson & Co., Inc., and their "alternate personalities", Stevenson Lines and Ocean Freighting and Brokerage Corp., had a large and very well-run office organization to oversee the operation of ships. I understand that during WWII they operated more than 150 ships from their New York headquarters. I mentioned that Stevenson Lines and Ocean Freighting and Brokerage Corp. were "alternate personalities" because they used to switch the ship's operator (of record) among these companies frequently, sometimes on successive voyages, for bookkeeping and tax purposes.

**Stevenson Lines Logo
and
Smoke Stack Symbol**

Commencing soon after WWII, they organized and operated an ocean freight shipping business between the U. S. East Coast and Mediterranean Sea ports, with a heavy emphasis on cargo to and from Italy. They had an American Resident Agent, Mr. Harold Vinick, stationed in Genoa and that was the port that handled the most European cargo for Stevenson Lines.

In its formative period, the Company made a bad decision when it decided to operate this steamship line using only Liberty Ships. These ships were cheap to buy and were easy and economical to operate but they only made eleven knots under ideal conditions. In the long run, that made them unable to compete with other steamship companies that had fleets of ships that made sea speeds of fifteen or more knots. T. J. Stevenson & Co., Inc. bought five Liberty Ships from the U. S. Government and renamed them as follows: the SS T. J. Stevenson, the SS Henry Stevenson, the SS Kenneth H. Stevenson, the SS Dorothy Stevenson, and the SS Helen Stevenson. There was so much freight business available in the early years that from time to time they had to charter additional ships to carry it.

One improvement that the Company made on its five owned Liberties was to install larger propellers. Instead of operating at 76 rpm when running at full ahead sea speed, they only needed to turn 60 rpm to make the same sustainable 11 knots.

Having slow ships caused problems, particularly with perishable cargoes, such as tobacco from Turkey. If it was in the ship's holds more than a certain number of days, it could be ruined or would greatly lose value. An additional difficulty was that Liberty Ships had no air conditioning nor even any fan-forced ventilation in the cargo holds. It was up to the crews to keep the vents properly trimmed for the wind/rain conditions. Also, slower ships could only make fewer voyages in a given period of time and therefore earned less revenue.

During the ten or so years after the end of WWII, many entrepreneurs took advantage of the low price for which they could buy surplus ships from the U. S. Government. Liberty Ships could be had, at times, for as little as $230,000. When freight rates were up, it was possible to pay for a ship in one or two voyages.

It was not feasible for Owners, who only had a few ships, to organize and support office staffs to operate their vessels. Many of them turned to companies, such as T. J. Stevenson & Co., Inc., to operate them on a contract basis. T. J. Stevenson & Co., Inc. got its share of this business which justified them keeping such a large, complete and competent staff.

The Company occupied two entire floors at 80 Broad Street in Lower Manhattan in New York City. This was a very high-class office building in an expensive neighborhood. The Operating Staff was on one floor and the Cargo Procurement, Chartering and Accounting personnel were on another. I only frequented the Operations Floor where the Vice President for Operations, Mr. John F. Shea, was the only one who had a private and enclosed office. All other personnel on this floor had desks in one very large open area.

To give an idea of the size of the operation, I will list the Headquarters Personnel as it existed in the early 1950's— Vice President (Operations)- Mr. John F. Shea; Operations Manager- Captain William J. Campbell; Marine Superintendent- Mr. John F. Bernard; Port Engineer- Mr. Charles Anderson; Assistant to Operations Manager- Mr. Eugene F. Mooers; Assistant to Operations Manager- Mr. Edmund S. Holmes; Insurance & Claims- Mr. Wilfred D. Keeson; Clerk, Insurance & Claims- Mr. J. F. Dowling, Jr.; Port Steward- Mr. Herbert F. Green; Assistant Port Steward- Mr. Charles E. Etches; Purchasing Agent- Mr. C. R. O'Neill, Jr.; Inventory Clerk- Mr. Leo Jasser; Pier Superintendent- Mr. William H. Hunt; Chief Clerk- Mr. Ralph Rogers; Supervisor, Paymaster & Personnel- Mr. John A. Moore; Crew Personnel Manager- Mr. Felix Trotta; and Paymaster- Mr. Alex J. Johnson. The Freight Procurement Department, Chartering and Accounting Departments were located on the floor above along with Mr. T. J. Stevenson, Sr. They included— General Traffic Manager- Mr. August Rambousek; Assistant Traffic Manager- Mr. David Duncanson; Inward Freight & Passenger Dept- Mr. John A. Peaty; Traffic Representative- Mr. John R. Fitzpatrick; Traffic Representative- Mr. Michael J. Senko; Treasurer-Secretary- Ms. Marie V. Gunson; Comptroller & Assistant Treasurer- Mr. James O. Fredricksen; Assistant Comptroller- Mr. Robert DeRose; Freight Collections and Demurrage Manager- Mr. R. M. J. Farrington; Secretary to Mr. T. J. Stevenson, Sr.- Ms. C. M. Werner; and Secretary to Mr. M. V. Gunson- Ms. Cecelia Giani. Of course, most of these executives had a private secretary.

Although I worked for his Company for eleven years and served as Captain on seven of his ships, I never met or even saw Mr. T. J. Stevenson, Sr. or Jr.

The Company had its own pier in Hoboken. It was about 500 feet long and appeared to be very ancient. It was completely wooden and had the shape of a huge Quonset Hut. Its appearance resembled some illustrations that I have seen depicting what Noah's Ark might have looked like. It was within easy walking distance of the Hoboken Institute of Technology.

Joining the *SS T. J. Stevenson* in Norfolk

I had left the *SS Waltham Victory* in New York on October 11, 1952, and traveled by train to my home in Sedalia, MO. I then had about a month of mostly unpaid vacation. About November 10th I received a telephone call from Mr. John A. Moore, Chief of Personnel for T. J. Stevenson & Co., Inc., and was told that I should travel to Norfolk and be ready to take command of the *SS T. J. Stevenson* on or about November 14th. Of course in those days, all of the travel to and from home and ships in the various ports was at my own expense.

I was still in a bit of shock at being given, at age 27, the command of the Company's flagship. I think in the Company's offices, it was just considered to be another one of the five ships that they owned but, to the personnel on the ships, there was considerable prestige involved in being on the Company's Flagship. Captain Venicia had been Flagship Captain for some years and had a good reputation in the sea-going community. I never heard why he was being fired. There must have been hard feelings because he left before my arrival and normally he would have been expected to assist in turning the records, etc. over to me.

The *SS T. J. Stevenson* had been built in 1944 at Jacksonville, FL under the name of *SS Raymond Clapper*. She was a standard Liberty Ship, being 441 feet long, 57 feet in beam, and with an allowed summer draft 27 feet, 8 7/8th inches. When fully loaded to her summer Plimsoll marks, she displaced about 14,000 long tons which would normally include about 10,800 long tons of cargo, fuel, water and stores. The summer loaded freeboard (distance from the water to the main deck) was nine feet 8 3/4th inches. The 2,500 hp steam reciprocating engine propelled her at about eleven knots in smooth water. Two boilers supplied the steam and the ship could operate at about eight knots on one boiler when necessary. There were 36 men in the crew, counting the Captain. She was not equipped with radar.

One nice renovation was that the bulkhead between the Captain's bedroom and the room astern of it had been removed, making my quarters into a three-room suite. That room had originally been the quarters for the Navy Gun Crew Commanding Officer and was now, of course, available for other uses. A settee, table and refrigerator had been installed which made it into a nice entertainment center.

I was going to sorely miss my long-time shipmate, Louis Murphy, but I could look forward to otherwise having better deck and engine officers and a better Chief Steward that had been available on my previous "non Company-owned" ships. They would all be "company men" with established employment records. "Company men" were assigned from a roster kept by the Company but, of course, they had to be members of the various maritime unions and be in good standing. On my previous commands, most of the officers had been supplied by the maritime unions in response to requests for specific ratings.

Although it was a long time ago, I remember the names and personalities of all of my ship's officers on the *SS T. J. Stevenson*.

Captain's BR & Hospitality Room, *SS T. J. Stevenson* (1952)

Chief Mate Bill Bunting (1952)

Third Mate Tony Koerner (1952)

Chief Mate William H. Bunting was a handsome man in his late twenties. He had a Master's license and was from Kennebunk ME. He was a graduate of the Massachusetts School ship. Bill was a serious family man, very sober and conscientious. I would recommend him to my relief in about a year when I would take a trip off for vacation.

Second Mate Joseph Koller was a red-head also in his late twenties. Joe was a fellow Kings Pointer and was very reliable and competent. He was married, but his marriage was in trouble and he would end up divorced a few years later. He had a Chief Mate License and I would recommend him for that position, when Bill Bunting moved up to Acting Captain to relieve me for vacation.

Third Mate Anthony Koerner was a thirty year old bachelor German-American devout Catholic. He was well-read and very much intellectually inclined. Tony was a bit overweight and was a "Professional Third Mate". He only had a Third Mate license and was not interested in raising his grade. But he was a very good Third Mate and dependable in every way.

Radio Operator (Sparks)
Raymond Brazner
SS T. J. Stevenson **(1952)**
He would later be lost at sea when his
ship went down with all hands.

Second Mate Joe Koller
SS T. J. Stevenson (1952)

Left to Right, 2nd Engr. Alex Bentsen, 3rd Engr. Donald Taylor, Chief Engr. George Thomas, 1st Engr. Neil Thomas

Radio Officer Raymond Brazner (Sparks) was from Baltimore. He was a vigorous and fun-loving married man in his mid-twenties. I later visited his home and met his wife and four year old son. He performed his duties properly and never presented any problems. A few years later he would be lost at sea when an ore ship, that he was serving on, went down with all hands, under unknown circumstances. There had been no indication of trouble before the tragedy.

The Portuguese Bosun on the SS T. J. Stevenson

Chinese/American Deck Maintenance Man (1952)

Chief Engineer George Thomas, from Fair Lawn, N. J., was a family man in his mid-fifties. He ran a good department. I later visited his home and met his wife. By coincidence, he had a brother, Ben Thomas, who was a Panama Canal Pilot. Five years later, I would work with him in the Panama Canal.

First Assistant Engineer Neil Thomas (no kin to George) was a vigorous man in his late forties. He was a little over six feet tall and was about thirty pounds overweight. But he was not flabby at all. Neil was an excellent engineer and would later serve with me on other ships. He was not married.

Second Assistant Engineer Alex Bentsen was in his early thirties and was very fair in complexion. Like the others, he was a good man all around. Alex was not married.

Donald Taylor was the Third Assistant Engineer. He was a fine widower gentleman about sixty-five years old. He was very quiet and minded his own business.

The Chief Steward was a Filipino, about fifty years old, by the name of Cornelio Bayubay. He had been with Stevenson Lines for some years and did a good job.

Among the unlicensed crew, the ones that stand out in my memory are the Bosun, who was a resident alien from Portugal, and the Deck Maintenance Man, who was an American citizen of Chinese descent. The Bosun was a huge bear of man, about six feet four inches tall and weighing about 240 pounds. There was not an ounce of fat on his frame and he was always ready for hard duty.

By contrast, the Deck Maintenance Man was small but muscular and probably weighed no more that 120 pounds. He was also very industrious and was very competent in many seamanship skills.

So, that was my cast of characters on the *SS T. J. Stevenson.* Except for taking vacations, all except Chief Mate Bunting, would remain with me for the entire additional two years that this ship was to operate for this Company.

First Voyage

Norfolk, New York, Praia (Terceira Island Azores), Gibraltar, Genoa, Trieste, Sibenik, Philadelphia, New York

Having traveled by train from my home in Sedalia, MO, I joined the *SS T. J. Stevenson* at the Norfolk Army Base on Friday, November 14, 1952. As had been my previous experiences here, I was required to walk from the entry gate to the ship, carrying my luggage and sextant.

The ship had returned from Europe in ballast (empty of cargo) and was in the process of loading general cargo for the U. S. Military. There was no longer sufficient Stevenson Lines cargo business to keep the five Company-owned ships occupied so they were seeking other cargoes for their vessels. The ship was now time-chartered to the U. S. Military.

I first had conference meetings/discussions with my key personnel, such as Chief Mate Bunting, Chief Engineer Thomas and Chief Steward Bayubay. They all gave an excellent first impression. It was clear that I had inherited a good crew.

Our local agent was still Hasler & Son and they were still doing their "thing" efficiently, albeit on a low budget. Although they were very busy men, Robert Hasler, Sr., and Robert Hasler, Jr., always had time for a little personal conversation and they were very interesting guys.

Mr. Herbert Green, the Port Steward for T. J. Stevenson & Co., Inc., was on hand to oversee our taking of voyage stores. He had great confidence in our ship's Chief Steward, Mr. Cornelio Bayubay.

Bunker "C" prices in New York were considerably lower than in Norfolk, so after completing loading, we sailed on Thursday, November 20, 1952, to New York, taking arrival at Scotland Light Vessel the next day. My notes show that the wind was on our starboard quarter, Beaufort Force 4-5. We anchored off Staten Island and our fuel was delivered by barge.

The passage data: Distance 228 miles, Speed 10.1 knots, Slip plus 3.4%, RPM 57.2, Barrels per mile 0.725, Mean Departure Draft 28' 9".

One of the advantages of sailing on tramp freighters was that you got to "see the world". It also meant, if you were in charge of the safe navigation, that you had to continually study and learn the approaches and regulations of many different ports. Our first port of discharge this voyage was to be Praia, Terceira Island, Azores.

So, I obtained and studied charts and Sailing Directions for the Azores and particularly, Terceira Island. The U. S. had constructed and was operating an important Air Base in this location. The port of Praia, if you can call it a port, was a small village in the middle of the east coast of the Island. There was a shallow indent in the coast, that hardly rated being called a "bay", and that was the location where ships anchored to discharge cargo into barges. The water was very deep right up to the shore, so it was not good "holding ground". Shelter from the wind and sea was only provided from SSW around through west to NNW. If the wind blew from any other direction, you would have to get underway quickly to avoid being blown ashore.

Terceira Island

We arrived and anchored on Tuesday, 12/2/52. My notes state that we had better than average weather for the time of year, but our low average speed and large positive slip for the passage indicate that we had some storms

The passage data: Distance 2.163 miles, Speed 9.75 knots, Slip plus 12.3%, RPM 57.8, Barrels per mile 0.755, Mean Departure Draft 27' 5".

During our time at anchor, we experienced excellent weather. The wind was blowing from the west which gave us the lee of the land. Although I anchored as close as I dared to the shore, the water was over 100 feet deep and the bottom sloped sharply downward from there. I put out seven shots of anchor chain (each shot was 15 fathoms or 90 feet), to guard against dragging anchor. The coast of the island rose in high bluffs, abruptly from the sea, pretty much everywhere. The vegetation was plentiful and was a beautiful green. Obviously, the island received adequate rainfall.

The Azores Islands belong to Portugal and our Agent was, of course, Portuguese. He was anxious to practice his English, so he paid an extensive visit to my ship, to converse about a wide range of subjects.

I was invited by the U. S. Army Officer, in charge of the cargo discharge operations, to visit the Officers Club and PX at the Base. So, I went ashore, intending to have dinner there. In the PX, I ended up buying a Leica IIIf rangefinder camera, and a couple of additional lenses, at what was considered to be a bargain price. The problem was that I only had $1.13 left after the purchase, so I was going to miss supper. Since there was nothing much to lose, I put all of my left-over change into a slot machine. Amazingly, my very last dime hit the jackpot, winning twenty-three dollars (in dimes). So, my luck was fantastic and I was able to buy a fine meal at the Officer's Club.

Our cargo discharging operations went well, especially when you consider that we had to discharge into relatively small barges, in what was almost the open and unprotected Atlantic Ocean, and we could only work cargo during daylight hours. We were finished in five days. We heaved up the anchor and got underway on Sunday, 12/7/52, for Gibraltar, where we were scheduled to refuel.

We had very good weather on our passage to Gibraltar and arrived there on Thursday, 12/11/52.

The passage data: Distance 1,049 miles, Speed 10.84 knots, Slip plus 9.3%, RPM 59.9, Barrels per mile 0.705, Mean Departure Draft 26' 0".

Gibraltar

There were several old Shell Oil Company Tankers, anchored in Gibraltar Bay, to serve as refueling stations. Soon after our arrival, a British Pilot boarded to direct our maneuvers to go alongside one of the hulks. The berthing was expertly done and the fueling operation was efficient. We were ready in a few hours to proceed. There was no shore leave allowed in either Gibraltar, nor in the adjoining Spanish territory. We took departure later that day, on 12/11/52, bound for Genoa, Italy.

My notes show that we had following wind and sea and that we proceeded west of the Balearic Islands. We arrived in Genoa Monday, 12/15/52.

The passage data: Distance 852 miles, Speed 10.84 knots, Slip plus 6.8%, RPM 60.4, Barrels per mile 0.693, Mean Departure Draft 27' 5".

Genoa

Genoa is a very interesting place. It was Columbus' home town and the house that he was believed to have lived in is open for tourists to inspect. The old city comes right down to the water front and it is only a short taxi ride from the docks to where it gets interesting.

I met, for the first time, Mr. Harold Vinick, Stevenson Line's rep in Genoa. He seemed to be very "Ivy League" and reserved in his manners. I got the impression that he had been a good friend of Captain Venetia, the fired Captain who I had replaced, and that he (Mr. Vinick) resented me taking his place.

During Mussolini's time, the port facilities in Genoa were greatly expanded, with the new and very large docks being given the names of some of his "conquests". We berthed at the Ethiopia Dock, which was next to the similar Eritrea and Somalia Docks. A huge breakwater protects the port. It would otherwise be completely exposed to southerly winds and seas. We discharged here about half of our remaining general cargo.

The food and drink here were exceptionally good and the sidewalk cafes were delightful.

I had purchased an English-Italian dictionary and was learning to converse a little in the local lingo. The people were extremely friendly, especially the ladies, and many romances occurred.

Christmas was just ahead and the people were getting ready for it. Italy did not have the buying and giving frenzy that seems to attack the U. S. at this time of year. Christmas was more of a religious occasion.

Genoa Harbor, Old Section (1952)

SS Andrea Doria, which was sunk 7/15/56 in a collision with the Swedish MV Stockholm. Of the 1,200 passengers and 500 crew members, 1,660 survived.

We finished discharging the cargo for Genoa and departed on Thursday, 12/18/52, bound for Trieste. I still could not name the country for this port, because it still had not been decided whether it should go to Italy or to Yugoslavia.

We steamed past the island of Stromboli, which was a spectacular sight. It is essentially a symmetrically shaped and smoking volcanic mountain, rising right out of the ocean.

This would be my first passage through the Straits of Messina, which requires some radical course changes, while meeting opposing traffic. But it provided interesting scenery.

After we rounded the south end of the Italian Boot, and started north in the Adriatic Sea, the topography changed

The Italian Island of Stomboli (1952)

radically. The east coast of Italy is low and flat, with relatively shallow coastal waters, and the opposite, facing west coasts of Greece, Albania and Yugoslavia, are mountainous with deep coastal water.

Trieste

We experienced strong headwinds the last day but otherwise the weather was good for this passage. We arrived at the Trieste breakwater at 1030 on Thursday, 12/23/52. The passage data: Distance 1,147 miles, Speed 10.14 knots, Slip plus 11.6%, RPM 59.4, Barrels per mile 0.746, Mean Departure Draft 26' 3".

The city/port of Trieste is located at the northeast corner of the Adriatic Sea, opposite Venice, which is located at the northwest corner. For a very long time it was part of the Austro-Hungarian Empire and was awarded to Italy after World War I. Tito's Yugoslavia was staking claim to it and Italy wanted to keep it. The population was overwhelmingly of Italian extraction and spoke the Italian language. Yugoslav troops occupied territory right up to and including sub-urbs of the city. A contingent of British Troops were stationed on the Italian side to maintain the status quo. The U. S. and the British supported Trieste going to Italy, if for no other reason, to prevent the further spread of communism. The situation was tense. Stevenson Lines had been shipping tanks and other military hardware to both sides for some time.

We were obviously going to spend the Christmas holidays here and cargo discharge was going to be slow, or nil, for many days. It turned out that we would also still be here for the New Years holiday and beyond. The thirteen days that we were to spend here gave us time to explore the places of interest and enjoy the local culture.

Third Mate Tony Koerner talked me into attending, with him, a presentation of Wagner's "Twilight of the Gods", at the Trieste Opera House. The theater was very old and had proud tra-ditions. Unfortunately, the seats were sized for the population as it existed a hundred or so years ago and were too tight a fit for both Tony and me. This was opening night and we were about the only men in attendance not wearing tuxedos. Most of those tuxedos had spent much time stored in mouth balls, and the stench of them was overpowering. This opera lasts for five hours. We made a break for it at the intermission. I believe that the performance was most likely good. It was put on by a German Opera Company and was sung in German. The audience, except for us, seemed to enjoy it.

Our cargo here, on the rare days that it was being worked, was being discharged with very old electric shore cranes. They were barely tall enough for the task and for the last several days, we had to put an ever increasing list on the ship, toward the dock, so that the cranes could reach over the rail and into the cargo holds. This made on-board living rather unpleasant and, as it turned out, caused a bad personal inconvenience. I had purchased, in a shop, a large wheel of Gorgonzola cheese and placed it in my small personal refrigerator in my back room. This reefer did not have a compressor and, instead, used electricity to heat and cause gas to circulate in a cooling cycle. Unbeknown to me, it did not work when it was not level. When I opened my

Superb British Troops in Trieste (1952)
Their presence prevented Yugoslavia from taking the city.

reefer a couple of weeks later, the smell of spoiled Gorgonzola cheese was remarkable, to say the least. My reefer box had to be taken out on deck to air out and the cheese went over the side.

This run that our ship was on, to the Mediterranean ports, was called "the romance run". The young ladies, particularly in Italy, but also in Spain, France, Greece and Turkey, were very desirable and many were also "available". Being a normal male, I was looking forward to participating in this bounty, but I did not intend to get serious with any of these girls. Generally speaking, the ones that I would meet, under casual circumstances, would not be the kind of girls that I would want to introduce to my parents.

In spite of my resolve, I fell hard for a beauty that I met in Trieste. Her name was Ana and she was gorgeous, vivacious and smart. She was twenty-three years old and recently divorced, from a husband who had abused her. Her beauty was so exquisite that I have trouble trying to describe her. She was about five feet six inches tall and about 120 pounds. Her hair was jet black, shoulder length and almost straight. Her face was slightly heart shaped, with finely chiseled features, and with full lips. Her complexion was fair, with no visible blemishes. She had blue eyes, which is not unusual for northern Italians. She was fluent in English and spoke it with a cute little Italian accent. And of course, she was fantastic as a bed partner. If I was designing the "perfect girl" from scratch, I don't know how I could improve on Ana. I had met her in a night club on Christmas Eve and so I got to enjoy her company for ten full days. She worked as a receptionist for a medical doctor. She seemed taken with me as much as I was with her. We both wanted our relationship to continue, so we agreed that she would travel to meet me in the various ports in Italy, that my ship might come to in the future.

As our cargo discharge in Trieste was nearing completion, I received orders from T. J. Stevenson & Co., Inc., to proceed to Sibenik, Yugoslavia, to take on a cargo of about 4,000 tons of chrome ore.

This was a port that none of us had ever heard of and, of course, we did not have charts or sailing directions for it. Sibenik is located in about the mid-position of the Yugoslav coast. I was able to obtain Italian charts locally for the approaches to the port, but no Sailing Directions. The charts were not up to the U. S. Hydrographic Office, or British Admiralty, standards and were not large scale. Never-the-less, they would have to do. The option to refuse the order was not on the table.

On Monday, 1/5/53, we departed Trieste and proceeded south along the coast to the entry to Sibenik Bay. The weather was stormy with headwinds and frequent rain showers. Since we now had no cargo in the ship, the wind affected us greatly. I was wishing, especially after dark, that I had that beautiful radar that I had enjoyed on the *SS Waltham Victory*. But we would have to do without that great aid to navigation. It was almost a day's run against the wind.

About 1500 on Tuesday, 1/6/53, we had reached a position opposite the entry to Sibenik. It was blowing hard from the south and raining almost continually. There was a scattering of small islands, on each side of a torturous channel, to the narrow entry to the large and deep bay, where the port was located. Sibenik was also the site of Yugoslavia's principal Naval Base, which is probably why no large scale charts were available. To my delighted surprise, I sighted the Pilot Boat. It was out braving this weather, and I proceeded to where it was hove-to.

I made a lee for the Pilot Boat and the Pilot climbed up our now very long pilot ladder. He was shown to the bridge, where I greeted him with a handshake and a cup of hot coffee. He was the first Montenegrin man that I had met, and man, was he impressive! He was at least six and a half feet tall and seemed very competent and commanding in his manner. His long black overcoat, and navy-style hat, tended to make his presence even more commanding. The ship's Agent and the boss Stevedore here were also Montenegrins, and were also about six and a half feet tall. I had encountered a race of "giants".

Sibenik

The Pilot was very expert and directed our maneuver through the narrow entrance to the bay and alongside a very long bulkhead pier, port side to the dock. He did not have any tug boats available to assist him, and he used an anchor skillfully to enable the safe berthing of our ship in this windy situation. He did the docking maneuver very quickly, so that we could finish before dark. I learned from watching how he used the anchor and would later copy his method in some of my own dockings. I was later told that his "nickname" was "Captain No Tugboats".

Entrance to Sibenik Bay, with City in Distance
Tourism Picture from Internet

The passage data: Distance 183 miles, Speed 9.25 knots, Slip plus 21.8%, RPM 61.3, Barrels per mile 0.754, Mean Departure Draft 10' 11".

Sibenik Bay is beautiful and surprisingly large. The entrance was only about five hundred feet wide with high bluffs on each side. The bay extended about a mile to the south and about five miles north from the entry channel. It was about half a mile wide in this area, but much wider farther north. The port was opposite the entry and it had a long bulkhead pier, about two thousand feet long. The landscape was rugged, hilly and very rocky, with only a few smallish trees. The population of the city was, I would estimate, about 20,000.

Yugoslavia was made up of six provinces which, alto they had a long history of conflict with each other, were held together by the iron fist communist rule of Marshal Tito. Sibenik was located in the province of Dalmatia, which included most of the coastal area of the country. It did not extend inland very far and was sparsely populated.

There was a smattering of Montenegrins in Sibenik, who stood out because of their size, and a pitiful minority of ethic Italians, who were very much oppressed by the Yugoslavs. They

177.

Climbing Sibenik Hill
Chief Mate Bill Bunting (left) Third Mate Tony Koerner (right) (1953)

were still very angry over Italy's conduct under Mussolini.

There was a beautiful old Catholic Cathedral here that had been completed in 1532, after being under construction for over 100 years. Third Mate Tony Koerner was Catholic, and he established a rapport with the Head Priest, who showed us around. The communist government discouraged religious activities, so the congregation was small. There was also a large, also mostly unattended, Orthodox Church in the town

There were the ruins of a very old castle on top of the hill, overlooking the city. Chief Mate Bunting, Third Mate Koerner and I climbed the hill to inspect it. When we reached the top, we found that it was difficult and dangerous to scale the wall. Neither the Venetian or Turkish Armies had been able to breech these walls. The view from the top made the climb worth the effort.

The Author scaling the old Castle Wall above Sibenik (1953)

178.

View of Sibenik Bay from Old Castle above Sibenik (1953)
One of our "Guides" posing in foreground

The only adequate restaurant in the city was in the Hotel Krka, which was named after the river that empties into the Bay at this location. The Manager spoke English and was very friendly. I asked him what were the points of interest that we should see while here. He suggested that we hire a bus to take a group of us to the Krka Water Falls, where we could roast a suckling pig, and have a fine picnic. He offered to make all of the arrangements, for a reasonable price, and we agreed to do it on the following Sunday.

So, since no cargo was to be worked on Sunday, we left only the duty watch officers on shipboard duty, and the rest of the Officers and I boarded a bus for the trip. It was about a six kilometer trip up the river to the spectacular rapids and falls, that are called the Krka Water Falls. This was a fantastic tourism site and we, and our Yugoslav cook and bus driver, had it all to ourselves.

The weather was perfect for our outing and I took a number of photographs. I was getting good use from the Leica camera that I had purchased at the U. S. Military PX at Terceira Island in the Azores, earlier on this voyage. The 35mm slides that I took, using Kodachrome or Ansco-chrome film are still good, after more than fifty years of indifferent storage conditions. The Ektachrome ones have shifted color balance and have not lasted very well.

Krka Waterfalls six kilometers upriver from Sibenik (1953)

The suckling pig was delicious, and we all had a great time. We also discovered that some of the Yugoslav wine was not too bad.

In the Hotel Krka, I became acquainted with a Yugoslav named Ivan. He was in his mid-twenties and wanted to practice his English. He invited me to go sailing with him in Sibenik Bay. His father owned a sailboat and would not mind us using it. It was agreed that he would bring the sailboat alongside our ship the following afternoon, and I would provide a basket lunch for four. Ivan was going to bring his girl friend, who sang at the local Opera House, and she would bring a friend (also a singer at the Opera House) to be my date.

It went as planed and again, we had perfect weather and had a great time. I took many pictures, which could have gotten me in trouble with the authorities. After a few hours of sailing around, they delivered me back to the ship. The young ladies did not speak any English, which was a bit awkward. They were living in a communist country, and so did not have any make-up or nice clothes. One thing that I hadn't considered before was that American, and many West European girls, must shave under their arms. These girls had a heavy clump of hair under their arms, which I found to be repulsive.

I didn't see Ivan again in town because, unbeknown to me, he was in jail. When they returned to the yacht moorings, the police arrested him and the girls, and interrogated them intently. They were asked if I had had a cigarette lighter, and when the answer was yes, the police told them that it might be a spy camera, and I might be trying to photograph the Yugoslav Naval Facilities. They didn't mention to the police that I had a regular camera with me, and was taking pictures openly. That would have gotten them into real trouble. Our ship would come back to Sibenik in about eight months and, at that time, Ivan would tell me about these things.

Sailing in Sibenik Bay, 1953. Shown is a new military installation that I was not supposed to photograph.

The Author's Yugoslav Friend, Ivan (1953) Sailing in Sibenik Bay. SS T. J. Stevenson in background

The chrome ore was loaded into our ship, using our ship's gear, with locally supplied grab buckets, that picked it out of railroad cars. The ore remaining after the grab buckets picked up all they could, was then shoveled by hand into big buckets. The track ran close alongside the berth. During the loading process, quite a bit of ore was spilled onto the ground around the railroad cars. A work gang was brought out to pick up the ore dropping. This work gang consisted of all women laborers, with a man foreman. The following photograph shows them in action. The fore**man** was not observed to do any work.

Yugoslav Women Work Gang with a (non-working) Male Foreman (1953)

As you can tell from this narrative, Sibenik had been an interesting port to visit. The people were stoic, but friendly to us, and seemed anxious to make a good impression on the Americans.

We had actually loaded almost 6,000 long tons of chrome ore, instead of the 4,000 that had first been proposed. To avoid having the ship be too stiff in the seaway, I had several hundred tons loaded into number three and four 'tween decks. This portion had to be trimmed, so as not to shift during rolling. The 6,000 tons would have easily fit into the lower holds, but that would have caused a dangerous rapid rolling motion in a seaway.

Prior to sailing from all foreign ports, we routinely searched for stowaways in such places as the store rooms, under the lifeboat covers, and in the steering gear room. In Sibenik, the local police came aboard, and searched with us, being sure that we were thorough. They probably knew that some of the oppressed local Italians would attempt to escape this communist "paradise" in this manner. Sure enough, five of them were found, and marched off to some dire future consequences. We were sorry for them but could not help.

The cargo was all aboard and we sailed from Sibenik on Monday, 1/12/53, bound for Philadelphia. Captain "No Tug Boats" came aboard and skillfully directed our undocking and exit from the Bay, and until we were clear of the restrictive outer approach channels. It had been a delightful six-day stay in this port.

My notes show that we had better weather than average for the time of year. However, the slow speed and high slip percentage for the passage indicate that we had our share of stormy weather. We proceeded east of Vis, west of Caza, and via the Messina Straits. The farthest south we went in the Atlantic Ocean was 34 degrees and 58 minutes north. We arrived at the Five Fathom Light Vessel, enroute to Philadelphia, on Tuesday, 2/3/53.

The passage data: Distance 4,936 miles, Speed 9.63 knots, Slip plus 17.0%, RPM 58.0, Barrels per mile 0.647, Mean Departure Draft 22' 5 1/2".

Philadelphia

We proceeded to a discharge berth and immediately started unloading the chrome ore, using shore cranes. While we were discharging, we had our voyage payoff, but did not sign new foreign articles, because we were due to be drydocked for hull and other inspections. This was necessary to keep the ship "in class" with the American Bureau of Shipping (ABS). No profitable cargo and no charter were immediately available. We had a happy ship, and most of the crew and all of the officers, signed coastwise articles, all hoping that the ship would continue to operate. We only took a limited amount of fresh stores (milk, bread, etc.).

Our cargo discharge took four days and we then departed Philadelphia, in the wee hours of Saturday, 2/7/53, for New York. We arrived at Scotland Light Vessel later that same day, after a difficult passage. We had dense fog and heavy traffic, and had to proceed with various slow and stop bells, as we listened for whistle signals. Most of the other ships had radar, but we did not, and so had to navigate in fog "the old fashion way".

The passage data: Distance 129 miles, Speed 8.84 knots, Slip plus 8.5%, RPM 51.7, Barrels per mile 0.504, Mean Departure Draft 9' 5".

Second Voyage
New York, Norfolk, New York, Rijeka, Pula, Genoa, Savona, New York
New York

We proceeded to a lay pier to await our turn in the drydock, which came after a day or two. All of the unlicensed crew was laid off and only the Captain, Chief Mate, Chief Engineer, First Assistant Engineer and Chief Steward were kept on the payroll. The boilers were secured and, since the weather was cold, we had to move to a hotel during this time. We commuted to and from the ship by taxi for duty.

The laid-off officers were told to keep in touch, as they would be called back to work as soon as the ship came out of the drydock, provided a cargo or charter could be found.

All necessary repairs and upgrades were completed and we came out of drydock on 2/15/53. The boilers were fired up and the ship was crewed up. We got all of our former officers and most of our old unlicensed crew back from the various union halls. We took voyage stores and signed foreign articles. On Tuesday, 2/17/53, we sailed for Norfolk.

The passage data: Distance 228 miles, Speed 11.52 knots, Slip plus 2.5%, RPM 61.2, Barrels per mile 0.729, Mean Departure Draft 10' 6".

Norfolk

We arrived on Wednesday, 2/18/53, and proceeded to the Norfolk Army Base, where we commenced to load military cargo, including light army tanks for Yugoslavia. On the previous voyage, we had delivered similar ones to Italy. They worked all five hatches 24 hours per day. We loaded mostly military trucks and tanks, so the ship filled up fast. It was very important that they were all firmly lashed and chocked in place, particularly the tanks. They were classified as being "light" tanks, but they weighed in at about five tons each. We sure did not want them shifting back and forth during rolling at sea.

On 2/19/53, we sailed for New York, where we were scheduled load additional cargo and to take full bunkers, since our cargo did not have much weight. We proceeded at reduced speed, so as to time our arrival in New York at a time convenient for the scheduled operations. We arrived at Scotland Light Vessel on 2/20/53. We proceeded to Port Newark to load more military cargo. Our fuel was delivered by barge. We felt lucky to have jobs since the shipping industry was obviously in quite a slump.

The passage data: Distance 228 miles, Speed 8.67 knots, Slip minus 5.6%, RPM 44.5, Barrels per mile 0.531, Mean Departure Draft 20' 0".

New York

On Wednesday, 2/25/53, we sailed from New York, with our first discharge port scheduled to be Rijeka, Yugoslavia.

This was to be a crossing during the height of the winter-time storms, so we had to double check all cargo lashings. My notes show that we were actually very lucky this passage with the weather.

Due to a problem in the Boiler Room, we had to steam on one boiler for 22 hours, but then Chief Engineer Thomas, and his gang, got the errant boiler back on line. We proceeded south of Sicily, west of Caza, east of Vis, close along the Yugoslav islands between Lussino and Unie, and close west of Levrera. We arrived in Rijeka on 3/16/53, which was my 28th birthday. I did not mention the BD to anyone.

The passage data: Distance 4,866 miles, Speed 10.88 knots, Slip plus 1.5%, RPM 59.6, Barrels per mile 0.628, Mean Departure Draft 25' 0".

Rijeka

This was Yugoslavia's most important seaport and, in 1953, had a population that I would estimate at about 150,000. It was located at the north end of the Adriatic Sea, on the opposite side of the Istrian Peninsula from Trieste. It had been an important seaport since medieval times. It was in the Yugoslav province of Croatia.

We proceeded to a pier and discharged vehicles. On Tuesday, 3/17/53, which was St. Patrick's Day (but not celebrated here), we left Rijeka and sailed for the much more interesting port of Pula, which is located on the west coast of the Istrian Peninsula.

The passage data: Distance 52 miles, Speed 10.61 knots, Slip plus 12.3%, RPM 54.2, Barrels per mile 0.596, Mean Departure Draft 24' 6"

Pula (formerly Pola)

Pula was at this time being used exclusively as a military port/base for an expected conflict with Italy over the disposition of Trieste. We discharged our tanks here. They were similar to ones that we had previously unloaded in Italy.

What made Pula such an interesting place were the Roman ruins. There was a smaller version of the Coliseum of Rome here that was in amazingly good condition. I could not believe

Roman Coliseum in Pula, Yugoslavia (1953)

that I had never heard of it. All of the world should be beating a path here to see these magnificent 2,000 year old ruins.

My Kodachrome slides taken in 1953 are still excellent after being kept in indifferent storage for over fifty years. One of them is reproduced here.

There were no local guides available to show us around and there were no pamphlets available to tell about the ruins. No one was guarding them against vandalism or theft. We and anyone else were free to wander among these ruins freely. And, of course, there were no regular tourists there to see them. This touristic treasure was going to waste. What a shame!!!

The shore personnel that I dealt with here were all uniformed Yugoslav military officers. It appeared that only a few civilians lived here. Everyone was polite but reserved.

In two days, we had finished discharging the tanks and sailed on Thursday, 3/19/53, for, guess where, Genoa, Italy, to discharge military hardware for the other side.

My notes show that we had excellent weather and a calm sea. We proceeded west of Jabuka, between Pianosa and Pelagosa, via Messina Straits, west of Stromboli, close west of Plarola, east of Giannutri, Giglio, Elba, Palmaila and Gorgona.

The passage data: Distance 1,061 miles, Speed 11.45 knots, Slip plus 0.47%, RPM 59.8, Barrels per mile 0.586, Mean Departure Draft 22' 10 1/2".

Genoa and Savona

It was a great relief to be back among the Italians, who were unreservedly friendly.

I had sent a radiogram to Ana in Trieste to see if she could come over to Genoa for a visit. Of course, I had been much closer to her when in Rijeka, but travel between Italy and Yugoslavia was not allowed. I was delighted to find that she was in a hotel waiting for me. She was as beautiful as ever, and it was sure good to see her. I had a strict rule that no ladies were to be allowed aboard and, of course, I had to follow my own rule. I did not neglect any duties, but when free, I spent a lot of time with Ana in town.

The cargo that we had for Genoa was discharged in two days, and we then moved eighteen miles south, to the port of Savona on Wednesday, 3/25/53. Ana moved to a hotel there. We were to spend five days in Savona. The weather was pleasant and Ana had found a hotel on the water that had its own private beach. The weather was too cool to go swimming, but the beach was pretty to look at. It seemed sinful to be drawing a salary while enjoying life so much. Of course, all of his enjoyment was costing considerable money, but it seemed to be worth it.

My paradise came to an abrupt end on Monday, 3/30/53. Our cargo was all discharged. I bid a sad farewell to Ana, and we sailed for New York.

My notes state that we proceeded west of the Balearic Islands. As we were approaching the U. S., we had a very severe westerly gale, off St. Georges Bank, for three days.

We arrived at Ambrose Light Vessel, enroute to New York, on Saturday, 4/18/53.

The passage data: Distance 4,508 miles, Speed 9.77 knots, Slip plus 9.91%, RPM 56.99, Barrels per mile 0.6074, Mean Departure Draft 11' 4".

Third Voyage

New York, Norfolk, Praia, Vila do Porto, Rijeka, Istanbul, Derince, New York

New York

Our U. S. Military Time Charter was being continued and we were all pleased to still have employment.

We proceeded to Port Newark, where we were to load more military trucks and light tanks. We conducted our voyage payoff, stored for the next voyage, and signed foreign articles.

On 4/22/53, we sailed for Norfolk, and arrived at Cape Henry on Friday, 4/24/53. My notes show that we had headwinds Beaufort Force 5 to 7.

The passage data: Distance 230 miles, Speed 8.05 knots, Slip plus 27.22%, RPM 57.4, Barrels per mile 0.765, Mean Departure Draft 13' 6".

Norfolk

We proceeded on arrival to the Norfolk Army Base, where we again loaded military cargo, both general cargo and more vehicles. The cargo operations took three days and then we sailed for Praia, Terceira Island, Azores, which was to be our first port of discharge. My notes show that we had mostly following wind and sea.

The Norfolk stevedores had not done a good job of lashing and chocking the vehicles in place. Some of the so called "light" tanks, which weighed about five tons, broke loose and started sliding back and forth in Number 2 and Number 3 'tween decks, as we rolled in the seaway.

This was a very serious problem and could result in them knocking the side out of the ship if we could not secure them. Our crew had to enter the cargo areas through the mast houses, and had to rig portable cluster lights in the 'tween decks, to see to work. Fortunately, we were not taking any seas on deck. I changed our course and reduced speed to minimize rolling, and fortunately, was able to almost eliminate it. With the rolling pretty well stopped, the crew was able to attach new lashings, with turnbuckles, to the ship's side and from one tank to the next. This took the efforts of all of the deck crew for many hours. Our big powerful Portuguese Bosun distinguished himself greatly during this effort.

Chief Mate Bunting oversaw operations in #2 'tween deck while Second Mate Koller was in charge in #3 'tween deck. We had to work both locations at the same time since either one could have resulted in us losing the ship. Third Mate Koerner and I stayed on the bridge. He steered, so that the AB/Helmsman could assist with the work in the 'tween decks. We could sure have used "walkie talkie" radios to communicate, but they were some years in the future

When we had things under control, we again resumed an easterly course toward our first port of discharge. The rolling that then ensued caused the tanks in #2 hatch to again break loose, so we had to hove to again so as to chock and lash them another time. By the time we were again secured, we had a very exhausted deck crew. Chief Mate Bunting was doubtful that the lashings would hold, so I maintained the northerly course, on slow speed, for minimal rolling, for another eight hours, so that everybody could get rested up in case we had to go through the routine again.

It was fortunate that I did this because, when we again set an easterly course, heavy rolling occurred, and once again the tanks in #2 'tween deck were sliding back and forth. I hove to again, and our now rested and experienced crew went back into the cargo compartment, and renewed the lashing and chocking operation. Fortunately, steering a northerly course pretty well eliminated the rolling.

Azores

On Tuesday, 5/5/53, we arrived at **Praia** and anchored. The wind was now blowing from the west, so we had the lee of the land and were able to discharge our cargo for this port into barges.

The passage data: Distance 2.341 miles, Speed 8.41 knots, Slip plus 2.78%, RPM 54.08, Barrels per mile 0.635, Mean Departure Draft 18' 7".

We discharged general cargo onto the barges in Praia for two days without any problems. The wind continued to be from the west which gave us smooth seas at the anchorage.

Now that were could open the hatches, and see to work properly, we finished securing the tanks in place in #2 and #3 'tween decks, being damn sure this time that they were not going to shift again.

As soon as our cargo operations here were finished, we proceeded on Thursday, 5/7/53, to our next Azores port, **Vila do Porto**, arriving there at daybreak the following morning.

The passage data: Distance 139 miles, Speed 11.97 knots, Slip plus 1.42%, RPM 63, Barrels per mile 0.712, Mean Departure Draft 16' 9".

Our cargo for Vila do Porto, on Santa Maria Island, had to be discharged at another open roadstead anchorage. It was even less protected than Praia. If you anchored in as close as safety allowed, you would only have the lee of the land from WNW through north to ENE. It would take a lot of luck to have the wind only blow from these directions.

The cargo would have to be discharged into "ducks", amphibious trucks that could drive right up on the beach, and to where they wanted the cargo.

We were fantastically lucky with the weather in Vila do Porto. The wind stayed northerly for the entire nine days that we needed to unload the cargo for this port. Even though we had the lee of the land, the water was still choppy enough to cause the "ducks" to bounce around quite a bit when alongside the ship.

Bearing WNW from our anchored ship at Via do Porto. Our only lee was from WNW thru North to ENE.

This was a very dangerous anchorage and I kept alert sea watches, with the engine on standby, for immediate use if needed. We kept a close watch on the barometer and wind direction, and took frequent anchor bearings to be sure we were not drifting. There was no shore leave allowed here and even the "ducks" had a rough time proceeding onto the beach with their loads from the ship.

The principal civilian airport for the Azores was located on Santa Maria Island. In those days, most planes did not have enough fuel capacity to allow them to fly non-stop from the U. S. to Europe, so they stopped here to refuel.

Finally, on Sunday, 5/17/53, we finished discharging our cargo for Vila do Porto and happily heaved up the anchor and got safely away from this dangerous place.

Our next port was familiar to us, it was to be Rijeka, Yugoslavia, again. My notes show that we had excellent weather, proceeded via Messina Straits and Vis Channel. We arrived in Rijeka on Wednesday, 5/27/53.

The passage data: Distance 2,595 miles, Speed 11.61 knots, Slip plus 5.36%, RPM 63.76, Barrels per mile 0.646, Mean Departure Draft 15' 0".

Rijeka

We only had light tanks and military trucks to discharge here. I guess that it was so that the Yugoslavs could better prepare to fight Italy over Trieste. It only took one day to discharge them and we were on our way.

It was good to be able to stretch our legs on dry land here in Rijeka, after being afloat for so long. Some of the crew had old girl friends here, from our last voyage, to look up. It was also good to have a restaurant meal for a change. The exchange rate was favorable, which made meals and other things cheap for us. But, we only had one day and night to enjoy the pleasures, and then we were again on our way.

Our next port of discharge would be Istanbul, Turkey. Most Ship Captains picked a Pilot, in the Dardanelles, to direct the navigation through the Straits and the Sea of Marmara. Although this was my first time in these water, I had good charts and Sailing Directions, and did not see any need for this added expense and delay. I proceeded through the Dardanelles Straits and the length of the Sea of Marmara, to the approaches to Istanbul, on my own. I did not have any undue problems. We arrived at Istanbul at 0900 on Tuesday, 6/2/53.

The passage data: Distance 984 miles, Speed 11.23 knots, Slip plus 8.55%, RPM 63.81, Barrels per mile 0.612, Mean Departure Draft 13' 6".

Istanbul

We had a number of interesting events occur while here. We proceeded into the harbor and made our bow fast to a large mooring buoy. Barges were brought alongside to receive our cargo.

The first interesting event was the shock that I got when I saw the callous way, in which the Turkish stevedores, walked on top of nice new automobiles in our cargo, with their hobnail boots. They badly dented and scratched them, and seemed oblivious to the damage that they were doing. They must have all been raised in horse barns.

The second shock was the earthquake that we experienced. I didn't know how an earthquake would feel on a ship. I don't think that it was any different from how it felt ashore. There was a rumble and a heavy vibration that lasted about fifteen seconds. As earthquakes go in this part of the world, it was a mild one, with no appreciable damage.

The third shock was a pleasant one. The Turks were celebrating the five hundredth year since "liberating" Constantinople (now called Istanbul) from the Greeks. Each night while we were here, fireworks were fired from a barge in the Bosporus. A German pyrotechnic crew had been hired to manage the nightly displays. From our ship, we had a perfect and unobstructed view of the displays, which were truly spectacular.

Istanbul is very interesting city. The number one sight, in my opinion, is an old church, that I was mistakenly told was named St. Sofia's. To set the matter straight, I will reprint some tourist info that I found on the internet.

"Aya Sofya (known as Haghia Sofia in Greek and also called the Church of the Divine Wisdom) was regarded as the greatest church in Christendom up until the fall of Constantinople, when it was put back into service as a mosque. The edifice is crammed with fine mosaics and topped by a magnificent dome.

Exterior and Interior views of the Aya Sofya, completed in 537 AD.
The interior of the dome contains about a million golden tiles.

Aya Sofya was not named after a saint; its name means holy wisdom. It is called Sancta Sophia in Latin. Emperor Justinian (r. 527-65) had the church built as yet another effort to restore the greatness of the Roman Empire. It was completed in 537.

Examining the interior of the church is more a metaphysical than a physical experience. Visitors entering through the main entrance, via the low original steps, experience both a gradual sense of being drawn upwards and a sense of gloomy darkness being dispelled by the inner light of 30 million gold *tesserae* (mosaic tiles).

The dome is supported by 40 massive ribs constructed of special hollow bricks made in Rhodes from a unique light, porous clay, resting on huge pillars concealed in the interior walls.

It was through the Imperial Door that Mehmet the Conqueror came in 1453 to take possession for Islam of the greatest religious edifice in the world. Before he entered, historians tell us, he sprinkled earth on his head in a gesture of humility. Aya Sofya remained a mosque until 1935, when Atatürk proclaimed it a museum. It must be seen to be believed."

The dome of this old church has survived the hundreds of earthquakes that have occurred here since it was constructed. It is a true architectural wonder, and is believed to be the first large dome ever constructed in a building.

When the Turks took the city in 1453, thousands of Christians took refuge in the church. The Turks rode in on horseback and slaughtered them all. They waged war for keeps in those days. This was revenge for actions that the Crusaders had performed when they rampaged through the Near East.

I had dinner in a restaurant that featured "Belly Dancing". I had no idea that it was possible for the human belly to go through such gyrations. Of course, the young lady doing the dance was rather scantly clad in colorful silk veils, which tended to make the performance more eye catching.

One interesting side issue worth mentioning. The professional ladies of the evening, in Istanbul, shave everywhere except, of course, the top of their heads. At least, that is what I was told.

The author posing in front of the "Blue Mosque" in Istanbul. Aya Sofya is at the far right. (1953)

I met an interesting Turkish man, who was about thirty years old, in the bar at the Park Central Hotel. It was, at that time, the best hotel in town. He wanted to practice his English. He had just finished serving his required time in the Turkish Army, where he had been assigned as an interpreter for American soldiers that had been sent to Turkey. They were there to instruct how to use some military hardware that we were supplying to the Turks. Prior to that, he had worked for an American Oil Company, that was prospecting for oil in Asiatic Turkey.

He told Chief Engineer Thomas and me some interesting stories. One was that he had witnessed, in this very bar, the invention of the drink known at the "screwdriver". The American GI's could not afford the

Istanbul Harbor as seen from the Golden Horn.
SS T. J. Stevenson **in background.**

local price of American whiskey, or Scotch from the U. K., and they didn't like the popular local hard drink, Raki. So, they settled for Turkish Vodka, and mixed it with the local orange juice, which was plentiful, good and cheap. While searching for a proper name for the drink, with our new friend in the group, it was said that this was a "screwy drink but that it had a lot of drive". That was soon shortened to "screwdriver".

His second story was of more immediate interest to us. He knew and had worked for the Turkish Colonel who was in charge of the military port of Derince, where we were headed next. The Colonel, our friend told us, dealt severely with dissenters and trouble makers. Helicopters would take off with them aboard but would return without them after a short flight over the water.

Derince

Our next and final discharge port this voyage was to be Derince, Turkey. This was a Turkish military port in the southeastern corner of the Sea of Marmara. No large scale charts and no sailing directions were available, so I decided to order a Turkish Pilot, who would board us in Istanbul, and ride the ship to Derince.

We departed Istanbul on Saturday, 6/6/53, and arrived in Derince later that day. It was only about a fifty-mile run.

The port only had one dock, which was barely long enough for our ship. We saw no civilians here, only uniformed Turkish military officers and men.

The Colonel in charge of the port paid a courtesy call, which in turn led to some unusual events. As we had just heard, while in Istanbul, he enforced severe discipline, and that the enforcement included dropping trouble makers out the door of helicopters over the Sea of Marmara. So, he was both an interesting and dangerous person.

He came to call at about 1600, and Chief Engineer George Thomas and I entertained the Colonel in my back party room. We plied him with hors d'oeuvres and Scotch whiskey. He was an unusually small man, who had ram-rod straight posture. He spoke only a little English, but with almost no accent. He seemed very much aware of his own importance. His two body guards maintained an alert vigil in the alleyway, outside my office door. He was fiercely proud of his drinking capacity. The Colonel invited Chief Thomas and me to come to his Officer's Club for dinner that evening, and he was going to show us how to drink Raki, the local hard drink.

We dressed in our best suits and presented ourselves at the appointed time of 1900. The Club was expecting us and we got VIP treatment. The Colonel arrived about half an hour later, wearing his dress uniform, with all of his many metals and decorations. This little man was obviously quite a hero and a brave fellow. He had the objective of getting George and me drunk on Raki, but we were in good training for this sort of contest. The Colonel got drunk but we didn't. We ended up, after dinner, inviting him to come back aboard for a "night cap". He should have declined, but he accepted. Back in my party room, he had another drink, and was by now very drunk. He suddenly realized it, and was angry about it. I think that he thought that we had tricked him. He called out loudly to his two body guards, who then charged in through my quarters to his side. He was in no shape to walk. The two soldiers got, one on each side of him, and carried him out, keeping him in a vertical position. We had caused him to lose face, and we were sorry about that, but there was no way to repair the damage. We did not see him again.

We finished discharging our cargo in three days and left Derince on Tuesday, 6/9/53, bound for New York. This was to be a return voyage in ballast, but we could normally expect good weather this time of year. I again crossed the Sea of Marmara, and transited the Dardanelles Straits, without using Turkish Pilots.

Unfortunately, in the Atlantic, we encountered strong headwinds most of the time. The schedule became critical and, during the later part of the passage, we were ordered to make all possible speed. We therefore ran the engine wide open for the last five days.

For the first time since I had joined this ship, we were to load a full cargo for Stevenson Lines from their Hoboken Pier, bound for Mediterranean ports. We arrived at the Ambrose Light

Vessel at 0400 on Monday, 6/29/53. We immediately proceeded to the Stevenson pier and started loading cargo.

The passage data: Distance 5,004 miles, Speed 10.5 knots, Slip plus 10.45%, RPM 62.19, Barrels per mile 0.7056, Mean Departure Draft 12' 51/2".

Fourth Voyage

New York, Genoa, Naples, Tripoli, Casablanca, Dingwall, Baltimore
New York

This was to be my first interaction with Mr. Bill Hunt, who was the longtime Pier Superintendent for T. J. Stevenson & Co., Inc. He was in his mid-fifties and was the unquestioned boss of this operation. He was a bonafide "Mafia-type". He had to be to deal successfully with the crooked New Jersey water-front labor unions. There was a measured amount of stealing and pilferage expected and tolerated, so as to avoid much worse consequences. He monitored all of this and everything was done with his tacit approval. Surprisingly, he wore a suit, tie and a felt hat at all times, even when the summer heat made it uncomfortable. I had some run-ins with him regarding the deck cargo, but I got no satisfaction from him. Some of the more delicate items were being stowed on the foredeck, but should be put on the after deck, where they would be less likely to suffer damage from any seas that we took on deck. I had better luck dealing with the Stevedore Foreman, who was more cooperative.

We took a full load of general cargo, including a full deck load. Crossing the ocean while carrying deck cargo always worried me. If we should encounter a bad storm or a hurricane, severe cargo damage would be unavoidable. I got no sympathy from Mr. Bill Hunt, who told me that it was my job to get it to the destination, intact and in a timely manner. One good thing was that we would not be deeply laden this voyage, so the deck cargo would have a better chance of survival. Also, we would have summer-season weather.

We departed New York on Monday, 7/8/53, bound for Genoa. My notes show that we had excellent weather and that, in the Mediterranean, we proceeded west of the Balearic Islands. We arrived in Genoa on Wednesday, 7/27/53.

The passage data: Distance 4,048 miles, Speed 10.96 knots, Slip plus 5.02%, RPM 59.99, Barrels per mile 0.6583, Mean Departure Draft 21' 1".

Genoa

I had been corresponding by mail with Ana, in Trieste, two or three times per month. I was beginning to wonder if I could afford to have such a part-time mistress as her. I was getting the impression that her main object in life was to get the maximum amount of money from me. Several times she had written with sad stories and desperately needing funds, which I always sent. Anyway, since we were going to Genoa, I sent her a radiogram and invited her to meet me there, which she did.

Ana and I had an enjoyable time at the hotel and in the restaurants in Genoa, but it was clear that the hot romance had dimmed a bit. Our cargo discharge here only took one day and a half, and we were then bound for Napoli. We departed Genoa late on 7/25/53, and arrived at Naples early on Monday, 7/27/53.

My notes show that we had excellent weather and a calm sea. We proceeded east of Elba, west of Ischia and ran at reduced speed to time early daylight arrival in Naples.

The passage data: Distance 337 miles, Speed 10.15 knots, Slip plus 0.589%, RPM 54.6, Barrels per mile 0.5789, Mean Departure Draft 18' 5 1/2".

Naples

Ana took the train and was again waiting for me. She had found a hotel with a beautiful view of the harbor.

Naples is an interesting city, with a great museum, and has the nearby ruins of Pompeii and Herculeam. Our time in port was too short to do any sight-seeing this trip.

One thing that I disliked about Naples was the rampant corruption. The Boarding Officials were unusually greedy in their demands for cartons of cigarettes and bottles of whiskey. We had to hire a team of three local watchmen to keep thieves from hauling away everything that was not nailed down. The thieves here would even cut the ship adrift and steal the mooring lines, if you didn't keep constant 24-hour vigil.

After a day and a half, our Naples cargo was all discharged. Ana and I bid each other another sad farewell. Our time together this voyage had been too brief. We didn't say so, but we both knew that our romance had cooled considerably. I guess that is the natural way of things. I was sure that she had boy friend back in Trieste, which I didn't mind, but I resented having to support him.

My notes state that we still were having excellent weather for our passage from the Naples breakwater to the Tripoli breakwater. We proceeded west of Sicily. We had an early daylight arrival at Tripoli on Thursday, 7/30/53.

The passage data: Distance 503 miles, Speed 11.05 knots, Slip minus 0.61%, RPM 56.22, Barrels per mile 0.5784, Mean Departure Draft 17' 2". Negative slip is unusual. The ship went more miles than the engine had pushed her.

Tripoli

Tripoli is the capital of Libya, which had been a colony of Italy before WWII. The U. S. had established an airbase in Libya at Wheeler Field, and we had cargo that was destined for that base. At this time there was a King, but his government appeared to be ineffectual. In a few years Colonel Muammar al-Qadhafi would take over this impoverished and backward land, and demand that we pull our forces out of Libya.

In the old part of town, nearly all of the men wore Arab style clothing and all of the women were heavily veiled, with only their eyes visible

One of my crew members requested to see a Doctor because of stomach aches that he had been having. The Agent was able to get an appointment for him with one of the few Italian Doctors still practicing medicine here. I went with him and the Agent for the appointment. We were appalled at the conditions that we observed.

On one of the street corners, a dentist had set up practice. His only equipment appeared to be a chair and a pair of pliers. He should have been charging admission to the audience that was being entertained by his tooth extractions.

The Crewman needed to use a bathroom and the only public one that we could find was unbelievably foul. It was a room about six feet square with a hole in the middle of the floor, about eight inches in diameter. Many previous users had completely missed the hole and the stench was horrible. The Crewman decided that he could hold "it".

We waited in the Doctor's reception room for about half an hour with some of the worst smelling people imaginable. The Crewman decided that his ailment was not really so bad after all, and we returned to the ship without seeing the Doctor.

If you were able to get away from the riffraff, there were some interesting things to see here. Archaeologists had been busy uncovering massive Roman ruins from about 2,000 years ago. They were right in the middle of the city, so a lot of people had to be displaced to make the ruins available.

We only had a few tons of cargo to discharge here and it was all out in one day.

So we departed Tripoli late on Thursday, 7/30/53, the same date on which we had arrived. The remaining cargo that we had on board was for Casablanca. My notes show that we had strong headwinds for two days. We had five hours of dense fog going through the Straits of Gibraltar, while encountering heavy traffic.

Soon after leaving Tripoli, I received a radiogram from T. J. Stevenson & Co., Inc., instructing that I should take bunkers as needed in Casablanca, and proceed to Dingwall to load

King's Palace, Tripoli (1953)

gypsum.

The big question was, where in the world is Dingwall? I got out my book of ports and found a Dingwall in Scotland, but on the chart, it did not appear to be a sufficient port for our ship. So I radioed back and inquired the location of Dingwall. They replied that it is located on Cape Breton Island, in Nova Scotia. It turned out that we had no charts for that area, so I asked that they airmail some to Casablanca.

We arrived in Casablanca on Tuesday, 8/4/53.

The passage data: Distance 1,264 miles, Speed 10.91 knots, Slip plus 6.44%, RPM 60.61, Barrels per mile 0.715, Mean Departure Draft 16' 8".

Casablanca

Casablanca is a large important port/city on the

2,000 Year Old Roman Ruins in Tripoli (1953)

northwest shoulder of Africa. It is the largest city in Morocco but it is not the capital. Rabat, which is located only a few miles away, is the seat of government.

The port is has no natural shelter from the elements and is exposed to the wide sweep of storms blowing in from the Atlantic Ocean. It is protected by a super huge breakwater, which at times in not completely effective. The Harbor Pilot boards the ships just after they have entered into the harbor and obtained some shelter from the ocean swells, which are pretty much constant.

In 1953, Morocco was still a colony of France, but there was a revolution brewing. Three years later they would obtain their independence and establish a constitutional monarchy.

Casablanca provided a mixture of the old and new. You saw women fully veiled and you saw women dressed in the current fashions from Paris and New York. Old traditional mosques with minarets were mixed in with modern buildings. There was an era of bustle and prosperity.

The port facilities were far superior to any other port in north Africa and the work was reasonably efficient. The Harbor Pilot skillfully directed our maneuvers to a modern dock, which had an adjacent sheltered storage area, and we soon commenced discharging our general cargo for this port.

It was only a $20 taxi ride to the beautiful city of Rabat, and several of us took the trip.

The French are famous for having the world's fanciest and best brothels, and one with the highest-rating was reputed to be in Rabat. It was named the "Sphinx". It had a fifteen-foot replica of the Sphinx by the front door but this one was fitted with finely detailed female breasts.

The building was set back a good way from the street, and the grounds were beautifully landscaped. Customers, arriving in private automobiles, could drive into garages in the rear, that had doors that automatically closed after their entry.

In the interior, you would have thought that you had been transported back to the time of King Louis XIV. The furnishings, lighting and music were tastefully executed. The gorgeous young ladies were dressed in evening gowns and had exquisite hairstyles, perfume and make-up.

Excellent wine and hors d'oeuvrés were served in the reception area. It was a real bachelor's paradise. Of course, my information only came from some of the other guys who actually partook of these pleasures.

Our cargo discharge in Casablanca would take four days. I was waiting on "pins and needles" to see if the charts for Dingwall would arrive soon enough to avoid delaying our departure. They arrived just at the last minute.

Casablanca Docks (1953)

Casablanca "Taxi Stand" (1953)

We departed Casablanca on Saturday, 8/8/53, bound for Dingwall, NS. We had done a voyage calculation and took sufficient bunkers to fuel our voyage to Dingwall and on to a port of discharge.

My notes show that we had moderate headwinds for most of the passage.

The passage data: Distance 2,543 miles, Speed 10.14 knots, Slip plus 13.7%, RPM 61.05, Barrels per mile 0.7062, Mean Departure Draft 10' 11".

Dingwall

We arrived off the entrance to Dingwall port about 1000 on Tuesday, 8/18/53. There was on pilot boat waiting for us so I went to anchor. After less than an hour, a boat came out from the port with the boarding party and the Pilot. Entry had to be timed for slack water, because the tidal current was very strong. The spring tidal range was, as I recall, more than thirty feet. Although our maximum draft was only about 15', we would likely ground at low water, so we needed to wait for high water slack tide. When the tide was just right, we heaved up and entered the port.

This was not a suitably developed port and T. J. Stevenson & Co., Inc., should not have booked this cargo. Their underwriters should have objected.

Rabat Street Scene and Laundromat (1953)

Rabat School Room (1953)

A very tricky maneuver is required to get to the dock, which was just inside the entry channel on the starboard side, and was at a ninety degree angle to the channel. The dock was about one hundred feet shorter than our ship.

The Harbor Pilot was a hard-drinking, very talkative Scotchman, in his fifties. He did a credible job and scared the heck out of me at the same time. We had to proceed into the harbor at a good speed, because of a cross current outside the entry, and then immediately after arriving inside, we had to go full astern and drop an anchor, so as to make an immediate ninety degree turn to starboard toward the dock.

When the tide went out, we were sitting on the bottom, which was a very bad situation. The bottom was not level so we leaned away from the dock seven or eight degrees. I wrote up and served the Charterers with a "Note of Protest", in case bottom damage might result to our ship. They were used to this and did not take it personally.

I mentioned that the Pilot was hard-drinking. After we got docked, I invited him to have a "heave ahead" in my back party room. I thought that I was never going to get rid of him. Finally, after a couple of hours, the Agent helped with the situation, and pretty much carried him off the ship.

There was a mine nearby that produced gypsum and they had accumulated a full cargo for us, more than 10,000 long tons.

Other than the gypsum industry, the main activity here was fishing for swordfish. Early each morning, about eight or ten especially rigged boats, which were about eighty feet long, would leave port to go fishing. They each had a raised platform on the bow, which was fitted with a circular waist-high steel safety rail. From there they would throw a hand harpoon into a swordfish. A typical swordfish would weigh several hundred pounds. The catch was poor while we were there, and the only swordfish that I could purchase for our ship was a "little fellow" that dressed out at seventy pounds. We had delicious swordfish steaks for several meals. It had slept in the ocean the night before we got it, so it was as fresh as it could be.

Shore leave was not restricted, but there was no place to go. The little town did not have a restaurant and not even a bar.

They finished loading us in four days. Figuring out how much cargo was aboard and getting a proper draft reading was difficult, because we were aground most of the time.

The friendly and very talkative Scottish Harbor Pilot came aboard and appeared to be sober. We had to leave port at exactly high tide, and it was another tricky maneuver. We backed away from the dock, dropped an anchor so as to be able to turn in a sort radius, about 90 degrees to starboard, toward the exit channel. We then we heaved up the anchor, after we had turned on it. Even at high tide, we were very close to the bottom, and our prop wash stirred up huge quantities of mud. It was a great relief to be clear of this port and back into deep water. I didn't offer the Pilot a departing drink, but presented him with a bottle that he could take home.

We left Dingwall on Saturday, 8/22/53, bound for Baltimore. My notes indicate that we had moderate headwinds most of the passage. We took arrival at the Chesapeake Light Vessel on Wednesday, 8/26/53.

The passage data: Distance 982 miles, Speed 10.21 knots, Slip plus 9.81%, RPM 59.00, Barrels per mile 0.689, Mean Departure Draft 27' 8 3/4".

Our cargo of 10,000 long tons of gypsum was discharged in four days. During this time we had our voyage pay-off and signed foreign articles. On Sunday, 8/30/53, we moved down the Chesapeake Bay to Norfolk to begin loading for our next voyage.

Fifth Voyage

Norfolk, New York, Casablanca, Leghorn, Sibenik, Gibraltar, Philadelphia

Norfolk

We were again going to load cargo for Mediterranean ports. It was to be a strange mix of about 9,500 tons of bulk coal and vehicles in #2, #3 and #4 'tween decks. We had to wait a day for our turn at the loading berth in Norfolk. They then dumped the 9,500 tons of coal into our ship in a few hours. The number 2, 3 and 4 'tween decks were left empty and clear. We then shifted to the Norfolk Army Base, where we loaded military trucks into #2 and #3 'tween decks.

We then got underway for New York, leaving Norfolk on 9/2/53, and arriving at Ambrose Light Vessel on Thursday, 9/3/53. The schedule was tight, so we were ordered to make all possible speed, and made the passage running the engine wide open.

The passage data: Distance 230 miles, Speed 11.27 knots, Slip plus 2.13%, RPM 62.3, Barrels per mile 0.748, Mean Departure Draft 28' 1" with 4 inches allowance for brackish water.

New York

This was indeed a strange stop for cargo. We went to the Stevenson Lines dock in Hoboken to load five black Lincoln sedans, that were armor-plated and had bullet proof glass in the windows. We had hurried to get here but cars were not yet on at the dock. When they finally arrived, they were carefully loaded and well-lashed and chocked in #4 'tween deck. Big shipping costs were being incurred for these five automobiles. Our stop in New York was just for them, and they were destined for Casablanca, and were our only cargo for that port.

We departed New York on Saturday, 9/5/53, bound for Casablanca.

This passage was memorable mainly for the severe hurricane that we encountered. The storm had originated off the coast of Africa at about twenty degrees north latitude and had traveled due west for several days, gathering strength, and then started moving WNW. It had developed winds well over 100 mph by the time it was in mid-ocean. Storm positions were not exactly known in those days, but I believe that it was about fifty miles south of us when our paths crossed.

When encountering a hurricane at sea, you always try to get to the left or navigable semi-circle, which usually means that, in the northern hemisphere, you need to get south of the storm's center. The forward motion of the storm, usually about fifteen knots or so, is added to the counter clockwise rotational velocity in the right semi-circle and subtracted on the left side of the storm.

There was no way that I could maneuver to get south of the storm, so I steered north to try to get farther away from the center. In those days, the tracking of these storms was not based on the good information that we have today. It was mainly based on reports from ships at sea, giving the wind direction and velocity and the barometric pressure at their location. I was sure glad that we didn't have any deck cargo, because the seas that we were taking aboard would have totally demolished it.

At our location, the wind had been blowing from the east for quite some time and the seas were forty to fifty feet high. Fortunately, we had daylight during the worst part of the storm and I could see and plan how best to ride it out. The wind had caused a regular pattern to develop, a continuing series of waves, neatly lined up, like moving ridges of water. The waves were very high, but were uniform in size and were spaced far enough apart, so that we had time to recover from one before the next one hit. I steered to keep the wind and seas slightly on the port bow and used just enough engine power to be able to maintain our heading. The rotation of the propeller on a single screw ship, when there are no other forces involved, will tend to cause the ship to turn to port (left), so with the wind and sea slightly on the port bow, I was able to maintain our heading, while using the least amount of engine power. The storm was awesome to behold, but we rode it out very well and, by the time darkness came, the wind and seas were diminishing.

We arrived at the Casablanca breakwater on Saturday, 9/19/53. There were two large ships outbound from the port, so I had to back-down and wait for them to exit before I could enter. The ocean swells were unusually large, probably because of the recent hurricane, and we rolled heavily while awaiting a time that I could safely enter the port, and gain the lee of the huge Casablanca breakwater.

When the channel was clear, I had to enter with more headway that I was "comfortable" with, and that became a problem because no pilot was immediately available. I couldn't just back the engine because that would cause me to lose steering control in the narrow channel, and the ship would most likely veer sharply to starboard and run into the breakwater. So, I had Chief Mate Bunting drop the port anchor with one shot of chain (15 fathoms or 90 feet), and then set the windlass break, so as to drag the anchor and thereby slow and steady the ship, while I put the engine on full astern. I successfully got the ship stopped in the channel. After what seemed like an eternity, the Harbor Pilot boarded. We heaved up the anchor and proceeded to a dock to discharge our precious cargo of five armored Lincoln sedans.

Fifty Foot Seas during an Atlantic Hurricane (1953)

The author testing the wind during an Atlantic Hurricane (1953)

The passage data: Distance 3,225 miles, Speed 9.91 knots, Slip plus 11.59%, RPM 58.05, Barrels per mile 0.693, Mean Departure Draft 28' 0" (3 inches allowance for brackish water)

Casablanca

We proceeded to a dock but didn't finished tying up until about 1800. It was too late to get stevedore gangs for that day, so they were to be ordered for 0600 the next day. We broke sea watches and many of the officers and crew had a night 'on the town". I was kind of tired and had just "seen" the interesting sights of this city on the previous voyage, so I stayed aboard. Besides, I wanted to be on hand early the next morning, to see about getting these cars discharged promptly, so that we could get on our way.

The five cars were all out of the ship by 1000. We secured for sea and left Casablanca bound for Leghorn on Sunday, 9/20/53.

According to my notes, we had excellent weather and we proceeded west of the Balearic Islands. We arrived at the Leghorn breakwater on Thursday, 9/24/53.

The passage data: Distance 1.157 miles, Speed 10.58 knots, Slip plus 7.79%, RPM 59.53, Barrels per mile 0.7042, Mean Departure Draft 27' 2".

Leghorn (Livorno)

The only cargo that we had for this port were military trucks that were stowed in #2 and #3 'tween decks. It would only take a few hours to discharge them, so I decided not to go to the expense of having Ana come over from Trieste.

We finished tying up at 1900, just before dark. Stevedore gangs were ordered for 0600, so the schedule here was about like it had been in Casablanca. We broke sea watches and most of the crew and officers had a night "on the town". It didn't seem right to me to be in Italy and not to see Ana. I missed her and was kind of sorry that I had not invited her to come to Leghorn. I went ashore with Chief Engineer Thomas and we had a nice dinner. We then returned to the ship, to be ready for an early start the next morning.

Our Leghorn cargo was all out of the ship by 1300 the next day and we promptly sailed for Sibenik, Yugoslavia, on Friday, 9/25/53. We enjoyed smooth seas, but we had three and a half hours of dense fog in the Adriatic Sea.

We had greatly enjoyed our stay in Sibenik eight months earlier and we looked forward to spending time there again. But things were not going to be so good this time.

We arrived at the Sibenik pilot station on Monday, 9/28/53. The huge Montenegrin Harbor Pilot, Captain "No Tug Boats", came aboard and again did a very professional job of directing our maneuvers into the port and to the dock. All of our remaining cargo of 9,500 long tons of coal was to be discharged here.

The passage data: Distance 874 miles, Speed 10.28 knots, Slip plus 11.44%, RPM 59.8, Barrels per mile 0.7002, Mean Departure Draft 27' 0".

Sibenik

We tied up to the long bulkhead pier, starboard side to the dock. Within an hour we had started discharging our cargo of coal, using the ship's gear, with grab buckets supplied by the port, into railroad cars. The rail road track ran alongside our berth.

On our first evening in port, I walked the six or seven blocks into town and to the Krka Hotel/Restaurant. I was hoping to find my local friend, Ivan, with whom I had gone sailing in Sibenik Bay during our previous time here.

It was a small town and Ivan had also come here, hoping to see me. What he had to say was troubling. When he and the two young ladies had returned to the yacht moorings, the police had arrested them. They had released the young ladies the next day but had kept Ivan for further interrogation for several days. They were concerned that I had been spying on the Yugoslav Naval Facilities. They had asked him if I had had a cigarette lighter, which might have been a spy camera to photograph the local military facilities. Ivan didn't tell them that I had a regular camera and was taking pictures openly, not knowing that photography here was not allowed. Anyway, they had frightened Ivan to the extent that he now told me that he could not be seen fraternizing with me. He was sorry but that was the situation. After telling me these things, he left the restaurant via the kitchen and back door. I never saw him again.

A couple of days later, at about four o'clock in the afternoon, the local police returned one of our ship's Oilers (a rating in the Engine Room), who was obviously intoxicated, to the ship. They gave me stern instructions that he was not to be allowed to go ashore here any more.

I requested, through the ship's Agent, that they give me something in writing regarding this, so that I would not be liable for a claim against the ship for overtime pay from the Oilier.

If I had refused to let him go ashore, without having been instructed by the local authorities, the ship would be required to pay him at his overtime rate for the time that he was illegally restrained. All I required was a simple note, but what I got was an amusing and very detailed accounting from the Chief of Police detailing what had transpired.

This incident seems a bit amusing to us, but these people took it very seriously, so I had to do the same. I posted a notice in the crew recreation room reminding them to respect the sovereignty and dignity of our host country.

A copy of the report from the Sibenik Chief of Police follows.

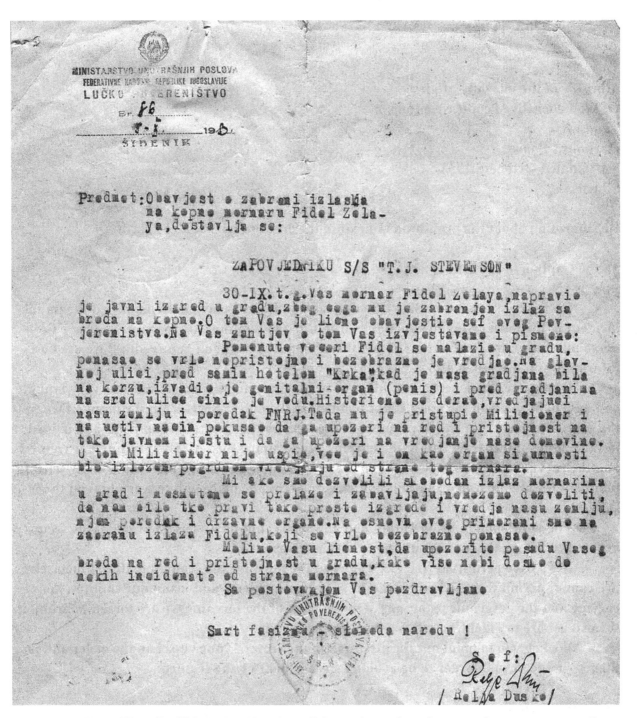

MINISTARSTVO UNUTRAŠNJIH POSLOVA
FEDERATIVNE NARODNE REPUBLIKE JUGOSLAVIJE
LUČKO POVERENIŠTVO

Br. 86

7-I.   19 .

ŠIBENIK

Predmet: Obavjest o zabrani izlaska
na kopno mornaru Fidel Zelaya, dostavlja se:

ZAPOVJEDNIKU S/S "T.J. STEVENSON"

30-IX.t.g. Vaš mornar Fidel Zelaya, napravio
je javni izgred u gradu, zbog čega mu je zabranjen izlaz sa
broda na kopno. O tom Vas je lično obavjestio šef ovog Pov-
jereništva. Na Vaš zantjev o tom Vas izvjestavamo i pismeno:
        Pomenute večeri Fidel se nalazio u gradu,
ponašao se vrlo nepristojno i bezobrazno je vredjao na glav-
noj ulici, pred samim hotelom "Krka", kad je naša gradjanka bila
na korzu, izvadio je genitalni organ (penis) i pred gradjanima
na sred ulice činio je vodu. Histerično se derao, vredjajuci
našu zemlju i poredak FNRJ. Tada mu je pristupio Milicioner i
na uctiv način pokušao da ga upozori na red i pristojnost na
take javnom mjestu i da ga upozori na vredjanje naše domovine.
U tom Milicioner nije uspio, već je i on kao organ sigurnosti
bio izlozen pogrdnom vredjanju od strane tog mornara.
        Mi ako smo dozvolili slobodan izlaz mornarima
u grad i nesmetano se prolaze i zabavljaju, nemozemo dozvoliti,
da nam oilo tko pravi take proste izgrede i vredja našu zemlju,
njen poredak i državne organe. Na osnovu ovog primorani smo na
zabranu izlaza Fidelu, koji se vrlo bezobrazno ponašao.
        Molimo Vašu licnost, da upozorite posadu Vašeg
broda na red i pristojnost u gradu, kako više nebi došlo do
nekih incidenata od strane mornara.
        Sa postovanjem Vas pozdravljamo

        Smrt fasizmu - sloboda narodu !

                                        Š e f:
                                        / Rel a Dus k o /

Letter from Sibenik Chief of Police describing misconduct by one of our seaman and
instructing that he not be allowed ashore any more. (10/5/53)

Translation (by Ship's Agent) into English follows on the next page.

207.

TRANSLATION

Ministry of the internity affairs
Of the Federative People,e republic
Yugoslavia
Harbour,s Board
No 86.dated October5,1953
Sibenik

Re.Informing about the prohibition of exit to the crew member Fidel Zelaya

To the Captain of ss "T.J.Stevenson"

On the day September 30,1953 your seaman Fedel Zelaya has committed the public incident in the town,owing to which it is prohibited to him the exit xashore. You have been personally informed by the chief of this Board about this and on your request we are now informing you in written also.

On the mentioned evening Fidel was in the town and his behaviour was very inpolite and rudely insulted on the main street just before the hotel "KRKA" in the moment when the mass of citizens was on the promenade, he took out his genital organ/penis and urined in the middle of the street before the citizens. He sorumed hustericaly insulting our country and the regyme of FHRJ/FPRY/. When the policeman approached him and politely tried to point out his attention to order and politeness on a public place and to warn him on the insultations of our country.

The policeman in his intention had no success, but he was as an organ of the security exposed to the ignominious insultations of this seaman.

If we have permitted free exit ashore to the town for the seaman to divert themselves ,we cannot permit that anybody committ so vulgar incidents and insult our country, her regyme and the governments organs . On the basis of the forgoing we are forced to prohibit the exit ashore to Fidel whose behavious was very rude.

We beg you to point out the attention to the crew of your vessel on the order and politeness in the town in order to be avoided any incident by the seamen.

Yours respectfully,

    L.S.

                    Death to fascismus –liberty to the people !

                              Chief

                    /Relja Disko/ signed

Since our last call in this port the previous January, hard feelings had been developing between Yugoslavia, which had the backing of the USSR, on the one hand; and Italy, which had the backing of the United States and Great Britain on the other hand, over the disposition of Trieste. British military forces had been posted in Trieste for the purpose of keeping the Yugoslav army from overrunning the city. It was a very uneasy truce, along the lines of the standoff in Berlin. Marshall Tito probably had little respect for the Italian army, which had disgraced itself in WWII, but, for good reason, he hesitated about taking on the British.

The situation, unfortunately for us, came to a head while we were docked in the port of Sibenik. It was formally announced that Italy would retain possession of Trieste. We had no access to English radio broadcasts, and so had no knowledge of the happenings.

Suddenly, at about 2300, a huge and very angry mob of townspeople gathered alongside our ship. There were several thousand people, that were shouting at us in a very angry manner, and were throwing pieces of coal at us from the dock. I sounded the General Alarm System on the ship to get all hand up. We battened down the watertight doors on the main deck and closed all doors on the boat and bridge decks. We couldn't pull up the gangway, because a goodly number of the mob had already boarded the ship. If it had been possible, I would have let go the mooring lines and left the dock, but we had already been boarded in large numbers. I did order that the engine department get ready to get underway, should the situation allow it.

Most U. S. flag Merchant Marine ships only have one .38 caliber revolver, that is normally kept in the ship's safe in the Captain's office. The SS T. J. Stevenson had four such revolvers. It appeared that we were about to be physically attacked and perhaps killed, by this unruly mob. We had to defend ourselves as best we could. I therefore issued a loaded revolver to each of the Deck Officers, and kept one for my own use. It was unlikely that anyone would be able to open the watertight doors on the main deck, so the danger points became the wooden doors on the boat deck and bridge deck. These doors had no effective locks. I issued orders to fire a warning shot if any boarders forced open one of these doors.

Looking back on the situation, I now see that this "spontaneous" demonstration was actually well-organized and well-orchestrated. The population of the town had been routed out of their homes, at night, and ordered to demonstrate at the docks. The "leaders" had electric megaphones, with which they addressed and controlled the crowd. No one tried to break into our quarters. After a couple of hours terrorizing us, the mob disbursed. The crew members that had been ashore, when this started, had not been harmed. They had been rounded up and told to get back aboard immediately.

The mob painted a message in large letters on the side of our ship. It read "Trieste Yugoslav, doli (translation "down with") Imperialistic America and England".

A couple of days later, the ship's Agent asked if I wasn't going to paint out the sign. I replied that I intended to steam into New York harbor with the sign intact, to show the American

Writing on Ship's side, "Trieste Yugoslav, down with Imperialistic America and England"

people how much appreciation we got for the coal that we were giving to the Yugoslav people. During that night, a shore gang came down to the ship and painted out the sign. I did photograph it as seen in the accompanying photographs.

After these events, none of our crew went ashore any more in this port. When we would go on deck to inspect the discharge operations, the stevedores frequently threw lumps of coal at us. Our remaining week or so in port was tense and unpleasant.

Finally, on Tuesday, 10/13/53, we finished discharging our cargo of coal. The big Harbor Pilot, Captain "No Tug Boats", came aboard and expertly directed our undocking and exit from the port. This time, it had been a tense and unpleasant stay in Sibenik.

As soon as we were in international waters, I sent a radiogram to the U. S. State Department. describing the Sibenik events. Operations Vice President, Mr. John F. Shea, later criticized my communication, on the basis that it might make it harder for Stevenson Lines to book further cargo to or from Yugoslavia.

We were bound for Gibraltar Bay to take fuel for our return to the U. S. We arrived off Europa Point on Sunday, 10/18/53. We had one day of dense fog on this passage. which made it necessary to run an additional fifteen miles, to minimize opposing traffic. We proceeded east of Vis and via the Messina Straits.

The passage data: Distance 1,505 miles, Speed 10.67 knots, Slip plus 4.4%, RPM 57.69, Barrels per mile 0.5847, Mean Departure Draft 11' 5".

Gibraltar

A British Pilot boarded and expertly directed our maneuver to alongside one of the old Shell Oil Company Tankers, that were being used as refueling stations in Gibraltar Bay. We got to the berth about 2000. Soon after midnight we had finished fueling. We were then on our way to Philadelphia. The date was 10/19/53.

We followed the 36th parallel of latitude westward and only had two days of bad weather. We arrived at the Five Fathoms Light Vessel, enroute to Philadelphia, on Saturday, 10/31/53

The passage data: Distance 3,382 miles, Speed 10.85 knots, Slip plus 5.84%, RPM 59.93, Barrels per mile 0.6277, Mean Departure Draft 12' 6".

Vacation

I was due a vacation and wanted to spend a Christmas at home. I had three nieces that were at an interesting age for Santa Claus, and I wanted to see some Christmas Spirit. My last Christmas at home was back in 1946, when I was attending Missouri School of Mines. Somehow I had now lost interest in becoming a Chemical Engineer.

I recommended that Chief Mate Bill Bunting relieve me as Captain, and that Second Mate Joe Koller take over as Chief Mate. Operations Manager, Captain William J. Campbell, approved my recommendations. I don't recall who they obtained to take the Second Mate position.

They had an interesting itinerary on this next voyage. It was as follows— Philadelphia, Norfolk, Praia, Gibraltar, Valencia, Piraeus, Venice, Norfolk.

I am glad that Bill Bunting got to make this voyage as Master, so that he could properly claim the title of "Captain". This was to be his last ship and he would soon "swallow the anchor" and go home to his family in Kennebunk, Maine.

The SS T. J. Stevenson got back to Norfolk on Wednesday, 1/16/54.

Chapter XI: SS T. J. Stevenson
(Second Tour of Duty)
Sixth Voyage

Norfolk, Philadelphia, New York, Norfolk, Praia, Vila do Porto, Genoa, Naples, Tripoli, Piraeus, Tampa

Norfolk

I traveled by train from my home in Sedalia, MO, and rejoined the SS T. J. Stevenson in the port of Norfolk. Bill Bunting resumed his position as Chief Mate and Joe Koller resumed his position as Second Mate. The Temporary Second Mate left before I arrived, and I never got to meet him.

We were to load general cargo for Stevenson Lines, with several loading and discharge ports. The cargo plan got to be very complicated and, of course, we had to handle it without the aid of computers, as they had not yet been developed. We used crayons of different colors on our drawings to indicate cargo for the different ports. There was also to be considerable deck cargo which greatly worried me. This was to be a winter-time voyage and stormy weather was to be expected.

We signed foreign articles with all of the Officers and most of the Crew signing over for another trip. We only took limited stores, since we would later be going to New York, where the prices were more competitive.

We left Norfolk on 2/27/54, and arrived at Overfalls Light Vessel, enroute to Philadelphia, on Thursday, 1/28/54. We encountered a strong NW gale. It was impossible to adequately control the ship, so I had to add ballast. I filled, with seawater, #1 and #2 Deep Tanks and #2 and #6 Double Bottom Fuel Tanks. It was a miserable passage with lots of rolling, pitching and pounding.

The passage data: Distance 133 miles, Speed 8.64 knots, Slip plus 29.2%, RPM 63.3, Barrels per mile 0.91, Mean Departure Draft 10' 2".

Philadelphia

We spent two days loading general cargo in Phily. I pumped out the clean ballast from #1 and #2 Deep Tanks while at the dock.

We sailed on Tuesday, 2/2/54, and arrived at Ambrose Light Vessel, enroute to New York, later that same day. We had excellent weather. As soon as we got out to sea, I started pumping the dirty ballast from #2 and #6 Double Bottom Fuel Tanks. This was, of course, polluting the ocean, but it was not illegal, and everyone did it.

The passage data: Distance 133 miles, Speed 11.3 knots, Slip plus 3.6%, RPM 60.48, Barrels per mile 0.70, Mean Departure Draft 22' 1".

New York

We proceeded to Stevenson Line's pier in Hoboken and loaded more general cargo for three days. Pier Superintendent Bill Hunt was closely monitoring things. I let him know that I was unhappy about taking deck cargo this time of year, and he let me know that he didn't care.

On Friday, 2/5/54, we sailed from New York bound for Norfolk to finish loading. We encountered moderate headwinds. We arrived at the Norfolk Buoy #2 the next day, 2/6/54, and immediately proceeded to the Norfolk Army Base, where we loaded general cargo for the Azores.

The passage data: Distance 234 miles, Speed 10.68 knots, Slip plus 6.77%, RPM 59.55, Barrels per mile 0.7222, Mean Departure Draft 21' 10".

Norfolk

Five days later, we finished loading and secured for sea. On Thursday, 2/11/54, we departed Norfolk bound for Praia, Terceira, Azores. We had two days of NW gales with the cargo shifting. I had to steer various courses to reduce rolling while our crew worked to re-chock and relash the cargo in #2, #3 and #4 'tween decks. The ship was in no danger from the shifting cargo, but the cargo itself was being damaged.

We arrived at the anchorage in Praia on Saturday, 2/20/54.

The passage data: Distance 2,376 miles, Speed 11.08 knots, Slip plus 4.19%, RPM 60.3, Barrels per mile 0.6717, Mean Departure Draft 25' 1".

Praia

A couple of hours after we anchored, the wind backed around to SSE, and we had to quickly get underway to guard against being blown ashore. I steamed around to the northwest side of the island and, since there was no good anchorage available, I steamed on the lee side in a large circle, with the engine on dead slow.

Early the next morning, the wind had shifted back to west and I returned to the anchorage at Praia. The wind was still strong, but we had the lee of the land, so the sea was calm. The water was deep here right up close to the shore, and the bottom sloped downward at a steep angle. The depth was almost 100 feet, so I put out seven shots (15 fathoms or ninety feet per shot) of chain, to be sure that the anchor would not drag down the slope.

About half an hour after we anchored, a Portuguese freighter, about 350 feet long, came in and anchored close to and directly upwind from us, between us and the shore.

Judging from the bells that they rang, they only put out three shots of chain, not enough in my judgment to hold in this wind. I saw immediate danger and put our engine on standby for immediate readiness. Sure enough, in a few minutes, the wind turned them sideways and they started rapidly dragging anchor toward us. I blew the danger signal on the whistle, and went hard left and full ahead to try to get out of their path. I did turn and move enough so that the flat port side of that ship landed flat against the flat starboard side of our ship, a little aft of amidships. If I had done nothing, they would have blown down, with their midship, striking hard against the stem of our ship. That would have holed the other ship, and maybe sunk it.

Soon after the other ship had dragged clear of us, they got their engine (diesel) started and commenced to heave up their anchor. As I expected, their anchor flukes were caught in our anchor chain.

I had Chief Mate Bunting and the Bosun go forward and start paying out our starboard anchor chain all the way, the full twelve shots. I had Sparks get in touch with the other ship, which was named the *MV Vila do Porto,* and suggested that we steam parallel, on a westerly heading, while the crew on the other ship disconnected their anchor chain at the first shackle. They agreed. Their dead slow speed was four knots, so I set our RPM to also make four knots. After an hour and a half, we were getting too far away from the island to have any effective lee. I suggested a wheeling turn to the left to steer back toward the island, and we were able to accomplish this maneuver. After about another thirty minutes, they succeeded in disconnecting their anchor and we both returned to anchor at Praia.

We heaved our starboard anchor and chain back in and found that the other ship's anchor was still caught on our chain. We re-anchored, using our port anchor. The next morning, we rigged our #1 booms with a running block and managed to heave the other anchor, together with its ninety feet of chain, up and stow it on our main deck. As a professional courtesy, I offered to return the anchor and chain. A barge was sent over to retrieve it.

There was no Surveyor available to determine the seaworthiness of our ship after this collision. Our damage was relatively minor. Parts of our starboard main deck bulwark was bent inward a foot or so and there was some minor damage to our boat deck on the starboard side. Chief Mate Bunting, Chief Engineer Thomas and I made a thorough inspection and determined that the *SS T. J. Stevenson* was indeed seaworthy. We all signed a statement to that effect and had it witnessed by our Praia Agent.

The other ship was owned by the same company that was acting as our Agent, so I could not expect him to act in our interest. I notified the Captain of the other ship, in writing, that I held him responsible for the incident, and for the cost of repairs that would be necessary. I could not legally correspond with my Owners by radio while we were in port, and was dependent on cables sent through the Agent.

We only had a small amount of cargo for Praia and it was discharged in one day.

On Monday, 2/22/54, we left Praia and proceeded to Vila do Porto, on Santa Maria Island. This was the port for which the ship was named that had collided with us. We arrived later that same day. We had excellent weather for the passage and a favorable wind direction for anchoring at Vila do Porto. We got anchored just before sunset and expected to start discharging our cargo the next morning.

As soon as I could legally do so, I sent by radio a full account of the incident that had occurred in Praia to T. J. Stevenson & Co., Inc.

Several months later, when I was in New York, I was deposed by attorneys regarding this collision. The Portuguese Captain had told some whopper lies. He claimed that he had anchored first and that I anchored later and dragged anchor into him.

The passage data: Distance 138 miles, Speed 10.87 knots, Slip plus 7.3%, RPM 62.0, Barrels per mile 0.696, Mean Departure Draft 24' 0".

Vila do Porto

In this dangerous anchorage, I kept alert sea watches with the engine on standby.

About midnight, the wind suddenly backed around to SW and started blowing hard. Also, the barometer was dropping. It was clear that we must immediately heave anchor and get out of there. In the dark, the white breakers on the nearby shore were frightening. As Chief Mate Bunting was heaving the anchor, I was helping the windlass by coming slow ahead on the engine. The seas were building up fast and the ship was starting to pitch some. As the bow rose on a sea, there was a loud snapping noise. Our anchor chain had broken with about one and a half shots of chain out. If we had waited a little longer to heave up, that fault in the chain might have given way and we would have quickly blown up onto the rocks.

This voyage was not going very well. First the collision and now we had lost an anchor.

There was a small bay on the east side of the island so I went around there and anchored in the lee. I was sure wishing that I had radar to aid in this night-time navigation.

About noon the next day, the wind had shifted back around to the north, and I returned to anchor at Vila do Porto. We were able to discharge about half of our cargo for this port that afternoon. We had another nervous night at anchor, but thankfully the wind continued from the north. By early afternoon the next day, we had finished discharging our cargo into the ducks (amphibious trucks) and gladly left that port bound for Genoa. The date was Wednesday, 2/24/54.

We had excellent weather and, in the Mediterranean, proceeded NW of the Balearic Islands. We arrived at the Genoa breakwater on Wednesday, 3/3/54.

The passage data: Distance 1,812 miles, Speed 11.54 knots, Slip plus 4.2%, RPM 62.65, Barrels per mile 0.6627, Mean Departure Draft 23' 1".

Genoa

It had now been eight months since I had seen Ana and was anxious for another meeting. I had written to her from New York and had sent her a radiogram when we left the Azores, inviting her to come over from Trieste for a visit in Genoa. I had had no reply and she was not waiting in Genoa. I had to assumed that our romance was over. I had mixed emotions about it. I truly enjoyed her company, but was alarmed at what it was costing me.

Prior to arrival, I sent a radiogram to Stevenson's Genoa Port Representative, Mr. Harold Vinick, and requested that he arrange for an ABS (American Bureau of Shipping) Surveyor to inspect our ship with reference to the collision damage in Praia, Azores, and also with respect to our lost anchor.

The Surveyor agreed with our finding that the ship was seaworthy, and he drew up a list of recommended repairs that could be accomplished "when convenient".

Our cargo for Genoa was discharged in two days and we departed Friday, 3/5/54, for Naples.

There was a strong SW gale blowing and, as I reflect on it, I believe that the Genoa Pilot, who directed our undocking and exit from the port, gave me advice intended to cause me to have a ship wreck. The strong wind was on our starboard beam as we were leaving the port of Genoa. The Pilot had to debark before we cleared the breakwater because it was much too rough outside.

Seas breaking on the Genoa breakwater (1954)
The head of the breakwater is just to the right of center in the picture.

A ninety degree turn to starboard (into the wind) was required as soon as we cleared the breakwater. Because of my youthful appearance, I think that the Pilot assumed that I was inexperienced about ship handling. As he was about to get off, he told me to just continue on dead slow after I cleared the breakwater. That action would have resulted in our going ashore on the rocks on the port side just beyond the breakwater entrance.

As soon as the Pilot was clear, I went full ahead and hard right and, even with that maneuver, it was nip and tuck whether or not I would be able to bring the ship around into the wind.

After we had made our turn to starboard and were headed south, I took the accompanying photograph from our starboard bridgewing. It shows the seas breaking on the Genoa Breakwater.

I did not follow the most direct course to Naples, but diverted a bit to the west to gain the lee of Corsica. The strong SW gale continued almost all of the way to Naples. I reduced speed so as to arrive at the breakwater at 0600 on Sunday, 3/7/54.

The passage data: Distance 363 miles, Speed 9.31 knots, Slip plus 9.25%, RPM 53.3, Barrels per mile 0.72, Mean Departure Draft 21' 10".

Naples

We proceeded immediately to the dock. We only had some vehicles to discharge here and they were all out of the ship by 1500. We secured for sea and were clear of the port by 1700, 3/7/54, bound for Tripoli, Libya.

We had excellent weather and proceeded west of Sicily. We arrived at the Tripoli breakwater on Tuesday, 3/9/54

The passage data: Distance 501 miles, Speed 11.73 knots, Slip plus 3.28%, RPM 63.0, Barrels per mile 0.6506, Mean Departure Draft 20' 10".

Tripoli

We again had military general cargo destined for Wheeler Airbase.

The *SS T. J. Stevenson* in Tripoli (1954)

The old Roman ruins were only a short taxi ride away from the dock, so several of us had a good look at them. There was a good English speaking guide available to tell us about them. The Romans had established a thriving colony, in the present day location of Tripoli, some 2,000 years ago. The ruins were quite extensive but had been damaged by earthquakes and wars over the centuries.

We were able to discharge all of our cargo for this port in two days. On 3/10/54, we left Tripoli and proceeded toward Piraeus, Greece. We had Beaufort Force five headwinds for most of the passage and arrived at the Piraeus breakwater on Saturday, 3/13/54.

The passage data: Distance 640 miles, Speed 10.44 knots, Slip plus 10.6%, RPM 60.67, Barrels per mile 0.7139, Mean Departure Draft 20' 6".

Piraeus

This was the very busy and congested port for Athens. The Greek Pilot very skillfully moored us between two other ships. Each ship had the bow secured by an anchor and the stern tied up to the main breakwater for the port. It was close quarters all around. After two days, a berth was available for us to discharge our cargo and we moved there on Monday, 3/15/54.

All of the remaining cargo on board was for this port and it would take four days to discharge it all. This gave us sufficient time to visit Athens and see the great sights of the Acropolis. This was physically hard work and required a lot of climbing. The Acropolis is, of course very high, but also, just walking in the streets of Athens means going up and down a lot of hills.

It was a long climb up to the Acropolis (1954)

The Author at the Parthenon on 29th Birthday

219.

After visiting the Acropolis and other ruins in and around Athens, and the Museums in Athens, we left with tremendous respect for the Ancient Greeks. You might even have wished to have lived in those times, until you took a look at the Dentist's tools from a couple of thousand years ago.

My 29th birthday occurred on 3/16/54. I did not mention it to anyone.

We finished discharging our cargo for Piraeus and sailed on Friday, 3/19/54, bound for Tamps, FL. We did not know it, but this was our swan song for the Med run. The *SS T. J. Stevenson* would never return to this lovely area of the world.

Seventh Voyage
The State Marine Time Charter
Tampa, New Orleans, Panama Canal, Long Beach, San Francisco, Seattle, Aberdeen, Yokohama, Yokkaichi, Kobe, Pusan, Sasebo, Keelung, Osaka, Yokohama

We arrived in Tampa on Sunday, 4/11/54, after a stormy crossing of the Atlantic. Arrangements had been made for us to go into the Tampa Shipyard to repair the damage from our collision in Praia, Terceira, Azores, and to replace the starboard anchor that we had lost at Vila do Porto, Santa Maria, Azores. We had also had lost a shot and a half of chain (a shot is 15 fathoms or 90 feet long), but they were not replaced. That left nine and a half shots with the starboard anchor and the original twelve shots on the port one.

While in the shipyard, we had our voyage payoff and signed foreign articles for the next voyage.

The *SS T. J. Stevenson* was being Time-Chartered to States Marine Line, which was at that time becoming a very large and apparently successful shipping company. Their operations were spectacular for quite a while, but they ended up going bankrupt.

States Marine Line presented me with detailed abstracts to be submitted. I was also to send our noon position every three days when at sea (Stevenson Line required a Noon Position report every five days), and report any unusual incidents immediately. We were going to load in several ports for discharge in several Far Eastern ports. We had an extensive on-hire survey in Tampa. Of course Stevenson Line also required their usual abstracts so the paper work was going to be considerable. Our smoke stack symbol was changed from T. J. Stevenson's logo to the States Marine logo.

We lost the services of Chief Mate William Bunting. He retired from the sea at age 30 and was going to start a business in his home town of Kennebunk, ME. He had been frugal during his sea-going days and had saved a nest-egg that should be sufficient to see him through to success. We all wished him well. He was retiring with the legitimate right to claim the title of "Captain" Bunting.

I promoted Joe Koller to Chief Mate and Kenneth Williams came aboard as Second Mate. He was a regular Stevenson Line Mate and came well-recommended, having sailed as both Second and Chief Mate. He was in his mid-thirties and very competent. One of his lungs had been removed, but was now cancer free. The other ship's officers all stayed on.

After two days, our repairs and the on-hire survey were completed and we sailed, in ballast, for New Orleans on 4/13/54.

It was expected that we would be loading heavy lifts during this charter and, in some ports,

Overhauling the 50-ton Jumbo Gear

Overhauling the 15-ton Jumbo Gear (1954)

shore cranes might not be available. Therefore, on the passage from Tamps to New Orleans, we took advantage of nice weather to overhaul and get ready our jumbo booms and gear.

New Orleans

We picked up the Pilot at South Pass on Thursday, 4/15/54 and proceeded up the Mississippi River to a cargo dock in New Orleans.

Loading Heavy Lifts in New Orleans (1954)

Navigating this river is a terrifying experience if you understand the dangers and pay close attention. The upriver traffic takes the inner side of the channel at the bends and the downriver traffic takes the outer side of the channel. Opposing ship traffic everywhere normally meets port to port, and the change-over needed at the bends is tricky and dangerous. Add strong currents, occasional poor visibility and tows with control that is, at times, inadequate, and you have a situation fraught with danger.

We only loaded two heavy lifts, which consisted of a landing ship/barge in two sections. This certainly didn't seem to be enough cargo to justify the expenses of calling here. This was to be the pattern in most of our ports of call under the States Marine Time Charter. I was not surprised when the Company later went bankrupt.

We sailed from New Orleans on Saturday, 4/17/54, bound for the Panama Canal.

Panama Canal

We arrived at the Cristobal Breakwater Entrance on Friday, 4/23/54, during the pre-dawn darkness. At the time, and until 1957, the 1,200 foot opening between the breakwater heads was restricted, by two pairs of buoys, to only 500 feet. The situation was further complicated by a cross current, ranging up to about three knots, outside the breakwater. There were many near collisions because of this channel restriction. In 1957, after a very close call, the Captain of a United Fruit Company ship, requested a answer, in writing, to his question of "why were these buoy there"? The embarrassed answer was that they were there for "training purpose". They were removed soon thereafter.

We managed to enter into Limon Bay during a rain squall, and in darkness, and got safely to anchor. Again I was wishing that my ship had been equipped with radar.

About 0700, Panama Canal Pilot, Captain William Calcutt, boarded along with the crew of Canal Seamen, who would handle the lines at the locks. We had an excellent transit and I got to know Captain Calcutt. He told me that I should put in an application to be a Canal Pilot, as they would soon be hiring. The principal requirement was to have sailed as Ship Master for a least one year, and I then had almost three years service as Captain. While we were in Miraflores Locks, Captain Calcutt asked the Lockmaster to telephone the Balboa Port Captain, and request that an application form be sent out to the ship, as we passed Balboa Basin. The Pilots, when working on transiting ships, had no independent radio communication in those days. The ship's radio station could only be used in case of an emergency. The needed form was sent out and I mailed it back from out next port, Long Beach.

We cleared the Pacific end of the Canal on 4/23/54, the same date that we had arrived at the Atlantic end.

West Coast Loading Ports— Long Beach, San Francisco, Seattle, Aberdeen

We arrived in **Long Beach** on Wednesday, 5/5/54, and loaded cargo for three days. On 5/8/54, we sailed for **San Francisco** where we arrived on 5/10/54, and only loaded a few tons. We sailed the next day for **Seattle,** where we arrived on Saturday, 5/15/54.

We had an extraordinarily beautiful day for our arrival in the Straits of Juan de Fuca. There were snow capped mountains visible all around, beautiful green forests with large trees, and magnificent blue water.

SS T. J. Stevenson docked in Seattle (1954)
Picture was taken from the Smith Tower
Note States Marine Stack Emblem

We loaded cargo in Seattle for two days and on Monday, 5/17/54, sailed for **Aberdeen,** arriving there the next day. This was our final loading port and we only loaded a few tons.

The cargo plan was the most complicated that I had ever seen. Since we had no computers, it was all on paper, with different color crayons marking the cargo for the different ports. We had loaded in five ports and were to discharge in seven. It was going to be necessary to move some cargo aside, in some ports, in order to get to the cargo to be discharged.

It certainly looked like it was to be a money losing voyage for the Charterer, States Marine Line. It was hard to imagine a freight rate high enough to justify port calls with so little cargo to load or discharge.

We secured for sea and sailed from Aberdeen bound for Yokohama on Wednesday, 5/19/54. This was to be a summer crossing, so we could expect good weather. I decided to take a Great Circle route which was, of course, the shortest. I did modify it a bit to avoid going up into the Aleutian Islands, but we did see some of them as we passed close south of them. The weather at that time was rainy, so we didn't get a a very good look at those desolate islands. We had some moderate gales but nothing severe.

As we approached the Japanese coast, we encountered thousands of fishing boats. At night, their lights made it look like a city at sea. I was worried that we might run into some of them and we had to change course many times. They did not seem to be keeping any lookout, but were concentrating entirely on fishing.

Far East Discharge Ports— Yokohama, Yokkaichi, Kobe, Pusan, Sasebo, Keelung, Osaka,Yokohama

On Wednesday, 6/9/54, we arrived at Fort #1 in Tokyo Bay, where we picked up the Pilot to direct our movement to a dock in **Yokohama**. It was a clear day and we could see the very impressive Mt. Fuji.

Picture that the author took of Mt. Fuji from Yokohama

We only had a few slings of cargo for this port and sailed later the same day.

Our next stop was at **Yokkaichi,** which was the next major port west of Yokohama on the south coast of Honshu Island. We arrived there on Thursday, 6/10/54. We picked up the Pilot just outside the entry to the large bay in which the port was located. The port was busy and crowded but there was a berth available for us. We docked port side to the pier between two other ships.

Yokkaichi was a very progressive city. They even had a seaman's club that was set up to cater to English speaking customers. It also had an active Rotary Club. There were a number of signs in English. There were large department stores, like in other big cities, and lots of automobile traffic. When crossing the street, we had to remember to look both ways, because they drive on the left side of the street in Japan.

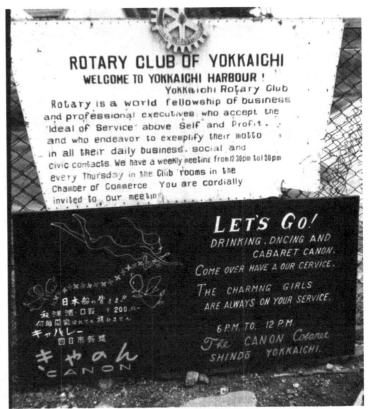

Sign in Yokkaichi, Japan (1954)

We didn't have much cargo for this port and sailed the next afternoon, 6/11/54, for Kobe.

We arrived at the **Kobe** breakwater and picked up the Harbor Pilot on Saturday, 6/12/54. We tied our bow up to a large mooring buoy.

I had previously been in Kobe in the summers of 1946, 1947 and 1948. The city had now been built up so much that I did not recognize anything. Instead of the small shops selling a great variety of goods, there were now big department stores. It was like being in New York. In 1946 there had been huge areas with no structures standing, except round commercial smoke stacks, that apparently withstood the blasts from aerial bombs.

Again, States Marine Lines had booked only a small amount of cargo for this port and we sailed the next day, Sunday, 6/13/54, for **Pusan, Korea.**

We picked up the Harbor Pilot for Pusan on Monday, 6/14/54.

The entrance to Pusan harbor now had a major new "landmark". An American Mariner-type freighter (570 feet long), the *SS Cornhusker Mariner,* had blown ashore here and broken in two during a Typhoon, a few months earlier. These were the newest and most modern ships in our Merchant Marine.

Bow Section of the *SS Cornhusker Mariner* (1954) Wrecked by Typhoon at Entrance to Pusan

The bow section was a hopeless wreck aground on rocks near the harbor entrance.

The after part of the ship was being salvaged, and had been towed back into Pusan harbor. I took photographs of both sections of the wreck as seen in the accompanying photos.

Stern Section of the *SS Cornhusker Mariner* (1954) Being salvaged in Pusan, Korea

The Korean ceasefire had gone into effect the previous July 27th, but war psychology still gripped the county. The people were grateful to the U. S. for saving them from Communism, and were very friendly to us. The U. S. military was still prominent all about.

I had previously been to Pusan in 1950, a few months before the North Koreans attacked the South Koreans. The city was much more modern and more prosperous now.

We spent a day at anchor awaiting a berth. After we shifted in to the dock, it was only a short rickshaw ride from the ship to town. There was nothing much of interest in the shops to buy.

Several of us overnighted in a local hotel to get a "feel" for the Korean culture. We left our shoes at the door and sat on the floor to eat our dinner of fish and rice, using chop sticks with varying degrees of success. We then slept on the floor on straw mats and used rice pillows. The wooden building had very thin walls and had very flimsy sliding doors to the rooms. None of us felt that this life style was for us.

Pusan was the first port for which we had enough cargo to make the stop seem financially viable for the Charterers. We spent four days total there and sailed on Friday, 6/18/54, for

Sasebo, Kyushu Island, Japan. We only had a few slings of cargo for that port and sailed early the next day, 6/19/54, for **Keelung, Taiwan.**

We had beautiful summer weather for our passage. Fortunately, there were no typhoons about.

Keelung is a large city and is the major port for Taiwan. It is located near the capital city, Taipei.

This port is located on the north coast of the island. I very nearly had a navigational disaster here, and my "intuition" apparently saved the day. I had adjusted our speed so as to make landfall just as it was breaking daylight. It was clear at sea, but along the coast there was a layer of heavy fog. I located the seabuoy and backed the ship to stop just beyond it, to wait for the Pilot to come out for us. There was a string of shoals about a mile and a half long on the west (port) side of the approach channel. The slight sea breaking on these rocks made them marginally visible. They extended seaward a little beyond the seabuoy. The visibility remained good in our location, but a few hundred yards farther toward the port, there was thick fog. The sea was almost calm. I had been able to get the ship stopped, and dead in the water, while maintaining a southerly heading toward the port. There was a steady flow of fishing boats coming out of the port, but no pilot boat. Suddenly, I felt that something was wrong. I hurried to the port bridge wing and discovered, to my horror, that the current had set us down on the string of shoals. I ordered full ahead and hard right rudder. We got out of there just in time.

Eventually the Harbor Pilot came out and took us into the port. It was very crowded and busy, but there was a berth for us. The port officials here were famous for being difficult to deal with, requiring very detailed store lists, which they would thoroughly check, unless they receive heavy gratuities in the form of cartons of cigarettes. The process was tedious but I eventually got through it.

It had been a long run down here from Japan and we again only had a small amount of cargo to discharge. How could States Marine Line be making any money on this Charter? We had arrived on Wednesday, 6/23, and sailed early the next day, 6/24/54, for **Osaka, Japan.**

The beautiful summer weather continued during our passage back north. We picked up the Osaka Harbor Pilot on Sunday, 6/27/54.

Osaka is on the east shore of the same bay as Kobe, which is on the west shore. We had been in Kobe two weeks before. Osaka is considerably larger than Kobe. We were to spend two days at this, our final discharge port in the Far East.

We had a couple of interesting experiences here. I had invited the Agent, and the Stevedore Boss, to have some hors d'oeuvres and drinks, with Chief Mate Joe Koller and me, in my back "party room". The Japanese fellows were anxious to practice their English and seemed like interesting guys. Somehow, after a few "heaves ahead", the Stevedore Boss and I ended up

"Indian Wrestling". I was much stronger than him and immediately bent his arm back to the table. The trouble was that he didn't consider the contest over and wanted to continue on indefinitely, hoping to wear me down and get his arm back up to vertical. This could have gone on for ever, but I declared myself the victor, and quit. Only he maintained that I had not yet won.

They then suggested that we should go ashore with them and they would show us the Osaka "red light district". This was a large area, of about ten square blocks, where every house, on both sides of the street, was stocked with "party girls". The houses all looked the same, being two stores high and of the same size and color. The Japanese men, the potential customers, were mostly staggeringly drunk, and walking down the middle of the rather narrow streets, in groups of from three to five. The girls would try to entice, and/or drag, them into the houses. The men would giggle and resist to various degrees. It was comical to watch. There was very strong racial discrimination, and Westerners, like Chief Mate Joe Koller and me, were not welcome in any of these establishments. Joe and I got the impression that Japanese men do not hold their booze very well and act silly.

After two days, we had discharged the last of our cargo for States Marine Line and sailed on Tuesday, 6/29/54, for **Yokohama**, where we would take bunkers and receive new orders.

We arrived at Fort #1 in Tokyo Bay, picked up the Pilot for Yokohama and proceeded to the fueling berth early on Thursday, 7/1/54.

In Yokohama I received new orders. States Marine Line had sub-Chartered us to the Matson Navigation Company. We were to load sugar in the Hawaiian Islands for a port or ports to be named later.

We were to have some dead time at the pier in Yokohama, so I decided to do some sight seeing in Tokyo. Third Mate Tony Koerner and I

Tokyo/Yokohama Subway (1954)

took the subway and, when we arrived at the Tokyo subway station, about 0900, hired a taxi driver. The driver spoke some English and agreed to show us "the sights". He drove to where we could see the Emperor's palace grounds, the official residence of the Japanese Prime Minister, and the Japanese Diet Building. We were able to enter the chamber where the Diet Upper House members meet.

Tony had agreed to get back to the ship to relieve the Second Mate, so that he could go ashore, so he caught the subway back to Yokohama about 1700. The security situation in Tokyo was very good and I felt save enough to stay on alone.

The taxi driver suggested that he had a recommendation for me, if I cared to spend the night in Tokyo. The former home, of an important Japanese general, had been converted to a "hospitality house", where I could get a good meal and have an entertaining and relaxing evening. He was not sure that I could get in without a reservation, but he was willing to check.

So, we drove up a winding road through a beautiful Japanese garden area, that covered about a city block, to a nice looking home. It was large but only of one story. There was a covered area for our automobile and a uniformed doorman on duty.

There were no other cars in sight, and the garages must have been in the rear. The driver spoke, in Japanese, with the doorman, and explained to him that I was Captain on an American ship. That carried

Scenes near Japanese Emperor's Grounds (1954)

Official Residence of the Japanese Prime Minister

229.

with it a lot of prestige in Japan. The doorman checked inside and then indicated that they could accommodate me.

I dismissed the taxi and the driver agreed to pick me up the next morning at 0700.

I exchanged my shoes for slippers at the door and proceeded to the reception area. The "mama san" signed me in, informed me that dinner would be served at 2000. She showed me into the bar area.

This was obviously going to be an expensive evening, but I was not asked for any payment in advance.

In the bar things got interesting. There were four very senior American Army Officers there, all of them were full Colonels or higher. They were on R & R. Each was paired off with a gorgeous Japanese girl, and all were seated on the floor at a large, low table.

Japanese Diet Building (1954)

Chamber Room for Upper House of Japanese Diet

The girls were dressed in kimonos and had their hair done up in high Japanese style. There were four or five others lounging there and it was obvious that I should choose one to be my companion. It was a hard choice, but I picked a beauty, and she joined me at one of the low tables. The other male customers were very friendly and were obviously enjoying themselves. They invited my date and me to join them at their large table.

My date spoke English very well and had been reading Time magazine, so as to be able to discuss the news of the day with an American.

The four Army Officers and I, and our dates, decided to all dine together. We moved to a dinning room and had a meal that consisted of several courses, some of which I liked, and some of which I didn't. I think that some of the stuff that I didn't like was raw fish. We drank saki in the traditional Japanese manner, which got complicated, with intertwined arms and sayings.

Knowing that we were not very adapt with chop sticks, they provided us with western style silverware. One of the Army Officers was good with the chop sticks and showed off by using them efficiently. The waitresses opened and closed the sliding doors with each entry/exit. They kneeled down to serve the food and drink on the low table. It was all done with impressive grace.

After dinner, my date suggested that I might enjoy a hot bath. I had been warned that when they say "hot" bath here, they mean very hot. That turned out to be the case.

She took me to a private bath room that had a large, tile covered tub about six feet by seven feet. It was about four feet tall. That is were the *hot* water was, but that is not where you bathed. I was instructed to sit on a low, three legged wooden stool, in the nude. There I got thoroughly sponge-bathed from a wooden bucket of warm soapy water. She then rinsed the soapy water off. All of this bath and rinse water went down a drain, in the floor, that was several feet away from the *hot* water tub. After I was immaculately clean, and only then, was I allowed to get into the *hot* water. At first I didn't think that I was going to be able to tolerate it, but after a while it felt good. My date joined me in the hot tub and commenced to massage me with a special rough sponge. The Army Officers were, I believe, having similar experiences in similar bath rooms.

We retired to a bedroom from the hot tub and things took their natural course. The "bed" was a straw mat (with white cotton sheets) on the floor and the very firm pillows were filled with rice. All in all, it was a delightful experience.

The next morning, after a western style breakfast of fried bacon and eggs, I settled up my understandably large bill by cash (credit cards were not yet widespread). My taxi driver, from the day before, was standing by, and drove me to the train station. I hated to return to the ordinary industrial working world.

The Matson Line Sub-Charter

Yokohama, Honolulu, Mahukona, Honolulu, Panama Canal, New Orleans

We sailed from Yokohama late afternoon on Friday, 7/2/54, and followed a Great Circle Route to Honolulu. There was an early typhoon churning up from the waters down in the area of the Philippines, but we were able to get well out into the Pacific before it got as far north as Japan. We had mostly good weather for this three-week passage.

We arrived at the **Honolulu** Pilot Station on Friday, 7/23/54, and proceeded to a dock. We commenced loading 100 pound bags of sugar. In San Juan, and earlier in Cuba, my ships had loaded 100 kilo bags of sugar, which were much harder to handle.

I telephoned my boyhood friend, Judson Banks, who lived here with his wife, Leloy, and child. They were not available that night, but they found a baby sitter for the following evening. We all had a good visit and dinner at a fine restaurant that they knew and recommended. Judson worked as a draftsman at a local architectural firm. He and his wife enjoyed living here, but complained a bit about high prices.

The Matson Line Representative presented me with another set of detailed abstracts to keep. They, like States Marine Line, wanted a noon position sent by radio every three days while at sea. Stevenson Lines required this every five days. Of course, States Marine and Stevenson Lines also continued to require their own abstract forms. I was beginning to feel like a "traveling clerk".

Loading Sugar at Open Roadstead at Mahukona (1954)

After loading about 6,000 long tons of sugar, we were ordered to proceed to a small open roadstead port on the northwest coast of Hawaii Island, named **Mahukona**. We were to load more bags of sugar from barges, which would be brought out from the local dock. We departed Honolulu Tuesday, 7/20/54, and anchored at Mahukona the following day.

When anchored in as close as I dared, we would only have a lee of the land from NNE through East to SSE. This was an extremely dangerous anchorage, and I decided that I would have to keep alert sea watches, with the engine on constant standby. We had a favorable easterly wind and so were able to anchor here and start loading cargo from the barges.

Porpoises that we encountered in mid-Pacific

Fortunately, there were only a few barge loads of bagged sugar available here and we were able to load it all in two days. We left this anchorage 7/22/54, bound back to Honolulu, We were to load more sugar that they had accumulated on the dock during our absence.

We arrived back in **Honolulu** on Friday, 7/23/54, and loaded more sugar for two additional days. We ended up with a little over 9,000 long tons of sugar.

The *USS Wisconsin*, locking down at Gatun Locks Panama Canal (1954)

Our discharge port had been declared to be New Orleans. We took aboard sufficient fuel to steam there.

We left Honolulu on Sunday, 7/25/54, bound for the Panama Canal. It was a nineteen day passage and we arrived at the **Panama Canal** Pacific anchorage on Friday, 8/13/54, at 0300.

By odd coincidence, I again had Captain William Calcutt as my Panama Canal Pilot. He was based in Cristobal and did not usually work northbound in the Canal. This gave me the opportunity to build on my relationship with this veteran Canal Pilot, who was actively helping me get an appointment as a Panama Canal Pilot. I, of course, told him that I had mailed in the application that he had arranged for me to get during our last Canal transit. He promised to check on it and did write me a letter, confirming that my application had been received and would be considered.

One interesting happening on this transit was that the Iowa class battleship, the *USS Wisconsin*, was locking down at Gatun Locks at the same time that we were. She had been called back into service during the Korean War and was now going to be deactivated. Her beam of 108 feet made her a tight fit in the 110 feet wide Panama Canal locks.

We completed an otherwise uneventful transit, on the same date that we had arrived, and departed Cristobal, on the Atlantic side, late on 8/13/54, bound for New Orleans.

It was a six day run. We arrived at South Pass and picked up the Pilot on Thursday, 8/19/54. We had the usual frightening run up the Mississippi River to **New Orleans**, switching sides of the channel, as necessary, to minimize the current flow against us, at the bends in the river. Many whistle signals were exchanged, with outbound ships and tows, to establish meeting arrangements.

We were berthed at a sugar refinery dock, on the opposite side and down river about fifteen miles from New Orleans. There was no public transportation and it was an expensive taxi ride to town.

Very upsetting news was received. Our ship, the *SS T. J. Stevenson*, was being sold to new Owners, and was going to be changed to the Liberian flag. Immediately after the voyage payoff, all hands were to be terminated from employment. The U. S. Merchant Marine was in a great and growing depression. We were all worried about getting another job.

The voyage payoff became very contentious. The NMU (National Maritime Union) watch standing crew members were claiming overtime pay, for twenty-four hours per day, while our ship had been anchored at Mahukona, Hawaii. I had kept alert seawatches there because the anchorage was exposed to the wind and sea from all directions except from the NNE through east to SSE. If the wind had shifted to be coming from any other direction, we would have had to immediately get underway, to avoid being blown ashore. I would have been recklessly negligent not to maintain this alert posture. I showed the NMU Patrolman the chart of the anchorage and explained this to him. He was adamant in claiming that I should have broken seawatches and therefore must pay the overtime. After several hours of arguing, I told them that there was no way that I was going to pay this overtime, and that the matter would have to be submitted to arbitration. I informed the Shipping Commissioner that the payoff was cancelled. To my surprise, they suddenly agreed to drop the claim, and the payoff continued. They knew that I was right, and just wanted to get on with things when they saw I would not yield.

We all scattered, some to go home and some to go to the various union hiring halls to seek new employment. Captain Campbell, the Operations Manager at T. J. Stevenson & Co., Inc., assured me that they would find something for me before long. So, I went home by train to Sedalia, MO, to enjoy a bit of an uneasy vacation, while hoping to get a telephone call from the New York office before too long.

(Note: According to "The Liberty Ships" by Captain Walter W. Jaffee, the SS T. J. Stevenson, which was originally named the SS Raymond Clapper, was purchased by the Niki Cia Nav. S. A. in 1954, reflaged Liberian, and renamed the SS Master Nicky. In 1960 she was reflaged Greece and renamed the SS Thrylos. In 1965 she was sold to Volbay Navigation Company and the name was changed to SS Elias Dayfas II. On 7/5/65, while on a voyage from Galveston to Saigon with a load of flour, she developed leaks while off the Yucatan Peninsula and was abandoned by her crew. She was taken in tow by the tanker, SS Sea Pioneer, but came adrift and was presumed sunk in Lat. 21 degrees, 11 minutes N., Long. 86 degrees, 26 minutes W.)

Chapter XII: The SS Kenneth H. Stevenson
First Voyage

New York, Praia, Casablanca, Genoa, Naples, Pula, Trieste, New York

My uneasy vacation/wait lasted less than a month. On September 15th, 1954, I received a call from Mr. John A. Moore, the personnel manager at T. J. Stevenson & Co., Inc. He told me that I could have the Chief Mate job on the *SS Kenneth H. Stevenson,* commencing in a few days, if I wanted it. He did not see any jobs as Master becoming available anytime soon, because more ships were being laid-up and/or sold. The Master of the *SS Kenneth H. Stevenson* was my old friend and mentor, Captain Demetrius Belesiotis. He knew that my ship had been sold, and he had requested me as his Chief Mate, if I was available.

New York

I decided to take the job and caught a train to New York, where I joined the ship on Monday, 9/20/54. It was good to see Captain Belesiotis again. We had had an excellent working and friendly relationship, when he was Master and I was Chief Mate on the *SS Sea Leader.* His recommendation was instrumental in me getting appointed to my first command, as Captain of the *SS Thomas Sumter,* back in May, 1951.

I joined the ship at Stevenson Line's cargo pier at Hoboken, NJ. We were loading Stevenson Line general cargo for Mediterranean ports. I got to deal again, this time as Chief Mate, with Mr. Bill Hunt, the Pier Superintendent. I found that he had not "mellowed" any since our previous encounters.

To be honest, I missed the prestige that went with being Captain, but it was relaxing not to have the 24-hour responsibility for managing and navigating the ship. The Chief Mate, on a three mate ship such as this, stands the 4 to 8 watches at sea, and is in charge of directing the maintenance and routine work of the Deck Department. The overtime earned (over forty hours per week) brings the take-home pay, for a Chief Mate, very close to that of the Captain.

**Taking the Local Apparent Noon Latitude Sights
Captain Belesiotis, left, 2nd Mate Kenneth Williams, right**

Of course, I felt no resentment toward Captain Belesiotis. I recognized that he was clearly a more qualified and experienced Ship Master than I was.

Praia

We sailed from New York on Friday, 9/24/54, and took the great circle route to Praia, Terceira Island, Azores. On my last time here, the Portuguese vessel *M/V Vila do Porto,* had dragged anchor and collided with my ship, the *SS T. J. Stevenson.* This time, our stay in the port would be more routine. We had moderate westerly wind, and therefore had the lee of the land in the anchorage. Of course, instead of navigating into the anchorage from the bridge, I was now forward, directing the dropping of the anchor, when so ordered by Captain Belesiotis.

We arrived on Friday, 9/24/54, and were able to discharge our cargo into barges without any trouble. We departed the next day, 9/25/54, for Casablanca, Morocco.

Casablanca

We arrived at the Casablanca breakwater on Thursday, 10/7/54. We experienced a moderate gale on the passage, but it fortunately gave us tail winds. I had been here in October 1953, and was again favorably impressed with the facilities and operations of this port.

There was a very heavy swell moving in from the northeast, which was striking the huge Casablanca breakwater directly at a ninety degree angle. Strangely, although the swells obviously could not get through the breakwater, they were being reproduced on the inner side, in the harbor, only a little reduced from their original size. Fortunately, the dock that we proceeded to was in the inner part of the port, and was therefore protected from the reproduced swells. Ships, at the more exposed docks, were surging at the berths and breaking many mooring lines.

We discharged cargo, using shore cranes, for two days and sailed from Casablanca on Saturday, 10/9/54.

We proceeded through the Straits of Gibraltar and passed the "rock" during daylight on a clear day. It is a remarkable geographical feature, which the British have succeeded in making self-sufficient. The concrete rain-water-catching surfaces are very large and are apparently effective.

Genoa

We proceeded west of the Balearic Islands and arrived in Genoa on Wednesday, 10/13/54. It was always a pleasure to come to this friendly port. Captain Belesiotis and I had an excellent dinner at a restaurant, that he knew from previous times.

We had quite a bit of cargo for Genoa and it took three days, working twenty-fours a day, to discharge it all, using shore cranes. We left Genoa on 10/16/54, headed south to Naples.

Naples

We arrived at the Naples breakwater on Sunday, 10/17/54, and immediately proceeded to a dock. We only had a few tons of cargo for this port, and were finished discharging and sailed the next day on 10/18/54.

Capo Spartivento (at "toe" of Italian "Boot")

Capo Santa Maria de Lucia at the "heel" of the Italian "Boot"(1955)

Pula

Our route was now through the Messina Straits, around the south end of the Italian boot, and north into the Adriatic Sea.

We proceeded north to the little Yugoslav military port of Pula (formerly Pola), on the west coast of the Istrian Peninsula, arriving on Thursday, 10/21/54. We waited outside the entrance for a Pilot for about an hour. Captain Belesiotis grew impatient and, since he knew the port, he decided to proceed in without a Pilot. A small Yugoslav Navy vessel fired a shot across our bow!!! This was outrageous and ridiculous, but Captain Belesiotis had no choice other than to back down and continue to wait for a Pilot.

The Harbor Pilot finally came out and boarded. I almost felt sorry for him for having to face the fury of Captain Belesiotis. He could be truly impressive when he was angry. When asked for an explanation, the Pilot acted as though he didn't understand English or Greek, but he could not have missed the implications.

When the boarding party came aboard, Captain Belesiotis gave them a good "chewing out" about the shot being fired across our bow. They were all uniformed military men and offered no apologies. Their English lingual skills were suddenly very poor.

The beautiful and well-preserved Roman ruins here were still freely open for inspection with no supervision. Nearly all of our crew went to have a look.

Our cargo for this port was mostly vehicles. There was no lighting on the pier, so the cargo was only discharged during the day. We were here for three days and sailed on Sunday, 10/24/54 for Trieste, Italy.

Trieste

We arrived in Trieste later the same on the same date, 10/24/54. I had been in Trieste on several previous occasions, but this was the first time since it had been officially declared to be part of Italy.

This was the home of my previous, very serious, girl friend, Ana. She had failed to respond to my correspondence the previous March, when I had invited her to come to Genoa for a visit. That was after about an eight month period since our previous tryst. It was now about eleven months since I had seen her. I was a little sheepish about contacting her now that I was no longer a ship captain. I decided not to try to find her.

We discharged the remainder of our cargo here in two days. Bunker fuel was available in Trieste at a reasonable price, so we took enough to get us back to the U. S. East Coast.

We departed Trieste on Saturday, 10/16/54, bound back to New York. Our route took us through the Messina Straits and the Straits of Gibraltar. There was a hurricane whirling away well south of us and it was moving west at about the same speed as us. It didn't bother us much because it was a good way south of us and was giving us moderate tail winds.

We arrived back in New York on Saturday, 11/13/54, after a reasonably good passage.

Second Voyage
New York, Norfolk, Casablanca, Cartagena, Tripoli, Rijeka, Norfolk
New York

We went to the Stevenson Line's cargo pier in Hoboken and spent a week loading general cargo for Mediterranean ports. My return bout with Pier Superintendent Bill Hunt was combative, as usual. He thrived on controversy and was always provoking it. We would be facing another winter-time crossing of the North Atlantic, and he was insisting on loading more deck cargo. Captain Belesiotis and I did succeed in limiting the amount of deck cargo that would be stowed on the foredeck.

During our stay in New York, I was asked to come to the Company office at 80 Broad Street, to be deposed regarding the collision that had occurred in Praia, Terceira Island, Azores, on 2/20/54, between the *SS T. J. Stevenson* and the *M/V Vila do Porto*. I had previously sent the Company a detailed report, copies of the log and bell book entries, and pictures of the damage. In brief, the other ship had recklessly anchored upwind from us and put out an insufficient scope of anchor chain, to hold the ship in that deep water and in that strong wind. It had dragged down on us and I alertly maneuvered so as to minimize the resulting damage. I had also directed the maneuvering that had gotten the two ship's anchor chains safely disconnected. As a professional courtesy, I had even salvaged the other vessel's anchor, plus ninety feet of chain, and had re-turned it to them without charge. Our damage had been repaired at the shipyard in Tampa, FL 4/11-4/13/54.

I was thoroughly disgusted to find that the Portuguese Captain had lied big-time about the accident. He claimed that he had anchored first and that I anchored later and then dragged down on his ship. The Ship's Agent at Praia worked for the same company that owned the other ship, and he was backing the story of the Portuguese Captain. Unless they had successfully falsi-fied their log and bell book entries, their lies would be exposed. I wish that I had been informed about the outcome. Settlement must have been made out of court, because I never heard more about the case.

After a week at the Hoboken dock, we sailed for Norfolk on Saturday, 11/20/54.

Norfolk

We arrived in Norfolk on 11/21/54, and immediately proceeded to the Norfolk Army Base. We were to load military general cargo and several "light" tanks, which would be stowed in #2 'tween deck. These were the same five-ton "light" tanks that I was familiar with, having hauled them to both Italy and Yugoslavia. I took special notice of the lashings and chocking for these tanks, because I had seen them break loose on two occasions during heavy rolling. They seemed to be secured as well as possible.

We worked cargo around the clock for two days and then secured for sea. We sailed on Monday, 11/22/54, into a very stormy North Atlantic Ocean, bound for Casablanca.

Nearly Losing the Ship

We had one heavy gale after another, and the ship did a lot of pitching and rolling.

What we had most feared happened when we were in the midst of a severe easterly gale in mid-Atlantic. At about 0400, the army tanks in #2 'tween deck broke their lashings and began shifting from side to side, slamming into the ship's side with great force. Captain Belesiotis hove to so as to reduce the rolling as much as possible. In spite of using only minimal engine power and heading into the wind and seas, the ship continued to pitch and roll heavily. The seas that we were taking on the foredeck had completely demolished the deck cargo there and made it ex-tremely dangerous for us to try to get to the #2 Deck House, so as to get into #2 'tween deck to try to secure the tanks. We had to take action because we were in danger of having the sides of the ship knocked out. I was the Chief Mate and it was up to me to get the job done.

Captain Belesiotis put the wind and sea slightly on the port bow to minimize the ship's movement and to give us a little lee on the starboard side.

At daybreak, I mustered all ten of the available deck crew (the Bosun, Deck Mainte-nance Man, five AB's and three Ordinary Seamen) on the Boat Deck on the starboard side. All had their heavy weather gear on, and were carrying flashlights. The Bosun, Deck Maintenance

Man and I timed the seas and made a dash to #3 deck house. We rigged a safety rope, using one and a half inch manila line, from the main deck house to #3 deck house. We got swamped a couple of times by seas that broke on deck, but we survived. We then timed the seas again, and made a dash to #2 deck house. We rigged an extension of the safety rope from #3 deck house.

Seas continued to break on deck from time to time and thoroughly drenched us. The water was very cold. We were wearing heavy rain gear, but that didn't seem to make any difference.

We all had flashlights, but would also need to rig cluster lights in #2 'tween deck. They were stowed in the #3 Deck House.

The three of us again timed the seas and made a dash from #2 Deck House to #3 Deck House, and opened the locker where the cluster lights were stowed. We then signaled the eight deck hands, who were standing by on the boat deck, to join us, which they bravely did. We collected three cluster lights with long cords, and all eleven of us managed to get to #2 Deck House.

It was somewhat of a relief to get into the Deck House and away from the constant wetting that we were getting on deck. To my surprise, the Second and Third Mates joined us to give a hand. We commenced climbing, one at a time, through the opening and down the ladder into the 'tween deck. Captain Belesiotis was on the bridge alone, except for one AB/Helmsman.

The power cords for the cluster lights had to be plugged in on the outside of the deck house. There was a double watertight plug-in electrical fixture, with screw-on caps, outboard on all four corners of the deck house. We could not use the ones on the port side because the seas were striking on that side. It was too dangerous to get to the fixture on the forward starboard corner, so I decided to only use the fixture on the after starboard side. This meant that we would only have power for two of the cluster lights. Just getting them plugged in was a life risking affair, but I did manage to do that myself, with the Bosun assisting.

The tanks that were sliding back and forth were, fortunately, in the after end of #2 'tween deck. Since the entry from the Deck House was at the forward end, we could safely get into the compartment and rig the lights.

There were five tanks, side by side, so that made a total of twenty-five tons of tanks sliding back and forth. They had developed a total of about eight feet of slack between them. It turned out that the welded pad eyes, on both sides of the hull, had torn out. I took some comfort in the fact that the lashings, that I had inspected and approved, had not given-way and were not at fault.

There was some excess dunnage in the general cargo in the forward part of the 'tween deck, and we immediately started chucking that into the open spaces between the tanks. It was not going to be nearly enough, so we also started throwing in cartons and bundles of general cargo from the forward end of #2 'tween deck. It would be badly damaged or destroyed, but that was of small concern now. We also started bringing excess dunnage up from #2 Lower Hold. We were working hard, fast and efficiently, because our lives depended on it.

The ship's motion, without being able to see the horizon, made it difficult to keep our footing. The slamming noise made when the tanks hit the side of the ship was frightening and we clearly felt the jolt that followed each slide. Before long, we had significantly reduced the amount of open space, and the impact following each slide commenced to diminish. Since the pad eyes had pulled out, there was no way to renew the lashings. We would have to depend entirely on chocking. After a couple of hours we had stopped the cargo movement. We continued to stuff more and more dunnage and general cargo in between the tanks. They ended up being completely covered.

Our heroic efforts had saved the ship and probably all of our lives. We could never have launched lifeboats in this storm. By 1100, we were satisfied that the tanks were secured, and we all climbed back up from the cargo compartment. Seas were still breaking over the main deck and it was dangerous, even with the safety lines, making the run back to the Main Deck House. But we all made it.

We were proud of our accomplishment, and Captain Belesiotis was lavish in his praise.

The deck cargo on the foredeck was all gone. The cargo on the after deck was badly damaged, as seen in the accompanying photographs.

Casablanca

We finally arrived at the Casablanca breakwater on Sunday, 12/5/54.

All of the deck cargo that had been stowed on the foredeck had been torn loose and washed overboard. There was also a lot of damage to the deck cargo that had been on the

After Deck Cargo Following Severe Gail (1954)

after deck. Many thousands of dollars worth of general cargo had been destroyed or severely damage when we chucked it in between the shifting tanks. There was moderate damage to the army tanks also. All of this had to be sorted out by the Underwriters.

I was going to be able to tell Pier Superintendent Bill Hunt "I told you so" with regards to deck cargo in the winter season.

There was not much cargo to discharge here, but we would spend a week in Casablanca as a result of our storm-damaged cargo. New, stronger pad eyes were welded back onto the inner hull in #2 'tween deck. The tanks were relashed and rechocked.

We sailed from Casablanca on Sunday, 12/12/54, bound for Cartagena, Spain.

Cartagena

We arrived in Cartagena early on Tuesday, 12/14/54. We went immediately to the dock and started discharging our cargo for this port.

This was a beautiful old city of historic interest. It is very hilly and has many beautiful vistas. Captain Belesiotis and I walked to town from the dock and attracted a group of about ten children who followed along. They were clean,well-dressed, and had good manners.

We were joined in town by the Chief Engineer and Radio Operator. Together, we had lunch in a nice café and ordered lobster. Mediterranean lobster is so much different from Maine lobster, that they seem to be different species. It was huge, with a body about eighteen inches long and a diameter of about eight inches. Its claws were very small and contained no useful meat. The lobster was served cold in the middle of the table for us to cut meat from as desired.

SS Kenneth H. Stevenson in Cartagena (1954)

We didn't have much tonnage for Cartagena and sailed late that evening, 12/14/54, for Tripoli, Libya.

Tripoli

We arrived at the Tripoli breakwater soon after daybreak on Saturday, 12/18/54. After a reasonable wait for the Harbor Pilot (about 30 minutes), Captain Belesiotis lost patience and entered the port and went to anchor. The Boarding Party and Pilot finally came out in the same boat. We soon

Cartagena School Children (1954)

got underway and proceeded to the dock. We had general cargo for our military base at Wheeler Field. There were no working lights on the dock, so we could only work cargo during daylight. We would be here three days.

Hostility against Westerners was building in this part of the Arab world, and you could sense it as you moved about town.

I was most impressed at the great fraternal relationship that exists within the world-wide Greek community. In almost every port that we called in, Captain Belesiotis located a fellow Greek, with whom to visit. They were usually Ship Chandlers, and frequently some business was transacted. Their conversations, in Greek, were always animated and usually much louder than we are accustomed to hear in English conversations. Captain Belesiotis even found a fellow countryman in this forlorn place.

We sailed from Tripoli on Tuesday, 12/21/54, bound for Rijeka, Yugoslavia.

Rijeka

We arrived in Rijeka early on Christmas Day, and were destined to spend the Christmas holidays in a Communistic country. What lousy luck!!! Of course it could have been worse— we could have been in Libya, or some other Muslim country.

Yugoslavia was officially atheist, so Christmas Day was not a holiday. We went to the dock and started discharging cargo.

Although it was not an official holiday, there was some observance for Christmas. Some of us went to a night club on Christmas evening and there was a good crowd in attendance.

Those tanks in #2 'tween deck, that had caused us to much grief, were to come out here. In fact, all of our considerable cargo remaining aboard, was destined for Rijeka. The damage to the tanks was noted and protested by the Receivers.

New Years Day was a holiday in Yugoslavia but, as luck would have it, we missed it. We sailed at midday on New Years Eve, Friday, 12/31/54, bound for Norfolk.

Night Club near Rijeka on Christmas evening (1954)

Coastwise— Norfolk, Wilmington, Savanna

After a stormy winter-time ocean crossing, we arrived in Norfolk on Wednesday, 1/18/55, and went to the Norfolk Army Base. We were to again load military general cargo. It included some of the same "light" tanks that we had taken on the previous voyage to Yugoslavia. These were going to Italy. I guess that we were trying to maintain a balance of power between these two countries that wished each other ill.

We departed from Norfolk late on 2/2/55, bound for Wilmington, NC, where we arrived on Friday, 2/4/55. We loaded more military general cargo and left on 2/8/55, for Savannah, arriving there on Wednesday, 2/9/55.

Captain Belesiotis left the ship to take a trip off for vacation. As per his recommendation, I relieved him as Master for this voyage.

Kenneth Williams, who had been my second mate on the last voyage of the *SS T. J. Stevenson,* was also second mate here. He was promoted to Chief Mate.

Third Voyage

Savannah, Naples, Norfolk

Our holds were full of general cargo, but we had no deck cargo. The military authorities had been in charge of loading, and they were not as gung-ho to earn the maximum revenue as was Stevenson Lines' Pier Superintendent, Bill Hunt. So we did not have any deck cargo for this winter season crossing of the Atlantic Ocean.

Again we did a super thorough inspection of the lashing and chocking for the "light" tanks, which were again stowed in #2 'tween deck.

We left Savannah on Friday, 2/18/55, headed out into the stormy winter-season North Atlantic. As would be expected, we had one gale after the other. We were fortunate to have tail winds in some of them. The tanks in #2 'tween deck held in place okay.

We experienced dense fog while proceeding through the Straits of Gibraltar. There was a lot of opposing traffic, and I again was wishing that Stevenson Lines would change their policy, and equip their ships with radar. We had to stop several times, exchanging whistle signals with other ships. We passed some of them too close for comfort.

Naples

We arrived in Naples on Friday, 3/11/55. We immediately went to the dock and started discharging our cargo.

This time I would be able to do some sight-seeing. I visited the Naples Museum. The thing that impressed me the most was a marble statue of Hercules by an unknown Greek sculpturer. It conveyed massive and brutal strength. There were many artifacts that had been recovered from Pompeii and Herculean. I also got to spend an afternoon exploring Pompeii.

Our cargo was worked around the clock and we sailed on Wednesday, 3/16/55, which was my 30th birthday. I did not let anyone know about my B. D. We were bound for Norfolk.

Enroute back to the U. S., I received a radiogram informing that I should plan to leave the ship in Norfolk, and that I would be taking command of the *SS Sea Leader*.

Our return voyage, in ballast, was not as stormy as normal for this time of year. Most of the gales that we encountered gave us tail winds.

"New" Castle in Naples (1955)

**The Author at Pompeii.
Mt. Vesuvius in background (1955)**

Norfolk

We arrived in Norfolk on Saturday, 4/9/55. Captain Belesiotis was waiting on the dock and came aboard as soon as we got the gangway out. He look fresh and hardy after his vacation and was "raring to go".

We had the voyage payoff the next day. I stayed on one more day to fill Captain Belesiotis in on various things. I was not going to have time to go home between ships. I would shortly have to start my travel, by train, to Houston, the port to which the *SS Sea Leader* was bound.

My demotion to Chief Mate for two voyages had been a sobering experience. The U. S. Merchant Marine was in a fast decline. I decided to write the Panama Canal Company and remind them that I was hoping for an appointment as a Panama Canal Pilot.

(Note: According to "The Liberty Ships" by Captain Walter W. Jaffee, the SS Kenneth H. Stevenson was originally named the SS Charles Paddock. She was built by the California Shipbuilding Corporation and launched 12/26/43. She was first operated by the Seas Shipping Co and was laid up in the Hudson River Reserve Fleet 4/27/46. In 1948 and 1949 she was operated by T. J. Stevenson & Co., Inc. and then put in the Reserve Fleet at Mobile Bay. She was withdrawn from there in January 1946, and purchased by the Ocean Freighting and Brokerage Corp. and renamed the SS Kenneth H. Stevenson. In 1962 she was sold to the Artemision Steamship Co., S. A., renamed the SS Skiathos and reflaged Liberia. In 1966 she was sold to the Hercules Nav. S. A. and renamed the SS Demitrios. On 7/12/67, while on a voyage from Bombay to Poland with a cargo of ore, she developed leaks and sank off Diego Suarez, Madagascar (Lat. 9 degrees 20 minutes South, Long. 48 degrees 30 minutes East.)

Chapter XIII: The SS Sea Leader
(as Master)
First Voyage

Houston, Jacksonville, Gibraltar, Haifa, Gibraltar, Mobile

Houston

The Master that I was relieving was being "bumped" by me into unemployment, and was understandably resentful. He was hostile and not cooperative in turning over command to me. For one thing, he was given no warning ahead of time, and didn't know that he was being fired until I came aboard and told him. It was a bit tense and unpleasant. He was a big and powerful man, and I think that he considered getting physical about it. In those days, I was thirty years old and in my "prime". I was ready to take him on if necessary.

I had previously spent two years (1950-51) on this ship as Chief Mate. That was no particular advantage to me now, because all Liberty ships were about the same.

I had three former shipmates from the *SS T. J. Stevenson* aboard. Joe Koller, who I had promoted to Chief Mate, was Chief Mate here; George Thomas, who had been my Chief Engineer, was Chief here; and Neil Thomas, who had been First Assistant Engineer on that ship, was now First Assistant on the *SS Sea Leader*. They were all good men and I was glad to see them. They seemed glad to see me and let me know that they had not been happy with the previous Captain.

In Houston, we had to wait four days for the berth to become available. We then shifted to a grain elevator where we took on a full load of wheat, about 10,000 long tons. It was destined for Haifa, Israel. During the loading, the grain dust in the air was very heavy, and it gave me a severe allergic reaction. I spent one night in a hotel to get away from it.

We sailed from Houston on Saturday, 4/16/55, bound for Haifa, with a stop scheduled at Gibraltar for fuel.

Breakdown at Sea

Three days out while in the midst of a moderate easterly gale, suddenly at about 2300, the engine started racing and had to be shut down. We were completely without engine power. All we could do was to put up two red lights, one over the other, to let other ships know our condition. After daylight, we changed the two red lights to two black balls, one over the other, to give the same information. Fortunately, we had plenty of sea room in which to drift.

I don't know enough about the problem to give a technically perfect explanation, but the problem was something like this. An essential cam in the drive mechanism broke, and prevented us from powering the drive shaft ahead. There was a similar cam that was used when we put the engine astern. Chief Engineer Thomas put his crew to work removing the astern cam and installing it in place of the broken cam. This was difficult work and the rolling that we were doing made it worse. It took several hours to complete. When they were done, we could power the engine ahead just fine, but could no longer back the engine.

I deemed that we must get this fixed before proceeding to Gibraltar and Haifa. I requested T. J. Stevenson to find a port and shipyard where this could be done. Operations Vice President, Mr. John F. Shea, urged me to continue on the voyage, but I insisted that it must be repaired before crossing to Europe.

After a few hours, they found a solution, and ordered me to proceed to Jacksonville, FL

Jacksonville

The *SS Sea Leader*, being fully loaded, was displacing about 14,000 long tons, and we had no backing power. Obviously, we would have a problem getting stopped when that became necessary.

The port of Jacksonville, at that time, did not have any tugboats that could be considered to be modern or high-powered. They had a Harbor Pilot, who was extremely competent, and not afraid to handle our ship under these conditions. In short, he had balls!!!

We arrived and started up the Jacksonville River about 0730 on Friday, 4/22/55. The Harbor Pilot had sent the biggest of his old tugs meet us at the entrance to the river. It put lines up to each quarter and followed along, dead astern, so as to be able to provide some backing action. It was so low-powered, that I couldn't keep up with us, and we ended up towing it up river.

When we were to arrive at the port and the shipyard, a ninety degree turn to starboard was going to be necessary, and we would be docking starboard side to the berth. Four additional large, old, and low-powered tugs came alongside on our port side. They covered our port side completely, each contacting and leaning against the tug astern of them. This was in the days before walkie talkies, so the pilot had to control all five of these tugs with hand and mouth whistle signals. There was also the problem of current in the river and that had to be taken into account. We had the starboard anchor backed out and ready to let go at a moment's notice. We couldn't use the port one because of the tugs on that side.

The Pilot skillfully timed when to stop our engine to drift our speed down, against the river's current, so as to be in position to make the starboard turn into the berth. In the proper location, with all of the tugs pumping away at full astern, and with skillful use of our engine on slow and dead slow ahead, with hard right rudder, we were able turn into the berth and to get stopped in good order. The stopping was mainly accomplished by the timely dropping of and holding the starboard anchor. I was very tense during these maneuvers and, when we were safely berthed, I lavished praise on the Pilot for his remarkably fine shiphandling.

The needed replacement cam was not available locally. There was a company in Houston that maintained a large inventory of Liberty ship parts, and they had one that was being trucked over. We had to wait two days for it and then a day to install it. When I think how Chief Engineer

Thomas, and his men, changed the part at sea, with the ship rolling, in less time that the shipyard crew could, I became their admiring fan.

On Friday morning, 4/24/55, we departed Jacksonville, bound for Gibraltar. We had a couple of moderate gales, but overall our sixteen day passage to Gibraltar was not bad.

Gibraltar

We arrived at Gibraltar Bay at 0430 on Tuesday, 5/10/55. It was a nice clear night with only a light breeze blowing from the north. We received the usual challenge by flashing light and identified our ship. They replied that the Pilot was on his way. I had to wait almost an hour for the pilot boat to show up, and was a bit peeved about that. He finally came aboard and directed our maneuver to go port-side-to one of the old Shell Oil Company tankers, that were anchored here as bunkering stations.

The Pilots here had to do all of their work without the assistance of tugs, and had therefore become very good shiphandlers. The hulks were free to rotate 360 degrees on their anchors, and so they always rode headed into the prevailing current or wind, whichever one predominated. Thus, by approaching from the direction of the stern of the anchored hulk, they were stemming the current and/or heading into the wind, which was helpful. They always berthed the ships port side to the hulks, which was the easiest maneuver for single screw ships. Being able to avoid the cost of tug boats was a major factor in making this a desirable bunkering port.

While in Gibraltar, the then new American passenger ship, the SS Independence, made a port call and I was able to photograph it. Years later, I would pilot her through the Panama Canal.

We finished bunkering and departed Gibraltar at 1400 on 5/10/55. It had been the usual efficient operation here.

The then new American passenger ship, the SS Independence, calling at Gibraltar (1955)

It was a nine day run over to Haifa and we had excellent weather. As we were running along the north coast of Africa, we observed an almost continual oil slick caused by tankers cleaning their tanks while enroute, via the Suez Canal, back to the oil loading ports in the Persian Gulf. We had also observed this on previous voyages. The pollution was becoming massive.

Haifa

None of us had ever been to Israel before, and we were looking forward to some interesting sight-seeing. The city was beautiful in the early morning sun when we arrived on Thursday, 5/29/55.

The port was busy and we had to wait two days for a berth. A grain sucker had not yet been installed, so our cargo had to be discharged using canvas slings, which were then dumped into trucks, that came alongside the ship in an efficient operation. We would end up spending thirteen days here. The weather was perfect and it was to be an interesting and pleasant stay here.

Saturday was, of course, the Sabbath and it was observed strictly. The Jewish dietary laws were also enforced in the restaurants. The people were generally very well educated and many spoke English as well as other languages.

Haifa was a large and bustling city dominated by Mount Carmel. There was a beautiful Bahai Temple, about half way up Mount Carmel, which had a large, breath-taking, real golden dome. It glistened brightly in the sun.

View of Mount Carmel, photographed from our ship at the dock in Haifa (1955)

View of Haifa from the top of Mount Carmel. The *SS Sea Leader* is docked center, distant.

Jerusalem was divided, with the Arabs holding the old part of the city. We ascended the YMCA tower, in the part of the city held by the Jewish forces, where we could see into the old city. Some of the main points of interest pointed out to us.

We were very favorably impressed with the industry, enthusiasm and patriotism shown by the Jewish people, with whom we dealt. The land was not very fertile and was full of rocks. The Arabs had been starving on it. The Jewish farmers cleared away the rocks, often having to do it by hand, fertilized, irrigated and intently cultivated. They were getting two and three crops a year on the same land that the Arabs had not been able to farm.

They had been greatly out-numbered by the Arab military forces, but, as they told us, they had a secret weapon— no other choice except to win or be driven into the sea. We saw several burned-out Syrian tanks along the

Bahia Temple, Haifa (1955)

251.

roadways. These were left over reminders of the heavy fighting that had accompanied the establishment of their country in May of 1948.

A group of us hired a very well-informed and pragmatic guide, who drove us around the country in his Chrysler limousine. He could conduct tours in several languages. Initially, he inquired as to our religious preferences (Catholic, Orthodox, Muslim, Protestant and if so what denomination, etc.). He would then cater to interests of the audience that he had. Since we were a mangy group of seamen, he tried to cover all bases. He himself was an atheist.

He showed us the place from where Mohammed had ascended into heaven, taking his horse with him. He showed us the tombs of a number of biblical characters, and then pointed out that there was no tomb for Mary, because she took her body with her when she went to heaven.

He showed us partial geological diggings around Jerusalem, that the Pope had forced to be stopped and abandoned, because they showed that the Mount of Olives had been enclosed within the ancient city. This was counter to Catholic doctrine.

He took us into a mosque, where a prayer service was under way, and embarrassed us by talking loudly and interrupting it. We got glares of hatred from some of the Arab participants.

We went to Nazareth, and he showed us where the Holy Ghost had informed Mary that she was to give birth to Jesus. The colored Second Cook on our ship was also shown this place, on a separate tour. He described his experience as having been in "the very room where the Holy Ghost done knocked-up the Virgin Mary".

Nazareth Street Scenes (1955)

252.

We also walked about the area in Nazareth where Joseph was believed to have worked as a carpenter.

Bethlehem was still under Arab control and we had to observe it from a distance. It looked pristine and beautiful.

He also took us to King David's cave where there is a stone altar which, he explained, was the best place in the world to have your sons circumcised. Here again he embarrassed us by talking loudly and interrupting a Jewish ceremony.

The tour would have been much more interesting if we had had access to the old city of Jerusalem. Hard and angry relations were apparent, and there was no travel or exchange of any kind between the Jewish and Arab controlled areas.

Nazareth Butcher Shop (1955)

The biggest bargains in Israel were books. They are heavily subsidized, and the several large book stores had good deals, that were hard to pass up. I bought several books on history, which has always been of great interest to me.

We finished discharging our cargo of wheat and sailed on Wednesday, 6/1/55, for Gibraltar.

Gibraltar

We arrived back in Gibraltar at 2200 on Wednesday, 6/8/55, and were met almost immediately by the Pilot. The evening was windy, so our berthing to one of the old Shell oil tankers was going to be difficult, with no tug being available. The pilot told me that he planned to drag an anchor up to the hulk, and I agreed that it was indicated due to the conditions. Chief Mate Joe Koller backed out the starboard anchor, so as to have it ready to drop without delay, when so ordered. When we were properly lined up and making about three knots, the Pilot ordered the anchor dropped. We were about three ship lengths from the hulk. The windlass brake was set when one shot (15 fathoms or 90 feet) of chain was paid out. It worked beautifully, slowing us and allowing slow ahead on the engine to keep steering control in the wind, without gaining too much headway.

The hose hook-up and bunkering was done expeditiously, and we got underway five hours later, leaving early on 6/9/55, bound for Mobile. We were looking forward to a nice summer season ocean crossing, and that is what we had.

Voyage Two

Mobile, Panama Canal, San Pedro, Muroran, Moji, Inchon, Moji, Seattle

Mobile

We arrived in Mobile early on Sunday morning, 6/26/55. We had our voyage payoff and signed foreign articles the next day.

Our cargo this voyage was to be a full load of coking coal for Korea. It was all aboard and we sailed on Wednesday, 6/29/55, for the Panama Canal.

Enroute to the Canal, our cargo in #4 'tween deck commenced to give off a considerable amount of water vapor, and it was noticeably getting warm. By radio, I requested that a Surveyor check the cargo in Panama, to verify that it was not going to catch fire by spontaneous combustion.

Panama Canal

We arrived at the Cristobal breakwater at 2300 on Tuesday, 7/5/55, and went to anchor in Limon Bay. I was again annoyed by the two pairs of buoys, between the breakwater heads, that restricted the entry to only 500 feet wide, instead of the 1,200 feet that it could have been. We had heavy rain as we arrived, which caused poor visibility made the entry a bit frightening, especially since we had no radar.

The Canal Boarding Party Officials told me to expect a Canal Pilot at about 0530, so we had a short night of it.

My Agent boarded and said that he had arranged for a Surveyor to board in the morning and survey the cargo during the transit.

I could not believe my luck when the Pilot turned out to be none other than Captain William Calcutt. He had been my Pilot now for three consecutive transits, spread over a period of a year and a half on two different ships. I was delighted to see him, as he was actively supporting my application to become a Panama Canal Pilot. The job was beginning to look very desirable, in view of the fact that more and more American ships were being sold or laid-up.

The Surveyor checked the temperature in the sounding pipes, port and starboard, of all five cargo holds. He found elevated temperatures everywhere, and also that water vapor was coming from all of the 'tween decks, especially #2 and #4. His conclusion was that the situation was not dangerous. He recommended that we keep the cargo vents trimmed for maximum ventilation, He also suggested that we check the temperature in the sounding pipes daily. I ordered a proper thermometer to be sent aboard as we passed Balboa.

We had a good transit, and Captain Calcutt promised to check on my application and let me know. He said that some new Pilots had recently been hired and more were needed.

We cleared the Pacific Channel of the Canal at 1700 on 7/6/55, the same date that we had arrived on the Atlantic side. We were bound for San Pedro, CA, for bunkers.

Passage Panama Canal to San Pedro

It was a thirteen day run up to San Pedro. The weather was perfect, except for a bit of a gale as we passed the Gulf of Tehuantepec. I almost never passed there without a blow of some sort. Some of the Captains that came this way frequently, run in close along the shore, so that the off-shore wind does not have the sweep necessary to build up the sea.

I was getting really worried about the possibility of having spontaneous combustion in our cargo of coking coal. We were getting temperatures of up to 140 degrees in some of the sounding tubes, and vapor was visibly coming from the cargo vents in all five holds. I reported this by radio to our San Pedro Agent, and also to the home office of T. J. Stevenson & Co.. Inc. in New York. I stressed the importance of having a really competent surveyor examine our cargo in San Pedro.

The San Pedro Agent reported our problem to the Coast Guard and to the "notorious" head of security for the Port of Los Angeles, retired Coast Guard Admiral Higby.

To my surprise, a Coast Guard cutter met my ship, as we approached the entry to the San Pedro breakwater, early morning on Tuesday, 7/19/55. By flashing light, they ordered me to proceed to an anchorage, that they designated, inside the breakwater. I did as directed.

San Pedro

Admiral Higby came aboard along with the Boarding Party and read me the riot act for entering the harbor, with a dangerous cargo, without authority and without a Pilot. I told him that I had been instructed by the Coast Guard cutter to proceed to this anchorage. He was not satisfied and was living up to his reputation of being perpetually angry. The Agent got me aside, and advised me not to step on the dock, because the Admiral would likely have me arrested and fined.

The Admiral would not allow us to go to the dock until a Surveyor had declared it safe to do so. That happened pretty quickly, and we heaved up the anchor and went to a fueling berth.

The Surveyor took samples of our coal cargo to a laboratory to be checked out. His conclusion was that there was not any danger of spontaneous combustion. They advised that I provide maximum ventilation to the cargo.

I took the Agent's advice seriously and did not set foot on the dock. There was a policeman standing by at the foot of the gangway, probably waiting for me to pass his way.

We departed San Pedro at 2200 on 7/19/55, the same date that we had arrived. We were bound for Inchon, Korea.

Transpacific with a Burning Cargo of Coal

I was very worried about our cargo, which continued to heat up and give off vapor. It was hard to understand how a laboratory could check a small sample, and be able to tell whether or not it might catch fire, when stored in large quantities in a ship.

We continued to take the temperatures in the sounding pipes. We were concerned enough to start doing this twice a day. The hottest spots were in #3 Lower hold and #2 and #4 'tween decks. The vapor coming from the cargo vents was becoming heavier everywhere.

This was a summer time passage so I was following a Great Circle route, which meant that we would be too far north for the Hawaiian Islands to be a possible harbor of refuge.

I was keeping T J. Stevenson & Co., Inc. advised of our situation. It was a helpless and frightening thing to be sitting on all of this stored energy, which was "coming to life" on its own.

When we were in mid-ocean, beyond the point of return, we started getting obvious fires in #2 and #4 'tween decks.

I decided to reverse our policy of maximum ventilation to one of no ventilation. I had the crew install the canvas covers on all of the cargo ventilators, and to trim them away from the wind. We only had about fifty tons of fresh water, and so could only run the steam smothering system for a token, symbolic, amount of time, mainly so as to be able to say that we had done it.

Had I done the right thing by cutting off all ventilation? My object was to deprive the coal of oxygen which is needed for combustion. The canvas covers would greatly reduce oxygen getting to the cargo, but they were not air tight by any means. But this measure also "bottled up" the heat that was being produced, and the temperature was building up dramatically. Was the cargo likely to explode? This was a real and frightening danger.

In the sounding tubes we were getting very high temperature readings. The hottest place appeared to be #3 Lower Hold. Our thermometer only read up to 250 degrees and it was off the end of the scale there. Later was off the scale in all ten sounding pipes.

The surface of the main deck was hot in many places, and I directed that we run sea water continually over the deck throughout the length of the ship.

I was asking T. J. Stevenson & Co., Inc. if they had any advice. They replied that I should avoid, if possible, putting seawater into the coal, as it would ruin it for making coke. They arranged for the port of Muroran, on the south coast of Hokkaido Island in Japan, to receive us and assist with the situation. It was a coal exporting port, and therefore had some experience that may be helpful.

I did not know it at the time, but there were five cargoes of this coal, enroute from Mobile to Korea, and all were now on fire. A British flag freighter was four days ahead of us, and they were also diverted to Muroran. They were in desperate condition. They had opened #3 hatch, in front of the bridge, to pour seawater on the fire, and now had open flames burning the paint off the front of the main deck house.

As we approached Muroran in the early morning hours of Tuesday, 8/9/55, we encountered dense fog. Again I was cursing the policy that Stevenson Lines had, in not equipping their ships with radar. To make things worse, we were encountering many fishing boats in the fog. I felt my way toward what I believed to be the port, frequently checking the soundings and taking bearings with the Radio Direction Finder. I finally decided to anchor until it cleared up.

I had done a pretty good job of navigating in the fog, and was close enough for the Harbor Pilot and Boarding Party to find us at anchor. Of course, they had radar to help them. To my great surprise, Mr. Harold Vinick, who had been Stevenson Lines Representative in Genoa, came aboard with the Japanese Boarding Party. Stevenson Lines had flown him over to assist with the situation.

About 1030, the fog began to lift. So we heaved anchor and proceeded to an anchorage inside the harbor.

Muroran

The Muroran Harbor Master proposed to do with us what he had done with the British ship, which had arrived four days before us. Namely, ground our ship, in an area of soft mud, and fill our holds with fresh water from barges, until the fires were out. Fresh water would not damage the cargo but sea water would ruin it for coking purposes.

The active fires that we had were in #2 and #4 'tween decks. #3 lower hold was suspect because of the heat that we found in the sounding pipes there, and also because the bulkhead at the after end of #3 hold was very hot to the touch (in the Second Deck, in the area of the Steward's store rooms). I did a calculation and determined that there was no need to ground the ship and risk damage to the bottom. We could spray water onto #2 and #4 'tween decks, and put out those smoldering fires, without a great tonnage of water being required. We could start pumping fresh water into #3 lower hold, until it got high enough in the hold to put out the fire, again without a great tonnage of water being required. The port had a couple of large water barges, and they were put to work hauling water to us. After three days, the fires were out, and all compartments had cooled down. We were able to get the fires out without an excessive increase in our draft, which would have made it necessary to ground the ship.

There was going to be the problem of pumping out the water when we got to our discharge port. It was decided to stop and pick up some heavy duty pumps at the Japanese port of Moji, in the Shimonoseki Straits. We sailed from Muroran on Friday, 8/12/55, bound for Moji.

I proceeded down the west coast of Honshu and approached the port from the west.

During all of this time we were having nice summer weather. It was in the midst of Typhoon Season, and there was one down south, but the weather was great in our location.

Moji

We arrived at Moji on Monday, 8/15/55. The entry to this port is very torturous and in close quarters. There was opposing ship traffic and many fishing vessels. I was a bit nervous navigating there, but it went well. A Japanese Pilot boarded, and we proceeded to a dock, and loaded the pumps. The big diesel-powered pumps were on the dock, ready for us. We hauled them aboard and stowed them on deck. There were two of them and they each weighed about three tons. They were truly heavy duty.

We had concluded that these pumps were probably not going to be necessary. Enroute from Muroran, Chief Engineer Thomas had put the bilge pump to work and, to our surprise, the water was pumping out freely. It was crystal clear and was, after all, being passed through a big carbon "filter".

As soon as the pumps had been loaded, we got underway for Inchon, Korea. The date was 8/15/55.

As we proceeded up the west coast of Korea, the weather turned rotten. There was almost constant heavy rain, with a moderate gale blowing from the West. This coast is treacherous to navigate in poor visibility with no radar. There are many small islands and rocks along the coast, and the entry channel at Inchon is very difficult, even in good weather. Inchon has a forty-foot tidal range, along with the strong currents that go with such a drastic change. I was plenty worried and concentrated hard on the navigation.

Meanwhile, as soon as we had the water pumped out of #3 lower hold, it started getting very hot again.

This cargo was the "pits". Also, the coal in #2 and #4 'tween decks was also heating up again.

Inchon

I reduced speed to time arrival at the Inchon entry channel to be at daybreak on Wednesday, 8/17/55. It was a miserable rainy morning, but I was able to find and identify the lighthouse and buoys. We proceeded into the port. There were already two ships anchored there, which made it a bit crowded.

Soon after anchoring, we had an emergency situation. A U. S. Army launch came alongside and informed me, by megaphone, that a North Korean mine was floating down the river toward us.

The tide was ebbing at about four knots. I could see the mine with the binoculars. It was a motley, gray, ugly, round thing, about three feet in diameter. It had several contact horns. It must have been in the water for a long time, because it also had what looked like barnacles on it.

It appeared to be drifting directly down on a Chinese (Taiwan) Liberty ship, that was anchored off our port beam. I believe that it would have struck that ship, if the army launch operator had not, at great personal risk, run his boat at full speed between the ship and the mine, causing the boat's bow wave to wash the mine away from the ship. Those guys performed bravely. I captured their action in the accompanying photograph.

U. S. Army Launch using bow wave to fend mine away from ship
Inchon, Korea (1955)

After mine floated past us, the Army launch continued to escort as it went out of sight. I imagine that they detonated it, when it arrived at a place where it was safe to do so.

The Agent already knew about the fires that we had. I had advised him, by radiogram, that we would need one or more barges of fresh water to spray on our cargo, to keep the coal from catching fire again. He had arranged for both the ones that were available.

When we opened the hatches, the coal, especially in #2 and #4 'tween decks, started smoldering. Stevedores, just about anywhere else in the world, would have refused to go down into these cargo compartments. But these guys, without hesitation, climbed down into the 'tween decks and started wetting it down, and shoveling the coal into canvas slings for discharge. It would not have been so bad if there had been grab bucket type cargo gear available, but we had to discharge by hand-shoveling it into canvas slings, that were then emptied into barges alongside. The coal was giving off heavy vapor. It was hot and the stevedores were only wearing canvas shoes. The water barges were supplying fresh water that was being constantly sprayed onto the cargo, to keep it cool enough to work. It was unbelievably difficult conditions. My admiration for the Korean stevedores, who endured these conditions, was immense.

The water barges were only able to supply spray-water to two hatches at a time. So, we worked two hatches around the clock. We were able to get all 10,000 tons of the coal cargo out in eleven days.

It turned out that the water pumps, that we loaded in Moji, were not needed. Chief Engineer Thomas was able to pump out all of the water, using only our regular bilge pump. The water being pumped from our bilges was crystal clear. The coal was acting as a huge carbon filter.

With all of the problems going on, I did not leave the ship. I kept alert sea watches, mainly because I was worried that we would have a collision with the other anchored ships, when the tide changed. The tide reversed about every twelve hours and fifteen minutes. I had to use the engine and rudder to be sure that we swung in the same direction as the other ships. Both of the ships that had been there when we arrived, left during our stay, but two others arrived to replace them. One was anchored so close that I sent the Captain a written note, asking him to move. He ignored it.

We were able to sail from Inchon on Sunday, 8/28/55, bound to Moji. We were to return the pumps (unused) and take bunkers for our return to the U. S. West Coast. I was never more relieved to get safely away from a port, and situation, than I was this time.

Korean Stevedores working in cargo of hot coal. Note the vapor rising from the cargo. (1955)

We had light fog leaving Inchon, and it increased to heavy fog a short time later. There were many fishing vessels working off the west coast of Korea, and also there was some coastwise shipping. We had to run slow, and stopped a couple of times, while exchanging fog signals with other vessels. After about ten hours, the fog lifted and we had good weather.

It was a two day run to Moji.

Moji

We again entered the confined and busy waters of the Shimonoseki Straits from the west, entering at 0700 on Tuesday, 8/30/55, enroute to Moji. This port is located on the north, or Honshu side, of the channel. The Japanese Pilot, that came out to board us, appeared to be very old, maybe about eighty. Anyway, he was sharp and handled our port entry and docking very expertly. The only English words that he knew were the engine and helm orders, which were sufficient.

View of the shore in the Shimonoseki Straits

We discharged the unused diesel-powered pumps, and our bunkering operation proceeded efficiently.

We sailed at 1500 that same day, this time bound east from Moji, through the Shimonoseki Strait, and through a portion of the Japanese Inland Sea. I proceeded south of Shikoku Island. When we were clear of the Japanese Islands, we started on a Great Circle course toward Seattle. I later modified the Great Circle course so as not to go up among the Aleutian Islands. Our weather for this passage was generally good.

Seattle

On my last arrival in the Straits of Juan de Fuca, we had experienced beautiful, clear weather, and got to enjoy some of the world's most beautiful scenery. This time, when we arrived on Monday, 9/19/55, it was a rainy and dreary day. We picked up the Pilot at Port Angles, and steamed on to Seattle, where we docked at a lumber loading pier.

Voyage Three

Seattle, Olympia, Aberdeen, Panama Canal, New York, Philadelphia, Wilmington, New York

We had our voyage payoff and signed coastwise articles. We were going to take a full load of lumber for the East Coast.

I now ran into a serious financial problem, in that the ship-chandlers would not extend the credit needed to purchase voyage stores. It seems that the Owner of the *SS Sea Leader*, for a period of time, had contracted with a different company, other than T. J. Stevenson & Co., Inc., to manage the ship. During that time, the *SS Sea Leader* had run up bills in several West Coast ports, and had not paid them. The fact that the ship now had a different operator did not impress the local ship-chandlers in the least.

The only way that we could get anything sold to us was by paying cash in advance. The problem was immediate, because we needed things such as milk, bread, fresh vegetables, etc., as soon as possible. Later we would need full voyage stores. So, I had to contact T. J. Stevenson & Co., Inc.'s New York office, and arrange for them to authorize the Agent in Seattle, and the other West Coast ports at which we would be loading, to advance sufficient cash to me to make the needed purchases. This required me to go to local banks, cash checks, and then carry large amounts of money back to the ship. I didn't know exactly how much would be needed, but I had to be sure to have enough money. Also, this situation caused me to lose bargaining power about prices, because I was lucky to be able to find anyone who was willing to do business with me. Then, of course, I had to be sure to be aboard when the stores were delivered alongside, because nothing would be put aboard until the bills were paid in advance by cash. This was an extra chore that I really didn't need.

We took a partial load of lumber in Seattle and then, on Saturday, 9/24/55, moved to Olympia.

Olympia

The weather cleared up and we did have pretty scenery during our shift to Olympia.

While going to sea, I maintained an active membership in the International Order of Elks. This membership gave me someplace to go in cities where I did not know anyone, or have local knowledge about restaurants, etc.

I went to the Elks Club in Olympia, on a Sunday, and had a friendly conversation at the bar with a fellow, who turned out to be the Principal at a local elementary school. After I had had enough "heaves ahead" to cloud my judgment, I agreed to his proposal to bring a bus full of his school kids to my ship for a guided tour on Monday morning.

I alerted my officers and the Chief Steward about this, but hoped that he would not show up. I had a tour arranged that would show them the wheelhouse, flying bridge, the engine room from the upper platform, the Steward's refer boxes and storerooms, the Galley and the Saloon Mess. I had the Steward set to serve lemonade and cake.

At 1000 Monday morning, not one but two school buses arrived and pulled up alongside our gangway. These were sixth and seventh graders. Many of the little girls were wearing "frilly" dresses. There were about sixty children. Stevenson's insurance people would have had me keel-hauled if they had known about this. Thank God everything went okay and no one was injured or had any problems. My new friend, the Principal, thought that it all went very well, and that the kids learned some interesting things.

We loaded lumber in Olympia for three days and then sailed on Tuesday, 9/27/55, for Aberdeen, to finish loading.

Aberdeen

We arrived at Aberdeen on Wednesday, 9/28/55. It was here that we would top off with our deck load, and our stability would become critical.

The *SS Sea Leader* had loaded lumber the voyage before I joined her, and the resulting problems were the reason that the previous Captain had been fired. I had to make sure that I didn't make the same mistakes.

There are special problems when carrying lumber on a freighter that is not specifically designed for it. When all of the lower holds and 'tween decks are loaded full of lumber, the ship is far from being down to her allowable draft. As a result, a large deck load of lumber is put on, so that the ship can earn the maximum amount of freight revenue. This, in turn, raises the center of gravity and causes stability problems.

With a Liberty ship, every double bottom tank must be full, except the one that you are burning fuel from. When that tank becomes empty, it must be filled with sea water ballast before a new tank is tapped. All tanks must be kept pressed up with no, absolutely no slack tanks ,that would allow a "free surface" effect. A big problem exists with regards to the large #3 Deep Tanks which are located in #4 Lower Hold. It is usually also used for fuel, and no Chief Engineer that I know of would allow sea water ballast to be put into that tank. So it, by necessity, will be a slack tank until all fuel in it is consumed. The double bottoms tanks alone would not hold enough fuel for our voyage.

When the *SS Sea Leader* had been loading on that previous voyage, there had been slack double bottom tanks, while they were taking fuel in #3 Deep Tanks. As the longshoremen were loading deck cargo, the ship suddenly heeled over about thirty degrees toward the dock. The longshoremen abandoned the ship in panic. There was damage to the ship and dock. Fortunately, there were no injuries, but there very well could have been. The fault was with the Engineers, for not keeping the Double Bottom tanks pressed up, and also, while taking fuel into #3 Deep Tanks, they had not keep the level even between the port and starboard tanks. If anyone got fired, it should have been them, but instead, it was the Captain.

Prior to loading, I had a serious conference with Chief Engineer Thomas, and stressed in the strongest possible terms, the necessity to keep all double bottom tanks pressed up with either fuel or sea ballast. He agreed to closely supervise this matter, and not to blindly trust underlings to properly see to it.

There is a large tidal range at Aberdeen ,and ships routinely sit on the bottom at low water. This happened to us, and it made it impossible to get an accurate draft reading. We had to take the Cargo Supervisor's word for it on how many tons of lumber they could keep piling on.

They put on a bit too much, because when the tide came back in, we had a list and the ship was very "tender", that is, she easily listed to port or starboard from minor things, such as swinging the cargo booms from one side to the other. We sounded all double bottom tanks and all were pressed up. The current consumption was from #3 Deep Tanks. There was no way that we could improve our stability, and it was not satisfactory. I insisted that some of the deck cargo be removed. This created a big fuss that was heard all of the way to New York, but I stuck by my guns. The local Coast Guard Inspector backed me up.

The stability was finally improved to my (bare) satisfaction, and we sailed from Aberdeen on Sunday, 10/2/55. We were bound for the Panama Canal.

As we proceeded on our way, our stability was barely adequate. We had a very slow top heavy rolling motion. We were going to have to be very careful in keeping all double bottom tanks pressed up. I was praying that we would not run into any rain squalls, because the lumber on deck would soak up water and worsen our stability.

For our Panama Canal transit, we were going to have to manage our fuel so that there would not even be one slack Double Bottom tank. They would all have to be full with either fuel or sea water. With even one slack tank, I feared that just the locomotives pulling or braking at the locks, would cause us to heel over with possible disastrous consequences. The Engineers would have to work this out, and they did. During our transit, they were using fuel from only the settling tank.

Except for the usual blow passing the Gulf of Tehuantepec, we had pretty good weather for this passage. We arrived at the Panama Canal at 2100 on Tuesday,10/18/55 and anchored off the Pacific entrance.

Panama Canal

On my three previous transits, I had Captain William Calcutt as my Pilot. Would I luck out again?

The Pilot assigned to our ship turned out to be Captain Fred Poore. He boarded at 0530 the next morning, and turned out to be a pleasant and competent fellow. I told him that I had an application in to be a Pilot. He himself was pretty new on the job, but highly recommended it. He said that the available housing was not very good, and that new Pilots started with no seniority for housing. They had to fall in behind Canal Zone "brats" that started building up seniority by ushering in the local movie theaters as kids, and then later took other jobs with the Canal Company. I sent a note ashore with him to Captain Calcutt, giving him my "regards".

We cleared the Cristobal breakwater at 1600 on 10/19/55, bound for New York.

There was a hurricane working its way across the Caribbean Sea, but it was going to be passed on by the time we got that far north. That was fortunate, because I sure would not want to encounter a bad storm with a big deck load of lumber.

Panama is lucky in that hurricanes just about never get that far south.

Coastwise— New York, Philadelphia, Wilmington, New York

Our weather was reasonably good and we arrived at the Scotland Light Vessel, enroute to New York, on Friday, 10/28/55. We proceeded to a dock in Port Newark, and commenced discharging lumber. I was very glad to get this deck load off, and have proper stability.

We did not have the voyage payoff yet, since we were going to be discharging in additional ports. I gave out a generous draw to the crew.

Stevenson Lines Operations Manager, Captain William Campbell, sent word for me to come to the office. Although I regarded him as my friend, the way the message was sent had me a bit worried.

Figuring out the trains and subways to travel from Port Newark to lower Manhattan was complicated, but I managed to get there. Captain Campbell, Personnel Manger Mr. John A. Moore, the then current Marine Superintendent, Mr. Bill Ottaway, and others, were all very cordial in their greetings. Captain Campbell swore me to secrecy, because he did not want the rest of the crew to get the news yet, but the *SS Sea Leader* was going to be sold to other interests as soon as this voyage was over. He said that he would try to find me another ship as soon as possible. I overcame his reluctance, and got him to agree to my telling Chief Mate Joe Koller and Chief Engineer George Thomas the bad news.

This was an alarming development, and it again emphasized how the American Merchant Marine was going down hill rapidly. I was glad that I had the application in to become a Panama Canal Pilot.

Upon my return to the ship, I told Chief Mate Koller and Chief Engineer Thomas the news about our pending lay-off, but I swore them to secrecy, as per orders from Captain Campbell.

We left Port Newark on 11/1/55, and steamed to Philadelphia, arriving there on Wednesday, 11/2/55. We only discharged lumber there for a day and a half, and then moved on to Wilmington, DE, where we completed discharge and had our voyage payoff.

We signed coastwise articles and sailed on 11/4/55, in ballast, enroute back to New York, arriving at Scotland Light Vessel on Saturday, 11/5/55. By now all hands knew the bad news.

We went into a drydock in Brooklyn, and had our paid-off there. Everyone was laid-off, and left the ship promptly after getting their money.

I ended up alone on the ship, winding up details. My relief and the new crew had not yet arrived. I left the new Captain an inventory of the slop chest items and wrote a note, asking that he please send payment to me for them, and also for the case of whiskey that the Customs Official had sealed in with the cigarettes. The new Greek Captain stiffed me on this and sent no payment. I later protested to Stevenson Lines about this, and they reimbursed me for everything except the case of whiskey.

It was a Sunday when I left the ship. No one in the shipyard was working and it was a spooky place. I had all of my gear and sextant to carry off the ship and down the long ladder from the drydock. I had a one hundred and fifty pound set of bar bells and exercise weights that I had to leave aboard. It was a wonder that I hadn't injured myself lifting weights, including the clean and jerk routine, on a rolling ship.

Now that I had plenty of time, I managed to do the four things that I always tried to do when in New York—

- 1. Take a trip to the top of the Empire State Building with a camera and a pair of binoculars.
- 2. Have a steak dinner at the Black Angus.
- 3. Have a lobster dinner at the Lobster Restaurant on 45th Street.
- 4. See the current show at the Radio City Music Hall.

I then boarded a train at Penn Station for travel home to Sedalia, MO, to have a "nervous" vacation, while hoping to get called for another job before too long.

(Note: According to "The Liberty Ships" by Captain Walter W. Jaffee, the SS Sea Leader was originally named the SS Joseph I. Kemp. She was built by the New England Shipbuilding Corporation. Her keel was laid on April 5, 1944 and she was launched on May 16, 1944. She was sold by the Whitehall Steamship Corporation in 1956 and renamed the SS Chelsea and then the SS Adolp Sperling. In 1961, she was lengthened to 511 feet in Tokyo, reflaged to Liberia and renamed the SS Cyclone, later the SS Mystras. On 6/29/66, while on a voyage from Chimbote, Peru to Rostock, Germany with a cargo of fishmeal, she went aground at full speed near the Elbe lightship. She was refloated in heavily damaged condition and towed to Cuxhaven, Germany, then to Rostock where she was declared a constructive total loss. She was scrapped in October 1966 by shipbreakers in Santander, Spain.)

Vacation/Honeymoon

This was not destined to be a routine vacation. For one thing, it turned out to be a long one, which gave me time to speculate, about my bachelor status and my life from a long-term perspective. I would soon be thirty-one years old.

For about five years, I had known certain a young women in Sedalia. I hadn't dated her because she had the reputation of not "sleeping around". I was mostly, in those days, looking for girls that did. Another thing was that she made me feel a bit inadequate, because I was not a good dancer, and she was one of the best. A third factor was that she had a son, Dewey Blaine Whittaker, from a divorced marriage, who was then thirteen years old.

Anyway, we started dating and I fell in love. I proposed to Dorothy Marie (Schneck) Whittaker, and she accepted.

We got married on February 1, 1956, at the home of Dorothy's Baptist Pastor, who was obviously favoring her. He left out the "obey" part of her oath of marriage, which gave me problems in the years ahead. The ceremony was witnessed by her mother, Emma Schneck, her son Dewey Blaine Whittaker, and the aunt and uncle who had raised me, Horace L. and Ora Lee Netherton. Dorothy's father, George Schneck, had died several years earlier.

The author, Pastor Thomas Cruxton, bride Dorothy Wedding Day, 2/1/56

Now days it is common for couples in love to have sex before marriage. We did not believe in that and we waited.

Unfortunately, I used Ektachrome film to take pictures of our wedding and they did not keep their color balance. They are so hopeless, that I decided to convert them to black and white for insertion in this Chapter. They also collected a lot of dust particles that will not blow or brush off.

While we were planning our wedding, I received a call from Mr. John A. Moore, the Personnel Manager for T. J. Stevenson & Co., Inc. He offered me a Chief Mate job on a Liberty ship that was due to arrive in San Francisco in about two weeks. I had been hoping for another Captain's job, but I had now been unemployed for three months, so, I gladly accepted the Chief Mate assignment. We made plans to have a honeymoon while traveling west.

Dorothy and Dewey had been living at the home of her mother until a few months earlier. She had purchased a duplex house, across the street from her mother's house, and she and Dewey had moved into half of the duplex. We now put Dewey in care of his grandmother, Emma Schneck, so that Dorothy and I could go on our honeymoon.

Stepson Dewey, the Author, Bride Dorothy 2/1/56

We took the Missouri Pacific railroad from Sedalia to Kansas City, where we spent a night at the Muelbach Hotel.

The next day, we caught a flight to Reno, where we had a reservation at the Riverside Hotel.

It was the first time either of us had been in a casino and, of course, the hotel lobby was just an extension of their main casino. Dorothy decided to pay roulette and put a dollar on a number that immediately hit. She had thirty-six dollars from her one, and decided that this was fun. Being a thrifty

Our Parents, Horace and Ora Lee Netherton, and Emma Schneck (2/1/56)

country girl, she kept back five, and so ended up with a profit of four after more play.

We spent a week in Reno and then caught a flight to San Francisco, where we stayed in the Palace Hotel on Market Street. It was a fine old hotel where the entry-way, which extended through to the street behind the hotel, was wide enough to allow a horse and carriage to pass through. We were told that they at one time did.

The big news of the day was that Princess Margaret was being forced, by the Royal Family in Great Britain, to break up her romance with race-car driver Peter Townsend. As we were going up in a full elevator at our hotel, Dorothy asked me if I had heard the story that the

Princess might join a convent, now that she was giving up Peter. The laughter from the sophisticated crowd in the elevator was immediate, and Dorothy did not understand why.

I was checking daily by telephone with the San Francisco Agent for T J. Stevenson & Co., Inc., regarding the ETA (Estimated Time of Arrival) of the *SS Harold D. Whitehead,* the Liberty ship that I was scheduled to join as Chief Mate. It was due on 2/12/56, and would be docking at the Oakland Army Base. It was a standard Liberty ship and, of course, I was thoroughly familiar with them. I was disappointed to find that, like the other ships that T. J. Stevenson & Co., Inc. operated, it was not equipped with radar.

Chapter XIV: SS Harold D. Whitehead
(First Cargo)

Joining the Ship in San Francisco

Stevenson Lines, at the last minute, decided to have me relieve the Captain of the ship instead of the Chief Mate. I don't know why they had decided to bump him, but they sent him a letter and explained that I had more seniority than him. They offered him the Chief Mate job, but he declined. I was glad to be sailing as Ship Master again. I enjoyed being in charge and felt completely capable.

The ship was loading general cargo at the Oakland Army Base. It was a difficult commute, but I was returning to the Palace Hotel every evening, and getting up at 0530 so as to be able to get back aboard before 0800. There were many nice shops near the hotel, so Dorothy was able to keep herself busy and entertained during the day time.

The Chief Mate, from the previous voyage, Mr. Paul Simonsen, stayed on. He was well-qualified and had considerable experience. He was in his mid-forties, about six feet tall, trim and energetic. Paul turned out to be an excellent and competent shipmate.

We got a new second mate, thirty-year old Chad Brandson. He had a remarkable resemblance to how Winston Churchill looked at that age. He also, probably on purpose, talked like the fine old British Statesman. We naturally called him "Winston", and he didn't mind. He was very good at his job and we all liked him.

The real jewel of a crew member, that I lucked out with, was Chief Engineer John Pottinger. He was very knowledgeable and competent and was the best Chief Engineer with whom I had ever sailed. John was a vigorous forty-five year old, just under six feet and of proper weight for his height. He had blue eyes, a round face with pleasant features, and wore his brown hair in a short crew cut. He was single, but he had a serious relationship, and planned to get married, probably after this voyage. We would become good friends.

The Military Charter
San Francisco, San Pedro, Panama Canal, Aruba, Zeebrugge, Bremerhaven, St. Nazaire, Bordeaux

This would turn out to be, by far, the longest voyage that I had ever made. As a newly-wed, this was unfortunate. It originally was scheduled to be about a month and a half long, but the Army kept extending our Charter, while we were in Europe. Because of the extensions, it was going to be eight months before Dorothy and I would be reunited. Her friends back in Sedalia would be wondering if she had really gotten married.

On Saturday, 2/18/56, we sailed from Oakland bound for San Pedro, where we would be loading additional military cargo. Dorothy caught a flight to Los Angles, and checked into a hotel in San Pedro to await my arrival.

San Pedro

We arrived at the Los Angles breakwater on mid-day on Monday, 2/20/56, and went to anchor. Early the next morning, we shifted to a dock in San Pedro, and resumed loading general cargo for the Army. Dorothy had contacted the Agent, who in turn let me know what hotel she had checked into. It was rather crummy, so we moved to a different one, that had a nice view of the harbor. I was again commuting daily between the ship and the hotel. Dorothy noticed that the commute, added to problems involved in getting a new crew and ship organized, was wearing me out. There wasn't much of interest for her to do while alone during the days. We were going to be loading here for about another week. Dorothy suggested that it might be best that she fly on back home now, instead of later. It was the sensible thing, so I managed to get her on a Sunday flight. I saw her off at the LA International Airport. Our honeymoon was over, but it had been a good one. We would next see each other in New York, about eight months later.

We sailed from San Pedro on Tuesday, 3/6/56, for the Panama Canal. We had mostly good weather but, as usual, had a strong easterly gale while passing through the Gulf of Tehuantepec.

Panama Canal

We arrived at the Pacific Anchorage for the Panama Canal in late afternoon on Sunday, 3/18/56. My thirty-first birthday had occurred two days earlier. No one on the ship would have known about it, but Dorothy sent me a Happy Birthday radiogram. I cautioned Sparks not to tell anyone, and he didn't.

Early the next morning, Veteran Panama Canal Pilot, Captain Harrington, boarded and directed our transit expertly. It was a pleasant windy dry season day. He confirmed that the Panama Canal Company needed to hire more Pilots, and that one or two new ones had recently arrived. Now that I was a married man, the urgency in finding a shore job had increased greatly.

We cleared the Cristobal breakwater at 1700 on 3/19/56, bound for Aruba.

Aruba

We arrived at the Aruba breakwater at 0900 on Wednesday, 3/21/56.

The refineries in Aruba got their crude oil from nearby Venezuela. The price was right and the Dutch ran a very efficient refining and bunkering operation.

As you entered this port, it appeared to be a transplant from old Holland. The city was laid out beautifully and was neat as a pin. The entry channel extended for a long distance along the side of the city. Our stay here was only going to be three or four hours long, so I did not allow any shore leave.

By early afternoon, we were on our way and again enjoyed seeing this picture post card city/harbor as we sailed away.

On 3/21/05, the same day that we had arrived, we set a great circle course for Zeebrugge, Belgium.

It was an eighteen day passage and we only encountered a couple of moderate gales. One of them was from the north, on our port beam, and caused a good deal of rolling. Our cargo included some vehicles in the 'tween decks. Chief Mate Simonsen went down into the 'tween decks and determined that everything was holding firmly in place.

Zeebrugge

We arrived at the huge Zeebrugge breakwater mid-morning on Sunday, 4/8/54, and immediately went to the cargo berth.

The breakwater for this port is one of the most impressive anywhere. It needs to be massive because there is no natural harbor here. It would otherwise be completely exposed to the many North Sea winter storms. During out time there, it was being further reinforced.

During the First World War, a British demolition team was landed here, at night, from a submarine. They succeeded in blowing a hole in the breakwater. It is difficult to see how any explosive charge could have been powerful enough to significantly damage this structure. Belgium was occupied by the German Army at the beginning of that war.

Zeebrugge Harbor (1956)

Zeebrugge Municipal Buildings

Zeebrugge is the seaport for the city of Brugge, Belgium. The name of the city translates to "bridge", which is very appropriate. It is known as "the Venice of North Europe", because it is interlaced with many navigable canals. Of course, the canals must have bridges over them. Many of the bridges are only walking bridges, and it is a delightful city to walk about. You could also tour the city by motor boat, and I did that also. The weather was beautiful, with the temperature in the fifties and sixties, with clear skies.

There were many cargo barges in the canals, similar to the ones that we had seen in Rotterdam. They were all the same size, about two hundred feet long, sized to just fit in the many locks that connect the waterways of Europe. They were equipped with regular pointed bows and had the wheelhouse and quarters aft. They were all neatly painted and many had families living aboard.

As a newly-wed, I was on the lookout for proper things to obtain for our new household. I bought here a complete set, for twelve, of Val St. Lambert crystal glass-ware. The set included water glasses, two sizes of wine glasses, champagne glasses, and small liqueur glasses. The shop pulled a sneaky trick on me by substituting two green water glasses because, I guess, they did not have a full set of plain ones. The set was all packed up and shipped to Dorothy back in Sedalia. We were happy with the odd green glasses, and they turned out to be the

Brugge is know as the "Venice of North Europe"

There are many swans in Brugge

ones that we used personally when we had company. As I reflect on this purchase, it was nervy of me to buy something so important, on my own, without input from Dorothy. Fortunately, she liked them.

We discharged cargo for two days and then sailed for Bremerhaven, Germany on Monday, 4/9/54.

Bremerhaven

We arrived in Bremerhaven early on Wednesday, 4/11/54, and immediately docked to discharge some vehicles from our cargo. I did not have time to go ashore, but I had been here a number of previous times, so I did not feel any particular need to see it again.

Crystal Store in Brugge
where the author bought a set of Val St. Lambert crystal ware. He and his wife, Dorothy, would return here twenty years later to replace broken pieces.

The vehicles were quickly out and we sailed that afternoon for St. Nazaire, France.

St. Nazaire

We had now left the efficient ports, run by the Belgiums and Germans, and were in old "easy going" France. This was the land of many holidays, long lunch breaks, and wine-drinking stevedores. I did not think much of their work ethnic, but it was pleasurable to only work cargo during the day, have work-free weekends, and end up with an extended stay in port.

During WWII, the Germans had built bomb-proof submarine pens in the middle of the St. Nazaire Harbor, They occupied prime real estate and needed to be removed. The problem was that they were so heavily built, that they were just about impossible to take out.

We would end up spending six days here to discharge tonnage that the north European ports would have had out in two days. This gave us time to enjoy some good French food and wine. The prostitutes were about the only people that were friendly to us. The others pretty much avoided eye contact and none of them spoke English.

St. Nazaire is located on the Bay of Biscay at the mouth of the Laire River. Forty miles up this river is the major French city of Nantes. Chief Engineer John Pottinger and I took a train

German Bomb-proof Submarine Pens in St. Nazaire
They needed to be removed, but how?

St. Nazaire Public Transportation (above)
Nantes Street Scene (right) (1956)

to see the sights there. It is a beautiful city and we found a very well-preserved old castle that had a moat and draw bridge

We had a fine dinner is a nice restaurant and caught a late train back to St. Nazaire.

Our cargo discharge operations finally finished, and we departed St Nazaire early on Saturday, 4/21/56, bound for Bordeaux.

Bordeaux

I adjusted our speed so as to arrive at the mouth of the Gironde River at daybreak on Sunday, 4/22/56. There was no pilot boat on station, so I went to anchor.

After a couple of hours, the Pilot came aboard and we heaved anchor. We proceeded up the river and berthed at a pier in Bordeaux.

Most of the cargo sent to support our troops, stationed in south Germany, came through this port. An American Army Colonel was in charge of U. S. cargo operations, and he paid a courtesy visit. There was not much that he could do to improve efficiency, because he had to use the regular French stevedores, and follow their work rules. We would spend an unbelievable sixteen days here, discharging cargo that should have been out in no more than four days.

SS Harold D. Whitehead **docked in Bordeaux (1956)**

The weather continued to be perfect and we were enjoying our extended and relaxed stay in port.

Chief Engineer Pottinger & his Peugeot motorbike.
Bordeaux Bell Tower, right (1956)

Chief Engineer Pottinger and I each purchased a motor bicycle. They were low powered with 125 cc two-cycle engines. I made a mental excuse to myself, justifying this expense, by thinking of it as a gift for step-son Dewey, when I got home.

Cargo operations shut down completely on weekends, and John and I took a number of excursions into the countryside on our new machines. On one Sunday trip, we discovered the delightful French village of Cadillac.

On another Sunday, we found a monastery in the midst of beautiful vineyards and we got to sample the most delicious wine that I have ever tasted. It was unbelievably good. We couldn't drink it with the abandon that we wanted, because we still had to drive our bikes several miles back to the ship. Our trip back was frightening because it was late Sunday afternoon and the French people, who had left the city for the weekend, were now returning in great numbers. The shoulder of the road was rough and the traffic made it too dangerous to ride on the pavement. The rough surface slowed us so much that it got dark before we could get back. We had no lights and it was a real scary situation. Intelligent grown men should not

Bridge near Bordeaux (1956)

Winery in Cadillac (1956)

Sunday Bicycle Race passing through Cadillac

277.

One legged Sheep Herder near Cadillac, France (1956)

have gotten themselves into this situation.

We finally finished discharging all of our cargo and left Bordeaux on Tuesday, 5/8/56. Our military charter was being extended and I was ordered to proceed to Milford Haven, Wales, to load another general cargo for the U. S. Army.

Chapter XV: SS Harold D. Whitehead
(Second and Third Cargoes)

Milford Haven, Livorno, Piraeus, Iskenderun, Livorno, Iskenderun, Piraeus, Casablanca

Milford Haven

It was a two day run from Bordeaux to Milford Haven and we arrived there mid-morning on Thursday, 5/10/56. It is located in a large, deep and beautiful bay at the southwestern tip of Wales. We proceeded to a dock and commenced loading general cargo. It was mostly supplies that had been shipped here from the U. S. and put into local storage.

The U. K. Customs officials were very nice and allowed Chief Engineer John Pottinger and me to use our French motor bicycles here, without having to pay the normally high duty. They essentially agreed to look the other way.

John and I explored the countryside during the continuing good weather that Europe was experiencing. On the back county roads, we could hardly go two or three miles without encountering the ruins of another castle. Nearly all had impossible Welch names, some with words containing about twenty letters, with lots of double l's.

The author castle exploring in Wales (1956)

Carew Castle near Milford Haven, Wales (1956)

We found an interesting Bed and Breakfast place named the "Pencock Inn". It was a huge rambling old one story building, furnished with large and beautiful antiques. It had a quaint little bar. We became acquainted with the Owner, Mr. Pencock. We asked him about the origin of his name. He replied that a few generations back it had been shortened from "Pen Spurs on Cock", which pretty well explained what trade his forbearers practiced.

I learned that our first port of discharge was going to be Livorno (Leghorn), Italy. I knew that my old friend and long-time shipmate, Louis Murphy, was stationed in the U. S. Army in south Germany. I sent a radiogram to him and gave him our ETA (Estimated Time of Arrival) in Leghorn and inquired if he might be able to come down for a visit.

After six days, we were had loaded all of the cargo available. We were not full but we had a pretty good load. We left Milford Haven on Wednesday, 5/16/56, bound for Livorno.

I sent Murphy an updated ETA for Livorno. The next day he replied and I was delighted that he was going to meet us in Livorno.

Livorno

We arrived in Livorno early on Thursday, 5/24/56. We went to a dock and soon commenced discharging cargo.

To my delight, there was my good friend, Louis Murphy, standing on the dock. He was now a sergeant in the U. S. Army, a company clerk assigned to a U. S. Army division stationed in south Germany. He had driven down in his Oldsmobile, which he had shipped over from home.

He and I had been shipmates on three different ships dating from December, 1946 to October,1952. He had been Third Mate when I was Second Mate, Second Mate when I was Chief Mate, and Chief Mate when I was Captain. He had been slated to get a well-deserved command of his own when he got drafted into the Army. This was in spite of the fact that he had been sailing in the Merchant Marine since 1943 and the Merchant Marine had a casualty rate during WWII higher than that of any of the armed services, even higher than the Marine Corps. In spite of our WWII service, we were considered to be draft dodgers.

Soon after Murphy finished his military obligation, Stevenson Lines gave him command of a T-2 tanker (523' x 68'). The Grace Line passenger ship, *SS Santa Rosa,* collided with Murphy's ship off the east coast of the U. S. in dense fog. There was loss of life on the tanker. Newspapers around the world ran pictures of the *SS Santa Rosa* arriving in New York harbor, with the smoke stack of the tanker impaled on its bow. The Coast Guard investigation determined that the passenger ship Captain was solely at fault.

We had shared some remarkable experiences during our time together and we now enjoyed reminiscing. We drove, in Murphy's Oldsmobile, from Livorno to the beautiful city of Florence. The idea was to see some of the fantastic art works that are on display there, but instead, we mostly talked about old times. We did take a long look at "David", by Michelangelo, which is truly awe inspiring.

We overnighted in Florence and returned to Livorno the next morning.

Murphy told about a colored sergeant, in his outfit, that was called in for an interview, because he was always getting into trouble. The officer conducting the interview suggested that he have his wife sent over to Germany to join him. He replied "sir, that would be like taking spam to a banquet".

Murphy was still a bachelor, but he had a serious girl friend back home. Soon after getting out of the Army, he did get married and fathered a daughter. As a family man, he wanted a shore job and found one as Chief Surveyor for the National Cargo Bureau in Duluth, MN. He was scheduled to take over their very busy and important Norfolk office, when he suddenly died. His death was caused by an enlarged heart. I had urged him to come to Panama and be a Panama Canal Pilot with me, but his wife did not want to move there.

Our cargo operations in Livorno included some loading as well as discharging. On Sunday, 5/27/56, we finished and sailed for Piraeus, Greece.

During our four-day run to Piraeus, we continued to have nice summer weather. We arrived there on Thursday, 5/31/56.

Piraeus

I had spent some time in Piraeus two years earlier and had greatly enjoyed seeing the ancient Greek ruins in Athens. Athens contains archaeological sights that are worth viewing over and over so, Chief Engineer John Pottinger and I "made like tourists" again. The weather was beautiful, so I was able to get some good photographs.

The Acropolis of Athens (1956)

The Parthenon, the Building with Perfect Dimensions. It survived the ages very well until the Turks stored munitions in it during the 18th Century.

Since we were now overseas far longer than we had taken stores for, we needed many things. The ship chandlers in Piraeus were able to supply most of the food items that we needed. One problem was that they could not obtain duty-free cigarettes, that I needed to resupply our slop chest. Since we were chartered to the U. S. Military, I asked the Army liaison here for assistance in the matter. They were helpful and the Army agreed to sell us several cases. Security for this operation was tight and I personally rode in the Army launch that carried the cigarettes from their facility to alongside our ship. Even though we saved the hefty duty, they cost a lot more than we had paid in the U. S. The smokers were desperate and did not object to the higher prices.

Porch of the Maidens (1956)
The third figure from the left is a replica. (The original is in the British Museum.)

Our cargo operations were competed and we sailed on Saturday, 6/2/56 for Iskenderun, Turkey. We steamed for three days in nice weather and anchored there on Tuesday morning, 6/5/56.

Iskenderun

This ancient city is located at the extreme southeast coast of Turkey. The population in 1956 was, I estimate, about 40,000. The border with Syria is only about thirty miles or so to the east.

An unusual and lucky situation converted our stay in this sleepy, dusty outpost of civilization, which had no bars, no movie theaters and a dearth of good restaurants, into a most interesting

Bill Harris and his Land Rover (1956)

Bus Station

place to visit. This was doubly fortunate, because we were to spend more than three weeks discharging our cargo while anchored here.

Oddly, the United Seamen Service, which had pretty much closed down at the end of WWII, had a representative here. He was sponsored by a big American university, to study for his Doctorate in Archeology. My recollection was that it was Stanford University, but I am not at all sure about that. His name was Bill Harris. He was in his late twenties, and was delighted to show us some very interesting sights. He had a Land Rover at his disposal, and took us on some very interesting trips. Six of us crowed into it for several excursions.

Our friend was conducting some diggings locally and was finding a lot of old pottery.

It is hard to believe now, with all of the trouble in this area, but at that time the border with Syria was not guarded by either Turkish or Syrian forces. It was not even marked, so you could not tell when you crossed from one country to the next

Caves seen from road between Iskenderun and Antioch

Our new friend took us to old Antioch, Syria. On the road between Iskenderun and Antioch, there were many small caves that could be seen high up in the rocky cliffs. Bill Harris was "aching" to explore them, but access was difficult. Who knows, there may be more "Dead Sea Scrolls" to be found in one of them.

Also interesting, our scholarly friend showed us a number of ruined Crusader forts or castles, and the ruins of an ancient, at one time important city, named Arsua, that predated the Romans.

SEN PiYER

THE CHURCH OF ST. PETER

Ruins of the First Christian Church Antioch, Syria (1956) Bill Harris, seated far left, John Pottinger standing center, Paul Simonsen, far right.

Crusader's Fort that we explored and the view from the top.

In Antioch, we were shown the remains, including the alter, of what is claimed to have been the very first Christian Church. It was founded by St. Peter and, since this was the first place they were called "Christians", it is by definition the first "Christian" church (The ACTS, Chapter 11, Verse 26). I even picked up some floor tiling from it and have it among my treasured possessions.

In ancient times Antioch competed with Alexandria, and the two were the principal cities in the middle east. The present modern city (in 1956) is named Antakya, and is an unimpressive backward city with a population in 1956 of about 30,000 or so.

I will now insert some material from the internet to give a feel for the importance of the ancient city of Antioch.

Antioch Blacksmith Shop and Street Scene

"Antioch, in Paul's time, contained over 200,000 inhabitants. Since the city of Antioch was a great center of government and civilization, the Christian religion spread there early. Nicolas, one of the seven deacons in Jerusalem, was from Antioch. After Jerusalem fell in 70 CE, many Christian immigrants fled to Antioch. Other Christians fled to Antioch, from Cyrene, or Cyprus, or wherever they were being persecuted. This influx of peoples also brought an influx of ideas, which eventually strengthened the roots of the Eastern Church.

Turkish Couple at the Iskenderun Farmer's Market

It was in Antioch that the new sect was first called Christian, perhaps a derogatory nickname, but the label stuck."

We found both the Turkish and Syrian people to be very friendly. When driving back to Iskenderun from Antioch, we again found no noticeable border and, of course, no border formalities.

On late Sunday, 7/1/56, we completed discharge and heaved anchor. We were bound back to Livorno, where we would load more cargo for the U. S. Army.

An easterly gale slowed our passage and it took us six days to steam back to Livorno. We arrived early on Saturday, 7/7/56.

Livorno

We were to load more military cargo, part of which was to go to Iskenderun, Turkey. The berth was not immediately available so I went to anchor. The next morning we heaved up and proceeded to the dock.

We loaded cargo around the clock for three days and immediately secured for sea. We set sail back to Iskenderun. Our nice weather continued for the three day passage. We arrived and anchored again in Iskenderun on Tuesday, 7/17/56.

Iskenderun

On our last stay here we had discharged only into barges while at anchor. This time was to be different. Early on 7/18/56, we heaved anchor and proceeded to a dock. There was no tug boat available here. The Turkish Pilot did a good job berthing us port side to the dock. We had the starboard anchor backed out and ready for immediate use, but we didn't need it.

I looked up Bill Harris and had him aboard for dinner. He was so highly over-qualified for being Agent for the United Seamen Service, that I suspected that the job may be a cover for something more important, like being a spy. Just speculation on my part. We were super lucky to have him here to show us the many interesting historical sites on our last visit. Our stay in port this time was too short and did not allow for any more trips.

We didn't have much cargo for Iskenderun this time, and it was all discharged in two days. Late on Thursday, 7/19/56, we left the dock and set course for Piraeus, Greece.

Piraeus

The good summer weather continued to hold and three days later, early in the morning of Sunday, 7/22/56, we arrived at the Piraeus breakwater. There was no Pilot on station so I went to anchor.

About 1000, the Harbor Pilot boarded and we moved to a dock. All of our remaining cargo was to be discharged here and we were to head back to the good old USA. In two days we were empty, and we immediately secured for sea. We were scheduled to take bunkers in Casablanca, and left Piraeus at mid-day on Tuesday, 7/24/56.

We encountered a northerly gale, that caused considerable rolling, but did not slow us down much. Since it was summer- time, I did not, as yet, put sea ballast in the forward deep tanks, nor in number five lower hold. I was keeping an eye on the weather and would have added ballast if it became stormy.

We proceeded via the Messina Straits and this time, we had clear weather passing through the Straits of Gibraltar.

Casablanca

I reduced speed a little so as to make arrival at the Casablanca breakwater at daybreak on Tuesday, 7/31/56. The usual swell was pouring in from the Atlantic, causing heavy rolling until gaining the lee of the big breakwater. This time the Pilot was standing by for us and boarded promptly. We proceeded to the bunkering pier.

The Agent boarded with some important news. Our military charter was being extended again. We were to proceed to Bremerhaven and load vehicles for Karachi, Pakistan. Since fuel was reasonably priced here, and since the next cargo was going to be vehicles with but little weight, we decided to take maximum bunkers, filling all double bottom tanks and number three deep tanks with Bunker "C". We were going to need Steward's stores, but a better selection would be available in Bremerhaven, so we would wait for that.

I believe that the reason, that they kept extending our charter, was that we were giving superior service. Chief Engineer Pottinger, and his Deck Engineer, were keeping our old steam winches purring like they were new. Our Charter Party called for partial off-hire when ever one broke down, and that had not happened a single time as yet. This was truly amazing. And, of course, all of our departures and arrivals had been expeditious.

We sailed from Casablanca at 2300 on 7/31/56, the same date that we had arrived.

Chapter XVI: SS Harold D. Whitehead
(Fourth Cargo)
Bremerhaven, Suez Canal, Karachi, Suez Canal, Casablanca, New York

It was a seven day run up to Bremerhaven from Casablanca. We had a westerly gale in the Bay of Biscay which caused a lot of rolling. That died down to almost a dead calm by the time that we reached the English Channel. We had heavy fog in the narrowest part, while encountering the usual heavy traffic, both cross-channel and opposing. We exchanged whistle signals with either the *SS Queen Mary* or the *SS Queen Elizabeth.* The power and majesty of their whistle was thrilling to hear, and is notably different from any other ship. As I recall, the "Mary" had three smoke stacks and the "Elizabeth" had two. We did not get a good enough look to tell which one it was, but from the size of the bulk that we saw through the fog,, it had to be one or the other. We had close call with one of the cross-channel ferries, which was making at least fifteen knots. We could see his radar antenna rotating as he passed close ahead of us. We got pretty well into the North Sea before the fog lifted.

We arrived at the mouth of the Weser River and picked up the German Pilot at 1000 on Tuesday, 8/7/56. We were secured, port side to the dock in Bremerhaven, by 1600.

Bremerhaven

We had arrived sooner that they had expected us, so no stevedores had been ordered to work until 0600 the following day. When they did get started, they were very efficient. Every bit of space was used, in all cargo compartments, to load cars and trucks, Every one was carefully and thoroughly lashed and chocked in place. Everything was stowed below and there was no deck cargo.

We ordered Steward's Stores and the quality was high. The Chief Steward and I were very pleased. The cost was higher that in the U. S., but that was to be expected.

We were fully loaded and secured for sea early on Saturday, 8/11/56, and sailed for the Suez Canal. We had good weather and clear visibility this time, through the English Channel and all the way to Gibraltar. I was getting a complex about the Straits of Gibraltar because I had fog so often there. It happen again. One good thing is that the inbound traffic usually steamed in the middle of the Straits, to take advantage of the inflow current, and the outbound traffic hugged the coast to avoid the current. Our whistle was getting a good work-out giving fog signals this voyage.

Suez Canal

This would be my first time in the Suez Canal and special problems were developing. Nasser announced in July, 1956, that he was nationalizing the Canal. Great Britain and France, which ran the Canal, were resisting strongly. Most of the Pilots were European, and Nasser was making life miserable for them. They were being paid in Egyptian pounds, which could not exchange to other currencies at a reasonable rate. They could not send their pay home. They were required to live in closely secured and watched compounds. Many had quit, including Captain Fred Weade, who had left a Piloting job in the Panama Canal. He would return to Panama, and I would later work there with him.

(Note: I am writing this in May, 2005. I received word last month that Captain Fred Weade had died at age 95. He is survived by his wife, Mary Jane, who lives in Littleton, Colorado.)

We arrived at Port Said at 0700 on Saturday, 8/25/56, and went to anchor. The Boarding Party and Agent came aboard about 1000, and the Pilot soon afterward. We got underway and tied up to big clusters of pilings in the port. A big special light was hung over our stem. It was designed to send a strong light beam to each bank of the canal.

We were boarded by a multitude of thieves. We had to fight to keep them out of our quarters. The weather was hot, but the crew could not put out the usual port hole vents, because the Egyptian thieves would remove them and steal anything that was within reach from the port holes. They even stole the brass screw-in sounding pipe covers on the main deck. Normally a square "T" wrench was used to unscrew them. These thieves were bare footed on the hot deck, and would use their big toes, in the square holes in the

Statue of Ferdinand de Lesseps
that was placed at the north end of the Suez Canal. He was the promoter and Chief Engineer of the project. The Egyptians later tore down the statue.

SS Harold D. Whitehead berthed in Port Said (1956)

sounding tube caps, to unscrew them. We hired a team of watchmen, as recommended by the Agent, but they were not effective. We got no help from the authorities. It was disgusting.

I was asked, in a very serious tone, if this ship had ever called at a port in Israel. I replied in the negative, but they insisted on examining our log books for the last five years. I was nervous about this, because I knew very little about the past history of this ship. If they had found that the ship had been in Israel, we would have been denied transit, and I would be arrested and fined for lying about the matter.

The Suez Canal is 101 miles long. It runs roughly north and south from the Mediterranean Sea to the Red Sea, through what is mostly sandy desert. About thirty miles from the north end, there was a double channel, which was used so as to allow two-way traffic in the northern part of the Canal. All of the southbound ships would tie up to big bundles of pilings along the bank of the Canal, and await the northbound traffic to pass in the alternate channel. Farther south, in the Great Bitter Lake, there was another passing arrangement. Ships bound in one direction would anchor, while opposing traffic passed. This was to avoid meeting in the one-way channel south of the Great Bitter Lake. The Pilots worked about half way through. They were relieved at the city of Ismailia by a fellow Suez Canal Pilot, who would then finish the transit.

**The *SS Harold D. Whitehead* transiting the Suez Canal
A Dutch Dredging Company was widening the canal.**

The Canal operates at sea level. There must have been an interesting mix of sea life when the digging was finished. There were no powerful environmental groups, in 1869, to object about these things.

Our own transit started at 1400 on 8/25/56, and we were able to reach our tie-up station in the by-pass just as it was getting dark. We tied up for about five hours, and then our convoy got underway. The special canal light, that had been hung over our stem, did pretty well lighting up both banks. It was a great aid to the Pilot. It was very important to stay in the middle of the channel, especially with deeply loaded ships, and thereby avoid bank suction. The straight stretches in the Canal were far too long for there to be any leading range lights (to mark the center of the channels) as we had in the Panama Canal.

Our convoy proceeded to and anchored in Great Bitter Lake. We dropped the hook about 0300. We got underway at 0900 and cleared the Canal at Port Suez at 1500 on Sunday, 8/26/56. A work boat came alongside to take away the special canal light and the Egyptian Canal Crew that had operated it. The Pilot disembarked. We were in the Red Sea and glad to be out of this Canal.

Red Sea

The Red Sea is an unusual body of water. From Port Suez it runs in a SSE'ly direction for about 1,100 miles. Throughout most of its length it is over 100 miles wide. At the south end, it suddenly narrows to about twenty miles wide. In those days it was French Somaliland on the Africa side and Aden on the Asia side. The names are different now.

We cleared the Red Sea and were in the Gulf of Aden for about forty miles, and then we were crossing the Arabian Sea, enroute to Karachi.

During our time in the Red Sea and the Gulf of Aden, we met many loaded tankers, most of them were what were then called super tankers. Today they would be considered "handy size", because ships, especially tankers, have grown enormously in size. It takes about the same size crew and office staff to operate a tanker displacing 15,000 tons as it does to operate one displacing 300,000 tons. The difference in earning potential is obviously enormous.

The weather during our steaming time in the Red Sea was almost dead calm. It was very hot. In the Arabian Sea we had seasonal steady trade winds, blowing from east to west. The seas were moderate to slight.

I adjusted our speed so as to arrive at the Karachi breakwater at daybreak on Thursday, 9/6/56.

Karachi

This is a very large city of many millions of people. The weather on the morning of our arrival was almost calm. The city produced a massive amount of air pollution that was clearly visible from sea.

The Pilot Boat was standing by for us. I made a lee and the Pilot climbed our Pilot Ladder, and proceeded to the bridge. He was a large man with medium complexion. He wore a white turban, but a European style suite, coat and tie. He spoke English with a cultured British accent. I antici-

The Port of Karachi (1956)

pated that he might prefer tea to coffee, and had some ready for him. He seemed to appreciate this gesture. He used two tug boats to assist in our docking maneuver, which when well.

I found the tremendous mass of humanity to be depressing and frightening. Masses of people were everywhere, and it seemed as though hardly anyone had "elbow room". I didn't do much shopping because of my uneasiness.

Word was sent to me that Operations Vice President, Mr. John F. Shea, wanted me to acquire, for him, a certain brand of chutney sauce named "Captain Grey's Chutney". Since I didn't want to go shopping, I asked the agent for assistance, and he sent one of his runners to obtain several bottles for me.

I did make one significant purchase here. The ship-chandler told me that he had a good buy on "Beck's" beer, a famous brand from Germany. Thinking of that long hot voyage back up the Red Sea, I decided to get a couple of cases. I asked Chief Engineer Pottinger and Chief Mate Simonsen, and they each also wanted a couple of cases. So I ordered six cases. I was ashore at the time they were delivered. When I returned to the ship, Second Mate "Winston"

Karachi Street Scene (1956)
Camels were used extensively to pull wagons.

met me at the gangway and gravely told me that the slop check was "chocker block" full of Beck's beer. The Indian Customs had sealed the door, so I could not look at the delivery until after we sailed. Instead of cases of twenty-four twelve ounce bottles, these were large wooden cases, each containing fifty one-liter bottles of beer. Of course the cost was a lot more that we intended to spend for beer, but the deal could not be undone, so we had to pay for it. We were going to be hard-pressed to consume three hundred liters of beer before we got back to the U. S.

We finished discharging our cargo of vehicles and left the dock on Saturday, 9/8/56. We were bound back to the Suez Canal, with bunkering scheduled to take place again in Casablanca.

It was a twelve-day run back up to Port Suez. The weather was mostly good and, as before on our southbound run, it was almost a dead calm during our time in the Red Sea, making it hot and unpleasant.

A medical emergency situation was developing. Our forty-year old colored Second Cook was one of those people who avoid the dentist, and later get into trouble because of this. He had a severe tooth ache, and his jaw was badly swelled. I sent a radio message to our Agent in Port Suez, and requested that arrangements be made for him to see a dentist as soon as possible after our arrival.

Meanwhile, disturbing news was reaching us about the situation in the Suez Canal. The European Pilots were in a big dispute with the, now nationalized, Canal Authority. On the day before our arrival, 9/20/56, they went on strike, and most of them were in the process of leaving.

Suez Canal
We arrived at Port Suez at 1700 on Thursday, 9/20/56. There was no Pilot on station. I waited for half an hour, but there was no visible activity. I assumed that, because of the dispute between the European Pilots and the and the new Nationalized Administration, there may not be a Harbor Pilot available. It was about to get dark, so I decided to enter the port and find a spot, in the now crowded anchorage, without further delay.

About 2200, the Agent boarded and informed us that we would commence our transit, using Egyptian Pilots, in the morning at 0600. I reminded him about the urgent need for our Second Cook to see a dentist. He promised to take care of it. I went to bed soon after he left.

At 0130 Second Mate "Winston" awakened me. The Agent had sent a Barber/Dentist aboard, and he was asking if we had any Novocain. I was not going to allow a part-time unqualified dentist to work on my crewman, and sent him packing. The Agent boarded again as we were about to get underway, and took the Second Cook ashore with him to see a proper dentist. He would rejoin at Port Said when we had finished our transit.

A representative of the Suez Canal Authority boarded with the Pilot, and asked to speak with me confidentially. I asked him to have a seat on my office settee, and I closed the door.. He offered me a job as a Suez Canal Pilot, with a pay rate of $50,000 per year plus benefits, including free housing. That was a lot of money in 1956. If I had not been married, I believe that I would have given it a try. As Ship Captain, my pay, in 1956, was about $12,000 per year.

Our northbound convey was to get an expeditious transit. We would not need the special light on the bow, because we would be through before dark. We heaved anchor and got underway at 0615. I was carefully monitoring the actions of the Egyptian Pilot, who was about thirty-five years old. He was nervous, but seemed competent. Our transit was easy and uncomplicated. We had a clear shot and did not have to anchor in the Great Bitter Lake ,or tie-up at the By-pass Channel. We had a deeply loaded tanker ahead of us and another one following. Because of the Pilot shortage, our Pilot did not get relieved at the midway place of Ismailia, as was the custom. I think that this was true for all of the ten or so ships in our convoy.

We finished our transit at Port Said at 1800. The Second Cook came aboard and was greatly relieved to have had his infected tooth extracted.

The date was Friday, 9/21/56. We set course for Casablanca where we were scheduled to take bunkers.

Our weather was mostly good and, again, we observed the almost continuous oil slick along the north coast of Africa. The tankers returning from their discharge ports routinely cleaned their tanks here, and the pollution was immense.

Distressingly, the Second Cook's problem was not solved. It was, if anything, worse than before. He was in severe pain and his jaw was greatly swelled. I sent a radio message to the Agent in Casablanca, and told him that we must have the services of a really good dentist.

Casablanca

We arrived at the Casablanca breakwater at 0900 on Sunday, 9/30/56. The fueling berth was not immediately available so we went to a lay-berth. We were all tied-up at by 1030.

The fueling berth would not be available until the next afternoon. We broke sea watches and the crew had a night on the town. Compared to Egypt and Pakistan, this was paradise.

The Agent had made an appointment with his own Dentist, one of the few French Dentists still practicing here. The Second Cook was in terrible shape. I decided to accompany him to the Dentist. After a minimal wait in what appeared to be a well-run and equipped facility, the Dentist called him in and seated him in his treatment chair. I was allowed in the room to observe. X-rays were taken and they showed that the Egyptian Dentist had just broken off the top of the tooth. The roots would have to be surgically removed. Even though he was deadly afraid of dentists, the Second Cook was desperate and he sensed that this man was expert. He willingly put himself in his hands. The Dentist dug out two pieces of tooth and took another X-ray, which revealed that there was still a sliver remaining. He went after it and finally had it all. He matched to pieces to the X-ray to be sure. It had been a terrible ordeal for the Second Cook. He was very grateful to have had competent treatment. He tanked the Dentist profusely, as did I. The Second Cook was unsteady on his feet, and I had to assist him to walk.

Chief Engineer Pottinger and I had an excellent meal, in a French restaurant that evening, and visited a night club that had a good floor show. We had become good friends and this would turn out to be our last outing together.

At 1600 the next afternoon, we shifted to the fueling berth and immediately commenced bunkering. We finished taking fuel at 0100 the next morning and sailed shortly thereafter. We took departure from the Casablanca breakwater on Tuesday, 10/2/56, at 0212, bound for New York.

I didn't depend on my letters reaching Dorothy in time, so I also sent her a radio message soon after leaving Casablanca, giving her our ETA in New York. I asked her to fly to New York, and suggested that she check in to the Governor Clinton Hotel, which she did.

The weather pattern looked good so I decided to take a Great Circle course, which took us just north of the Azores Islands. We had mostly good weather and made the passage in thirteen days.

New York

We took arrival at Ambrose Light Vessel at 1000 on Monday, 10/15/56. We went to a lay berth in Brooklyn and were all tied up by 1400. As soon as I could get to a phone, I called the Governor Clinton hotel and had my first conversation with my bride in almost eight months. I was able to get away from the ship about 1800, and caught a subway to Penn Station. I then only had to walk across the street to the Governor Clinton Hotel.

We had all signed on this ship, the previous February, expecting to made a voyage of about a month and a half long. After eight months, we all had had enough of the sea for a while. All of the Officers, and nearly all of the Unlicensed Crew, got off to take a vacation.

We had our voyage payoff (a very good one) the next day, and just about everyone took off. My most senior officers (the Chief Mate, Chief Engineer, First Assistant Engineer and the Chief Steward) and I stayed on another few days, to make an orderly turn-over to our reliefs.

(Note: According to "The Liberty Ships" by Captain Walter W. Jaffee, the SS Harold D. Whitehead was built by the Todd Houston Yard and was launched on December 7, 1944. She was originally operated by Alcoa Steamship Co. and was briefly put into the Astoria Reserve Fleet in late 1946. From December 1946 to 1950 she was operated by the U. S. War Department and then the Alaska Steamship Co. In 1950 she was put in the Olympia Reserve Fleet. In 1951 she was again activated and sold to the Boise Griffin Agencies Corp. In 1954, the Whitehall Steamship Corp. purchased and operated her. Over the succeeding years the ship had thee changes of ownership and names. She continued to operate under the U. S. flag until December 1969, when she was scrapped by Shipbreakers in Chittagong, Pakistan.)

Chapter XVII: SS Federal Jurist
(My Last Command)

Vacation

Once I finished turning over command of the *SS Harold D. Whitehead* to the new Captain, I was free to show Dorothy the sights in New York City. They included my favorites, the Empire State Building and the show at the Radio City Music Hall. One unforgettable experience was seeing Edith Piaf perform at the Versailles Night Club. She sang beautiful songs, that told haunting tales, that brought tears to our eyes.

I am going to tell of one incident that Dorothy will not like. Remember, we were newly weds. When she checked in at the Governor Clinton Hotel, the clerk asked if twin beds were okay and, embarrassed, she replied in the affirmative. These were true twin-size beds and they was very crowded with two people.

I was now very much looking for a shore job. I requested an appointment with Mr. John F. Shea, the Operations Vice President of T. J. Stevenson & Co., Inc. He told me that he was having to reduce his staff and could offer no hope of a shore job in the foreseeable future. He thanked me for the fine work that I had done while serving as Master of several ships for the Company.

After several days in New York, we had had enough, and caught a plane at La Guardia to Kansas City, MO, which had the closest airport to our home in Sedalia, MO. We caught the Missouri Pacific Railroad from KC to Sedalia on 10/25/56.

Dorothy had fixed up the downstairs apartment, in the duplex that she owned, very nicely to be our first home. She was the perfect wife in just about every way.

I became more acquainted with Dewey, my then fourteen-year-old stepson. I was new at this father business and made my share of mistakes. As I expected, the motor bicycle ,that I bought in France, made a big hit with him. Then the local police informed us that he had to be sixteen to use it in the public streets. Over his strong protests, I stored it in the basement, and told him that he could not ride it for two more years.

One evening when he was supposed to be staying at his grandmother's, I got a call at 2300, informing that he was riding the bicycle in the streets. I went to check it in the basement. I slipped on the ice and fell down the outside steps to the basement. I thought that I had badly injured my back, so Dorothy called an ambulance to take me to the Bothwell Hospital emergency room. It turned out that I had no broken bones, but my relationship with fourteen year old Dewey was badly bruised.

As soon as I was organized for correspondence, I wrote a letter to Panama Canal Pilot, Captain William Calcutt, and asked him to check on the status of my application. He replied that they had passed me over because I had five children. They had a shortage of quarters for large families. I replied and told him that I only had one fourteen-year-old boy. He checked again and found that they had considered the application from Captain Robert Valentine, who did have five children, and thought that it was me. He straightened them out. In less than a year, my application would be approved. About a year after that, they also took Bob Valentine's application although his family required two adjoining apartments.

It was becoming obvious that I was going to have to go back sea to make a living. I was worried about whether or not another Master's job would come along. The American Merchant Marine continued in its spiral downward.

Christmas 1956 was not too far in the future and it looked like I would be home for this one, spending money instead of earning it.

On 12/12/56, I got a call from Mr. John A. Moore, the Personnel Manager of T. J. Stevenson & Co., Inc. He offered me the Master's job on a Victory ship named the *SS Federal Jurist*. It was due to arrive in Norfolk 12/15/56, so I was going to have to hurry to take command.

Dorothy and Dewey drove me to the Kansas City airport, where I caught a flight to Norfolk, on Friday, 12/14/56.

SS Federal Jurist

Joining the Ship in Norfolk

I spent the night in the Monticello Hotel and the next morning went to the office of Stevenson Lines Norfolk Agent, Hasler & Son. It was Saturday, but they were fully ready for business. We were old friends and greeted each other as such. The *SS Federal Jurist* was a standard 6,000 horse powered Victory ship. They were 455 feet long, 62 feet in beam, had a deadweight capacity of about 10,800 long tons, and made fifteen knots when turning 100 RPM. One thing that delighted me was that she was equipped with one of the top rated Raytheon Pathfinder Radars. She was to take a full load of coal for a north European port to be named later.

The Master that I was bumping was Captain Leo Critides, who would later become a good friend and fellow Panama Canal Pilot. He was a super competent Mariner and was a fellow Kings Pointer, class of 1944. The only reason that he was being bumped was because Stevenson Lines wanted to give me a job.

As a result of my behavior during taking over the ship, Leo developed an understandable dislike for me. The events unfolded like this.

Stevenson Lines required that the Ship Captains own the slop chest inventory. It consisted of work clothes, work shoes, tooth brushes and paste, shaving supplies, miscellaneous small items and cigarettes. These items were sold at sea with an allowed 10% mark-up. Some Captains handled the actual sales themselves. I did not think it suited the dignity of the position, so I always got one of the Mates, or the Radio Operator, to take the job of operating the slop chest. I gave them the 10% profit for their trouble.

From Leo's last name, I knew that he was of Greek descent. The Greek Captain that had relieved me on the *SS Sea Leader,* in November of 1955, had stiffed me. He had not sent payment for the slop chest items and case of whiskey that I left aboard. Although Stevenson Lines had later reimbursed me for the slop chest items, they had refused to pay for a case of whiskey that I had to leave on the ship. Leo was a very honorable man, but I did not know that, and I required that we take a joint detailed inventory. This required getting a U. S. Customs Official to come to the ship to break the seal on the slop chest so, that we could count the cigarettes. Everything was in order as per his inventory and Leo was understandably pissed.

During our conversation, I mentioned to Leo that I had an application in to become a Panama Canal Pilot. He took note and later applied himself. He became a Panama Canal Pilot about a year after me and, in Panama, we became good friends.

A previous Captain of this ship, Captain Stanton, frequently came to my mind, usually about once per day when I had my daily commune with Mother Nature. When he was in command, and the ship was making landfall enroute to Bordeaux, France, on a foggy morning, a touch of diarrhea caused him to make a fast run to his toilet. The lid was counterweighted to go into the up position when not in use. In one hurried movement, he dropped his pants, swung into position, lowered the seat and sat down. Unfortunately, his scrotum swung to the side under the seat and one of his testicles was crushed as he sat down. Needless to say, the Chief Officer had to complete the navigation to the Pilot Station. The French Doctors wanted to surgically remove the crushed testicle. Captain Stanton declined their kind offer and caught a plane to the U. S. His U. S. Surgeon agreed with the French Doctors, and Captain Stanton was thereafter known as "One Ball Stanton".

We signed foreign articles and went to a coal loading dock where they dumped about 10,000 long tons of coal into our ship in about fourteen hours.

Voyage One

Norfolk, Antwerp, Philadelphia

We sailed from Norfolk on Tuesday, 12/18/56, bound for a port to be named later in North Europe, so I set course for the English Channel. Several days later, I received radio orders to proceed to Antwerp, Belgium, for discharge.

On Christmas Day, we were in the midst of a northerly gale, with considerable rolling taking place. The Stewards Department did their best to give us a special meal, with turkey as the main course. We had to put up the side boards on the dinning tables and wet the table cloths so that the dishes would more or less stay in place. During the noon meal hour, I adjusted course to reduce rolling as much as possible.

As we were approaching the English Channel, we saw an inspiring sight. It was a four-masted sailing vessel running before the wind. I altered course so as to pass close enough to photograph it. We were making fifteen knots when we overtook it. I estimate that they were doing about nine or ten knots under sail. I later found out that it was a training ship for the German Merchant Marine.

German Training Vessel in the English Channel (1956)

Except for the gale that we encountered on Christmas Day, we had reasonably good weather for the twelve day passage to Antwerp. We arrived at the mouth of the Schelde River, enroute to Antwerp, late on 12/30/56. We picked up the Belgium Pilot and made the forty-mile run up the river to Antwerp. The weather was overcast and cold.

Antwerp

The cargo would be discharged by shore cranes into railroad cars, but the berth was not yet available. We were put to a lay berth. Our deck crew had to get out their warmest clothes to go out and handle the mooring operation. We did not get tied up until about 0430 on Monday, 12/31/56.

The next two days were national holidays in Belgium, so we were free to enjoy New Years Eve with wild abandon. This was widely known as a good and friendly port for Merchant Seamen. There are many nice clubs and a good supply of beautiful and friendly girls. What was unusual was that, because of the efficient operations here, we normally only had one or two days in this port. We were about to enjoy six. The only downside was that it was cold and windy. And, now as a married man, my nightclub activities were considerably curtailed.

The discharge berth did not become available until about noon on Thursday, 1/3/57. We shifted there and the big shore cranes commenced discharging our cargo of coal that afternoon.

They had all cargo out late on 1/4/57. We secured for sea and left the dock at 2300. It was a forty mile run to the North Sea and we took departure at 0312 on Saturday, 1/5/57.

We had remarkably good weather for this time of year for the run back to the U. S. East Coast. We took arrival at 1700 at the Overfalls Light Vessel, enroute to Philadelphia, on Wednesday, 1/16/57. We had snow flurries as we steamed up the Delaware Bay and it was bitterly cold.

Philadelphia

There was no cargo immediately available and it was not certain whether or not the ship would continue to operate. We went to anchor at 0100 in the port to await orders. The Pilot went ashore. We were not allowed to use the ship's radio station while in port, so we were had no knowledge, but had lots of curiosity regarding our future employment.

At 0700 the Philadelphia Agent came aboard with news. He had found a lay berth for us and we were due to move there about 0900. We would have our voyage payoff followed by a partial layoff. Only the Captain, Chief Mate, Chief Engineer, First Assistant Engineer and the Chief Steward would be kept on the payroll. The boilers were to be secured and we would move to a hotel to keep from freezing to death. We would commute by taxi daily to the ship to oversee routine voyage repairs. It was expected that a cargo would be found in a week or two. The laid-off officers were to keep in touch with the Agent by phone. Shore electric power would be provided to the ship and electric heaters would be provided in the engine room and officers saloon.

This was further confirmation that the American Merchant Marine was on the skids. I was hoping that the Panama Canal Pilot's job would be forthcoming soon.

A tug came alongside a and Harbor Pilot came aboard at about 0900 on Thursday, 1/17/57. We shifted to a lay-berth and had our voyage payoff that afternoon. We secured the boilers and got hooked up with shore electricity. Heaters were installed in the engine room and in the Officer's Saloon.

Mr. Ladislas Pathy, President and CEO of the company that owned this ship, paid a surprise visit to my quarters, aboard the *SS Federal Jurist,* that afternoon about 1600. He had decided to expand the number of ships that he had under the U. S. flag, and wanted to set up to operate them from his own office, instead of having T. J. Stevenson & Co., Inc. do that. He chatted a while and looked around my quarters, with particular attention to the books that I had on my book shelf. To my great surprise, he offered me the position of Marine Operations Manager of Federal Bulk Carriers, Inc. The company only had this one ship at that time, but he planed to obtain more vessels. The starting salary would be $9,000, which was $3,000 less than I was making as ship master. I would be working from their offices, located on the thirty-third floor of the Lafayette Building. It was across the street from Grand Central Station, in Manhattan.

I thanked Mr. Pathy for considering me for the position and told him that I believed that I was capable of handling the job. I told him that I needed some time to consider his proposal, to talk it over with my wife, and to make "peace" with T. J. Stevenson & Co., Inc, for whom I had worked these past ten and a half years.

The *SS Federal Jurist* was owned by "Federal Bulkcarriers, Inc." An affiliated company, based in Montreal, operated several ships under the Canadian and Egyptian flags. The New York office was, among other things, currently organizing financing for the construction of a super-tanker in Japan. The *SS Federal Jurist* was the only ship that they owned, under the U. S. flag, and they had engaged the services of T. J. Stevenson & Co., Inc., to operate it. They had also organized the ship registration service based in Liberia, which had been tremendously successful. They had sold that operation and were now in the process of organizing a ship registration operation to be based in Haiti. The political instability there would later cause that ship registration business to fail. All of these operations, and others, were presided over by Mr. Ladislas Pathy, an immigrant Hungarian Jew who, in 1957, was in his early seventies. He was a "hands on" manager. His younger brother, Mr. George Pathy, assisted in managing the various enterprises. A Mr. Dunn was the Chief Financial Officer, and was a key figure in the organization.

As soon as I was able to finish taking care of details in connection with our partial lay-up, I went ashore to confer with Dorothy. She had flown to Philadelphia and had visited aboard ship that morning, but was now back in the hotel..

We did not know how well we could live in New York on $9,000 per year, but that was more money than most people made in those days. We didn't owe any money and had about $10,000 in the bank. We decided to accept the position, which would give us a chance to have a normal home life.

Mr. Pathy wanted me to start work immediately after our next voyage. This meant that Dorothy was going to have to arrange the move of our things from Sedalia on her own.

Author's Spouse, Dorothy Vantine (1957)
Visiting aboard the *SS Federal Jurist* in Philadelphia

I left Chief Mate Richardson in charge of the ship and the routine voyage repairs that were taking place. Dorothy and I caught a train to New York and started looking for a place to live. A Real Estate Agent guided us to the New Rochelle area, and to a brand new apartment complex named the Drake Apartments. They suited us and we agreed to lease an unfurnished two bedroom, one bath apartment. It would be an easy commute to work for me, since the frequent

NEW YORK TERMINAL
PIER 5, 1 HOBOKEN, N. J.

WASHINGTON, D. C.
INTERSTATE BLDG.

GENOA, ITALY
VIA ROTTERDAM 1

TOKYO, JAPAN
VIA FUKOKU BLDG.

Stevenson Lines
T. J. Stevenson & Co., Inc.

Steamship Operators, Managers and Berth Agents

80 Broad Street
New York 4, N.Y.

AGENTS
N. Y. PRODUCE EXCHANGE
MARITIME EXCHANGE

REGULAR SERVICES
U. S. ATLANTIC AND GULF PORTS
TO
MEDITERRANEAN CANAL PORTS

PLEASE ADDRESS YOUR REPLY TO

J. F. Shea
PIER 5, HOBOKEN RIVER
NEW JERSEY 13, N. Y.

CABLE AGENTS
NATIONAL SHIPPING AUTHORITY
(U. S. MARITIME ADMINISTRATION)

CABLE ADDRESSES
STEVESHIPS NEW YORK
STEVOTRANS NEW YORK
STEVEN MOR SAN FRANCISCO

February 6, 1957

Captain W. H. Vantine
c/o Federal Bulk Carriers, Inc.
50 East 42nd Street
New York 17, N. Y.

Dear Captain Vantine:

I acknowledge receipt of your letter under date of January 28th, to which was attached a copy of your letter of resignation to Captain Campbell.

It goes without saying that I deeply regret having you resign from this organization, however I realize that there is a grand opportunity awaiting you with Messrs. Federal Bulk Carriers, Inc. I have been associated with Mr. Ladislas Pathy and Mr. George Pathy for some years and I found them to be very wonderful people and I sincerely trust that you will make your way with them.

If there is anything that we can ever do for you please do not hesitate to call upon us. Good luck in your future position.

Sincerely yours,

John F. Shea
Executive Vice President

JFS:bo

Letter from Mr. John F. Shea, Executive Vice President
T. J. Stevenson & Co., Inc.
February 6, 1957

302.

WASHINGTON, D. C.
SHERATON BLDG.

Stevenson Lines
T. J. Stevenson & Co., Inc.
Steamship Owners, Operators, Managers, Berth Agents

80 Broad Street
New York 4, N.Y.

March 2, 1957

GENERAL AGENTS
NATIONAL SHIPPING AUTHORITY
(U.S. MARITIME ADMINISTRATION)

DOMINICAN STEAMSHIP LINE
(FLOTA MERCANTE DOMINICANA, C. POR A.)
PIER 2, ERIE BASIN, BROOKLYN, N. Y.
CABLE ADDRESS: "FLOMEROOM" NEW YORK

REGULAR SERVICES
U. S. ATLANTIC TO
MEDITERRANEAN-LEVANT PORTS
PIER 9, HOBOKEN, N. J.

CABLE ADDRESS: NEW YORK
"STEVELINE" "STEVEWIND"
"TEJAYSTEVE"
CODES: BOE-BENTLEY'S-SCOTT

PLEASE ADDRESS YOUR REPLY TO
W. J. Campbell

TO WHOM IT MAY CONCERN:

Captain W. H. Vantine has been employed by this organization from December 1946 to the present date. Captain Vantine was originally employed as Second Mate, having served approximately two years in that capacity, then a further approximate two years in the capacity of Chief Mate. Beginning June 1951 Captain Vantine was promoted to Master and has served continuously from that date to the present time as Master on Liberty and Victory vessels, either owned and/or operated by this Organization.

We have always found Captain Vantine to be honest, conscientious, industrious and are of the opinion that he could definitely fill any position assigned to him, either ashore or afloat in the operating end of the shipping business.

Captain Vantine advises that he is resigning his present comand to accept a position ashore in the operating end of another steamship corporation. It is with reluctance that we accept his resignation and feel quite confident he will be highly successful in any position to which he may be assigned by other interests.

STEVENSON LINES
T.J. STEVENSON & CO., INC.

Manager
Operations Department

WJC:ced

Letter from Captain William J. Campbell, Operations Manager
T. J. Stevenson & Co., Inc
March 2, 1957

trains, from the station at New Rochelle, ended up fifty minutes later at Grand Central Station, across the street from the Lafayette Building, where my office was located.

I had worked for T. J. Stevenson & Co., Inc. since December, 1946. They had given me a ship command at the tender age of 26. I felt loyalty to them and had mixed emotions about leaving the company. I wrote letters of resignation to Operations Manager, Captain William J. Campbell, and Operations Vice President, Mr. John F. Shea. Copies of their replies are reproduced above..

I recommended to Mr. Ladislas Pathy that Chief Mate Richardson be promoted to Captain of the *SS Federal Jurist* at the end of the next voyage, when I left the ship. He had done an outstanding job as Chief Officer. Mr. Pathy agreed and Richardson was delighted with the promotion.

Voyage Two

Philadelphia, Dunkerque, Philadelphia

Finally, after twelve days in limbo, on Monday, 1/28/57, a cargo was found, at a freight rate that would provide but little profit, but was better that nothing. We crewed up, fired the boilers and took voyage stores the next day. Late on 1/29/57, we shifted to the coal loading dock. They dumped in the usual 10,000 long tons of coal and we left the dock, bound for sea, late on 1/30/57. We took departure from the Overfalls Light Vessel early on Thursday, 1/31/57. Our destination was a port in France to be named later. We were all thankful to have a job. I had mixed emotions, because this was likely the last voyage of my seagoing career. That, indeed, turned out to be the case.

A few days out, I was advised by radio that our discharge port would be Dunkerque, France. This was to be a new port for me, so I got out the charts and Sailing Directions to study up on this port. The name was famous from WWII days, when the remnants of the British Expeditionary Force were rescued from the beach here by British fishing boats, yachts, Merchant and Naval Vessels. It had been a truly heroic effort.

We were at the height (or depth) of the winter storm season, and so could expect the worst. Actually, we had better than average weather, for the time of year, and were able to make the passage in eleven days. We arrived at the Dunkerque breakwater at 0400 on Monday, 2/11/57. It was nice to have radar to assist in making a landfall during darkness. We had to wait about an hour for the Pilot, and then proceeded to the dock.

Dunkerque

The pier to which we tied-up had shore cranes to discharge our cargo of coal into railroad cars. The tracks were conveniently located alongside the ship.

The weather was miserable. It was continuously overcast, windy and cold. Snow was on the ground, but it was old and had become dirty and ugly.

The city had been completely destroyed during WWII and was now rebuilt. It had a modern and neat appearance, and seemed unusually clean and well kept for a French city.

The cranes were idle much of the time awaiting empty railroad cars. It would take five days to discharge our 10,000 tons of coal. They finished Friday night, 2/15/57, at 2200.

We immediately secured for sea and left the dock at 0100. We took departure from the Dunkerque breakwater at 0148 on 2/16/57.

We had the usual winter storms and it took us twelve days to travel back to Philadelphia. We had gone the other way in eleven days. We took arrival at the Overfalls Light Vessel at 2000 on Thursday, 2/28/57, enroute to Philadelphia.

Philadelphia

We picked up the Pilot an proceeded up Delaware Bay. We had a young Pilot, in his mid-twenties, who was making his first solo trip. They should have given him more training because he was incompetent. I needed to work on the voyage payroll, but was unable to do so because this Delaware Pilot required my constant attention. He was extremely nervous. The weather was clear and we had an excellent radar. Our trip up the Bay should have been routine.

He required a consultation with me on which side to pass every sighted buoy. On reflection, I wonder if he might have been color blind, or maybe he couldn't remember "red-right-returning" for the buoy system.

A dredge was working in the channel and he did not know the light arrangement that designated the side of the dredge on which we should pass.

Then, to top things off, he anchored us, in the early morning darkness, in Philadelphia in a shallow area where we would be aground when the tide flowed out. Later that morning, at about 0900, a tug and Harbor Pilot came out to provide a free shift to a proper anchorage. The Pilot Association was covering for incompetent member.

It would not be known for another couple of weeks, but because of the incompetent Delaware Bay Pilot, the ship suffered bottom damage and was holed in one of the double bottom tanks.

At noon, on Friday, 3/1/57, we shifted to a lay-berth and had our voyage payoff.

Chief Mate Richardson became Captain Richardson, and had my congratulations. I left the *SS Federal Jurist,* my "Last Command", and went ashore to assume my new position as Operations Manager of Federal Bulkcarriers, Inc.

Dorothy and Dewey had driven to New Rochelle from Sedalia, MO, in our 1957 DeSoto sedan (with big tail fins) . They were camped out in our empty apartment there, awaiting the arrival of our furniture which had been shipped from Missouri.

My seagoing career had lasted from June 1943 to March 1957. This spanned the years that the U. S. Merchant Marine was in its prime and continued over to the years when it started into a disastrous decline.

Chapter XVIII: Federal Bulkcarriers, Inc.

Handling the Job

On Monday, 3/4/57, I turned over command of the *SS Federal Jurist* to Chief Mate, now Captain Richardson. I was then officially Operations Manager for the Company and responsible for the shore operations of this, the one and only, ship that the Company owned.

On the return voyage from France, I had labored hard in writing up Operating Instructions to be issued to key personnel on the ships. I borrowed heavily from a similar document from T. J. Stevenson & Co., Inc., that had been my guide for these past years. I gave a copy to the Captain, Chief Engineer and Chief Steward.

My first job was to collect the stores requisitions from the ship, approve them, and contact the local Ship Chandlers to make bids. There were some minor repairs required in the Engine Room, so I had to contact local Ship Repair companies to check them out and make bids.

Mr. Ladislas Pathy had hired a Broker, who was busy trying to find us a cargo at a rate which would be profitable. There were several proposals and I was given the task of estimating the time that each proposed voyage would take. That information would then lead to a profit/loss calculation, applying the known daily average operating cost of the ship, plus the fuel required at the prices available at convenient fueling ports. I calculated that the break even freight rate for hauling coal to North Europe from the US East Coast was about $6.50 per ton. Of course, keeping the ship on idle status, while rate shopping, also cost money and that had to be worked into the equation. It was "slim pickings" all around but we decided, with Mr. Ladislas Pathy's approval, to accept a charter to carry a cargo of coal from Philadelphia to Antwerp, Belgium, for $6.85 per ton. The fact that the ship was already in Philadelphia was the deciding factor.

Since we were operating on such a thin margin, I took another hard look at the store requisitions and cut out items that were not essential.

I checked the price of Bunker "C" in several ports in Europe. and concluded that we had best reduce our cargo tonnage as necessary. and fuel in the U. S. for the round trip.

I informed the Ship Chandlers and Ship Repair Companies in Philadelphia, that there were to be no gratuities to me or to any ship personnel. They were to give us the best possible prices, devoid of any "kick-backs".

The ship shifted to the coal loading dock and took aboard the proper tonnage of cargo. Bunker "C" was a lot cheaper in New York, so I arranged to take fuel by barge at the Staten Island anchorage. The ship left Philly early on Wednesday, 3/13/57, and arrived at the Staten Island anchorage late that evening. The bunkering went as planned and the *SS Federal Jurist* sailed from New York early on Thursday, 3/14/57.

Personal Problems

My new job had been demanding all of my attention, so Dorothy was left to handle our personal affairs on her own. The furniture that she had purchased in Kansas City, and shipped to New Rochelle, had apparently been lost somewhere and no one seemed to know how to find it. It was over-due and might arrive at any minute, which meant that Dorothy and Dewey were stuck all day in the empty apartment, waiting for it. The truck with our stuff finally arrived, a week after the promised delivery date. I was still tied up in Philadelphia and was of no help in the situation. Dorothy handled everything very competently and when I finally arrived on the scene, everything was where it belonged and the place looked great. She had even hung curtains in all of the windows.

I was finally able to check out of my hotel in Philadelphia and go to my new home at the Drake Apartments in New Rochelle.

Dewey was very unhappy about this move. He missed his friends and grandmother back in Sedalia. Dorothy had enrolled him in a middle school in New Rochelle to continue his studies in the eighth grade. We didn't yet know it yet, but he was failing in school and playing hooky many days. He was a truly troubled teenager. He needed a full-time, wise and expert father. I was not performing as needed.

One Friday night, Dewey told us that a friend had invited him to spend the night at his house. We were pleased that he was making new friends and readily agreed to the arrangement. He had had the boy to our apartment to meet us and he seemed like a nice kid.

That night we received a call from the police about 0030, telling us that they had Dewey and our car at the Police Station. We didn't think that was possible because we had both sets of car keys. I checked in the parking lot and the car was missing. We called the house of the boy where he was supposed to be staying, and they thought that their son was staying at our house for the night. Obviously, I should have checked this story out earlier. I called a taxi, and Dorothy and I went to the Police Station.

The Officers in a patrol car had seen a fifteen year old boy driving our car at midnight, and naturally pulled him over. He and the other boy were joy riding. On one of the days that he was playing hooky, Dewey had taken a set of car keys from the house and had duplicates made. I could handle a ship and crew, but I was failing at handling a teenager. Being a good stepfather to a teenager was more difficult than being a good ship master.

Dorothy and I tried to talk sense to Dewey. It was obvious that he was not repentant. We did not know what to do. As punishment, I stopped his allowance for a couple of weeks and restricted him to the house. That was hard on all of us.

Meanwhile, back at the office

When the *SS Federal Jurist* was about two thirds way across the Atlantic, they discovered that they had seawater instead of fuel in one of the double bottom tanks. Fortunately, it appeared that no other tank was breached and, since we had bunkered for the round trip, they were not going to run out of fuel.

The only reasonable explanation for this had to be that the bottom had been holed when the young, inexperienced and incompetent Delaware Pilot anchored the ship improperly in Philadelphia in the early morning of 3/1/57. This was technically my fault, since I had been in command when it happened. Captains are always deemed responsible for damage such as this, although it is obviously not possible for them to have expert local knowledge in all the ports. Captains must, by necessity, depend on Pilots in the ports that their ships call.

He didn't say so, but I sensed that Mr. Ladislas Pathy blamed me for this disaster. It was very serious, mainly because it was going to be hard to find a port that would allow a ship, that was leaking a considerable amount of oil to enter. Certainly Antwerp, which was some forty miles up the Schelde River, would not let the *SS Federal Jurist* enter and pollute their river.

Fortunately, Mr. George Pathy had a close personal friend who owned a shipyard, with an adequate drydock, in France. For the life of me, I can't remember which in which port it was located. Anyway, the Shipyard Owner had enough influence in his port to get permission for entry. The ship would have to be drydocked while fully loaded, which was difficult but not impossible. The shipyard did creditable work, which was approved by the ABS (American Bureau of Shipping) Surveyor. Although this was handled expeditiously, the incidence added ten days to the voyage, and converted a slight profit into a large loss. Insurance would pay for the repairs, but not for the lost time.

When the repairs were completed, the ship proceeded to Antwerp and discharged the cargo of coal.

Meanwhile, our Broker was getting information about a number of possible cargoes for the next voyage. I was doing voyage calculations to determine which one looked the best. None of them were outstanding, but the best appeared to be taking a cargo of wheat from Houston to North Europe. So, we sent orders to Captain Richardson to take bunkers, in Antwerp, sufficient to steam to Houston. He was also requested to have the crew wash down the cargo holes to prepare for a cargo of grain.

My time was also taken up in checking out and setting up Agents to handle our ship in the various ports. For the most part, I used the same Agents that I had become acquainted with while working for T. J. Stevenson & Co., Inc.

With all of the delays that had been encountered, the *SS Federal Jurist* was not going to get to Houston until about 5/1/57. I was going to again have to leave the problem of how to handle our rebellious teenager entirely in Dorothy's hands, while I traveled to Houston to handle the ship's affairs for the upcoming voyage.

The first thing was to evaluate the performance of Captain Richardson. This had been his first voyage as Captain, which is a difficult hurdle. From the reports and correspondence, I had the impression that he was doing just fine. Evaluating things aboard confirmed that things were going okay. He had, with considerable help from the Radio Operator, figured the payoff and entered the amounts due on pay envelopes for each crewmember and officer. I had the envelopes delivered to the Houston bank that the Agent used. There they will filled and delivered aboard for the payoff. I arranged for the Shipping Commissioner to be aboard, which was a requirement in those days (but long since dispensed with). The payroll was handled well which further confirmed my good impression of Captain Richardson.

Foreign Articles were signed for the upcoming voyage.

It was going to be necessary to arrange for shifting boards (bulkheads) to be installed in the 'tween decks to prevent dangerous shifting of the grain cargo. The National Cargo Bureau had strict requirements that had to be followed exactly. The Houston Agent was familiar with a firm that was expert in these installations. He arranged for them to do the work, and they did so expeditiously.

When the National Cargo Bureau Inspector was satisfied with the cleanliness of the cargo holds and the shifting board installation, we had the ship moved to the grain elevator. The cargo of almost 10,000 long tons of wheat was dumped into the ship in about eight hours.

My voyage calculations concluded that we should take fuel in Houston sufficient to return to the East Coast. Bunkers in Europe continued to be very expensive.

Of course I also had to approve the voyage requisitions and arrange storing. Also there were some voyage repairs and the ship's laundry to take care of. Until I actually got involved in doing it, I had never realized how much effort it took to supervise the port operations for a ship.

The Houston Agent was very helpful and we managed to get the ship out in three and a half days. She sailed on Saturday, 5/4/57.

The wheat cargo was destined for North Europe, where the handling would most likely be expeditious. The weather for the ocean crossing should be good and it was too early for any hurricanes. It looked like smooth sailing, a big change from the last voyage.

Meanwhile, back on the Home Front

Things were not going any better with our Rebellious Teenager. The Truant Officer came to see us and we found out that Dewey had been playing hooky almost as much as he had been attending classes. He was not doing his home work and, although we knew that he was plenty smart, he was failing all classes. The school year was a disaster and would have to be repeated. We lined him up to take some summer courses and tried to properly motivate him.

How were our finances holding up? My salary of $9,000 per year worked out to only $750 per month. That sounds like very low pay now in 2005, but, adjusted for inflation, it was well above the average pay in 1957. My pay as shipmaster had been $12,000 per year and, while a bachelor, could mostly be saved since my room and board, while working, was also included.

I could not drive our car to the rail station and park it in the mornings, because that would leave Dorothy without transportation. She could not drive me, because she was getting Dewey fed and off to school at the same time that I went to work. So, for the first month I took a taxi to and from the station. After work, I sometimes had a drink, in a nearby bar in Manhattan with coworkers, before catching the train to New Rochelle. When I added up the income and outgo at the end of that first month, I was shocked. I was spending more than I was making. I checked the bus schedules and started taking them to and from the station. I started getting cheaper lunches in town. There were no more stops at the bar on the way home. If the Company prospered and expanded, and if I had made an important contribution to all of that, I could, I was sure, look forward to a Christmas bonus. But that could not be counted on in view of the depression that the U. S. Merchant Marine was suffering.

End of the Job

The voyage with wheat was going well. Rotterdam was named as the port of discharge. I had set up an Agency there to handle our ship's affairs. There were no unusual problems and we had a two-day turn-around in port. This voyage was going to be profitable.

Our Broker had found several more possible cargoes for the next voyage. My calculations showed that a cargo of grain from Norfolk to North Europe was the best deal available, so we contracted for that.

I was also getting somewhat involved in the specifications for a 45,000 ton tanker to be built in Japan. At the time they were calling it a "super tanker" but, in view of the size of ships that later evolved, I can't bring myself to call it that. Now days it would be called "handy size". Mr. Ladislas Pathy was arranging the financing and investing heavily himself in this venture. His office in Montreal was mainly handling the matter. That office also managed the several ships that he had under the Canadian and Egyptian flags.

I was also advising on a major effort to organize a ship registry business to operate from Haiti. Mr. Pathy was dealing with dictator "Papa Doc" Duvalier, and because he would later be overthrown, that venture was doomed to failure. Mr. Pathy had been very successful in organizing the Ship Registry business in Liberia and had sold that business, making a substantial profit. He had agreed not to go back into the ship registry business for a certain period of time, and the time limit was about to expire. My input was mainly aimed at preventing abuse of seamen that would be manning the ships.

I proceeded to Norfolk to handle the ship's business there. Her arrival date was 6/4/57. I had arranged for my friends, the Haslers (father and son), to be my Agent there.

311.

I had a problem in that some of the grain shifting bulkheads had been damaged in Rotterdam and needed repair before we could again load wheat. To my disgust, the National Cargo Bureau Inspector, that I had dealt with as Chief Mate and Ship Master several times over the years, turned out to be "on the take". I had to bribe him with $500 to pass the repaired shifting boards. They were perfectly good, but he was nit-picking and was about to cause us to lose our turn at the grain elevator. I later heard that he had been fired and that was good riddance.

The ship shifted to the grain elevator late on Thursday, 6/6/57. They dumped about 10,000 long tons of wheat into the ship in about nine hours. At 1000 on the following day, they departed Norfolk, bound for the English Channel. A few days later we were advised that the cargo should go to Rotterdam, and we so advised Captain Richardson.

I contacted the Agent that I had set up in Rotterdam and asked them to handle ship's affairs for us, which they did excellently. There were no problems and the ship had the usual (for North Europe) two day turn-around.

I again did voyage calculations on the various possible charters for our next voyage. The freight rates everywhere were low and barely profitable. The best available cargo was coal from Hampton Roads to France, so we radioed orders to Captain Richardson to proceed to Norfolk. They arrived there on Wednesday, 7/3/57.

I traveled to Norfolk to husband the *SS Federal Jurist*. I watched the Fourth of July fireworks there. In the business world, holidays are not greeted with much joy. This one caused us to lose a day, which is bad when you are barely scraping by financially. We needed to tear out and salvage what value we could from the grain shifting boards in the ship and, of course, gangs to do the work were not available on the holiday.

We were not able to get to the coal loading dock until Monday, 7/8/57. The ship sailed for the English Channel at mid-day on Tuesday, 7/9/57. Later, Dunkerque was designated for discharge. The crew was going to get some easy duty in France, with a seven-day stay in port instead of the two or three days they would have had in the Dutch, Belgium, or German ports.

The freight rates continued to tank. Coal from Hampton Roads to Europe was going for $6.00 per ton, well below break-even. Mr. Ladislas Pathy, and his senior advisors, determined that operating American Flag Ships could not be profitable. They decided to cut their loses and put their one American ship up for sale.

New York was the best market for ship sales, so Captain Richardson was ordered to proceed there. They arrived on Sunday, 7/18/57. We arranged for a lay berth in Brooklyn. The voyage payoff was made the following day and all hands were sadly terminated.

Without any ships, there obviously was no need for an Operations Manager. So, what was going to become of me?

Mr. Pathy was always getting involved in unusual projects. He had landed a contract to supply part of the DEW (Distance Early Warning) Line that was being constructed across northern Alaska, Canada and Greenland. He offered me a job as Expeditor.

My fantastic good luck struck again. At this time, I was offered a position as a Pilot in the Panama Canal. My choices were the Arctic or the Tropics. That was a "no brainier".

My job with Federal Bulkcarriers, Inc. ended on 8/31/57.

With my good luck still running strong, we quickly found a nice couple to sub-lease our apartment, with no loss to us. The moving company, hired by the Panama Canal Company, expertly packed up our furniture and clothes for shipment to Panama. Nothing was lost— they even shipped the dirt in our flower pots.

Dorothy, Dewey and I made a quick drive to Sedalia, MO, to wind up some affairs there and to collect things that we wanted to take with us to Panama.

Poor Dewey was desperately unhappy about this latest development. He loved his mother and resented and hated me. Things got so bad and stormy on the drive back to New York, that I had to stop the car, pull off the highway, and have a brief fist fight with him. He was a big, strong fifteen-year-old and, I am sure, Dorothy was worried that he might win. After each time that I landed a punch, I asked him if he had had enough. About the third time that I hit him, Dewey declared that yes, he had had enough. This incident cleared the air for a while in our "young bull, old bull" conflict. Dewey still had a black eye when we arrived in Panama, which caused some comment.

The very fine Coach at the Cristobal High School, Mr. Luke Palumbo, provided the way to motivate my stepson. Dewey was a great athlete, but he had to pass his courses in order to play football and the other sports.

You would not have thought it possible at the time, but in later years, Dewey and I became good friends.

We boarded the *SS Cristobal,* which was one of the two passenger ships owned by the Panama Canal Company, and sailed from New York on 9/6/57. We were enroute to Cristobal, Canal Zone, with a stop scheduled in Port Au Prince, Haiti.

We would spend the next forty years as residents of the Canal Zone and (later) Panama.

The End